Resources for the Knowledge Based Economy Series

KNOWLEDGE AND STRATEGY
Michael H. Zack

KNOWLEDGE AND SPECIAL LIBRARIES
James M. Matarazzo and Suzanne D. Connolly

RISE OF THE KNOWLEDGE WORKER
James W. Cortada

KNOWLEDGE IN ORGANIZATIONS
Laurence Prusak

KNOWLEDGE MANAGEMENT AND ORGANIZATIONAL DESIGN
Paul S. Myers

KNOWLEDGE MANAGEMENT TOOLS
Rudy L. Ruggles, III

THE STRATEGIC MANAGEMENT OF INTELLECTUAL CAPITAL
David A. Klein

Table of Contents

▦ Introduction

KNOWLEDGE, GROUPWARE AND THE INTERNET

Today's world is a science fiction picture of what we lived in less than a decade ago. Today organizations and people talk about the accelerating pace of change, web years and other concepts that emphasize the point that the world is moving quicker, and organizations that cannot keep up with the new dynamics will not be able to effectively compete and win in the future. In the new world where knowledge and its application is replacing land, labor and capital as a measure of an organization's success, there are two keys to future successful competition. They are how effectively organizations can move from individual knowledge to group knowledge and how quickly they can make the tacit knowledge that is in an individual's head explicit for many people to use and apply.

The idea of the importance of knowledge is not new. Whether it was the advantage that was created through the first tribe that learned to control fire, the first civilization that learned how to make weapons of bronze or iron, or Henry Ford and his harnessing of the power of the assembly line, all of these advantages were created through applying the advantages that the individuals or groups knowledge created. In today's world we increasingly hear about the "knowledge based economy" or hear pundits speaking of "competing on knowledge." But today, these speakers are increasingly speaking of how one competes in the era of the globalization and rapid change. The way one competes is through the effective and efficient use of technology to enable knowledge activities.

Prusak and Davenport have defined knowledge as at a specific yet generic level when they say:

> Knowledge is a fluid mix of framed experiences, values, contextual information, and expert insight that provides a framework for evaluating and incorporating new experiences and information. It originates and is applied in the minds of knowers. In organizations, it often becomes embedded not only in

documents or repositories but also in organizational routines, processes, practices, and norms.[i]

Lotus Development corporation advances a different definition of knowledge management when they define it "as the systematic leveraging of information and expertise to improve organizational innovation, responsiveness, productivity and competence."[ii] They go on to say that "We see this in action when we form a team to create and market a new product, when we find the expert who can provide definitive information in a crisis, and during spontaneous hallway conversations with a colleague."[iii]

Both definitions recognize that people and organizations are a key element of knowledge management. Both definitions also understand that "good" knowledge management involves putting it into action.

When one gets to the specific level and decides how does one apply these generic frameworks across multiple continents, twenty-four time zones and many different cultures the enablement problem comes to the forefront. When one asks how to get people to collaborate in a timely fashion while working simultaneously in California, Tokyo, Zurich and London on similar projects organizations are increasingly looking to groupware and internet technologies. But as several of the articles show, technology is not the silver bullet. If an organization builds an intranet, no one is assured it will be used. If organizational as well as technical issues are not addressed, no knowledge management system will work.

Like any other business activity, knowledge management can be viewed as a process. Put simply, knowledge must first be created; then it can be distributed and diffused. And all previous knowledge process activities are of little value unless knowledge is used to benefit clients or internal firm operations.

All of us look for experts across our work, many times relying on people we know, or our "social network." But in the current environment of downsizing, mergers, and people being stretched to their limits, the social networks have become dispersed brittle and in some cases even broken. People now have limitations on their ability to form connections outside of their immediate organizational or geographic area. But the limitations are being overcome through the use of new technologies. Technologies that enhance collaboration and can produce improved "innovation, responsiveness, productivity . . . ."[iv] Technologies that enhance an organization's ability to develop the ability "for evaluating and incorporating new experiences and information."[v]

Throughout this, one is doing what Nonaka proposed when he suggested that knowledge in order to be exchanged, shared, distributed or combined it

---

[i] Thomas H. Davenport and Laurence Prusak, *Working Knowledge* (Boston: Harvard Business School Press, 1998), p. 5
[ii] Lotus Institute, Leveraging Expertise, Lotus White Paper, 1998, p. 1
[iii] Ibid
[iv] Ibid
[v] Davenport and Prusak, Ibid

must be made explicit prior to being internalized by the individual. In order to make the knowledge explicit, one must record it, store it, document it, and provide access to it so that communities can act on it. The creation sharing and combining of knowledge across an organization requires both a technical infrastructure as well as behavioral and organizational support. Only through these actions can the contextual knowledge potential of the explicit knowledge artifacts be unleashed.[vi]

As stated earlier, the key enablers for this revolution are groupware and the Internet. In many ways groupware almost presupposed the Internet in that it set up frameworks for collaboration and learning. The Internet has in many cases become the base over which groupware applications flow. With groupware, we have the basis for creating increasing group and organizational collaboration. We have places to store, access and collaborate structured and unstructured data and information. Through this collaboration one can create geographically dispersed teams and communities that add insights and experience to produce knowledge. Many times these teams or communities stored these insights in documents, especially prior to the innovation of groupware.

Prior to the invention of groupware and the Internet these documents were distributed on paper; what is relatively new is the use of information technologies to disseminate Professional Service knowledge. The widespread use of IT for PS firm knowledge management arose in the early 1990s with the advent of Lotus Notes. Price Waterhouse, IBM Consulting and Andersen Consulting were early adopters of this technology; IBM especially with its Intellectual Capital Management System. Since then many other firms have developed similar knowledge repositories using either Notes or Intranet Webs. Whether on Notes or the Web, this sort of document repository is undoubtedly the single most popular knowledge management application, in PS firms and elsewhere.

The Internet has and moved the look and feel of groupware from black and white to color. It has taken us from text and shared spaces to sametime communication and collaboration. It has added streaming videos, wider search capabilities, and worldwide connectivity over IP networks. It has combined the promise of GroupWare to bring widely dispersed individuals much closer to the desired face to face contact which increases knowledge sharing and trust. But the promise only is instantiated if an organization puts the organizational and human systems to support the desired outcomes.

BUSINESS ISSUES

Knowledge Management has no focus unless it addresses specific business issues. It is only through enabling the advancement of a business issue, that groupware or the Internet enable and enhance an organization's ability to act.

[vi] A knowledge artifact is any item that captures explicit or tacit knowledge. It can include documents, tape recordings, video, web pages, databases, CD ROMs, etc.

GroupWare and the Internet enable businesses in four primary ways: Collaboration, Learning, Innovation and Sense-making. The four "pillars" of business issues concentrate and enhance a firm's need to focus on knowledge performance given the increased business complexity in the twentieth and twenty-first century. Organizations are creating an urgency to work together, improve performance, develop new ideas faster and understand complexity. This is being brought on by organizations continually being asked to do more from less due to in part from downsizing. The downsizing erodes the established knowledge base. Another issue driving this urgency is the acceleration of competition as cross sector competition intensifies, windows of opportunity are increasingly becoming narrower and as a multiplicity of offerings increase. In addition, one is seeing the increase in smart products and an increased service intensity, and due to the fact that the world is becoming smaller and smaller.

Knowledge related business issues both go across enterprises and across the enterprise. When looking across the enterprise one can look at suppliers, integrators, distributors and customers. A supplier issue could include knowing who else could manufacture the item. For many organizations, today's primary focus is around getting closer to the customer. Many of today's high valuations placed on Internet companies are due to their interaction with the customer, early in the sell cycle.

When examining different types of organizations, many of them are trying to see how to share best practices with a discipline across project teams. Or, asking how to share the tacit and explicit knowledge of a project amongst various disciplines. In order to better manage all of these issues, one must either collaborate, learn, innovate or make better sense of the environment to be more successful. And in order to do this globally, the best enablers are groupware and the Internet.

COLLABORATION

If a firm's primary competitive advantage in the current and future world is its ability to learn and create ideas, and move them into the marketplace at ever increasing speeds, the firm needs to manage knowledge to create the distinctive competencies. Organizations must create and nurture an environment where sharing knowledge and helping others is an essential ingredient to future success. A more formal way of stating this is that organizations must collaborate across all boundaries; be they personal, organizational or geographical.

Collaboration issues arise when a given project or group of tasks requires more than one individual for their completion. In many cases there is a group of people required to complete the task or project. The project may require input from a many different individuals who are located at multiple sites.[vii] Or it might just require people who are physically closely co-located, but who are in different reporting structures and have no idea of what the other is doing.

Another area where collaboration is the key, is in the effective identification, development, and application of teams and communities. How an organization goes beyond the formal structures as described through organizational charts to the informal networks and groups of people who work together to share experiences in order to "get things done" is in many cases the critical mechanism for the application of informal organizational knowledge. The informal networks of people collaborating together is the glue that makes many organizations run.

The lack of collaboration leads to a series of less than optimal results. These include poor sharing among groups, longer timelines for completeness of projects, more errors and rework, and more "reworking of the wheel" where everyone invents the same thing over and over again, rather than working with and improving tested methodologies. An industry that benefits from collaboration is the professional services industry, or consulting industry.

As shown in "Growing Intellectual Capital at IBM: More than Technology," by Cohen and Azzarello, a major need for a consulting organization is to reuse intellectual capital and to encourage collaboration across the firm. Consulting engagements are usually small team based where every situation is new, but in many cases related closely to similar situations. In addition, you are dealing with geographically dispersed teams that have created the intellectual capital that others need to reuse. If consulting companies do not reuse intellectual capital, leveraging the expertise of others who are not on the current team, they cannot benefit from the organization's prior experiences, they cannot respond to their client needs in a timely fashion and the amount of new work that would need to be done on every engagement would raise costs to non-competitive levels.

LEARNING

In one sense, organizational learning is simply any learning that takes place within an organization. Learning in groups as part of an organization is more complex than learning by individuals. Within groups, individuals must first learn to understand what others in the group mean by what they are saying. They then must learn to trust each other so they can work as a cognitive unit. They have to learn to understand the others person's meaning based on their own set of experiences. They must set up standards that become a common learning ground for

---

[vii] In our experience, the individuals do not have to be widely dispersed. In several instances, we have identified individuals who were on different aisles of the same floor of the same office building who were working on similar projects where collaboration would be to their mutual benefit, but due to their lack of knowledge about what the other was doing, they did not collaborate or share anything.

the group, rather than leave it up to each individual and each individual's interpretation. Lastly the group must learn to respond to an everchanging world by learning quicker and applying the learning faster than their competitors.

At the MIT Center for Organizational Learning, originally founded by Peter Senge, they talk about the idea about how people need to reflect on new knowledge. It is through reflection that one can consider the purpose of learning and the knowledge it creates, and then how best to apply it to the business challenges, or even if the learning is applicable to the business challenges. For best results Jeff Clanon of the Center said that "learning is most effective when it is a part of a working life, embedded in business experiences, not set apart in an isolated classroom environment."[viii]

One of today's key challenges is how can one learn best in a time of limited physical resources, ever tightening controls on containing costs and geographically dispersed teams. In the past many organizations would allow personnel to either attend a central corporate training center or attend training sessions run by universities or education companies. This meant that a key asset of the organization, the employees, were "out of action" for the training time. They could not have their normal interfaces with customers or other parts of the job. In addition, they had to do the learning at times and places that were not necessarily cost effective or convenient to themselves. But the parent organization had a dilemma of how else did one impart knowledge through schooling and training to their employees, and how did one do it cost effectively, especially if they believed that the learning was a necessary differentiator in their competitive environment.

The answer that several organizations have come up with is to use the Internet or groupware to begin to solve these issues. Buckman Labs has come up with many innovative practices where they partner with different universities and learning institutions to produce courses that can be delivered over a modem. In many cases, they are using Lotus Notes or the Internet to deliver the richness that is needed. These courses range from specialty chemical training to accredited graduate level courses. Advantages of these courses include that they can be done at a convenient time for the student and that they lower the education costs for the organization.[ix] The course materials can be delivered through a replication

---

[viii] "Managing Knowledge for Business Success, A Conference Report" Cohen, Smith, Prusak and Azzarello, p. 15.

[ix] Education costs are lowered, as there is no cost for housing or transporting the student while they attend a course. In addition, the company is not paying for the use of physical assets such as classrooms. A proponent of distributed learning is Gary Becker, the Nobel Prize winning economist from the University of Chicago. At the 1999 LotusSphere Conference, he presented economic arguments for distributed learning that could be delivered at a time and place that was convenient to the user. He emphasized the need to move away from education being delivered primarily through a classroom environment for many reasons including the ability for many individuals to leverage the expertise of thought leaders. He also suggested that new technologies such as the Internet and wide bandwidth access are what has made this possible.

function; there can be interactive talk with Internet or Groupware sametime "chat" technologies which enable sametime as well as ongoing discussions. One can also store the discussion, creating a chat database so that one has the benefit of the interactive chat combined with the ability to reflect on and confirm what was said, for additional richness.

Organizations need to learn better to improve performance. This is done through learning from groups and communities as well as sharing effective practices. Performance variation is an instance where learning could have a positive effect on business results. Performance variation occurs when multiple groups of people perform the same or similar tasks in different locations. The different locations can be on one geographical site or they can be spread around the world. You could have a task that is performed by multiple groups located at multiple sites where the efficiency of the task is performed at different levels. Plant managers ask why does my line not run as fast or have as few errors as another plant. Business managers look for best practices that they can teach across geographies to bring competencies up to a higher level.

Examples of these and related issues can be found in the articles:

"Exploration and Exploitation in Organizational Learning," by James G. March and "Organizational Learning and Communities of Practice: Toward a Unified View of Working, Learning and Innovation," by John Seely Brown and Paul Duguid.

In both of these articles we first examine how organizations learn and work to achieve higher levels of organizational effectiveness.

INNOVATION

Innovation is a key to future business success. Business innovations include developing new ideas faster in products or processes, learning how to leverage innovations that in the past were only part of a R&D environment and creating conditions that foster innovation. Companies are born, have a life and then eventually die if they cannot continue to create more and better products than their competitors. Innovations are a key driver of corporate growth.

Innovation is also tied to an organization's ability to transfer and diffuse knowledge. The diffusion and transfer of knowledge through direct contacts between people is still an important factor in most organizations. The "communities of practice" in which knowledge is exchanged work best when participating individuals know each other and the context in which knowledge will be applied. Such communities are best developed through at least some face-to-face contact. It is also likely that when organizations have a common culture and way of operating around a firm. But through the groupware and the Internet, one is now able to do this across physical time and space. Technology applications that list "who knows what" in an expertise directory or skills database can facilitate face-to-face connections between professionals, and those physical contacts can then be further enabled through discussion databases and other collaborative tools.

Innovation issues exist due to a number of factors. Today we are seeing shorter product life cycles. Whether it is the advent of "web years,"[x] continual improvement or the eating your own children (products) before your competitors do, product lifecycles have grown shorter and shorter. In addition, we have seen the demand for mass customization, the demand for quality and intense pressure on prices, which is exacerbated by an economy that does not tolerate many price hikes. All of these factors drive the need for new and better products is increasingly shorter time frames.

Products are not just created on their own. They are most successful in a culture where knowledge is valued and shared effectively. In many cases, it is the author's belief that innovation best occurs in firms that see knowledge as a resource on par with land labor and capital. One must have support for innovation as well as a common "innovation language" so that when is collaborating through virtual mediums, there is a shared and common understanding of what is needed. The common language can therefore lead to a shared purpose across a globally dispersed organization. This with the proper technological enablers can enhance the innovation capabilities of a firm.

Some organizations could be classified as successful product innovators. These would include Sony with their Walkman and Diskman, as well as 3-M with their post it notes. Other organizations work on product innovation. This can be done through innovative work in operational efficiency or operational effectiveness. Examples of organizations that have excelled in operational efficiency include Dell in the PC business and FedEx and UPS in the distribution industry. Sony is also an outstanding innovator in the area of operational effectiveness with their high quality manufacturing for a wide range of consumer products. All of these organizations have proved that innovation is a key to continued business success. All of these organizations are also examples of companies that do not rest on a particular innovation or series of innovations. They instantiate the idea of continual innovation in their corporate culture, knowing if they begin to stand still, that someone will quickly pass them.

SENSE MAKING

The need for sense making is driven by the need to reach understanding from increasingly large volumes of data information and knowledge sources. A better understanding of the business and operational environment can lead to better organizational decision making. Prior to the information age, a manager's sense making apparatus was his personal network and a limited number of dated reports. Today, groupware and the Internet have expanded the potential for an

---

[x] There are four web years to a calendar year.

individual network, and the availability of data and information is only limited by the amount of time one wants to spend.

Good decision making increasingly depends on understanding how to capture and classify potentially useful information, understanding what information sources have validity, and what filters are being used to keep people from existing in a state of information overload. The decision making process can be around traditional needs such as competitive information, location of expertise or the identification and use of new good ideas. All of these are issues that are currently being developed and used in new groupware applications.[xi]

Many of these and related issues are addressed in the following articles:

"Designing GroupWare Applications: A Work Centered Design Approach," by Kate Ehrlich, "Information Technology and Strategic Knowledge Management," by The Economist Business Unit and "Knowledge Management and Collaboration Technologies," by Michael Zack and Michael Serrino.

KNOWLEDGE MANAGEMENT IN PROFESSIONAL SERVICE FIRMS

Early adopters of the issues raised in through managing knowledge and how to best instantiate it in an organization using groupware and the Internet were professional service firms. Most consulting firms have embraced KM in order to support geographically distributed professionals and to reduce the negative implications of growth, e.g., rapid turnover of personnel. Other "generic" principles of knowledge management in the industry include improving the speed, cost and quality of client service. In addition, there is a broadly held desire for better competitive positioning and higher marketplace awareness through "thought leadership," or generation of innovative knowledge about business and management. The tools chosen by the "Big 5" are either Groupware or Internet based.[xii] And it is probably safe to say that new information technologies—Lotus Notes and Intranet Webs in particular—have provided the impetus for widespread, global knowledge management in PS firms.

While consulting or professional service firms have embraced knowledge management for many different reasons, many have paid more attention to measuring benefits. Some of the financial measures employed in benefit cases include:

[xi] One can look at the new filters in internet browsers, expertise locators in new or future realizes of Lotus Notes, profilers as internet or groupware attachments that search for articles of interest to someone with the users current search and reading list. The list is endless, but the ability to enable better decision-making is a key that groupware is continuing to address.

[xii] Currently 4 out of the Big 5 consulting firms use Lotus Notes and Internet based systems.

- Productivity increases by consultants;
- Time decreases in proposal and workplan development (non-billable hours);
- Overall business value—anecdotal reports of time saved and work won;
- Value from change in win rate of proposals.

CONCLUSION

In today's competitive environment, developing and leveraging knowledge is a key competitive success factor. Leading edge firms actively manage their knowledge in order to apply it for business success. In doing so they do not manage Collaboration, Learning, Innovation and Sense as separate silos. In many cases they manage them so they overlap and enhance each other.[xiii] Knowledge Management technologies enable this through sharing, codifying, making accessible, documenting and help disseminating both internal and external knowledge for positive knowledge enabled business outcomes. However, to unleash this technical potential, organizations have created human factors that increase the incidence of these activities happening.

[xiii] Examples of this include: Increased collaboration between Research and Development sites which can increase the incidence of innovation. In addition, learning from each other can come through collaboration, and increase an organization sense of understanding of the outside environment in order to better respond to new events.

PART I

History

Chapter 1

A Dynamic Theory of Organizational Knowledge Creation[1]

Ikujiro Nonaka
Institute of Business Research, Hitotsubashi University, Kunitachi, Tokyo, Japan

*I recommend this paper to **Organization Science** readers because I believe that it has the potential to stimulate the next wave of research on organization learning. It provides a conceptual framework for research on the differences and similarities of learning by individuals, groups, and organizations.*

—Arie Y. Lewin

Abstract—This paper proposes a paradigm for managing the dynamic aspects of organizational knowledge creating processes. Its central theme is that organizational knowledge is created through a continuous dialogue between tacit and explicit knowledge. The nature of this dialogue is examined and four patterns of interaction involving tacit and explicit knowledge are identified. It is argued that while new knowledge is developed by individuals, organizations play a critical role in articulating and amplifying that knowledge. A theoretical framework is developed which provides an analytical perspective on the constituent dimensions of knowledge creation. This framework is then applied in two operational models for facilitating the dynamic creation of appropriate organizational knowledge.
(Self-Designing Organization; Teams; Knowledge Conversion; Organizational Innovation; Management Models)

[1] Reprinted by permission, Ikujiro Nonaka, "A Dynamic Theory of Organizational Knowledge Creation," *Organizational Science*, Vol. 5, No. 1, 1994, the Institute for Operations Research and the Management Sciences (INFORMS), 901 Elkridge Landing Road, Suite 400, Linthicum, Maryland 21090–2909 USA.

1. INTRODUCTION

It is widely observed that the society we live in has been gradually turning into a "knowledge society" (Drucker 1968; Bell 1973; Toffler 1990). The ever increasing importance of knowledge in contemporary society calls for a shift in our thinking concerning innovation in large business organizations—be it technical innovation, product innovation, or strategic or organizational innovation.[2] It raises questions about how organizations process knowledge and, more importantly, how they create new knowledge. Such a shift in general orientation will involve, among other things, a reconceptualization of the organizational knowledge creation processes.

The theory of organization has long been dominated by a paradigm that conceptualizes the organization as a system that "processes" information or "solves" problems. Central to this paradigm is the assumption that a fundamental task for the organization is how efficiently it can deal with information and decisions in an uncertain environment. This paradigm suggests that the solution lies in the "input-process-output" sequence of hierarchical information processing. Yet a critical problem with this paradigm follows from its passive and static view of the organization. Information processing is viewed as a problem-solving activity which centers on what is given to the organization—without due consideration of what is created by it.

Any organization that dynamically deals with a changing environment ought not only to process information efficiently but also create information and knowledge. Analyzing the organization in terms of its design and capability to process information imposed by the environment no doubt constitutes an important approach to interpreting certain aspects of organizational activities. However, it can be argued that the organization's interaction with its environment, together with the means by which it creates and distributes information and knowledge, are more important when it comes to building an active and dynamic understanding of the organization. For example, innovation, which is a key form of organizational knowledge creation, cannot be explained sufficiently in terms of information processing or problem solving. Innovation can be better understood as a process in which the organization creates and defines problems and then actively develops new knowledge to solve them. Also, innovation produced by one part of the organization in turn creates a stream of related information and knowledge, which might then trigger changes in the organization's wider knowledge systems. Such a sequence of innovation suggests that the organization should be studied from the viewpoint of how it creates information and knowledge, rather than with regard to how it processes these entities.

The goal of this paper is to develop the essential elements of a theory of organizational knowledge creation. In the sections which follow, the basic concepts and models of the theory of organizational knowledge creation are

---

[2] See Lewin and Stephens (1992) for arguments on challenges to and opportunities for organizational design in the post industrial society.

presented. Based on this foundation, the dynamics of the organizational knowledge creation process are examined and practical models are advanced for managing the process more effectively.

2. BASIC CONCEPTS AND MODELS OF ORGANIZATIONAL KNOWLEDGE CREATION

The following subsections explore some basic constructs of the theory of organizational knowledge creation. They begin by discussing the nature of information and knowledge and then draw a distinction between "tacit" and "explicit" knowledge. This distinction represents what could be described as the epistemological dimension to organizational knowledge creation. It embraces a continual dialogue between explicit and tacit knowledge which drives the creation of new ideas and concepts.

Although ideas are formed in the minds of individuals, interaction between individuals typically plays a critical role in developing these ideas. That is to say, "communities of interaction" contribute to the amplification and development of new knowledge. While these communities might span departmental or indeed organizational boundaries, the point to note is that they define a further dimension to organizational knowledge creation, which is associated with the extent of social interaction between individuals that share and develop knowledge. This is referred to as the "onto-logical" dimension of knowledge creation.

Following a consideration of the two dimensions of knowledge creation, some attention is given to the role of individuals and, more specifically, to their "commitment" to the knowledge creating process. This covers aspects of their "intention," the role of autonomy, and the effects of fluctuations or discontinuities in the organization and its environment.

Next, a "spiral" model of knowledge creation is proposed which shows the relationship between the epistemological and ontological dimensions of knowledge creation. This spiral illustrates the creation of a new concept in terms of a continual dialogue between tacit and explicit knowledge. As the concept resonates around an expanding community of individuals, it is developed and clarified. Gradually, concepts which are thought to be of value obtain a wider currency and become crystalized. This description of the spiral model is followed by some observations about how to support the practical management of organizational knowledge creation.

2.1. Knowledge and Information

Knowledge is a multifaceted concept with multilayered meanings. The history of philosophy since the classical Greek period can be regarded as a never-ending search for the meaning of knowledge.[3] This paper follows traditional epistemology and adopts a definition of knowledge as "justified true belief." It should be noted, however, that while the arguments of traditional epistemology focus on "truthfulness" as the essential attribute of knowledge, for present purposes it is important to consider knowledge as a personal "belief," and emphasize the importance of the "justification" of knowledge. This difference introduces another critical distinction between the view of knowledge of traditional epistemology and that of the theory of knowledge creation. While the former naturally emphasizes the absolute, static, and nonhuman nature of knowledge, typically expressed in propositional forms in formal logic, the latter sees knowledge as a dynamic human process of justifying personal beliefs as part of an aspiration for the "truth."

Although the terms "information" and "knowledge" are often used interchangeably, there is a clear distinction between information and knowledge. According to Machlup (1983), information is a flow of messages or meanings which might add to, restructure or change knowledge. Dretske (1981) offers some useful definitions. In his words:

> Information is that commodity capable of yielding knowledge and what information a signal carries is what we can learn from it (Dretske 1981, p. 44). Knowledge is identified with information-produced (or sustained) belief, but the information a person receives is relative to what he or she already knows about the possibilities at the source (ibid. p. 86).

In short, information is a flow of messages, while knowledge is created and organized by the very flow of information, anchored on the commitment and beliefs of its holder. This understanding emphasizes an essential aspect of knowledge that relates to human action.

The importance of knowledge related to action has been recognized in the area of artificial intelligence. For example, Gruber (1989) addresses the subject of an expert's "strategic knowledge" as that which directly guides his action, and attempts to develop the tools to acquire it. Since the 1980s, the development of cognitive science has been based on a serious reflection on behavioralist psychology's neglect of such traditional questions as, "Why do human beings act in a certain way?", which was a central issue for so-called "folk psychology" (Stich 1986). Searle's discussion on the "speech act" also points out a close relationship between language and human action in terms of the "intention" and "commitment" of speakers (Searle 1969). In sum, as a fundamental basis for the theory of organizational creation of knowledge, it can be argued that attention should be

---

[3] Discussion on epistemology here is based on such classical accounts as Plato's *Theaetetus* and *Phaedo,* Descartes's *Discourse on Method,* Locke's *An Essay Concerning Human Understanding,* Hume's *An Enquiry Concerning Human Understanding,* and Kant's *Critique of Pure Reason.* For interpretation of these works, see Hospers (1967), Dancy (1985), Hallis (1985), Moser and Nat (1987), and Winograd and Flores (1986).

focused on the active, subjective nature of knowledge represented by such terms as "belief" and "commitment" that are deeply rooted in the value systems of individuals.

The analysis of knowledge and information does not stop at this point. Information is a necessary medium or material for initiating and formalizing knowledge and can be viewed from "syntactic" and "semantic" perspectives. The syntactic aspect of information is illustrated by Shannon's analysis of the volume of information which is measured without regard to its meaning or value. A telephone bill, for example, is not calculated on the basis of the content of a conversation but according to the duration of time and the distance involved. Shannon said that the semantic aspects of communication, which center on the meaning of information, are irrelevant to the engineering problem (Shannon and Weaver 1949). A genuine theory of information would be a theory about the content of our messages, not a theory about the form in which this content is embodied (Dretske 1981).

In terms of creating knowledge, the semantic aspect of information is more relevant as it focuses on conveyed meaning. The syntactic aspect does not capture the importance of information in the knowledge creation process. Therefore, any preoccupation with the formal definition will tend to lead to a disproportionate emphasis on the role of information processing, which is insensitive to the creation of organizational knowledge out of the chaotic, equivocal state of information. Information, seen from the semantic standpoint, literally means that it contains new meaning. As Bateson (1979, p. 5) put it, "information consists of differences that make a difference." This insight provides a new point of view for interpreting events that make previously invisible connections or ideas obvious or shed light on unexpected connections (Miyazaki and Ueno 1985). For the purposes of building a theory of knowledge creation, it is important to concentrate on the semantic aspects of information.

2.2. Two Dimensions of Knowledge Creation

Although a great deal has been written about the importance of knowledge in management, relatively little attention has been paid to how knowledge is created and how the knowledge creation process can be managed. One dimension of this knowledge creation process can be drawn from a distinction between two types of knowledge—*"tacit knowledge"* and *"explicit knowledge."* As Michael Polanyi (1966, p. 4) put it, "We can know more than we can tell".[4] Knowledge that can be expressed in words and numbers only represents the tip of the iceberg of the entire body of possible knowledge. Polanyi classified human knowledge into two categories. "Explicit" or codified knowledge refers to knowledge that is transmittable in formal, systematic language. On the other hand, "tacit" knowledge has a personal quality, which makes it hard to formalize and communicate.

---

[4] See also Polanyi (1958) and Gelwick (1977).

Tacit knowledge is deeply rooted in action, commitment, and involvement in a specific context. In Polanyi's words, it "indwells" in a comprehensive cognizance of the human mind and body.

While Polanyi articulates the contents of tacit knowledge in a philosophical context, it is also possible to expand his idea in a more practical direction. Tacit knowledge involves both cognitive and technical elements. The cognitive elements center on what Johnson-Laird (1983) called "mental models" in which human beings form working models of the world by creating and manipulating analogies in their minds. These working models include schemata, paradigms, beliefs, and viewpoints that provide "perspectives" that help individuals to perceive and define their world. By contrast, the technical element of tacit knowledge covers concrete know-how, crafts, and skills that apply to specific contexts. It is important to note here that the cognitive element of tacit knowledge refers to an individual's images of reality and visions for the future, that is to say, what is and what ought to be. As will be discussed later, the articulation of tacit perspectives—in a kind of "mobilization" process—is a key factor in the creation of new knowledge.

Tacit knowledge is a continuous activity of knowing and embodies what Bateson (1973) has referred to as an "analogue" quality. In this context, communication between individuals may be seen as an analogue process that aims to share tacit knowledge to build mutual understanding. This understanding involves a kind of "parallel processing" of the complexities of current issues, as the different dimensions of a problem are processed simultaneously. By contrast, explicit knowledge is discrete or "digital." It is captured in records of the past such as libraries, archives, and databases and is assessed on a sequential basis.

The Ontological Dimension: The Level of Social Interaction

At a fundamental level, knowledge is created by individuals. An organization cannot create knowledge without individuals. The organization supports creative individuals or provides a context for such individuals to create knowledge. Organizational knowledge creation, therefore, should be understood in terms of a process that "organizationally" amplifies the knowledge created by individuals, and crystallizes it as a part of the knowledge network of organization.

In this line, it is possible to distinguish several levels of social interaction at which the knowledge created by an individual is transformed and legitimized. In the first instance, an informal community of social interaction provides an immediate forum for nuturing the emergent property of knowledge at each level and developing new ideas. Since this informal community might span organizational boundaries—for example, to include suppliers or customers—it is important that the organization is able to integrate appropriate aspects of emerging knowledge into its strategic development. Thus, the potential contribution of informal groups to organizational knowledge creation should be related to more formal notions of a hierarchical structure. If this is done effectively, new knowledge associated with more advantageous organizational processes or technologies will be able to gain a broader currency within the organization.

In addition to the creation of knowledge within an organization, it is also possible that there will be formal provisions to build knowledge at an interorganizational level. This might occur if informal communities of interaction, that span the link between customers, suppliers, distributors, and even competitors, are put on a more formal basis, for example, through the formation of alliances or outsourcing.

2.3. Commitment on the Part of the Knowledge Subject: Intention, Autonomy, and Fluctuation

The prime movers in the process of organizational knowledge creation are the individual members of an organization. Individuals are continuously committed to recreating the world in accordance with their own perspectives. As Polanyi noted, "commitment" underlies human knowledge creating activities. Thus, commitment is one of the most important components for promoting the formation of new knowledge within an organization. There are three basic factors that induce individual commitment in an organizational setting: "intention," and "autonomy," and a certain level of environmental "fluctuation."

Intention

Intention is concerned with how individuals form their approach to the world and try to make sense of their environment. It is not simply a state of mind, but rather what might be called an action-oriented concept. Edmund Husserl (1968) called this attitude on the part of the subject "intentionality." He denied the existence of "consciousness" per se, which was generally assumed by psychologists in 19th century, and argued that consciousness arises when a subject pays attention to an object. In other words, any consciousness is a "consciousness of something." It arises, endures, and disappears with a subject's commitment to an object.

Eigen (1971) argued, in his evolutionary theory, that evolution involves the process of acquiring environmental information for better adaptation. Eigen insisted that the degree of meaningfulness of information, or a value parameter, needs to be introduced to explain this system. Human beings, as organic systems, derive meaning from the environment which is based on their ultimate pursuit of survival (Shimizu 1978). Man cannot grasp the meaning of information about his environment without some frame of value judgment.

The meaning of information differs according to what a particular system aims to do (manifest purpose or problem consciousness) and the broader environment in which that system exits (context). It is more concerned with the system's future aspirations than its current state. Weick (1979) explains this "self-fulfilling prophecy" of a system as the "enactment" of the environment, which may be a projection of its strong will for self-actualization. While mechanistic information-processing models treat the mind as a fixed capacity device for converting meaningless information into conscious perception, in reality cognition is the activity of knowing and understanding as it occurs in the context of purposeful activity (Neisser 1976). Intention becomes apparent against this background. Without intention, it would be impossible to judge the value of the information or knowledge perceived or created. "The intentionality of the mind not only creates the possibility of meaning, but also limits its form" (Searle 1983, p. 166).

Autonomy

The principle of autonomy can be applied at the individual, group, and organizational levels either—separately or all together. However, the individual is a convenient starting point for analysis. Individuals within the organization may have different intentions. Every individual has his or her own personality. By allowing people to act autonomously, the organization may increase the possibility of introducing unexpected opportunities of the type that are sometimes associated with the so-called "garbage can" metaphor (Cohen et al. 1972). From the standpoint of creating knowledge, such an organization is more likely to maintain greater flexibility in acquiring, relating, and interpreting information. In a system where the autonomy of individuals is assured, or where only "minimum critical specification" (Morgan 1986) is intended, it is possible to establish a basis for self-organization.

Individual autonomy widens the possibility that individuals will motivate themselves to form new knowledge. Self-motivation based on deep emotions, for example, in the poet's creation of new expressions, serves as a driving force for the creation of metaphors. A sense of purpose and autonomy becomes important as an organizational context. Purpose serves as the basis of conceptualization. Autonomy gives individuals freedom to absorb knowledge.

Fluctuation

Even though intention is internal to the individual, knowledge creation at the individual level involves continuous interaction with the external world. In this connection, chaos or discontinuity can generate new patterns of interaction between individuals and their environment. Individuals recreate their own systems of knowledge to take account of ambiguity, redundancy, noise, or randomness generated from the organization and its environment. These fluctuations differ from complete disorder and are characterized by "order without recursiveness"—which represents an order where the pattern is hard to predict in the beginning (Gleick 1987).

Winograd and Flores (1986) emphasize the role of periodic "breakdowns" in human perception. Breakdown refers to the interruption of an individual's habitual, comfortable "state-of-being." When breakdowns occur, individuals question the value of habits and routine tools, which might lead to a realignment of commitments. Environmental fluctuation often triggers this breakdown.

When people face such a breakdown or contradiction, they have an opportunity to reconsider their fundamental thinking and perspectives. In other words, they begin to question the validity of basic attitudes toward the world. This process necessarily involves deep personal commitment by the individual and is similar in context to Piaget's (1974) observations about the importance of the role of contradiction in the interaction between the subject and its environment in such a way that the subject forms perceptions through behavior.

2.4. Knowledge Conversion and the Spiral of Knowledge

It is now possible to bring together the epistemological and ontological dimensions of knowledge creation to form a "spiral" model for the processes involved. This involves identifying four different patterns of interaction between tacit and explicit knowledge. These patterns represent ways in which existing knowledge can be "converted" into new knowledge. Social interaction between individuals then provides an ontological dimension to the expansion of knowledge.

The idea of "knowledge conversion" may be traced from Anderson's ACT model (Anderson 1983) developed in cognitive psychology. In the ACT model, knowledge is divided into "declarative knowledge" (actual knowledge) that is expressed in the form of propositions and "procedural knowledge" (methodological knowledge) which is used in such activities as remembering how to ride a bicycle or play the piano. In the context of the present discussion, the former might approximate to explicit knowledge and the latter to tacit knowledge. Anderson's model hypothesizes that declarative knowledge has to be transformed into procedural knowledge in order for cognitive skills to develop. This hypothesis is consistent with Ryle's classification (1949) of knowledge into categories of knowing that something "exists" and knowing "how" it operates. Anderson's categorization can be regarded as a more sophisticated version of Ryle's classification. One limitation of the ACT model is the hypothesis that transformation of knowledge is unidirectional and only involves transformations from declarative to procedural knowledge, while it can be argued that transformation is bidirectional. This may be because the ACT model is more concerned with maturation than with the creation of knowledge.

Four Modes of Knowledge Conversion

The assumption that knowledge is created through conversion between tacit and explicit knowledge allows us to postulate four different "modes" of knowledge conversion: (1) from tacit knowledge to tacit knowledge, (2) from explicit knowledge to explicit knowledge, (3) from tacit knowledge to explicit knowledge, and (4) from explicit knowledge to tacit knowledge.

First, there is a mode of knowledge conversion that enables us to convert tacit knowledge through interaction between individuals. One important point to note here is that an individual can acquire tacit knowledge without language.

Apprentices work with their mentors and learn craftsmanship not through language but by observation, imitation, and practice. In a business setting, on-the-job training (OJT) uses the same principle. The key to acquiring tacit knowledge is experience. Without some form of shared experience, it is extremely difficult for people to share each others' thinking processes. The mere transfer of information will often make little sense if it is abstracted from embedded emotions and nuanced contexts that are associated with shared experiences. This process of creating tacit knowledge through shared experience will be called "socialization."

The second mode of knowledge conversion involves the use of social processes to combine different bodies of explicit knowledge held by individuals. Individuals exchange and combine knowledge through such exchange mechanisms as meetings and telephone conversations. The reconfiguring of existing information through the sorting, adding, recategorizing, and recontextualizing of explicit knowledge can lead to new knowledge. Modern computer systems provide a graphic example. This process of creating explicit knowledge from explicit knowledge is referred to as "combination."

The third and fourth modes of knowledge conversion relate to patterns of conversion involving both tacit and explicit knowledge. These conversion modes capture the idea that tacit and explicit knowledge are complementary and can expand over time through a process of mutual interaction. This interaction involves two different operations. One is the conversion of tacit knowledge into explicit knowledge, which will be called "externalization." The other is the conversion of explicit knowledge into tacit knowledge, which bears some similarity to the traditional notion of "learning" and will be referred to here as "internalization." As will be discussed later, "metaphor" plays an important role in the externalization process, and "action" is deeply related to the internalization process. Figure 1.1 illustrates the four modes of knowledge conversion.

Three of the four types of knowledge conversion—socialization, combination, and internalization, have partial analogs with aspects of organizational theory. For example, socialization is connected with theories of organizational

	Tacit knowledge To Explicit knowledge	
Tacit knowledge From	Socialization	Externalization
Explicit knowledge	Internalization	Combination

FIGURE 1.1 Modes of Knowledge Creation

culture, while combination is rooted in information processing and internalization has associations with organizational learning. By contrast, the concept of externalization is not well developed. The limited analysis that does exist is from the point of view of information creation (see Nonaka 1987).

Theories of organizational learning do not address the critical notion of externalization, and have paid little attention to the importance of socialization even though there has been an accumulation of research on "modeling" behavior in learning psychology. Another difficulty relates to the concepts of "double-loop learning" (Argyris and Schon 1978) or "unlearning" (Hedberg 1981), which arises from a strong orientation toward organization development (OD). Since the first integrated theory of organizational learning presented by Argyris and Schon, it has been widely assumed, implicitly or explicitly, that double-loop learning, i.e., the questioning and reconstruction of existing perspectives, interpretation frameworks, or decision premises, can be very difficult for organizations to implement by themselves. In order to overcome this difficulty, they argue that some kind of artificial intervention such as the use of organizational development programs is required. The limitation of this argument is that it assumes implicitly that someone inside or outside an organization knows "objectively" the right time and method for putting double-loop learning into practice. A mechanistic view of the organization lies behind this assumption. Seen from the vantage point of organizational knowledge creation, on the contrary, double-loop learning is not a special, difficult task but a daily activity for the organization. Organizations continuously create new knowledge by reconstructing existing perspectives, frameworks, or premises on a day-to-day basis. In other words, double-loop learning ability is "built into" the knowledge creating model, thereby circumventing the need to make unrealistic assumptions about the existence of a "right" answer.

Modal Shift and Spiral of Knowledge

While each of the four modes of knowledge conversion can create new knowledge independently, the central theme of the model of organizational knowledge creation proposed here hinges on a dynamic interaction between the different modes of knowledge conversion. That is to say, knowledge creation centers on the building of both tacit and explicit knowledge and, more importantly, on the interchange between these two aspects of knowledge through internalization and externalization.

A failure to build a dialogue between tacit and explicit knowledge can cause problems. For example, both pure combination and socialization have demerits. A lack of commitment and neglect of the personal meaning of knowledge might mean that pure combination becomes a superficial interpretation of existing knowledge, which has little to do with here-and-now reality. It may also fail to crystallize or embody knowledge in a form that is concrete enough to facilitate further knowledge creation in a wider social context. The "sharability" of knowledge created by pure socialization may be limited and, as a result, difficult to apply in fields beyond the specific context in which it was created.

Organizational knowledge creation, as distinct from individual knowledge creation, takes place when all four modes of knowledge creation are "organizationally" managed to form a continual cycle. This cycle is shaped by a series of shifts between different modes of knowledge conversion. There are various "triggers" that induce these shifts between different modes of knowledge conversion. First, the socialization mode usually starts with the building of a "team" or "field" of interaction. This field facilitates the sharing of members' experiences and perspectives. Second, the externalization mode is triggered by successive rounds of meaningful "dialogue." In this dialogue, the sophisticated use of "metaphors" can be used to enable team members to articulate their own perspectives, and thereby reveal hidden tacit knowledge that is otherwise hard to communicate. Concepts formed by teams can be combined with existing data and external knowledge in a search of more concrete and sharable specifications. This combination mode is facilitated by such triggers as "coordination" between team members and other sections of the organization and the "documentation" of existing knowledge. Through an iterative process of trial and error, concepts are articulated and developed until they emerge in a concrete form. This "experimentation" can trigger internalization through a process of "learning by doing." Participants in a "field" of action share explicit knowledge that is gradually translated through interaction and a process of trial-and-error, into different aspects of tacit knowledge.

While tacit knowledge held by individuals may lie at the heart of the knowledge creating process, realizing the practical benefits of that knowledge centers on its externalization and amplification through dynamic interactions between all four modes of knowledge conversion. Tacit knowledge is thus mobilized through a dynamic "entangling" of the different modes of knowledge conversion in a process which will be referred to as a "spiral" model of knowledge creation, illustrated in Figure 1.2. The interactions between tacit knowledge and explicit knowledge will tend to become larger in scale and faster in speed as more actors in and around the organization become involved. Thus, organizational knowledge creation can be viewed as an upward spiral process, starting at the individual level moving up to the collective (group) level, and then to the organizational level, sometimes reaching out to the interorganizational level.

2.5. From Metaphor to Model: Methodology of Knowledge Creation

Before concluding this presentation of the basic constructs of the theory, it is helpful to consider some general principles for facilitating the management of knowledge conversion. One effective method of converting tacit knowledge into explicit knowledge is the use of metaphor. As Nisbet (1969, p. 5) noted, "(m)uch of what Michael Polanyi has called 'tacit knowledge' is expressible—in so far as

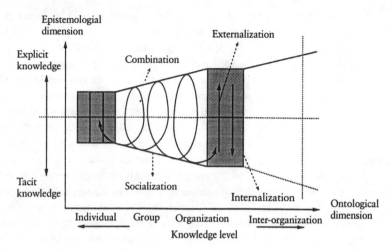

FIGURE 1.2 Spiral of Organizational Knowledge Creation

it is expressible at all—in metaphor." "The essence of metaphor is understanding and experiencing one kind of thing in terms of another (Lakoff and Johnson 1980, p. 5)." Even though the metaphor is not in itself a thinking process, it enables us to experience a new behavior by making inferences from the model of another behavior. The use of metaphor is broader than the traditional, lexical definition of the term (meta = change; phor = move). According to Lakoff and Johnson: "metaphor is pervasive in everyday life, not just in language but in thought and action. Our ordinary conceptual system, in terms of which we both think and act, is fundamentally metaphorical in nature" (Lakoff and Johnson 1980, p. 3).

As a method of perception, metaphor depends on imagination and intuitive learning through symbols, rather than on the analysis or synthesis of common attributes shared by associated things. Rosch (1973) suggested that man describes the world, not in the formal attributes of concepts, but in terms of prototypes. For example, the robin could be seen as a better prototype than the turkey for a small bird. Prototypes provide a mechanism for recognizing the maximum level of information with a minimum of energy.

Metaphor is not merely the first step in transforming tacit knowledge into explicit knowledge; it constitutes an important method of creating a network of concepts which can help to generate knowledge about the future by using existing knowledge. Metaphor may be defined as being "two contradicting concepts incorporated in one word." It is a creative, cognitive process which relates concepts that are far apart in an individual's memory. While perception through prototype is in many cases limited to concrete, mundane concepts, metaphor plays an important role in associating abstract, imaginary concepts. When two concepts are presented in a metaphor, it is possible not only to think of their similarity, but also to make comparisons that discern the degree of imbalance, contradiction or inconsistency involved in their association. The latter process becomes the basis for creating new meaning.[5] According to Bateson (1973) metaphors cut across different contexts and thus allow imaginative perceptions to combine with literal levels of cognitive activities. This experience, he further argues, will promote the type of "presupposition-negation" learning that is closely related with the formation of new paradigms.

Contradictions incorporated in metaphor may be harmonized through the use of analogies. Analogy reduces ambiguity by highlighting the commonness of two different things. Metaphor and analogy are often confused. The association of meanings by metaphor is mostly driven by intuition, and involves images. On the other hand, the association of meanings through analogy is more structural/functional and is carried out through rational thinking. As such, metaphors provide much room for free association (discontinuity). Analogy allows the functional operation of new concepts or systems to be explored by reference to things that are already understood. In this sense, an analogy—that enables us to know the future through the present—assumes an intermediate role in bridging the gap between image and logic.

It follows from the preceding discussion that tacit knowledge may be transformed into explicit knowledge by (1) recognizing contradictions through metaphor, and (2) resolving them through analogy. Explicit knowledge represents a model within which contradictions are resolved and concepts become transferable through consistent and systematic logic. In the business organization, a typical model is the prototype that represents the product concept. The prototype's specification is then explicit knowledge. It has been pointed out that metaphor, analogy, and model are all part of the process of scientific discovery.[6] Whether the metaphor-analogy-model sequence is indispensable in all such processes will depend upon the nature of the question under study; yet in creating new concepts, the model is usually generated from a metaphor.

3. THE PROCESS OF ORGANIZATIONAL KNOWLEDGE CREATION

The theoretical constructs and models described in §2 may now be related to organizational knowledge creation in a corporate organizational setting. This will be approached by assessing the processes that enable individual knowledge to be enlarged, amplified, and justified within an organization.

---

[5] Metaphor should not be understood as mere rhetoric or an issue of expression; it is deeply connected with knowledge creation. For this point, see Black (1962) and McCormac (1985).

[6] For comprehensive discussion on metaphor, analogy, and model, see Leatherdale (1974) and Tsoukas (1991).

3.1. The Enlargement of an Individual's Knowledge

The prime mover in the process of organizational knowledge creation is the individual. Individuals accumulate tacit knowledge through direct "hands-on" experience. The quality of that tacit knowledge is influenced by two important factors. One factor is the "variety" of an individual's experience. If this experience is limited to routine operations, the amount of tacit knowledge obtained from monotonous and repetitive tasks will tend to decrease over time. Routine tasks mitigate against creative thinking and the formation of new knowledge. However, increasing the variety of experience is not sufficient by itself to raise the quality of tacit knowledge. If the individual finds various experiences to be completely unrelated, there will be little chance that they can be integrated to create a new perspective. What matters is "high quality" experience which might, on occasion, involve the complete redefinition of the nature of a "job."

A second factor that determines the quality of tacit knowledge is "knowledge of experience." The essence of "knowledge of experience" is an embodiment of knowledge through a deep personal commitment into bodily experience. Varela et al. (1991) have pointed out that the embodied nature of human knowledge has long been neglected in Western epistemological traditions that have followed from Descartes. They define embodiment as: "a reflection in which body and mind have been brought together" (1991, p. 27). Yuasa (1987) describes this "oneness of body-mind" as the free state of minimal distance between movement of the mind and of the body, as for example in the dynamic performance of a master actor on a stage (1987, p. 28). As Merleau-Ponty (1964) pointed out, bodily experience plays a critical role in the process of crystallization. Commitment to bodily experience means an intentional self-involvement in the object and situation which transcends the subject-object distinction, thereby providing access to "pure experience" (Nishida 1960). This notion is prevalent in oriental culture. As Yuasa mentions:

> One revealing characteristic of the philosophical uniqueness of Eastern thought is presupposed in the philosophical foundation of the Eastern theories. To put it simply, true knowledge cannot be obtained simply by means of theoretical thinking, but only through "bodily recognition or realization" (*tainin* or *taitoku*), that is, through the utilization of one's total mind and body. Simply stated, this is to "learn with the body" not the brain. Cultivation is a practice that attempts, so to speak, to achieve true knowledge by means of one's total mind and body (1987, pp. 25–26).

A good case in point is "on-the-spot-ism" in Japanese management. In developing the products and identifying the markets, Japanese firms encourage the use of judgement and knowledge formed through interaction with customers and by personal bodily experience rather than by "objective," scientific conceptualization. Social interaction between individuals, groups and organizations are fundamental to organizational knowledge creation in Japan. Nevertheless, since this approach uses hands-on experience and action, it sometimes falls in the category of "experiencism" which neglects the importance of reflection and logical thinking. It tends to overemphasize action and efficiency at the expense of a search for higher level concepts which have universal application. While the concepts of "high-quality experience" and "knowledge of experience" may be used to raise the quality of tacit knowledge, they have to be counterbalanced by a further approach to knowledge creation that raises the quality of explicit knowledge. Such an approach may be called a "knowledge of rationality," which describes a rational ability to reflect on experience. Knowledge of rationality is an explicit-knowledge-oriented approach that is dominant in Western culture. It centers on the "combination" mode of knowledge conversion, and is effective in creating digital, discrete declarative knowledge. Knowledge of rationality tends to ignore the importance of commitment, and instead centers a reinterpretation of existing explicit knowledge.

In order to raise the total quality of an individual's knowledge, the enhancement of tacit knowledge has to be subjected to a continual interplay with the evolution of relevant aspects of explicit knowledge. In this connection, Schön (1983) pointed out the importance of "reflection in action," i.e., reflecting while experiencing. Individual knowledge is enlarged through this interaction between experience and rationality, and crystallized into a unique perspective original to an individual. These original perspectives are based on individual belief and value systems, and will be a source of varied interpretations of shared experience with others in the next stage of conceptualization.

3.2. Sharing Tacit Knowledge and Conceptualization

As we saw in the previous section, the process of organizational knowledge creation is initiated by the enlargement of an individual's knowledge within an organization. The interaction between knowledge of experience and rationality enables individuals to build their own perspectives on the world. Yet these perspectives remain personal unless they are articulated and amplified through social interaction. One way to implement the management of organizational knowledge creation is to create a "field" or "self-organizing team" in which individual members collaborate to create a new concept.

In this connection, it is helpful to draw on the concept of an organization's "mental outlook" as articulated in Sandelands and Stablein's (1987) pioneering work on "organizational mind." While making caveats about the dangers of reification and anthropomorphism, these authors use the analogy of "mind" to identify the process by which organizations form ideas. Mind is distinct from the brain in the same way that computer software is distinct from hardware. Against this background, intelligence may be seen as the ability to maintain a working similarity between mind and nature.

The development of ideas associated with organizational mind requires some form of physical substrate (i.e. hardware) which Sandelands and Stablein (1987) argue might be derived from "patterns of behavior traced by people and machines" (p. 139). Organizational behaviors can convey ideas and, like the firing of neurons in the brain, may trigger other behaviors and so form a trace of activation.

> In the brain, whether or not one neuron influences another depends on a complex set of factors having primarily to do with physical proximity, availability of pathways, intensity of the electrochemical signal, and whether or not the target neuron is inhibited by other neurons. Similarly, whether one behavior influences another in social organizations depends on a complex of factors primarily concerned with physical access, lines of communication, power, and competition from other behaviors. At an abstract formal level, at least, the politics of the social organization and the physiology of the brain share much in common (Sandelands and Stablein 1987, p. 140).

It is human activity that creates organizational mind as individuals interact and trigger behavior patterns in others. Managing a self-organizing team involves building an appropriate degree of flexibility into the system which can accommodate a diversity of imaginative thinking in the pursuit of new problems and solutions.

Constructing a Field: Building a Self-organizing Team

To bring personal knowledge into a social context within which it can be amplified, it is necessary to have a "field" that provides a place in which individual perspectives are articulated, and conflicts are resolved in the formation of higher-level concepts. Berger and Luchman (1966) say that reality in everyday life is socially constructed. Individual behavior ought to be relativized through an interactive process to construct "social reality."

In the business organization, the field for interaction is often provided in the form of an autonomous, self-organizing "team" made of several members coming from a variety of functional departments. It is a critical matter for an organization to decide when and how to establish such a "field" of interaction in which individuals can meet and interact. It defines "true" members of knowledge creation and thus clarifies the domain in which perspectives are interacted.

The team needs to be established with regard to the principles of self-organization. In Lewin's (1951) development of the field theory in social psychology, a group is defined as "a dynamic whole based on interdependence rather on similarity." Some indication of the number of members and the composition of their background can be achieved using the principle of "requisite variety" (Ashby 1956). According to our observation of successful project teams in Japanese firms, the appropriate team size may be in the region between 10 and 30 individuals, with an upper limit arising because direct interaction between all the group members tends to decrease as group size increases. Within the team, there are usually 4 to 5 "core" members who have career histories that include multiple job functions. These core members form focal points in the team and could be seen as the organizational equivalent of the central element in a series of nested

Russian dolls.[7] That is to say there is a radial pattern of interaction with other members, with closer links being associated with key individuals. Core members play a critical role in assuring appropriate "redundancy" of information within the cross-functional team. Other attributes of members such as formal position, age, gender, etc. might be determined with regard to Morgan's (1986) four principles of "learning to learn, requisite variety, minimum critical specification, and redundancy of functions."

The span of team activities need not confined to the narrow boundary of the organization. Rather, it is a process that frequently makes extensive use of knowledge in environment, especially that of customers and suppliers. As Norman (1988) argues, the mental outlook of an organization is shaped by a complex pattern of factors within and outside the organization.[8] In some Japanese firms, for example, suppliers of parts and components are sometimes involved in the early stages of the product development. The relationship between manufacturers and suppliers is less hierarchial and arms length than in Western countries. Some other Japanese companies involve customers in the field of new product planning. In both cases, sharing tacit knowledge with suppliers or customers through coexperience and creative dialogue play a critical role in creating relevant knowledge.

The significance of links between individuals that span boundaries, both within and outside the organization, has been highlighted by Brown and Duguid's (1991) revealing insight into the operation of "evolving communities of practice." These communities reflect the way in which people actually work as opposed to the formal job descriptions or task-related procedures that are specified by the organization. Attempts to solve practical problems often generate links between individuals who can provide useful information. The exchange and development of information within these evolving communities facilitate knowledge creation by linking the routine dimensions of day-to-day work to active learning and innovation. Collaboration to exchange ideas through shared narratives and "war stories" can provide an important platform on which to construct shared understanding out of conflicting and confused data.

[7] The self-organizing team may be depicted by Maturana and Varela's (1980) concept of an "autopoietic system." Living organic systems are composed of various organs, which are again composed of numerous cells. Each unit, like an autonomous cell, is self-regulating. Moreover, each unit determines its boundary through self-reproduction, and is separate from the environment. This self-referential or self-reflecting nature is a quintessential feature of autopoietic systems.

[8] Gibson (1979) suggested an interesting hypothesis that knowledge lies in the environment itself, contrary to the traditional epistemological view that it exists inside the human brain. According to him, man perceives information ("affordance") which natural objects afford to human cognitive activity, i.e., according the degree of affordance of the environment. Information on chair, knife, and cliff are revealed when the actions of sitting, cutting, and falling are made, in other words, in the course of interactions between the subject and the object of perception.

By contrast with conceptions of groups as bounded entities within an organization, evolving communities of practice are "more fluid and interpenetrative than bounded, often crossing the restrictive boundaries of the organization to incorporate people from outside" (Brown and Duguid 1991, p. 49). Moreover, these communities can provide important contributions to visions for future development. Thus these communities represent a key dimension to socialization and its input to the overall knowledge creation process.

The self-organizing team triggers organizational knowledge creation through two processes. First, it facilitates the building of mutual trust among members, and accelerates creation of an implicit perspective shared by members as tacit knowledge. The key factor for this process is sharing experience among members. Second, the shared implicit perspective is conceptualized through continuous dialogue among members. This creative dialogue is realized only when redundancy of information exists within the team. The two processes appear simultaneously or alternatively in the actual process of knowledge creation within a team.

Before discussing these two processes further, it is necessary to mention another dimension of the knowledge creating process that can be associated with the self-organizing team. Scheflen (1982) proposed an idea of "interaction rhythms," in which social interactions were viewed as being both simultaneous and sequential. The management of interaction rhythms among team members, i.e., that of divergence and convergence of various interaction rhythms, plays a critical role in accelerating the knowledge creation process. Within the team, rhythms of different speed are first generated and amplified up to certain point of time and level, and then are given momentum for convergence towards a concept. Therefore, the crucial role of the team leader concerns how to balance the rhythm of divergence and convergence in the process of dialogues and shared experience.

In sum, the cross-functional team in which experience sharing and continuous dialogue are facilitated by the management of interaction rhythms serves as the basic building block for structuring the organization knowledge creation process. The team is different from a mere group in that it induces self-organizing process of the entire organization through which the knowledge at the group level is elevated to the organizational level.

Sharing Experience

In order for the self-organizing team to start the process of concept creation, it first needs to build mutual trust among members. As we shall see later, concept creation involves a difficult process of externalization, i.e., converting tacit knowledge (which by nature is hard to articulate) into an explicit concept. This challenging task involves repeated, time-consuming dialogue among members. Mutual trust is an indispensable base for facilitating this type of constructive "collaboration" (Schrage 1990). A key way to build mutual trust is to share one's original experience—the fundamental source of tacit knowledge. Direct understanding of other individuals relies on shared experience that enables team members to "indwell" into others and to grasp their world from "inside."

Shared experience also facilitates the creation of "common perspectives" which can be shared by team members as a part of their respective bodies of tacit knowledge. The dominant mode of knowledge conversion involved here is socialization. Various forms of tacit knowledge that are brought into the field by individual members are converted through coexperience among them to form a common base for understanding.

As was mentioned earlier, tacit knowledge is a distinctly personal concept. Varela et al. (1991) point out the limitation of the cognitivist view of human experience in comparison with the non-Western philosophical view, and suggest that cognitive experience is "embodied action" rather than a mere representation of a world that exists independent of our cognitive system. The mutual conversion of such embodied, tacit knowledge is accelerated by synchronizing both body and mind in the face of the same experience. Coexperience with others enables us to transcend the ordinary "I-Thou" distinction, and opens up the world of common understanding, which Scheflen (1982) called "Field Epistemology." Condon (1976) shared this view that communication is a simultaneous and contextual phenomenon in which people feel a change occurring, share the same sense of change, and are moved to take action. In other words, communication is like a wave that passes through people's bodies and culminates when everyone synchronizes himself with the wave. Thus, the sharing of mental and physical rhythm among participants of a field may serve as the driving force of socialization.

Conceptualization

Once mutual trust and a common implicit perspective have been formed through shared experience, the team needs to articulate the perspective through continuous dialogues. The dominant mode of knowledge conversion here is externalization. Theories of organizational learning have not given much attention to this process. Tacit "field-specific" perspectives are converted into explicit concepts that can be shared beyond the boundary of the team. Dialogue directly facilitates this process by activating externalization at individual levels.

Dialogue, in the form of face-to-face communication between persons, is a process in which one builds concepts in cooperation with others. It also provides the opportunity for one's hypothesis or assumption to be tested. As Markova and Foppa (1990) argue, social intercourse is one of the most powerful media for verifying one's own ideas. As such, dialogue has a congenetic quality, and thus the participants in the dialogue can engage in the mutual codevelopment of ideas. As Graumann (1990) points out, dialogue involves "perspective-setting, perspective-taking, and multiperspectivity of cognition." According to the theory of language action suggested by Austin (1962) and Searle (1969), illocutionary speech does not only involve a description of things and facts but the taking of action itself. The expression "language is behavior," therefore, implies that language is a socially creative activity and accordingly reveals the importance of the connection between language and reality created through dialogue.

For these purposes, dialectic is a good way of raising the quality of dialogue. Dialectic allows scope for the articulation and development of personal theories and beliefs. Through the use of contradiction and paradox, dialectic can serve to stimulate creative thinking in the organization. If the creative function of dialectic is to be exploited to the full, it is helpful to pay regard to certain preconditions or "field rules." First, the dialogue should not be single-faceted and deterministic but temporary and multifaceted so that there is always room for revision or negation. Second, the participants in the dialogue should be able to express their own ideas freely and candidly. Third, negation for the sake of negation should be discouraged. Constructive criticism substantiated by reasoned arguments should be used to build a consensus. Fourth, there should be temporal continuity. Dialectic thinking is a repetitive, spiral process in which affirmation and negation are synthesized to form knowledge. Strict and noncontinuous separation of affirmation and negation will only result in logical contradictions and thus hamper the creation of knowledge. Team leaders, therefore, should not discourage the dramatic and volatile dimensions of dialogue. If these conditions are met, dialogue will add much to the potential of the group in knowledge creation.

The process of creating a new perspective through interpersonal interaction is assisted by the existence of a degree of redundant information. Making and solving new problems are made possible when its members share information by obtaining extra, redundant information which enables them to enter another person's area and give advice. Instances of "learning by intrusion" (Nonaka 1990) are particularly widespread in Japanese firms.[9] In the meantime, redundancy of information also functions to determine the degree to which created perspectives are diffused. It may sound paradoxical; yet the degree of information redundancy will limit the degree of diffusion. In this sense, information redundancy can serve to regulate the creation of perspectives.

It is now possible to turn to the question of how to conceptualize new perspectives created from shared tacit knowledge. According to Bateson (1979), concepts are created through deduction, induction, and abduction. Abduction has a particular importance in the conceptualization process. While deduction and induction are vertically-oriented reasoning processes, abduction is a lateral extension of the reasoning process which centers on the use of metaphors. Deduction and induction are generally used when a thought or image involves

---

[9] Jaikumar and Born (1986) pointed to this as the characteristic of Japanese firms' production methods. According to them, the production method for most American firms is clearly defined as the function of the basic manufacturing technology, assigned works, organizational goals, and environment. In this mode of production, then, workers are well aware of their work and thus simply follow the routine procedure. On the other hand, Japanese workers do not get prior knowledge and thus become part of the given work, rather than being separate from the work itself. Therefore, anomaly, or nonroutine nature, of the work itself becomes an important opportunity for learning.

the revision of a preexisting concept or the assigning of a new meaning to a concept. When there is no adequate expression of an image it is necessary to use abductive methods to create completely new concepts. While analytical methods can be used to generate new concepts via inductive or deductive reasoning, they may not be sufficient to create more meaningful—or radical—concepts. At the early stages of information creation, it is very useful to pursue creative dialogues and to share images through the metaphorical process by merging perspectives, i.e., tacit knowledge.

3.3. Crystallization

The knowledge created in an interactive field by members of a self-organizing team has to be crystallized into some concrete "form" such as a product or a system. The central mode of knowledge conversion at this stage is internalization. Crystallization may then be seen as the process through which various departments within the organization test the reality and applicability of the concept created by the self-organizing team. These internalization processes are facilitated by encouraging experimentation. It should be noted that because the instrumental skill, a part of tacit knowledge, is exploited in this process, a new process of knowledge creation is triggered by crystallization. While this usually leads to refinement of the concept, sometimes the concept itself is abandoned and fundamentally recreated.

The process of crystallization is a social process which occurs at a collective level. It is realized through what Haken (1978) called "dynamic cooperative relations" or "synergetics" among various functions and organizational departments. This relationship tends to be achieved most effectively when redundancy of information creates scope for critical knowledge conversion processes to take place. In an organization where there is redundancy of information, the initiative for action can be taken by the experts who have more information and knowledge. This characteristic is what McCulloch (1965) called "the principle of redundancy of potential command." In this principle, all parts of a system carry the same degree of importance, and each part's impact upon the system is determined by the importance of information it contains in each specified context. In sum, each part has the potential of becoming the leader of the entire system when there exists redundancy of information.

The speed at which Japanese firms develop new products seems to be assisted by information redundancy. In the product development process of Japanese firms, different phases of the process are loosely linked, overlapping in part, and the creation and realization of information is carried out flexibly. The loosely linked phases, while simultaneously maintaining mutual independence, have redundant information that activates their interactive inquiry thereby facilitating cyclical generation and solution of problems (Imai et al. 1985). This "rugby-style" product development is equipped with the flexible capability of knowledge conversion. Clark and Fujimoto (1991) showed that Japanese firms take relatively less time for product development than American and European firms.

The specific characteristics of the product development in Japanese firms is its lateral breadth covering the whole organization. In other words it is overlapping and synthetic rather than analytic or linear. In this system, development staff can traverse overlapping phases and, to a certain extent, share each other's functions. This is far different from the usual product development process of U.S. firms, which have definite partitions between phases over which a baton is relayed. In the Japanese "rugby-style" product development (Takeuchi and Nonaka 1986), staff involved in one phase also may be in the next phase. Thus, some development staff can be involved in all phases of development. Sometimes this process also involves those outside the organization such as suppliers and customers in order to mobilize and explicit environmental knowledge.

One problem with this developmental style is the potential risk of confusion if, for example, the design changes or other alterations take place. Participants might have to exert more effort to organize the process due to the lack of strict specifications at each phase and definite boundaries between them. However, these risks are counterbalanced by a tendency to create and realize concepts quickly and flexibly in an integral fashion. In this context, redundant information can play a major role in facilitating the process.

3.4. The Justification and Quality of Knowledge

While organizational knowledge creation is a continuous process with no ultimate end, an organization needs to converge this process at some point in order to accelerate the sharing of created knowledge beyond the boundary of the organization for further knowledge creation. As knowledge is conventionally defined as "justified true belief," this convergence needs to be based on the "justification" or truthfulness of concepts. Justification is the process of final convergence and screening, which determines the extent to which the knowledge created within the organization is truly worthwhile for the organization and society. In this sense, justification determines the "quality" of the created knowledge and involves criteria or "standards" for judging truthfulness.

What matters here are the evaluation "standards" for judging truthfulness. In the business organizations, the standards generally include cost, profit margin, and the degree to which a product can contribute to the firm's development. There are also value premises that transcend factual or pragmatic considerations. These might be opinions about such things as the extent to which the knowledge created is consistent with the organization's vision and perceptions relating to adventure, romanticism, and aesthetics. The inducements to initiate a convergence of knowledge may be multiple and qualitative rather than simple and quantitative standards such as efficiency, cost, and return on investment (ROI).

In knowledge-creating organizations, it is the role of top or middle management to determine the evaluation standard. Determining the turning point from dissipation to convergence in the creation process is a highly strategic task which is influenced by the *"aspiration"* of the leaders of the organization. Justification standards have to be evaluated in terms of their consistency with higher-order value systems. The ability of leaders to maintain continuous self-reflection in a wider perspective is indispensable when it comes to increasing the quality of knowledge created.

3.5. Networking Knowledge

The realization of new concepts, described above, represents a visible emergence of the organization's knowledge network. During this stage of organizational knowledge creation, the concept that has been created, crystallized and justified in the organization is integrated into the organizational knowledge-base which comprises a whole network of organizational knowledge. The organizational knowledge base is then reorganized through a mutually-inducing process of interaction between the established organizational vision and the newly-created concept.

Speaking in sociological terms, this mutually-inducing relationship corresponds to the relationship between a grand concept and a middle-range concept. A middle-range concept is induced from an equivocal knowledge base as a grand concept and then is condensed into concrete form. The grand concept is not fully understood at the organizational level unless these middle-range concepts are verified on site. This verification also induces the creation or reconstruction of a grand concept, causing the interactive proliferation of grand concepts presented by top management, and middle-range concepts created by middle management. This interaction, mediated by the concrete form as condensed information, is another dynamic self-organizing activity of knowledge network that continuously creates new information and meaning.

It should be noted that the process of organizational knowledge creation is a never-ending, circular process that is not confined to the organization but includes many interfaces with the environment. At the same time, the environment is a continual source of stimulation to knowledge creation within the organization. For example, Hayek (1945) pointed out that the essential function of market competition is to discover and mobilize knowledge "on-the-spot," i.e., the implicit, context-specific knowledge held by market participants.

In the case of business organizations, one aspect of the relationship between knowledge creation and the environment is illustrated by reactions to the product by customers, competitors, and suppliers. For example, many dimensions of customer needs take the form of tacit knowledge that an individual customer or other market participants cannot articulate by themselves. A product works as a trigger to articulate the tacit knowledge. Customers and other market participants give meaning to the product by their bodily actions of purchasing, adapting, using, or not purchasing. This mobilization of tacit knowledge of

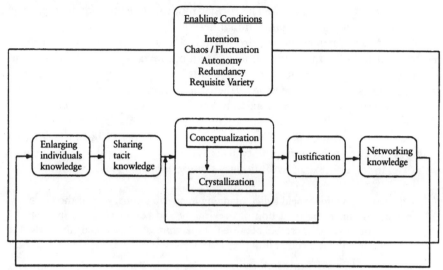

Process of generating information/knowledge in the market

FIGURE 1.3 Organizational Knowledge Creation Process

customers and market will be reflected to the organization, and a new process of organizational knowledge creation is again initiated.

The total process of organizational knowledge creation is summarized in Figure 1.3. Even though the figure is illustrated as a sequential model, the actual process progresses forming multilayered loops. Respective stages can take place simultaneously, or sometimes jump forward or backward.

4. MANAGING THE PROCESS OF ORGANIZATIONAL KNOWLEDGE CREATION: CREATIVE CHAOS, REDUNDANCY, AND REQUISITE VARIETY

This section draws on preceding arguments in order to develop a practical perspective on the management of organizational knowledge creation. Its main purpose is to complement the aspects of "individual commitment" to the knowledge creating process (i.e., intention, autonomy, and fluxuation, discussed in §2.2) with, what could be seen as, "organization-wide" enabling conditions that promote a more favorable 'climate for effective knowledge creation[10] (see Figure 1.3). An analysis of these enabling conditions—creative chaos, redundancy of information, and requisite variety—is developed below, prior to making specific proposals for two management models: "middle-up-down management"

---

[10] The development of these concepts are based on a series of theoretical and empirical research studies (Kagono et al. 1985, Takeuchi et al. 1986, and Nonaka 1988a).

and a "hypertext" organization. The former model relates to management style, while the latter centers on organizational design.

As was mentioned earlier, environmental fluctuation is one of the three factors that induce individual commitment. At an organizational level, environmental fluctuation can generate "creative chaos" which triggers the process of organizational knowledge creation. When the organization faces nonrecursiveness that cannot be dealt with by existing knowledge, it might try to create a new order of knowledge by making use of the fluctuation itself. According to the principle of "order out of noise" proposed by von Foerster (1984), the self-organizing system can increase its ability to survive by purposefully introducing its own noise. In the context of evolutionary theory, Jantsch (1980) argues:

> In contrast to a widely held belief, planning in an evolutionary spirit therefore does not result in the reduction of uncertainty and complexity, but in their increase. Uncertainty increases because the spectrum of options is deliberately widened; imagination comes into play (1980, p. 267).

This represents a circular process in which chaos is perceived in its interaction with cosmos and then becomes a cosmos, which in turn produces another chaos.

Creative chaos is generated naturally when the organization faces a real "crisis" such as rapid decline of performance due to changes in technologies or market needs, or the realization of a significant competitive advantage on the part of a rival firm. It can also be generated intentionally when leaders of an organization try to evoke a "sense of crisis" among organizational members by proposing challenging goals. This creative chaos increases tension within the organization and focuses attention on forming and solving new problems. In the information processing paradigm, a problem is simply given and a solution is reached through a process of combining relevant information based on a preset algorithm. But this process ignores the importance of problem setting—defining the problem to be solved. In reality, problems do not present themselves as given but instead have to be constructed from the knowledge available at a certain point in time and context.

It should be noted, however, that this process takes place only when organizational members reflect on their actions. Without reflection, the introduction of fluctuation tends to produce "destructive" chaos. As Schön (1983) observed, "When someone reflects while in action, he becomes a researcher. He is not dependent on the categories of established theory and technique, but constructs a new theory of the unique case" (1983, p. 68). The knowledge-creating organization is required to institutionalize this reflection-in-action in its process as well as in its structure to make the chaos truly "creative."

A second principle for managing organizational knowledge creation is redundancy. In business organizations, this means the conscious overlapping of company information, business activities, and management responsibilities. To Western managers, the term "redundancy," with its connotations of unnecessary duplication and waste, may sound unappealing. Nevertheless, redundancy (Landau 1969 and Nonaka 1990) plays a key role, especially in the process of knowledge creation at the level of the organization. Redundant information can be instrumental in speeding up concept creation. A concept that was created by an individual or a group often needs to be shared by other individuals who may need the concept immediately. The redundancy of information refers to the existence of information more than the specific information required immediately by each individual. The sharing of extra information between individuals promotes the sharing of individual tacit knowledge. Since members share overlapping information, they can sense what others are trying to articulate. Especially in the concept development stage, it is critical to articulate images rooted in tacit knowledge. In this situation, individuals can enter each others' area of operation and can provide advice. This allows people to provide new information from new and different perspectives. In short, redundancy of information brings about "learning by intrusion" into an individual's sphere of perception.

Redundant information can be an instrumental factor in reducing the impact of managerial hierarchy. That is to say, redundant information provides a vehicle for problem generation and knowledge creation which follows procedures that are different from those specified by the "official" organizational structure. This concept of "nonhierarchy" has been described by Hedlund (1986) as "heterarchy." The important point to note is that redundancy of information makes the interchange between hierarchy and nonhierarchy more effective in problem solving and knowledge creation. It enables all members of the organization to participate in the process on the basis of consensus and equal preparation. In this sense, redundancy of information is an indispensable element in inducing the "synergetics" and to realize the "principle of redundancy of potential command."

Deep, mutual trust between the members of the organization—the creators of knowledge—can be promoted through information redundancy and, in this way, the organization can control its knowledge creation. If an organization contains enough redundancy of information to deal with as many contingencies as possible, it can generate various combinations of information flexibly. This redundancy also facilitates interaction among organizational members and consequently makes it easier to transfer tacit knowledge among them. Redundancy can eliminate cheating among organizational members and facilitates establishment of mutual trust. Williamson (1975) argues convincingly that opportunism tends to appear less frequently in internally organized activities than in market transactions. Close interaction and trust based upon sharing of redundant information minimizes the possibility of cheating. Since "trust is a critical lubricant in social systems" (Arrow 1974), it would be impossible to form "synergetics" needed for knowledge creation without trust.

Sharing of extra information also helps individuals to recognize their location in the organization, which in turn increases the sense of control and direction of individual thought and behavior. This state is different from the one in which all members are scattered with no relationship to each other. Redundancy of information connects individuals and the organization through information, which converges rather than diffuses.

There are several ways to build redundancy into the organization. One is to adopt an overlapping approach and internal competition in product development. As was stressed in the section on crystallization, Japanese companies manage product development as an overlapping, "rugby-style" process where different functional divisions work together in a shared division of labor. Some of them also divide the product-development team into competing groups that develop different approaches to the same project and then argue over the advantages and disadvantages of their proposals. Internal rivalry encourages the team to look at a project from a variety of perspectives. Under the guidance of a team leader, the team eventually develops a common understanding of the "best" approach. In one sense, such internal competition is wasteful. But when responsibilities are shared, information proliferates, and the organization's ability to create and implement concepts is accelerated.

Another way to build redundancy into an organization is through strategic rotation, especially between different areas of technology and between functions such as R&D and marketing. Rotation helps members of an organization understand the business from a multiplicity of perspectives. This makes organizational knowledge more fluid and easier to put into practice. Wide access to company information also helps build redundancy. When information differentials exist, members of an organization can no longer interact on equal terms, which hinders the search for different interpretations of new knowledge.

Since redundancy of information increases the amount of information to be processed, it is important to strike a balance between the creation and processing of information. One way of dealing with this issue is to determine the appropriate location of information and knowledge storage within an organization. Ashby (1956) has suggested the concept of "requisite variety" which refers to the constructing of information process channels that match the information load imposed by the environment. According to the principle of requisite variety, an organization can maximize efficiency by creating within itself the same degree of diversity as the diversity it must process. Following Ashby, requisite variety may be seen as the third principle of organizing knowledge creating activities.

Efficient knowledge creation requires quick inquiry and preprocessing of existing knowledge and information. Therefore, it is a practical requirement here that everyone is given access to necessary information with the minimum number of steps (Numangami et al. 1989). For this purpose, (1) organizational members should know who owns what information, and (2) they should be related to the least number of colleagues so that they are not loaded with information in the excess of each one's cognitive capacity.

4.1. Middle-Up-Down Management: Leadership for Parallel Process

In earlier work, a new model of management called "middle-up-down management" was proposed and contrasted with typical "top-down" management or "bottom-up" management (Nonaka 1988b). This middle-up-down management model is suitable for promoting the efficient creation of knowledge in business organizations. The model is based on the principle of creative chaos, redundancy, and requisite variety mentioned above; much emphasis is placed on the role of top and middle management for knowledge creation, which has been almost neglected in traditional accounts of managerial structure.

The essence of a traditional bureaucratic machine is top-down information processing using division of labor and hierarchy. Top managers create basic managerial concepts (the premises of decision making) and break them down hierarchically—in terms of objectives and means—so that they can be implemented by subordinates. Top managers' concepts become operational conditions for middle managers who then decide how to realize the concepts. Again, middle managers' decisions constitute operational conditions for lower managers who implement their decisions. In consequence, the organization as a whole executes a huge amount of work that can never be done by individuals.

If we visualize the dyadic relations between top vs. middle managers, the middle vs. lower members, an organization assumes a tree-shaped or pyramidal structure. In this "top-down" model, it is desirable to organize the whole structure in the way it will conform to the above relations. To clearly break down the endmeans relations, it is necessary to get rid of any ambiguity or equivocality in the concepts held by top managers. In sum, the concepts anchor on the premise that they only have one meaning. By corollary, the concepts are also strictly functional and pragmatic. An implicit assumption behind this traditional model of organization is that information and knowledge are processed most efficiently in a tree structure. The division of labor taking place within such a bureaucratic organization is associated with a hierarchical pattern of information processing. Moving from the bottom to the top of the organization, information is processed selectively so that people at the peak would get simple, processed information only. Moving in the reverse direction, on the other hand, information is processed and transformed from the general to the particular. It is this deductive transformation that enables human beings with limited information processing capacity to deal with a mass of information.

It should be noted that information processing by middle and lower members in this model is of minor relevance to knowledge creation. Only top managers are able and allowed to create information. Moreover, information created by these top managers exists for the sole purpose of implementation; therefore it is a tool rather than a product. On the contrary, in the bottom-up model, those who create information are not top managers, but middle and lower managers. In a typical bottom-up managed company, intracompany entrepreneurs or "intrapreneurs" (Pinchot 1985) are fostered and developed by the system. In reality there are not many larger firms that have bottom-up management style. In this model, top managers remain sponsors for individual employees who function as intra company entrepreneurs—including knowledge creation. However, this model is also anchored on the own situation and perspectives. Thus, what makes sense critical role of the individual as independent, separate actor as in the top-down model.

Unlike the above two models, the middle-up-down model takes all members as important actors who work together horizontally and vertically. A major characteristic of the model regarding knowledge creation is the wide scope of cooperative relationships between top, middle, and lower managers. No one major department or group of experts has the exclusive responsibility for creating new knowledge.

But this is not to say that there is no differentiation among roles and responsibilities in this style of management. In the middle-up-down model, top management provides "visions for direction" and also the deadline by which the visions should be realized. Middle management translates these visions out of those from top and lower managers and materialize then vis-à-vis the two levels. In other words, while top management articulates the dreams of the firm, lower managers look at reality. The gap between these two forms of perspectives is narrowed by and through middle management. In this sense, it is a leadership style that facilitates the parallel knowledge creation process taking place simultaneously at top, middle, and lower management respectively.

Table 1.1 summarizes the comparison of the three models, top-down, bottom-up, and middle-up-down management, in terms of knowledge creator, resource allocation, structural characteristics, process characteristics, knowledge accumulation, and inherent limitation. The roles and tasks of lower, top and middle managers in the middle-up-down management will now be discussed in detail.

Frontline employees and lower managers are immersed in the day-to-day details of particular technologies, products and markets. No one is more expert in the realities of a company's business than they are. But, while these employees and lower managers are deluged with highly specific information, they often find it extremely difficult to turn that information into useful knowledge. For one thing, signals from the marketplace can be vague and ambiguous. For another, employees and lower managers can become so caught up in their own narrow perspective, that they lose sight of the broader context. Moreover, even when they try to develop meaningful ideas and insights, it can still be difficult to communicate the importance of that information to others. People do not just passively receive new knowledge; they actively interpret it to fit their own situation and perspectives. Thus, what makes sense in one context can change or even lose its meaning when communicated to people in a different context.

The main job of top and middle managers in the model of middle-up-down management is to orient this chaotic situation toward purposeful knowledge creation. These managers do this by providing their subordinates with a conceptual framework that helps them make sense of their own experience.

TABLE 1.1 A Comparison of Three Management Models

	Top-Down	Middle-Up-Down	Bottom-up
Agent of Knowledge Creation	Top management	Self-organizing team (with middle managers as team leaders)	Entrpreneurial individual (intrapreneur)
Resource Allocation	Hierarchically	From diverse viewpoints	Self-organizing principle
Pursued Synergy	"Synergy of money"	"Synergy of knowledge"	"Synergy of people"
Organization	Big and powerful hq. staff use manuals	Team-oriented Affiliated firms by intrapreneurs	Small hq. Self-organizing suborganizations
Management processes	Leaders as commanders Emphasis on information processing Chaos not allowed	Leaders as catalysts Create organizational knowledge Create/amplify chaos/noise	Leaders as sponsors Create personal information Chaos/noise premised
Accumulated Knowledge	Explicit computerized/ documented	Explicit and tacit shared in diverse forms	Tacit incarnated in individuals
Weakness	High dependency on top management	Human exhaustion lack of overall control of the organization	Time consuming difficult to coordinate individuals

Source: From Nonaka (1988b).

In both top-down management and bottom-up management, a high degree of emphasis is given to charismatic leadership. By contrast, middle-up-down management views managers as catalysts. In this role as a "catalyst," top management sets the direction, provides the field of interaction, selects the participants in the field, establishes the guidelines and deadlines for projects, and supports the innovation process.

Top management gives voice to a company's future by articulating metaphors, symbols, and concepts that orient the knowledge-creating activities of employees. In other words, they give form to "organizational intention" that is beyond the personal intention of top management as an individual. This is achieved by asking the questions on behalf of the entire organization: What are we trying to learn? What do we need to know? Where should we be going? Who are we? If the job of frontline employees and lower managers is to know "what is," then the job of top management is to know "what ought to be." In other words, the responsibility of top management in middle-up-down management is to articulate the company's "conceptual umbrella": the grand concepts expressed in highly universal and abstract terms identify the common features linking seemingly disparate activities or businesses into a coherent whole. Quinn (1992) called this conceptual umbrella a "future vision" that gives intellectual members of organizations some challenges for intellectual growth and develops their capacity for continuous change.

Another way in which top management provides employees with a sense of direction is by setting the standards for justifying the value of knowledge that is constantly being developed by the organization's members. As earlier comments on the "justification" of knowledge indicated, deciding which efforts to support and develop is a highly strategic task. In order to facilitate organizational knowledge creation, qualitative factors such as truthfulness, beauty, or goodness are equal important to such qualitative, economic factors as efficiency, cost or ROI.

In addition to the umbrella concepts and qualitative criteria for justification, top management articulates concepts in the form of committed, equivocal visions, which are open-ended and susceptible to a variety of, and even conflicting, interpretations. If a vision is too sharply focused, it becomes more akin to an order or instruction, which will not foster the high degree of personal commitment. A more equivocal vision gives employees and self-organizing teams the freedom and autonomy to set their own goals. The final role of top management in middle-up-down management is to clear away any obstacles and prepare the ground for self-organizing teams headed by middle management. Knowledge creation, in this type of management, takes place intensively at the group level, at which middle managers embody top managers' visions. Middle managers are selected by top management, and therefore staffing is an important strategic consideration. Top managers should be able to provide middle managers with a sense of challenge or crisis and trust them.

As we have seen before, teams play a central role in the process of organizational knowledge creation. The main role of middle managers in middle-up-down management is to serve as a team leader who are at the intersection of the vertical and horizontal flows of information in the company. The most important knowledge creating individuals in this model are neither charismatic top managers nor the entrepreneur-like lower managers, but every employee who works in association with middle managers. It is the middle manager that takes a strategic position at which he or she combines strategic, macro, universal information and hands-on, micro, specific information. They work as a bridge between the visionary ideals of the top and the often chaotic reality on the frontline of business. By creating middle-level business and product concepts, middle managers mediate between "what is" and "what ought to be." They even remake reality according to the company's vision.

In addition, middle management forms the strategic knot that binds the top-down and bottom-up models. As the self-organizing team, headed by middle management moves up and down the organization, much redundancy and fluctuation can be created. As such, the organization with middle-up-down management naturally has a strong driver of self-reorganization. The middle management sometimes plays the role of "change-agent" for the self-revolution of the organization.

In sum, middle managers synthesize the tacit knowledge of both frontline employees and top management, make it explicit, and incorporate it into new technologies and products. They are the true "knowledge engineers" of the knowledge creating organizations.

4.2. Hypertext Organization: A Design Prototype of a Knowledge Creating Organization

Finally, an image can be presented of organizational design that provides a structural base for the process of organizational knowledge creation. Middle-up-down management becomes most efficient if supported by this infrastructure. The central requirement for the design of the knowledge-creating organization is to provide the organization with a strategic ability to acquire, create, exploit, and accumulate new knowledge continuously and repeatedly in a circular process. Earlier work has described an image of organizational design equipped with such a dynamic cycle of knowledge under the concept of a "hypertext organization," (Nonaka et al. 1992). This term is borrowed from a concept of computer software where "hypertext" allows users to search large quantities of text, data, and graphics by means of a friendly interface. It links related concepts and areas of knowledge to allow a problem to be viewed from many angles. In many ways, this is analogous to the ability of individuals to relate stories in different ways according to the nature of the audience. The same knowledge might be used but in different formats, making it easier to draw relationships between different sets of information.

The core feature of the hypertext organization is the ability to switch between the various "contexts" of knowledge creation to accommodate changing requirements from situations both inside and outside the organization. Within the process of organizational knowledge creation, it is possible to distinguish several "contexts" of knowledge creation such as the acquisition, generation, exploitation, and accumulation of knowledge. Each context has a distinctive way of organizing its knowledge creation activities. Nonhierarchical, or "heterarchical" self-organizing activities of teams are indispensable to generate new knowledge as well as to acquire "deep" knowledge through intensive, focused search. On the other hand, a hierarchical division of labor is more efficient and effective for implementation, exploitation, and accumulation of new knowledge as well as acquisition of various information through extensive, unfocused search.

Hypertext organization design first distinguishes the normal routine operation conducted by a hierarchical formal organization from the knowledge creating activities carried out by self-organizing teams. But it does not mean that the two activities need to operate separately and independently. Rather, it stresses the need for the careful design of the two activities which takes account of their distinctive contributions to knowledge creation. The important point to note is that the design of the hierarchy and self-organizing teams should enable the organization to shift efficiently and effectively between these two forms of knowledge creation. In terms of the theory of organizational knowledge creation, while hierarchical formal organization mainly carries out the task of combination and internalization, self-organizing teams perform the task of socialization and externalization. This also improves the ability of an organization to survive. By establishing the most appropriate organizational setting for the two activities, an organization can maximize the efficiency of its routine operation, which is determined by bureaucratic principles of division of labor and specialization, and also the effectiveness of its knowledge creation activities. In this type of organization, the knowledge creating activities of self-organizing teams work as a measure which serves to prevent the so-called "reverse function of bureaucracy" (Merton 1957).

Thus the hypertext organization combines the efficiency and stability of a hierarchical bureaucratic organization with the dynamism of the flat, cross-functional-task-force organization. Nevertheless, it should be noted that a critical factor for the design of the hypertext organization lies in the coordination of time, space, and resources to realize the "requisite variety." Jacques (1979) pointed out that positions in the hierarchical organization have responsibility of different time-span. This implies that the hierarchical organization is a coordination device for these works of diverse time-span, and generates a "natural frequency" by "orchestrating" various rhythms. As the previous section indicated, each self-organizing team also creates its own "natural frequency" by synchronizing various rhythms brought into the field by members from diverse positions in hierarchical organization. The hypertext organization is an organizational structure that enables orchestration of different rhythms or "natural frequency" generated by various project teams and the hierarchical organization. It coordinates the allocation of time, space, and resource within the organization so as to compose an "organizational" rhythm that makes organizational knowledge creation more effective and efficient. In this sense, the hypertext organization is a structural device to build "requisite variety," which cannot be secured solely by middle-up-down management.

The image of the hypertext organization is illustrated in Figure 1.4. It can be visualized as a multilayered organization comprised of three layers: knowledge-base, business-system, and project team. At the bottom is the "knowledge-base" layer which embraces tacit knowledge, associated with organizational culture and procedures, as well as explicit knowledge in the form of documents, filing systems, computerized databases, etc. The function of this archival layer may be seen in terms of a "corporate university." The second layer is the "business-system" layer where normal routine operation is carried out by a formal, hierarchical, bureaucratic organization. The top layer relates to the area where multiple self-organizing project teams create knowledge. These teams are loosely

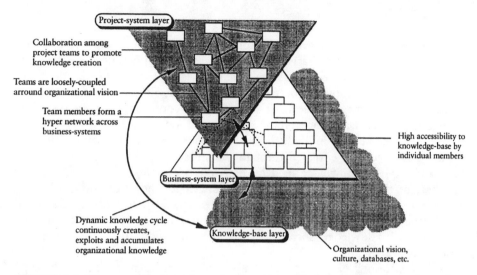

FIGURE 1.4 Hypertext Organization—An Interactive Model of Hierarchy and Nonhierarchy

Source: Nonaka, Konno, Tokuoka, and Kawamura (1992).

linked to each other and share in the "joint creation of knowledge" using "corporate vision." Thus the hypertext organization takes different "forms," depending on the perspective from which it is observed.

The process of organizational knowledge creation is conceptualized as a dynamic cycle of knowledge and information traversing the three layers. Members of project teams on the top layer are selected from diverse functions and departments across the business-system layer. Based on the corporate vision presented by top management, they engage in knowledge creating activities interacting with other project teams. Once the task of a team is completed, members move "down" to the knowledge-base layer at the bottom and make an "inventory" of the knowledge acquired and created in the project. After categorizing, documenting, and indexing the new knowledge, they come back to upper business-system layer and engage in routine operation until they are called again for another project. A key design requirement in the hypertext organization is to form such a circular movement of organization members, who are the fundamental source and subject of organizational knowledge creation. From the vantage point of strategic management, the true "core competence" (Prahalad and Hamel 1990) of the organization, which produces sustainable competitive advantage, lies in its management capability to create relevant organizational knowledge (Nonaka 1989, 1991). This is a continuous process and the ability to switch swiftly and flexibly between the three layers in the hypertext organization is critical to its success.

5. CONCLUSION

The theory of organizational knowledge creation proposed here has been constructed mainly on the basis of hands-on research and practical experience of Japanese firms. Nevertheless, it should be stressed that the principles described have a more general application to any organization, either economic or social, private or public, manufacturing or service, in the coming age despite their field of activities as well as geographical and cultural location. The theory explains how knowledge held by individuals, organizations, and societies can be simultaneously enlarged and enriched through the spiral, interactive amplification of tacit and explicit knowledge held by individuals, organizations, and societies. The key for this synergetic expansion of knowledge is joint creation of knowledge by individuals and organizations. In this sense, the theory of organizational knowledge creation is at the same time a basic theory for building a truly "humanistic" knowledge society beyond the limitations of mere "economic rationality."

Organizations play a critical role in mobilizing tacit knowledge held by individuals and provide the forum for a "spiral of knowledge" creation through socialization, combination, externalization, and internalization. All of these conversion modes interact in a dynamic and continuous "entanglement" to drive the knowledge creation process. These modes operate in the context of an organization and, while acknowledging the role of individuals as essential actors in creating new knowledge, the central theme of this paper has been to address the processes involved at an organizational level.

By concentrating on the concept of organizational knowledge creation, it has been possible to develop a perspective which goes beyond straightforward notions of "organizational learning." In the language of the present discussion, learning can be related to "internalization" which is but one of the four modes of conversion required to create new organizational knowledge. Taken by itself, learning has rather limited, static connotations whereas organizational knowledge creation is a more wide-ranging and dynamic concept.

Finally, hypertext and middle-up-down management have been offered as practical proposals for implementing more effective knowledge creation. As knowledge emerges as an ever more important feature of advanced industrial development, it is necessary to pay increased attention to the processes by which it is created and the assessment of its quality and value both to the organization and society.

ACKNOWLEDGMENTS

The author would like to thank Arie Y. Lewin, John Seeley Brown, Takaya Kawamura, doctoral student at Hitotsubashi University, and Tim Ray for their insightful comments and assistance.

REFERENCES

Anderson, J. R. (1983), *The Architecture of Cognition*, Cambridge, MA: Harvard University Press.

Argyris, C. and D. A. Schön (1978), *Organizational Learning*, Reading, MA: Addison-Wesley.

Arrow, K. J. (1974), *The Limits of Organization*, New York: John Brockman Associates.

Ashby, W. R. (1956), *An Introduction to Cybernetics*, London: Champan & Hall.

Austin, J. L. (1962), *How to Do Things with Words*, Oxford: Oxford University Press.

Bateson, G. (1973), *Steps to an Ecology of Mind*, London: Paladin.

———— (1979), *Mind and Nature: A Necessary Unity*, New York: Bantam Books.

Bell, D. (1973), *The Coming of Post-industrial Society: A Venture in Social Forecasting*, New York: Basic Books.

Berger, P. L. and T. Luchman (1966), *Social Construction of Reality*, New York: Doubleday.

Black, M. (1962), *Models and Metaphors*, Ithaca, NY: Cornell University Press.

Brown, J. S. and P. Duguid (1991), "Organizational Learning and Communities of Practice: Towards a Unified View of Working, Learning and Organization," *Organization Science*, 2, 1, 40–57.

Clark, K. B. and T. Fujimoto (1991), *Product Development Performance*, Boston, MA: Harvard Business School Press.

Cohen, M. D., J. G. March, and J. P. Olsen (1972), "A Garbage Can Model of Organizational Choice," *Administrative Science Quarterly*, 17, 1–25.

Condon, W. S. (1976), "An Analysis of Behavioral Organization," *Sign Language Studies*, 13.

Dancy, J. (1985), *Introduction to Contemporary Epistemology*, New York: Basil Blackwell.

Dretske, F. (1981), *Knowledge and the Flow of Information*, Cambridge, MA: MIT Press.

Drucker, P. (1968), *The Age of Discontinuity: Guidelines to Our Changing Society*, New York: Harper & Row.

Eigen, M. (1971), "Self-Organization of Matter and the Evolution of Biological Macro-Molecules," *Naturwissenshaften*, 58.

Gelwick, R. (1977), *The Way of Discovery: An Introduction to the Thought of Michael Polanyi*, Oxford: Oxford University Press.

Gibson, J. J. (1979), *The Ecological Approach to Visual Perception*, Boston, MA: Houghton-Mifflin.

Gleick, J. (1987), *Chaos*, New York, Viking.

Graumann, C. F. (1990), "Perspective Structure and Dynamics in Dialogues," in I. Markova and K. Foppa, (Eds.), *The Dynamics of Dialogue*, New York: Harvester Wheatsheaf.

Gruber, T. R. (1989), *The Acquisition of Strategic Knowledge*, San Diego, CA: Academic Press.

Hallis, M. (1985), *Invitation to Philosophy*, Oxford: Basil Blackwell.

Haken, H. (1978), *Synergetics: Nonequilibrium Phase Transitions and Self-Organization in Physics, Chemistry and Biology*, 2nd ed., Berlin: Springer.

Hayek, F. A. (1945), "The Use of Knowledge in Society," *American Economic Review*, 35, 4, 519–530.

Hedberg, B. L. T. (1981), "How Organizations Learn and Unlearn," in P. C. Nystrom, and W. H. Starbuck, (Eds.), *Handbook of Organizational Design*, Oxford: Oxford University Press.

Hedlund, G. (1986), "The Hypermodern MNC—A Heterarchy?," *Human Resource Management*, 25, 1.

Hospers, J. (1967), *An Introduction to Philosophical Analysis*, 2nd ed., London: Routledge & Kegan Paul.

Husserl, E. (1968), *The Ideas of Phenomenology*, Hague: Nijhoff.

Imai, K., I. Nonaka, and H. Takeuchi (1985), "Managing the New Product Development Process: How Japanese Companies Learn and Unlearn," in K. B. Clark, R. H. Hayes and C. Lorenz, (Eds.), *The Uneasy Alliance: Managing the Productivity-Technology Dilemma*, Boston, MA: Harvard Business School Press.

Jacques, E. (1979), "Taking Time Seriously in Evaluating Jobs," *Harvard Business Review*, September–October, 124–132.

Jaikumar, R. and R. E. Born (1986), "The Development of Intelligent System for Industrial Use: A Conceptual Framework," *Research on Technological Innovation, Management and Policy*, 3, JAI Press.

Jantsch, E. (1980), *The Self-Organizing Universe*, Oxford: Pergamon Press.

Johnson-Laird (1983), *Mental Models*, Cambridge: Cambridge University Press.

Kagono, T, I. Nonaka, K. Sakakibara, and A. Okumura (1985), *Strategic vs. Evolutionary Management*, Amsterdam: North-Holland.

Lakoff, G. and M. Johnson (1980), *Metaphors We Live By*, Chicago, IL: University of Chicago Press.

Landau, M. (1969), "Redundancy, Rationality, and the Problem of Duplication and Overlap," *Public Administration Review*, 14, 4.

Leatherdale, W. H. (1974), *The Role of Analogy, Model and Metaphor in Science*, Amsterdam: North-Holland.

Lewin, A. Y. and C. V. Stephens (1992), "Designing Post-industrial Organization: Theory and Practice," in G. P. Huber and W. H. Glick (Eds.), *Organization Change and Redesign: Ideas and Insights for Improving Managerial Performance*, New York: Oxford University Press.

Lewin, K. (1951), *Field Theory in Social Science*, New York: Harper

Machlup, F. (1983), "Semantic Quirks in Studies of Information," in F. Machlup and U. Mansfield (Eds.), *The Study of Information*, New York: John Wiley.

Markova, I. and K. Foppa (Eds.), (1990), *The Dynamics of Dialogue*, New York: Harvester Wheatsheaf.

Maturana, H. R. and F. J. Varela (1980) *Autopoiesis and Cognition: The Realization of the Living*, Dordrecht, Holland: Reidel.

McCormac, E. R. (1985), *A Cognitive Theory of Metaphor*, Cambridge, MA: MIT Press.

McCulloch, W. (1965), *Embodiments of Mind*, Cambridge, MA: MIT Press.

Merleau-Ponty, M. (1964), *The Structure of Behavior*, Boston, MA: Beacon Press.

Merton, R. K. (1957), *Social Theory and Social Structure*, New York: Free Press.

Miyazaki, K. and N. Ueno (1985), *Shiten* (The View Point), Tokyo: Tokyo Daigaku Shuppankai (in Japanese).

Morgan, G. (1986), *Images of Organization*, Beverly Hills, CA: Sage Publications.

Moser, P. K. and A. V. Nat (1987), *Human Knowledge*, Oxford: Oxford University Press.

Neisser, U. (1976), *Cognition and Reality*, New York: W. H. Freeman.

Nisbet, R. A. (1969), *Social Change and History: Aspects of the Western Theory of Development*, London: Oxford University Press.

Nishida, K. (1960), *A Study of Good* (Zen no kenkyu), Tokyo: Printing Bureau, Japanese Government.

Nonaka, I. (1987), "Managing the Firms as Information Creation Process," Working Paper, January (published in J. Meindl (Ed.), (1991), *Advances in Information Processing in Organizations*, 4, JAJ Press.

—— (1988a), "Creating Organizational Order Out of Chaos: Self-Renewal in Japanese Firms," *California Management Review*, 15, 3, 57–73.

—— (1988b), "Toward Middle-Up-Down Management: Accelerating Information Creation," *Sloan Management Review*, 29, 3, 9–18.

—— (1989), "Organizing Innovation as a Knowledge-Creation Process: A Suggestive Paradigm for Self-Renewing Organization," Working Paper, University of California at Berkeley, Berkeley, CA, No. OBIR-41.

—— (1990). "Redundant, Overlapping Organizations: A Japanese Approach to Managing the Innovation Process," *California Management Review*, 32, 3, 27–38.

—— (1991), "The Knowledge-Creating Company," *Harvard Business Review*, November–December, 96–104.

——, N. Konno, K. Tokuoka, and T. Kawamura (1992), "Hypertext Organization for Accelerating Organizational Knowledge Creation," *Diamond Harvard Business*, August–September (in Japanese).

Norman, D. A. (1977), *The Psychology of Everyday Things*, New York: Basic Books.

Numagami, T., T. Ohta, and I. Nonaka (1989), "Self-Renewal of Corporate Organizations: Equilibrium, Self-Sustaining, and Self-Renewing Models," Working Paper, University of California at Berkeley, Berkeley, CA, No. OBIR-43.

Piaget, J. (1974), *Recherches sur la Contradiction*, Paris: Presses Universitaires de France.

Pinchot, G. III (1985), *Intrapreneuring*, New York: Harper & Row.

Polanyi, M. (1958), *Personal Knowledge*, Chicago, IL: The University of Chicago Press.

—— (1966), *The Tacit Dimension*, London: Routledge & Paul.

Prahalad, C. K. and G. Hamel (1990), "The Core Competition of the Corporation," *Harvard Business Review*, May–June, 79–91.

Quinn, J. B. (1992), *Intelligent Enterprise*, New York: Free Press.

Rosch, E. H. (1973), "Natural Categories," *Cognitive Psychology*, 4, 328–350.

Ryle, G. (1949), *The Concept of Mind*, London: Huchinson.

Sandelands, Lloyd E. and R. E. Stablein (1987), "The Concept of Organization Mind," *Research in the Sociology of Organizations*, 5.

Scheflen, A. E. (1982), "Comments on the Significance of Interaction Rhythms," in M. Davis (Ed.), *Interaction Rhythms*, New York: Free Press.

Schön, D. A. (1983), *The Reflective Practitioner,* New York: Basic Books.

Schrage, M. (1990), *Shared Minds: The New Technologies of Collaboration,* New York: John Brockman.

Searle, J. R. (1969), *Speach Acts: An Essay in the Philosophy of Language,* Cambridge: Cambridge University Press.

——— (1983), *Intentionality: An Essay in the Philosophy of Mind,* Cambridge: Cambridge University Press.

Shannon, C. E. and W. Weaver (1949), *The Mathematical Theory of Communication,* Urbana, IL: University of Illinois Press.

Shimizu, H. (1978), *Seimei o toraenaosu* (Capturing the Nature of Life), Tokyo: Chuo koronsha (in Japanese).

Stich, S. (1986), *From Folk Psychology to Cognitive Science: The Case Against Belief,* Cambridge, MA: MIT Press.

Takeuchi, H. and I. Nonaka (1986), "The New New Product Development Game," *Harvard Business Review,* Jan.–Feb., 137–146.

——— K. Sakakibara, T. Kagono, A. Okumura, and I. Nonaka (1986), *Kigyo no jiko kakushin* (Corporate Self-renewal), Tokyo: Chuo koronsha (in Japanese).

Toffler, A. (1990), *Powershift: Knowledge, Wealth and Violence at the Edge of 21st Century,* New York: Bantam Books.

Tsoukas, H. (1991), "The Missing Link: A Transformation View of Metaphor in Organizational Science," *Academy of Management Review,* 16, 3, 566–585.

Varela, F. J., E. Thompson, and E. Rosch (1991), *Embodied Mind: Cognitive Science and Human Experience,* Cambridge, MA: MIT Press.

von Foerster, H. (1984), "Principles of Self-organization in a Socio-Managerial Context," in H. Ulrich and G. J. B. Probst, (Eds.), *Self-organization and Management of Social Systems,* Berlin: Springer-Verlag.

Weick, K. E. (1976). *The Social Psychology of Organizing,* 2nd ed., Reading, MA: Addison-Wesley.

Williamson, O. E. (1975), *Market and Hierarchies: Antitrust Implications,* New York: The Free Press.

Winograd, T. and Flores (1986), *Understanding Computer and Cognition,* Reading, MA: Addison-Wesley.

Yuasa, Y. (1987), *The Body: Toward an Eastern Mind-Body Theory,* T. P. Kasulis, (Ed.), translated by S. Nagatomi and T. P. Kasulis, New York: State University of New York Press.

Accepted by Arie Y. Lewin; received December 1992. This paper has been with the author for 1 revision.

Chapter 2
Understanding Organizations as Learning Systems

Edwin C. Nevis, Anthony J. DiBella, and Janet M. Gould[1]

How can you tell if your company is, indeed, a learning organization? What is a learning organization anyway? And how can you improve the learning systems in your company? The authors provide a framework for examining a company, based on its "learning orientations," a set of critical dimensions to organizational learning, and "facilitating factors," the processes that affect how easy or hard it is for learning to occur. They illustrate their model with examples from four firms they studied—Motorola, Mutual Investment Corporation, Electricité de France, and Fiat—and conclude that all organizations have systems that support learning.

Edwin C. Nevis is director of special studies at the Organizational Learning Center, MJIT Sloan School of Management Anthony J. DiBella is a visiting assistant professor at the Carroll School of Management, Boston College. Janet M. Goud is associate director at the Organizational Learning Center.

[1] Reprinted from "Understanding Organizations as Learning Systems" by Edwin C. Nevis, Anthony J. DiBella and Janet M. Gould *Sloan Management Review,* Winter, 1995, pp. 73–85, by permission of publisher. Copyright © 1995 by Sloan Management Review Association. All rights reserved.

* The research in this paper was supported by a grant from the International Consortium for Executive Development Research, Lexington, Massachusetts, and by the MIT Organizational Learning Center. The authors would like to thank Joseph Reelin, Edgar Schein, Peter Senge, and Sandra Waddock for their helpful comments on an earlier version of this paper.

With the decline of some well-established firms, the diminishing competitive power of many companies in a burgeoning world market, and the need for organizational renewal and transformation, interest in organizational learning has grown. Senior managers in many organizations are convinced of the importance of improving learning in their organizations. This growth in awareness has raised many unanswered questions: What is a learning organization? What determines the characteristics of a good learning organization (or are all learning organizations good by definition)? How can organizations improve their learning? In the literature in this area, authors have used different definitions or models of organizational learning or have not defined their terms.[2] Executives have frequently greeted us with comments like these:

- "How would I know a learning organization if I stumbled over it?"
- "You academics have some great ideas, but what do I do with a mature, large organization on Monday morning?"
- "I'm not sure what a good learning organization is, but you should not study us because we are a bad learning organization."

Our research is dedicated to helping organizations become better learning systems. We define organizational learning as the capacity or processes within an organization to maintain or improve performance based on experience. Learning is a systems-level phenomenon because it stays within the organization, even if individuals change. One of our assumptions is that organizations learn as they produce. Learning is as much a task as the production and delivery of goods and services. We do not imply that organizations should sacrifice the speed and quality of production in order to learn, but, rather, that production systems be viewed as learning systems. While companies do not usually regard learning as a function of production, our research on successful firms indicates that three learning-related factors are important for their success:

1. Well-developed core competencies that serve as launch points for new products and services. (Canon has made significant investments over time in developing knowledge in eight core competencies applied in the creation of more than thirty products.)
2. An attitude that supports continuous improvement in the business's value-added chain. (Wal-Mart conducts ongoing experiments in its stores.)
3. The ability to fundamentally renew or revitalize. (Motorola has a long history of renewing itself through its products by periodically exiting old lines and entering new ones.)

---

[2] C. Argyris, "Double Loop Learning in Organizations," *Harvard Business Review,* September–October 1977, pp. 115–124; K. Weick, *The Social Psychology of Organizing* (Reading, Massachusetts: Addison-Wesley, 1979); B. Leavitt and J. G. March, "Organizational Learning," *Annual Review of Sociology* 14 (1988): 319–340; P.M. Senge, *The Fifth Discipline* (New York: Doubleday, 1990); and E. H. Schein, "How Can Organizations Learn Faster? The Challenge of Entering the Green Room," *Sloan Management Review,* Winter 1993, pp. 85–92.

These factors identify some of the qualities of an effective learning organization that diligently pursues a constantly enhanced knowledge base. This knowledge allows for the development of competencies and incremental or transformational change. In these instances, there is assimilation and utilization of knowledge and some kind of integrated learning system to support such "actionable learning." Indeed, an organization's ability to survive and grow is based on advantages that stem from core competencies that represent collective learning.[3]

As a corollary to this assumption, we assume that all organizations engage in some form of collective learning as part of their development.[4] The creation of culture and the socialization of members in the culture rely on learning processes to ensure an institutionalized reality.[5] In this sense, it may be redundant to talk of "learning organizations." On the other hand, all learning is not the same; some learning is dysfunctional, and some insights or skills that might lead to useful new actions are often hard to attain. The current concern with the learning organization focuses on the gaps in organizational learning capacity and does not negate the usefulness of those learning processes that organizations may do well, even though they have a learning disability. Thus Argyris and Schön emphasize double-loop learning (generative) as an important, often missing, level of learning in contrast with single-loop learning (corrective), which they have found to be more common.[6] Similarly, Senge makes a highly persuasive case for generative learning, "as contrasted with adaptive learning," which he sees as more prevalent.[7] The focus for these theorists is on the learning required to make transformational changes—changes in basic assumptions—that organizations need in today's fast-moving, often chaotic environment. Their approach does not negate the value of everyday incremental "fixes"; it provides a more complete model for observing and developing organizational learning. After periods of significant discontinuous change, incremental, adaptive learning may be just the thing to help consolidate transformational or generative learning.

Another assumption we make is that the value chain of any organization is a domain of integrated learning. To think of the value chain as an integrated learning system is to think of the work in each major step, beginning with strategic decisions through to customer service, as a subsystem for learning experiments. Structures and processes to achieve outcomes can be seen simultaneously

[3] C. K. Prahalad and G. Hamel, "The Core Competence of the Corporation," *Harvard Business Review,* May–June 1990, pp. 79–91.
[4] J. Child and A. Kieser, "Development of Organizations over Time," in N. C. Nystrom and W. H. Starbuck, eds., *Handbook of Organizational Design* (Oxford: Oxford University Press, 1981), pp. 28–64; and E. H. Schein, *Organizational Culture and Leadership* (San Francisco: Jossey-Bass, 1992).
[5] J. Van Maanen and E. H. Schein, "Toward a Theory of Organizational Socialization," *Research in Organizational Behavior* 1 (1979): 1–37.
[6] C. Argyris and D. A. Schön, *Organizational Learning: A Theory of Action Perspective* (Reading, Massachusetts: Addison-Wesley, 1978).
[7] Senge (1990).

as operational tasks and learning exercises; this holds for discrete functions and for cross-functional activities, such as new product development. The organization encompasses each value-added stage as a step in doing business, not as a fixed classification scheme. Most organizations do not think this way, but it is useful for handling complexity. With this "chunking," we are able to study learning better and to see how integration is achieved at the macro-organizational level. This viewpoint is consistent with a definition of organizations as *complex arrangements of people in which teaming takes place.*

While we have not looked at organizations' full value-added chains, we selected our research sites so that we could examine learning in different organizational subsets. In addition, we gathered data indicating preferences or biases in investments in learning at different points of the chain and to understand how learning builds, maintains, improves, or shifts core competencies. Do organizations see certain stages of the chain where significant investment is more desirable than at others?

Our last assumption is that the learning process has identifiable stages. Following Huber, whose comprehensive review of the literature presented four steps in an organizational learning process, we arrived at a three-stage model:

1. Knowledge acquisition—The development or creation of skills, insights, relationships.
2. Knowledge sharing—The dissemination of what has been learned.
3. Knowledge utilization—The integration of learning so it is broadly available and can be generalized to new situations.[8]

Most studies of organizational learning have been concerned with the acquisition of knowledge and, to a lesser extent, with the sharing or dissemination of the acquired knowledge (knowledge transfer). Less is known about the assimilation process, the stage in which knowledge becomes institutionally available, as opposed to being the property of select individuals or groups. Huber refers to the assimilation and utilization process as "organizational memory." While this is an important aspect of knowledge utilization, it is limited and works better when discussing information, as distinct from knowledge. True knowledge is more than information; it includes the meaning or interpretation of the information, and a lot of intangibles such as the tacit knowledge of experienced people that is not well articulated but often determines collective organizational competence. Studies of organizational learning must be concerned with all three stages in the process.

---

[8] Huber identifies four constructs linked to organizational learning that he labels knowledge acquisition, information distribution, information interpretation, and organizational memory. Implicit in this formulation is that learning progresses through a series of stages. Our framework makes this sequence explicit and connects it to organizational action. Huber does not make this connection since to him learning alters the range of potential, rather than actual, behaviors. See: G. Huber, "Organizational Learning: The Contributing Processes and Literature," *Organization Science* 2 (1991): 88–115.

Early in our research, it became clear that organizational learning does not always occur in the linear fashion implied by any stage model. Learning may take place in planned or informal, often unintended, ways. Moreover, knowledge and skill acquisition takes place in the sharing and utilization stages. It is not something that occurs simply by organizing an "acquisition effort." With this in mind, we shifted our emphasis to look for a more fluid and chaotic learning environment, seeking less-defined, more subtle embodiments.

The first phase of our research was based on intensive field observations in four companies, Motorola Corporation, Mutual Investment Corporation (MIC), Electricité de France (EDF), and Fiat Auto Company.[9] We wanted to have both service and manufacturing settings in U.S. and European environments. We chose two sites where we had access to very senior management and two where we were able to study lower levels. We selected Motorola as an example of a good learning organization; we were able to observe organizational learning during its fourteen-year quality improvement effort.

We did not attempt to study entire firms or to concentrate on any single work units in these four organizations. For example, at Motorola, we began by studying two senior management teams of twenty to twenty-five executives each from all parts of the corporation. Each team focuses on a critical issue defined by the CEO and COO, to whom the groups report. The teams' structures were designed as executive education interventions and vehicles for "real-time" problem solving. Our objective was to see how these teams reflected and utilized organizational learning at Motorola.

From our interview data, we identified what organizational members claimed they had learned and why. We wrote case descriptions of the learning processes in their organizations, which we shared with the organizations to ensure their accuracy Using a grounded analysis, we identified categories that reflected learning orientations and then constructed a two-part model of the critical factors that describe organizations as learning systems.[10] We have since tested this model in data-gathering workshops with personnel from more than twenty *Fortune* "500" companies. Our testing led us to revise some of the model's components, while retaining its overall framework.

[9] At Motorola, we observed and interviewed fifty senior managers, visited the paging products operations, and had access to about twenty-five internal documents. At Mutual Investment Corporation (a pseudonym for a large financial services company based in the United States), we observed and interviewed corporation employees in the investment funds group and the marketing groups. At Electricité de France, we observed and interviewed employees in the nuclear power operations. At Fiat, we observed and interviewed employees in the Direzione Technica (engineering division) in Torino, Italy.

[10] A. Strauss, *Qualitative Analysis for Social Scientists* (Cambridge: Cambridge Universiry Press, 1987).

CORE THEMES

Next we discuss the core themes that emerged from our research and provided a basis for our model.

All Organizations are Learning Systems

All the sites we studied function as learning systems. All have formal and informal processes and structures for the acquisition, sharing, and utilization of knowledge and skills. Members communicated broadly and assimilated values, norms, procedures, and outcome data, starting with early socialization and continuing through group communications, both formal and informal. We talked with staff people in some firms who claimed that their companies were not good learning organizations, but, in each, we were able to identify one or more core competencies that could exist only if there were learning investments in those areas. Some type of structure or process would have to support the informed experience and formal educational interventions required for knowledge acquisition, sharing, and utilization. We found this in both our field sites and other firms. For example, one firm that considers itself to be a poor learning organization because of its difficulty in changing some dysfunction has a reputation in its industry for superior field marketing. It is clear that this group has well-developed recruiting, socialization, training and development, and rotating assignment policies that support its cadre of respected marketing people. Obviously, some learning has been assimilated at a fairly deep level.

Learning Conforms to Culture

The nature of learning and the way in which it occurs are determined by the organization's culture or subcultures. For example, the entrepreneurial style of MIC's investment funds group results in a learning approach in which information is made available to fund managers and analysts, but its use is at the managers' discretion. In addition, there is a good deal of leeway in how fund managers make their investments; some are intuitive, some rely heavily on past performance, and a few use sophisticated computer programs. Thus the find managers' use or application of learning is largely informal, not dictated by formal, firmwide programs. Meanwhile, the culture of MIC's marketing groups is more collaborative; learning is derived more from interaction within and between cross-functional work groups and from improved communication.

In contrast, there is no question that a great deal of organizational learning about quality has occurred at Motorola, but its emphasis on engineering and technical concerns resulted in an earlier, complete embrace of total quality by product manufacturing groups. In a culture that heavily rewards product group performance, total quality in products and processes that require integrated, intergroup action lags behind, particularly in the marketing of systems that cut across divisions.

Style Varies between Learning Systems

There are a variety of ways in which organizations create and maximize their learning. Basic assumptions about the culture lead to learning values and investments that produce a different learning style from a culture with another pattern of values and investments. These style variations are based on a series of learning orientations (dimensions of learning) that members of the organization may not see. We have identified seven learning orientations, which we see as bipolar variables.

For example, each of two distinct groups at both Motorola and MIC had different approaches to the way it accrued and utilized knowledge and skills. One Motorola group had great concern for specifying the metrics to define and measure the targeted learning. The other group was less concerned with very specific measures but, instead, stressed broad objectives. In the two groups at MIC, the methods for sharing and utilizing knowledge were very different; one was informal, and the other more formal and collaborative. From these variations, we concluded that the pattern of the learning orientations largely makes up an organizational learning system. The pattern may not tell us how *well* learning is promoted but tells a lot about what is learned and where it occurs.

Generic Processes Facilitate Learning

How well an organization maximizes learning within its chosen style does not occur haphazardly. Our data suggest that talking about "the learning organization" is partially effective; some policies, structures, and processes do seem to make a difference. The difference is in how easy or hard it is for useful learning to happen, and in how effective the organization is in "working its style." By analyzing why learning took place in the companies we studied, we identified ten facilitating factors that induced or supported learning. While we did not observe all the factors at each site, we saw most of them and at other sites as well. Thus we view them as generic factors that any organization can benefit from, regardless of its learning style. For example, scanning, in which benchmarking plays an important role, was so central to learning at Motorola that it is now an integral ongoing aspect of every important initiative in the company. Although MIC tends to create knowledge and skill internally, it maintains an ongoing vigilance toward its external environment. On the negative side, the absence of solid, ongoing external scanning in other organizations is an important factor in their economic difficulties.

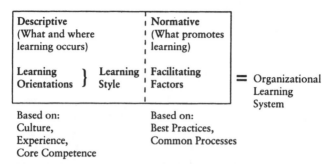

FIGURE 2.1 A Model of Organizations as Learning Systems

A MODEL OF ORGANIZATIONS AS LEARNING SYSTEMS

Our two-part model describes organizations as learning systems (see Figure 2.1). First, *learning orientations* are the values and practices that reflect where learning takes place and the nature of what is learned. These orientations form a pattern that defines a given organization's "learning style." In this sense, they are descriptive factors that help us to understand without making value judgments. Second, facilitating factors are the structures and processes that affect how easy or hard it is for learning to occur and the amount of effective learning that takes place. These are standards based on best practice in dealing with generic issues. (See the sidebar for definitions of the learning orientations and facilitating factors we identified.)

Both parts of the model are required to understand an organization as a learning system; one without the other provides an incomplete picture. In addition, separating the parts enables organizations to see that they do indeed function as learning systems of some kind, and that their task is to understand better what they do well or poorly. (The idea of assessing what exists is more useful than the pejorative notion that there is only one good way to be a learning organization.) Finally, a refined, detailed list of factors related to organizational learning may help companies select areas for learning improvement that do not demand drastic culture change but, rather, can lead to incremental change over time.

Learning Orientations

In the next section, we expand on the definitions of the seven learning orientations and provide examples of each.

1. **Knowledge Source.** To what extent does the organization develop new knowledge internally or seek inspiration in external ideas? This distinction is seen as the difference between innovation and adaptation—or imitation. In the

Seven Learning Orientations	Ten Facilitating Factors	
1. Knowledge Source: Internal–External. Preference for developing knowledge internally versus preference for acquiring-knowledge developed externally.	**1. Scanning Imperative.** Information gathering about conditions and practices outside the unit; awareness of the environment; curiosity about the external environment in contrast to the internal environment.	**7. Operational Variety.** Variety of methods, procedures, and systems; appreciation of diversity; pluralistic rather than singular definition of valued competencies.
2. Product-Process Focus: What?–How? Emphasis on accumulation of knowledge about what products/services are versus how organization develops, makes, and delivers its products and/services.	**2. Performance Gap.** Shared perception of a gap between actual and desired state of performance; performance shortfalls seen as opportunities for learning.	**8. Multiple Advocates.** New ideas and methods advanced by employees at all levels; more than one champion.
3. Documentation Mode: Personal–Public. Knowledge is something individuals possess versus publicly available know-how.	**3. Concern for Measurement.** Considering effort spent on defining and measuring key factors when venturing into new areas; striving for specific, quantifiable measures; discussion of metrics as a learning activity.	**9. Involved Leadership.** Leaders articulate vision, are engaged in its implementation; frequently interact with members; become actively involved in educational programs.
4. Dissemination Mode: Formal–Informal. Formal, prescribed, organization-wide methods of sharing learning versus informal methods, such as role modeling and casual daily interaction.	**4. Experimental Mind-set.** Support for trying new things; curiosity about how things work; ability to "play" with things; "failures" are accepted, not punished; changes in work processes, policies, and structures are a continuous series of learning opportunities.	**10. Systems Perspective.** Interdependence of organizational units; problems and solutions seen in terms of systemic relationships among processes; connection between the unit's needs and goals and the company's.
5. Learning Focus: Incremental–Transformative. Incremental or corrective learning versus transformative or radical learning.	**5. Climate of Openness.** Accessibility of information; open communication within the organization; problems/errors/lesson are shared, not hidden; debate and conflict are acceptable ways to solve problems.	

6. Value-Chain Focus: Design–Deliver. Emphasis on learning investments in engineering/production activities ("design and make" functions) versus-sales/service activities ("market and deliver" functions). 7. Skill Development Focus: Individual–Group. Development of individuals' skills versus team or group skills.	6. Continous Education. Ongoing commitment to education at all levels of the organization; clear support for all members' growth and development

BOX 2.1 Definitions of the Orientations and Factors

United States, there is a tendency to value innovativeness more highly and look down on "copiers." American critiques of Japanese businesses often mention that the Japanese are good imitators but not good innovators. In our opinion, both of these approaches have great merit as opposing styles rather than as normative or negative behaviors.

Although our data show a tendency in organizations to prefer one mode over the other, the distinction is not cleat-cut. While MIC does scan its environment, it prefers to innovate in responding to customer needs and problems and has been a leader in developing new financial products and services. EDF modeled its nuclear power plants on U.S. technology: Motorola appears to be equally vigorous in innovation and in reflective imitation; it has been innovative in developing new products and adroit at adapting others' processes, such as benchmarking and TQM procedures. Among firms not in this study, American Airlines, Wal-Mart, Merck, and Rubbermaid appear to be innovative in producing knowledge. And American Home Products is a good example of a highly successful, reflective imitator, as are AT&T's Universal Credit Card, Tyco Toys (a Lego "copier"), and Lexus and Infiniti automobiles.

2. Product-Process Focus. Does the organization prefer to accumulate knowledge about product and service outcomes or about the basic processes underlying various products? Many observers have stated that one reason Japanese companies are so competitive is that they make considerably more investments in process technologies in comparison to U.S. companies. The difference is between interest in "getting product out the door" and curiosity about the steps in the processes. All organizations give some attention to each side; the issue is to organize for learning in both domains.

Motorola makes learning investments on both sides. The executives we observed spent roughly equal amounts of time in collaborative learning about processes and out-comes. They paid less attention to "people processes" than to "hard" or technical processes, but many of them accepted the importance of process issues. MIC, EDF, and Fiat have traditionally focused almost exclusively on product issues but are now making greater learning investments in process issues.

3. **Documentation Mode.** Do attitudes vary as to what constitutes knowledge and where knowledge resides? At one pole, knowledge is seen in personal terms, as something an individual possesses by virtue of education or experience. This kind of knowledge is lost when a longtime employee leaves an organization; processes and insights evaporate because they were not shared or made a part of collective memory. At the other pole, knowledge is defined in more objective, social terms, as being a consensually supported result of information processing. This attitude emphasizes organizational memory or a publicly documented body of knowledge.

MIC's investment funds group focuses on a personal documentation style, eschewing policy statements and procedure manuals. In keeping with its entrepreneurial orientation, MIC makes it possible for individuals to learn a great deal, but there is little pressure to codify this. Though engaged in a business that values "hard data," the group supports subjective, tacit knowledge in decision-making processes. And at Fiat's Direzione Technica, where the individual has historically been the repository of knowledge, efforts are being made to establish a *memoria technica,* or engineering knowledge bank. Motorola shows evidence of both approaches but works hard to make knowledge explicit and broadly available.

4. **Dissemination Mode.** Has the organization established an atmosphere in which learning evolves or in which a more structured, controlled approach induces learning? In the more structured approach, the company decides that valuable insights or methods should be shared and used by others across the organization. It uses written communication and formal educational methods or certifies learning through writing the procedures down. In the more informal approach, learning is spread through encounters between role models and gatekeepers who compellingly reinforce learning. In another approach, learning occurs when members of an occupational group or work team share their experiences in ongoing dialogue.[11]

MIC's investment funds group clearly prefers informal dissemination in which learning develops and is shared in loosely organized interactions. This method occurs in other MIC areas, although the marketing groups are becoming more structured in their dissemination. Motorola supports both approaches, though it invests heavily in structured, firmwide programs when senior management wants a basic value or method institutionalized. It considered quality so critical that it now includes vendors and customers in its dissemination. (Recently, some vendors were told that they had to compete for the Malcolm Baldrige Quality Award in order to be on the company's approved vendor list.) EDF prefers formal modes, emphasizing documented procedures that all share.

---

[11] For a discussion of "communities of practice" see: J. S. Brown and P. Puguid, "Organizational Learning and Communities of Practice," *Organization Science* 2 (1991): 40–57.

Fiat's Direzione Technica formally spreads knowledge by accumulating it in specialist departments and then disseminating it to cross-functional design teams.

5. **Learning Focus.** Is learning concentrated on methods and tools to improve what is already being done or on testing the assumptions underlying what is being done? Argyris and Schön call the former "single-loop learning" and the latter "double-loop learning."[12] They have rightfully argued that organizational performance problems are more likely due to a lack of awareness and inability to articulate and check underlying assumptions than to a function of poor efficiency. In our opinion, these learning capabilities reinforce each other. Organizations may have a preference for one mode over the other, but a sound learning system can benefit from good work in both areas.

Our research sites displayed a range of behavior. EDF is primarily focused on incremental issues and does not question its basic assumptions. It prides itself on being the world's major nuclear power utility and devotes significant resources to being the most efficient, safe operator through small improvements rather than transformations. Though similar, Fiat's Direzione Technica is beginning to question assumptions about its new product development process. Since 1987, MIC has been in a transformational mode, particularly in the way that its marketing groups have focused on a questioning learning style. Motorola is fairly well balanced in its orientation; the founding family has historically accepted the concept of organizational renewal, which has led to far-reaching changes in the company's product lines through the years and to an inquisitive style. On the other hand, its strong dedication to efficiency learning often precludes questioning basic assumptions.

6. **Value-Chain Focus.** Which core competencies and learning investments does the organization value and support? By learning investments, we mean all allocations of personnel and money to develop knowledge and skill over rime, including training and education, pilot projects, developmental assignments, available resources, and so on. If a particular organization is "engineering focused" or "marketing driven," it is biased in favor of substantial learning investments in those areas. We divided the value chain into two categories: internally directed activities of a "design and make" nature, and those more externally focused of a "sell and deliver" nature. The former include R&D, engineering, and manufacturing. The latter are sales, distribution, and service activities. Although this does some disservice to the value chain concept, the breakdown easily accounts for our observations.

At MIC, the investment funds group focuses on the design and make side. While this is balanced by learning investments on the deliver side in the MIC marketing groups, there is a strong boundary between these groups, and the fund management side is regarded as the organization's core. Motorola's total quality effort clearly recognizes the importance of value-added at both sides, but "design and make" is significantly ahead of "deliver" in learning investments in quality. Fiat's Direzione Technica is clearly oriented toward design and make, although

[12] Argyris and Schön (1978).

its new system of simultaneous engineering is balancing its approach with increased sensitivity to the deliver side. EDF nuclear operations focuses squarely on efficient production. While not in our study Digital Equipment Corporation's learning investments traditionally were much more heavily focused on "design and make" than on "deliver."

7. **Skill Development Focus.** Does the organization develop both individual and group skills? We believe it helps to view this as a stylistic choice, as opposed to seeing it in normative terms. In this way, an organization can assess how it is doing and improve either one. It can also develop better ways of integrating individual learning programs with team needs by taking a harder look at the value of group development.

MIC designed the investment fund group to promote individual learning, which seems to fit with its culture and reward system. Heavy investment in team learning would probably improve its performance. On the other hand, MIC's marketing groups, more supportive of collective learning, are now investing in team development as one way to improve its total effectiveness. Fiat's Direzione Technica has been oriented toward more individual development, but, with its new reliance on cross-functional work teams, group development is increasingly more important. Recently, Motorola has become more team oriented and is making heavier investments in collaborative learning. It designed the two executive groups we observed to foster collective learning on two strategic issues affecting the entire company EDF develops both individual and group skills, especially in control-room teams. All EDF employees follow individual training programs for certification or promotion. Control-room teams also learn, in groups, by using plant simulators. Some other firms that emphasize team learning are Federal Express, which invests heavily in teams for its quality effort, and Herman Miller, which stresses participative management and the Scanlon plan.

We view the seven learning orientations as a matrix. An organizational unit can be described by the pattern of its orientations in the matrix, which in turn provides a way to identify its learning style. Given the characteristics of the sites we studied and other sites we are familiar with, we believe it is possible to identify learning styles that represent a distinct pattern of orientations. Such styles may reflect the industry, size, or age of an organization, or the nature of its technology.

Facilitating Factors

The second part of our model is the facilitating factors that expedite learning. The ten factors are defined in the sidebar.

1. **Scanning Imperative.** Does the organization understand or comprehend the environment in which it functions? In recent years, researchers have emphasized the importance of environmental scanning and agreed that many organizations were in trouble because of limited or poor scanning efforts. Thus many firms have increased their scanning capacity. Five years into Motorola's quality

program, a significant scanning effort showed it what others, particularly the Japanese, were doing. In reaction, Motorola substantially changed its approach and won the first Baldrige Award four years later. By contrast, the mainframe computer manufacturers (Cray, Unisys, IBM) and the U.S. auto companies in the 1970s failed to respond to developing changes that sound investigative work would have made painfully visible. Recent changes at Fiat result from a concerted scanning effort in which fifty senior managers visited the manufacturing facilities of world-class auto and other durable goods companies.

2. **Performance Gap.** First, how do managers, familiar with looking at the differences between targeted outcomes and actual performance, analyze variances? When feedback shows a gap, particularly if it implies failure, their analysis often leads to experimenting and developing new insights and skills. One reason that well-established, long-successful organizations are often not good learning systems is that they experience lengthy periods in which feedback is almost entirely positive; the lack of disconfirming evidence is a barrier to learning.

Secondly, is there a potential new vision that is not simply a quantitative extension of the old or goes well beyond the performance level seen as achievable in the old vision? One or more firm members may visualize something not previously noted. Awareness of a performance gap is important because it often leads the organization to recognize that learning needs to occur or that something already known may not be working. Even if a group cannot articulate exactly what that need might be, its awareness of ignorance can motivate learning, as occurred at Motorola after its 1984 benchmarking. Currently, this "humility" is driving Fiat's Direzione Technica to make a major study of what it needs to know.

In our findings, EDF provides perhaps the best instance of a performance gap leading to adaptive learning. Due to the nature of the nuclear power business, performance variations because the catalyst for a learning effort to again achieve the prescribed standard. We also found that future-oriented CEOs encouraged performance-gap considerations related to generative learning at Motorola and MIC (patent company).

3. **Concern for Measurement.** Does the organization develop and use metrics that support learning? Are measures internally or externally focused, specific, and custom-built or standard measures? The importance of metrics in total quality programs has been well documented and is used in target-setting programs such as management by objectives.[13] Our interest is in how the discourse about measurements, and the search for the most appropriate ones, is a critical aspect of learning, almost as much as learning that evolves from responding to the feedback that metrics provide.

Motorola executives believe that concern for measurement was one of the most critical reasons for their quality program's success. At three or four critical

---

[13] W. H. Schmidt and J. P. Finnegan, *The Race Without a Finish Line: America's Quest for Total Quality* (San Francisco: Jossey-Bass, 1992).

junctures, reexamination of measurement issues helped propel a move to a new level of learning. They are applying this factor to new initiatives, a major concern of the executive groups we observed. At EDF, the value of metrics is clearly associated with the performance gap. Its nuclear power plants are authorized to operate at certain specifications that, if not met, may suggest or predict an unplanned event leading to shutdown. Each occasion becomes an opportunity for learning to take place.

4. **Experimental Mind-Set.** Does the organization emphasize experimentation on an ongoing basis? If learning comes through experience, it follows that the more one can plan guided experiences, the more one will learn. Until managers see organizing for production at any stage of the value chain as a learning experiment as well as a production activity learning will come slowly. Managers need to learn to act like applied research scientists at the same time they deliver goods and services.[14]

We did not see significant evidence of experimental mind-sets at our research sites, with some notable exceptions at Motorola. At its paging products operation, we observed the current production line for one product, a blueprint and preparation for the new setup to replace the line, and a "white room" laboratory in which research is now underway for the line that will replace the one currently being installed. Motorola University constantly tries new learning approaches; the two executive groups we observed at Motorola were also part of an experiment in executive education.

We have seen evidence of experimental mind-sets in reports about other firms. For example, on any given day, Wal-Mart conducts about 250 tests in its stores, concentrated on sales promotion, display, and customer service. Although a traditional firm in many ways, 3M's attitude toward new product development and operational unit size suggests a strong experimental mind-set.

5. **Climate of Openness.** Are the boundaries around information flow permeable so people can make their own observations? Much informal learning is a function of daily, often unplanned interactions among people. In addition, the opportunity to meet with other groups and see higher levels of management in operation promotes learning.[15] People need freedom to express their views through legitimate disagreement and debate. Another critical aspect is the extent to which errors are shared and not hidden.[16]

Perhaps the most dramatic example of openness in our findings is EDF, where abnormalities or deviations are publicly reported throughout the entire system of fifty-seven nuclear power plants. The company treats such incidents as researchable events to see if the problem exists anywhere else and follows up

---

[14] For the idea of the factory as a learning laboratory, see: D. Leonard-Barton, "The Factory as a Learning Laboratory," *Sloan Management Review,* Fall 1992, pp. 39–52.

[15] This skill has been referred to as "legitimate peripheral participation." See: J. Lave and E. Wenger, *Situated Learning: Legitimate Periphereal Participation* (Palo Alto, California: Institute for Research on Learning, IBL Report 90–0013, 1990).

[16] C. Argyris, *Strategy, Change, and Defensive Routines* (Boston: Putman, 1985).

with a learning-driven investigation to eliminate it. It then disseminates this knowledge throughout the company. While this openness may be explained by the critical nature of problems in a nuclear power plant, we can only speculate as to what would be gained if any organization functioned as though a mistake is potentially disastrous and also an opportunity to learn.

6. **Continuous Education.** Is there a commitment to lifelong education at all levels of the organization? This includes formal programs but goes well beyond that to more pervasive support of any kind of developmental experience. The mere presence of traditional training and development activities is not sufficient; it must be accompanied by a palpable sense that one is never finished learning and practicing (something akin to the Samurai tradition). The extent to which this commitment permeates the entire organization, and not just the training and development groups, is another indicator. In many ways, this factor is another way of expressing what Senge calls "personal mastery."

MIC does an excellent job of exposing its young analysts to developmental experiences. Its chairman also seeks knowledge in many areas, not just direct financial matters. Motorola has a policy in which every employee has some educational experience every year; it has joint ventures with several community colleges around the country; joint programs with the state of Illinois for software competence development and training of school superintendents, and on-the-job and classroom experiences for managers up to the senior level. The company spends 3.6 percent of its revenues on education and plans to double this amount.[17] Among firms not in our study, General Electric, Unilever, and Digital Equipment Corporation have valued continuous education at all levels for many years.

7. **Operational Variety.** Is there more than one way to accomplish work goals? An organization that supports variation in strategy policy process, structure, and personnel is more adaptable when unforeseen problems arise. It provides more options and, perhaps even more important, allows for rich stimulation and interpretation for all its members. This factor helps enhance future learning in a way not possible with a singular approach.

We did not see a great deal of variety at our sites. EDF, perhaps due to the importance of total control over operations, shows little variation. Fiat's Direzione Technica follows similar response routines, although the change to a new structure should lead to greater variation because of its independent design teams. An exception is MIC investment funds group, where we identified at least three different methods that fund managers used in making investment decisions. Senior management, although a bit skeptical about one of the methods, seemed willing to support all three as legitimate approaches.

8. **Multiple Advocates.** Along with involved leadership, is there more than one "champion" who sets the stage for learning? This is particularly necessary in learning that is related to changing a basic value or a long-cherished method. The

---

[17] See "Companies That Train Best," *Fortune*, 8 February 1993, pp. 44–48; and "Motorola: Training for the Millenium," *Business Week*, 28 March 1994, pp. 158–163.

greater the number of advocates who promote a new idea, the more rapidly and extensively the learning will take place. Moreover, in an effective system, any member should be able to act as an awareness-enhancing agent or an advocate for new competence development. In this way, both top-down and bottom-up initiatives are possible.

One of the authors participated in two significant change efforts that failed, largely because there was only one champion in each case. One highly frustrated CEO said, "It doesn't do me or the company any good if I'm the only champion of this new way of doing business." At Motorola, we found that a major factor in the quality effort's success was the early identification, empowerment, and encouragement of a significant number of advocates. In a current initiative we observed, Motorola is enlisting a minimum of 300 champions in strategic parts of the company. Digital Equipment Corporation has had learning initiators throughout the company since its early days. Digital's problem has been in assimilating and integrating the lessons of its myriad educational and experimental efforts, rather than in creating an environment that enables broad-scale initiation. MIC's investment funds group encourages many individuals to initiate their own learning but not to proselytize.

9. Involved Leadership. Is leadership at every organizational level engaged in hands-on implementation of the vision? This includes eliminating management layers, being visible in the bowels of the organization, and being an active, early participant in any learning effort. Only through direct involvement that reflects coordination, vision, and integration can leaders obtain important data and provide powerful role models.

At Motorola, CEO Bob Galvin not only drove the quality vision, he was a student in the first seminars on quality and made it the first item on the agenda at monthly meetings with his division executives. Much-admired Wal-Mart CEO David Glass spends two or three days each week at stores and warehouses; employees can call him at home and are often transferred to his hotel when he is in the field. Mike Walsh of Tenneco (formerly of Union Pacific Railroad) meets with groups of employees at all levels in what Tom Peters calls "conversation."[18]

10. Systems Perspective. Do the key actors think broadly about the interdependency of organizational variables? This involves the degree to which managers can look at their internal systems as a source of their difficulties, as opposed to blaming external factors. Research in the field of systems dynamics has demonstrated how managers elicit unintended consequences by taking action in one area without seeing its dynamic relationship to its effects.[19]

Despite its importance, this factor was relatively lacking at our research sites. MIC and Motorola are structured so that there are strong boundaries between groups and functions. Both have changed their perspectives recently, MIC as a consequence of unexpected internal problems related to the October 1987 stock market crash, and Motorola after experiencing difficulties in selling

[18] T. Peters, *Liberation Management* (New York: Knopf, 1992).
[19] Jay W. Forrester is considered to be the founder of the field of systems thinking.

large-scale systems (as opposed to discrete products). In a 1992 survey of 3,000 Motorola employees that asked them to evaluate their unit based on Senge's five factors, they rated systems thinking the lowest and the one that required the most work to improve organizational learning. In contrast, Fiat's Direzione Technica took a systems approach to understanding the consequences of its structure on new product development. As a result, it changed the structure to establish mechanisms for simultaneous engineering. To reduce the new products' time to market, functions now work in parallel rather than sequentially.

GENERAL DIRECTIONS FOR ENHANCING LEARNING

We have divided the seven learning orientations and ten facilitating factors into three stages—knowledge acquisition, dissemination, and utilization. Figure 2.2 shows the orientations and factors within this framework. Within our two-part model, there are two general directions for enhancing learning in an organizational unit. One is to embrace the existing style and improve its effectiveness. This strategy develops a fundamental part of the culture to its fullest extent. For example, a firm that is a reflective imitator more than an innovator could adopt this strategy with heightened awareness of its value. A company that has benefited from heavy learning investments on the "make" side of the value chain would see the value of those investments and decide to build further on them. This approach builds on the notion that full acceptance of what has been accomplished is validating and energizing for those involved. It is similar to the appreciative inquiry numerous organizational change consultants advocare.[20] The task is to select two or three facilitating factors to improve on.

The second direction is to change learning orientations. The organizational group would make more learning investments at a different part of the value chain, try to be an innovator if it is now more of an imitator, and so on. These are different changes from those involved in enhancing the facilitative factors, and the tactics will be different. Some changes will be seen as an attack on the organization's basic values, and it may be possible to avoid this by moving toward balance between the two poles, so members of the organization will support te existing style and advocate the "new look" as a supplementary measure.

Supporting the Learning Orientations

In the second phase of our research, in which we worked closely with personnel from more than thirty Fortune "500" companies to identify their learning orientations, we validated our notion that organizations learn in varied ways. The singular "learning organization" should be a pluralistic model.

---

[20] S. Srivastra and D. L. Cooperrider and Associates, *Appreciative Management and Leadership* (San Francisco: Jossey-Bass, 1990).

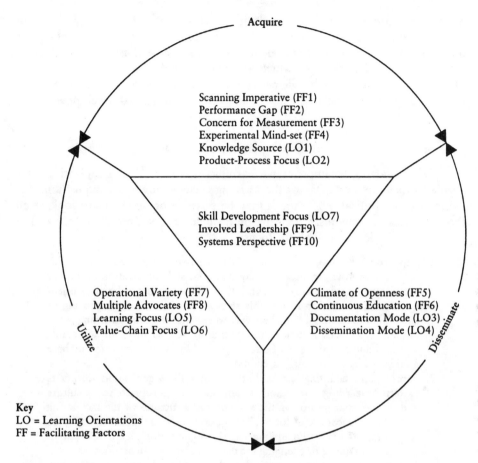

FIGURE 2.2 Elements of an Organizational Learning System

Looking at "what is" in a descriptive rather than normative way has another advantage in that you see better what you are *not* by examining better what you *are*. In the gestalt approach to dealing with resistance to organizational change, it has been well documented that change comes more readily if the targets of change first become more aware of and more accepting of their resistance.[21] In other words, it is important to gain full knowledge and appreciation of your organizational assumptions about learning whether you want to build on them or alter them.

This model may also be used to identify the complementary of styles between coordinating organizations and to recognize that circumstances may dictate conditions and orientations in particular settings. For example, EDF's

[21] E. Nevis, *Organizational Consulting: A Gestalt Approach* (Cleveland: Gestalt Institute of Cleveland Press, 1987).

nuclear operations are constrained from transforming real-time operations due to the potentially dire consequences (e.g., the Chernobyl disaster) of operating under novel assumptions. However, at EDF, testing system assumptions is characteristic of its R&D division, which uses new technologies in the design of new plants. Thus changing one's style needs to be considered from a systems perspective; it may also be associated with the stage of organizational development.[22]

Strategies for Improving Organizational Learning Capability

When starting to improve its learning capabilities an organization may decide to focus on any stage of the learning cycle—knowledge acquisition, dissemination, or utilization. While it may be possible or necessary to look at all three phases simultaneously, focusing on a single area is more manageable. The next task is to select an option for focus:

1. Improve on learning orientations. There are two reasons for selecting this option. First, the organization may decide to shift its position on one or more learning orientations. Second, the current pattern of learning orientations has resulted in identifiable strong competencies, so improving or expanding them may be the best way to enhance the unit's learning capabilities. This focus assumes that facilitating factors meet an acceptable standard and that more can be accomplished by adding to the strong base established by the learning orientations.
2. Improve on facilitating factors. In this option, the organization accepts its pattern of learning orientations as adequate or appropriate to its culture and decides that improving the systems and structures of the facilitating factors is the most useful course. This option assumes that maximizing the facilitating factors would add more to the organization's learning capabilities than enhancing or changing the current learning orientations.
3. Change both learning orientations and facilitating factors. An organization should select this option when it sees the other variables as inadequate. This option assumes that large-scale change is necessary and that changing one group of variables without changing the other will be only partially successful.

Each organizational unit or firm must make the decision to pursue one strategy or another for itself. While there are no rules for making this decision, the three options are incrementally more difficult to implement (i.e., one is the easiest to implement; three is the hardest). From the first to the third options, the resistance to change within the organization increases significantly. It is one thing to develop a plan for improving what is already done reasonably well; it is another to engage in nothing less than near-total transformation. It is one thing to stay within accepted, assimilated paradigms; it is another to replace institutionalized models.

[22] W. R. Torbert, *Managing the Corporate Dream* (New York: Dow Jones-Irwin, 1987).

Whatever the organization's choice, we offer three guidelines for developing and implementing a chosen strategy:

1. Before deciding to become something new, study and evaluate what you are now. Without full awareness and appreciation of current assumptions about management, organization, and learning, it is not possible to grasp what is being done well and what might be improved or changed.

2. Though the systemic issues and relationships in organizational life require that change be approached from multiple directions and at several points, organizations can change in major ways if people experience success with more modest, focused, and specific changes. As with many skills, there is a learning curve for the skill of managing and surviving transitions. Large-scale change requires that many initiatives be put into place in a carefully designed, integrated sequence.

3. Organizations must consider cultural factors in choosing and implementing any strategy, particularly when considering how it does specific things. For example, in a highly individualistic society like the United States or the United Kingdom, skill development focuses on individual skills; in comparison, more communitarian societies such as Japan or Korea have traditionally focused on group skill development. Moving from one pole to the other is a major cultural change; to simply improve on the existing orientation is much easier.

To help managers better understand the learning capabilities in their own organizations, we have developed and are testing an "organizational learning inventory." This diagnostic tool will enable an organization's members to produce a learning profile based on our model. The profile can guide managers to their choices for improving learning capability. Through further research, we intend to show how learning profiles vary within and across different companies and industries.

Chapter 3

Learning From Collaboration: Knowledge and Networks in the Biotechnology and Pharmaceutical Industries

Walter W. Powell[1]

In a number of technologically advanced industries, a new logic of organizing is developing. Rather than viewing firms as vehicles for processing information, making decisions, and solving problems, the core capabilities of organizations are based increasingly on knowledge-seeking and knowledge-creation. In technologically intensive fields, where there are large gains from innovation and steep losses from obsolescence, competition is best regarded as a learning race. The ability to learn about new opportunities requires participation in them, thus a wide range of interorganizational linkages is critical to knowledge diffusion, learning, and technology development. These connections may be formal contractual relationships, as in a research and development partnerships or a joint venture, or informal, involving participation in technical communities. Both mechanisms are highly salient for the transfer of knowledge and are reinforcing. Yet even though the awareness of the importance of both external sources of knowledge and external participation has grown, we know much less about how knowledge is generated, transferred, and acted upon in these new contexts.

[*1] Copyright ©1998, by The Regents of the University of California. Reprinted from the *California Management Review*, Vol. 40, No. 3. By permission of The Regents.
[*] This article draws on collaborative research done with colleague Ken Koput, and with our graduate research assistants Jason Owen-Smith and Laurel Smith-Doerr The financial support of the National Science Foundation (NSF grant #9710729) is greatly appreciated.

THE TWIN FACES OF COLLABORATION

By a variety of accounts, the number and scope of interorganizational collaborations have grown rapidly in many industries, most notably in the field of biotechnology.[2] In the world of practice, this heightened interest is captured in discussions of the "virtual firm," and evidenced in all manner of cooperative relationships that join two or more organizations in some form of common undertaking.[3] In the world of theory, research on various forms of collaboration has two principle foci: on the transaction and the mutual exchange of rights; and on the relationship and the mechanisms through which information flows and mutual adjustments take place. Typically, the more exchange-oriented analysis treats collaboration as a variant of the make or buy decision and analyzes key features of the transaction: how it is negotiated and which party retains what control rights.[4] Thus, it matters a great deal whether common assets are being pooled or different resources traded, what stage of development a project is at, and whether some form of ownership is involved.[5] This strand of research, based primarily in the fields of industrial organization economics and business strategy, focuses more on the contractual mechanisms for coordinating interorganizational relations.

The second line of inquiry, stemming more from sociology and organization theory, adopts a processual focus, analyzing whether features of the task require continuous communication and organization learning, and the extent to which the collaboration is embedded in multiple, ongoing relationships.[6] This approach focuses on the relational capability of organizations, how and when organizations are able to combine their existing competencies with the abilities of

[2] See data presented in National Science Board, *Science and Technology Indicators—1996* (Washington, D.C.: U.S. Government Printing Office, 1996).
[3] A good discussion is found in H. Chesbrough and D. J. Teece, "When Is Virtual Virtuous: Organizing for Innovation," *Harvard Business Review*, 74/1 (January/February 1996): 65–73.
[4] See O. Williamson, "Comparative Economic Organization," *Administrative Science Quarterly*, 36 (1996): 269–296; O. Hart, *Firms, Contracts, and Financial Structure* (New York, NY: Oxford University Press, 1995).
[5] Representative examples include Paul Joskow, "Contract Duration and Relation-Specific Investments," *American Economic Review*, 77 (1987): 168–195; Gary Pisano and P. Y. Mang, "Collaborative Product Development and the Market for Know-How," *Research on Technological Innovation, Management, and Policy*, 5 (1993): 109–136; Phillipe Aghion and Jean Tirole, "On the Management of Innovation," *Quarterly Journal of Economics*, 109 (1994): 361–379.
[6] See, for example, Mark Granovetter, "Economic Action and Social Structure: The Problem of Embeddedness," *American Journal of Sociology*, 91(1985): 481–510; Charles Sabel, "Learning by Monitoring," in N. Smelser and R. Swedberg, eds., *Handbook of Economic Sociology* (Princeton, NJ: Princeton University Press, 1994), pp. 137–165; Brian Uzzi, "The Sources and Consequences of Embeddedness for the Economic Performance of Organizations," *American Sociological Review*, 61 (1996): 624–648.

others. These capabilities are not viewed as static, but rather emerge and deepen over time as firms both develop existing relationships and explore new ones.

These two perspectives are, at times, viewed as competing explanations, but since they involve different units of analysis—the transaction and the relationship, respectively—they need not be. Key structural features of an industry may determine the relative weight that contractual and processual elements play in interorganizational collaborations.[7] Large-scale reliance on interorganizational linkages reflects a fundamental and pervasive concern with access to knowledge. In the rapidly-developing field of biotechnology, the knowledge base is both complex and expanding and the sources of expertise are widely dispersed. When uncertainty is high, organizations interact more, not less, with external parties in order to access both knowledge and resources. Hence, the locus of innovation is found in networks of learning, rather than in individual firms. How contracts are structured is not unimportant; in fact, getting the intellectual property rights specified clearly is critical. But focusing too closely on the transactional details of an exchange risks missing the boat as the larger field rides the waves of rapid technological change. Moreover, current work on contractual aspects of collaboration between biotech and pharmaceutical firms suggests that as the relationships unfold, many of the specific covenants contained in contracts are not invoked.[8] In short, process matters, and firms differ in their ability to do relational contracting.

In several key respects, arguments about the learning and strategic aspects of collaboration converge to produce new questions about the pivotal role of learning and interfirm relationships in rapidly developing industries. Firms in technologically intensive fields rely on collaborative relationships to access, survey, and exploit emerging technological opportunities. As the structure of an industry becomes shaped by interorganizational relations, the nature of competition is altered, but the direction of change is very much open. First, collaboration raises entry barriers. To the extent that the capabilities of organizations are based in part on the qualities or capabilities of those with whom they are allied, collaboration increases the price of admission to a field. If parties act either opportunistically or restrictively, collaborating only with a narrow range of partners whose behavior they can influence, then collaboration can exclude admission to many. But if the participants interact broadly and engage in mutual learning with the organizations they are affiliated with, the effects of collaboration are expansive, mobilizing resources throughout a field, with collaboration serving as an

[7] Walter W. Powell, Kenneth Koput, and Laurel Smith-Doerr, "Interorganizational Collaboration and the Locus of Innovation: Networks of Learning in Biotechnology," *Administrative Science Quarterly*, 41(1996): 116–145; Peter Grindley and David Teece, "Managing Intellectual Capital: Licensing and Cross-Licensing in Semiconductors and Electronics," *California Management Review*, 38/2 (Winter 1997): 8–41.
[8] Josh Lerner and Robert P. Merges, "The Control of Strategic Alliances: An Empirical Analysis of Biotechnology Collaborations," unpublished manuscript, Harvard Business School.

inclusive entry pass. Second, interfirm cooperation accelerates the rate of techno-logical innovation. In our earlier work, we demonstrated a ladder effect, in which firms with experienced partners competed more effectively in high-speed learning races.[9] Rather than seeking to monopolize the returns from innovative activity and forming exclusive Partnerships with only a narrow set of organiza-tions successful firms positioned themselves as the hubs at the center of overlap-ping networks, stimulating rewarding research collaborations among the various organizations to which they are aligned, and profiting from having multiple projects in various stages of development.

Third, reliance on collaboration has potentially transformative effects on all participants. Those positioned in a network of external relations adopt more administrative innovations, and do so earlier.[10] The presence of a dense network of collaborative ties may even alter participants' perceptions of competition. Inside a densely connected field, organizations must adjust to a novel perspective in which it is no longer necessary to have exclusive, proprietary ownership of an asset in order to extract value from it. Moreover, since a competitor on one project may become a partner on another, the playing field resembles less a horse race and more a rugby match, in which players frequently change their uni-forms.[11] Seen from this perspective, decisions that were initially framed as strate-gic have cumulative consequences that alter the economic calculus, while choices motivated by learning and experimentation remake the institutional landscape.

Finally, collaboration may itself become a dimension of competition. As firms turn to outside parties for a variety of resources, they develop a network profile, or portfolio of ties to specific partners for certain activities. Thus, for example, an emerging biotech company may have a research grant from a branch of the National Institutes of Health, a research collaboration with a leading uni-versity, licensing agreements with other universities or nonprofit research insti-tutes, clinical studies underway with a research hospital, and sales or distribution arrangements with a large pharmaceutical corporation. Others may have only one such relationship, or may hook up with the same partners for different

---

[9] Powell et al. op. cit.

[10] On the diffusion of matrix management, see L. R. Burns and D. R. Wholey, "Adoption and Abandonment of Matrix Management Programs," *Academy of Management Journal,* 36 (1993) 106–138; on the spread of the "poison pill," see G. Davis, "Agents Without Principles?" *Administrative Science Quarterly,* 36 (1991): 583–613; on the multidivisional form, see D. Palmer, P. D. Jennings, and X. Zhan, "Late Adoption of the Multidivisional Form by Large U.S. Corporations," *Administrative Science Quarterly,* 38 (1993): 100–131; on the diffusion of total quality management, see J. D. Westphal, R. Gulati, and S. Shortell, "Customization or Conformity," *Administrative Science Quarterly.* 42 (1997): 366–394.

[11] Walter W. Powell and Laurel Smith-Doerr, "Networks and Economic Life," in N. Smelser and R. Swedberg, eds., *Handbook of Economic Sociology* (Princeton, NJ: Princeton University Press, 1994), pp. 368–402; Richard S. Rosenbloom and Williams J. Spencer, "The Transformation of Industrial Research," *Issues in Science and Technol-ogy,* 12/3 (1996): 68–74.

activities, or with disparate partners for similar activities, or have complex relationships involving multiple activities with each partner. Analytically each combination of partnership and business activity represents a distinct collaborative relationship. A firm's portfolio of collaborations is both a resource and a signal to markets, as well as to other potential partners, of the quality of the firm's activities and products. Whether firms in a field are constrained to a narrow set of relationships or have broad options in determining their portfolios has profound consequences for competition. To draw on the language of political sociology, heterogeneity and interdependence are greater spurs to collective action than homogeneity and discipline.[12] If the members on an industry are constrained in their choice of partners to a small set of potential partners, competition is increased, but within a narrow sphere. The effect is like a tournament, in which the "winners" receive exclusive sponsorship in order to compete against each other in ever-fiercer rounds. On the other hand, if there is a broad and growing set of nonexclusive partners, then the participants will evince heterogeneous collaborations, and the avenues of rivalry are widened.

In sum, regardless of whether collaboration is driven by strategic motives, such as filling in missing pieces of the value chain, or by learning considerations to gain access to new knowledge, or by embeddedness in a community of practice, connectivity to an inter-organizational network and competence at managing collaborations have become key drivers of a new logic of organizing. This view of organizations and networks as vehicles for producing, synthesizing, and distributing ideas recognizes that the success of firms is increasingly linked to the depth of their ties to organizations in diverse fields. Learning in these circumstances is a complex, multi-level process, involving learning from and with partners under conditions of uncertainty, learning about partners' behavior and developing routines and norms that can mitigate the risks of opportunism, and learning how to distribute newly acquired knowledge across different projects and functions. But learning is also closely linked to the conditions under which knowledge is gained, and in this sense the motives that drive collaboration can shape what can be learned. Much sophisticated technical knowledge is tacit in character—an indissoluble mix of design, process, and expertise. Such information is not easily transferred ·by license or purchase. Passive recipients of new knowledge are less likely to fully appreciate its value or be able to respond rapidly. In fields such as biotechnology, firms must have the ability to absorb knowledge.[13] In short, internal capability and external collaborations are

[12] For introductions to the political sociology literature, see Gerald Maxwell and Pamela Oliver, *The Critical Mass in Collective Action* (Cambridge: Cambridge University Press, 1993); Sidney Tarrow, *Power in Movement: Social Movements, Collective Action, and Politics* (Cambridge: Cambridge University Press, 1994).

[13] This argument draws freely on Cohen and Levinthal's ideas about absorptive capacity, Nelson and Winter's work on developing routines for learning, and Brown and Duguid's ideas on situated learning. See Wesley Cohen and Daniel Levinthal, "Absorptive Capacity:

complementary. Internal capability is indispensable in evaluating ideas or skills developed externally, while collaboration with outside parties provides access to news and resources that cannot be generated internally. A network serves as the locus of innovation in many high-tech fields because it provides timely access to knowledge and resources that are otherwise unavailable, while also testing internal expertise and learning capabilities.

THE NETWORK STRUCTURE OF THE BIOTECHNOLOGY FIELD

The science underlying the field of biotechnology had its origins in discoveries made in university laboratories in the early 1970s. These promising breakthroughs were initially exploited by science-based start-up firms (DBFs, or dedicated biotechnology firms, in industry parlance) founded in the mid to late 1970s. The year 1980 marked a sea change with the U.S. Supreme Court ruling in the Diamond vs. Chakrabaty case that genetically engineered life forms were patentable. And Genentech, which along with Cetus was the most visible biotech company, had its initial public offering, drawing astonishing interest on Wall Street. Over the next two decades, hundreds of DBFs have been founded, mostly in the U.S. but more recently in Canada, Australia, Britain, and Europe.

The initial research—most notably Herbert Boyer and Stanley Cohen's discovery of recombinant DNA methods and Georges Köhler and Cesar Milstein's cell infusion technology that creates monoclonal antibodies—drew primarily on molecular biology and immunology. The early discoveries were so path-breaking that they had a kind of natural excludability, that is, without interaction with those involved in the research, the knowledge was slow to transfer. But what was considered a radical innovation then has changed considerably as the science diffused rapidly. Genetic engineering, monoclonal antibodies, polymerase chain reaction amplification, and gene sequencing are now part of the standard toolkit of microbiology graduate students. To stay on top of the field, one has to be at the forefront of knowledge-seeking and technology development. Moreover, many new areas of science have become inextricably involved, ranging from genetics, biochemistry, cell biology, general medicine, computer science, to even physics and optical sciences. Modern biotechnology, then, is not a discipline or an industry per se, but a set of technologies relevant to a wide range of disciplines and industries.

The commercial potential of biotechnology appealed to many scientists and entrepreneurs even at its embryonic stage. In the early years, the principal efforts

A New Perspective on Learning and Innovation," *Administrative Science Quarterly*, 35 (1990): 128–152; Richard Nelson and Sidney Winter, *An Evolutionary Theory of Economic Change* (Cambridge, MA: Harvard University Press, 1982); John Seeley Brown and Paul Duguid, "Organizational Learning and Communities-of-Practice," *Organization Science*, 2 (1991): 40–57.

were directed at making existing proteins in new ways, then the field evolved to use the new methods to make new proteins, and now today the race is on to design entirely new medicines. The firms that translated the science into feasible technologies and new medical products faced a host of challenges. Alongside the usual difficulties of start-up firms, the DBFs needed huge amounts of capital to fund costly research, assistance in managing themselves and in conducting clinical trials, and eventually experience with the regulatory approval process, manufacturing, marketing, distribution, and sales. In time, established pharmaceutical firms were attracted to the field, initially allying with DBFs in research partnerships and in providing a set of organizational capabilities that DBFs were lacking. Eventually, the considerable promise of biotechnology led nearly every established pharmaceutical corporation to develop, to varying degrees of success, both in-house capacity in the new science and a portfolio of collaborations with DBFs.

Thus the field is not only multi-disciplinary, it is multi-institutional as well. In addition to research universities and both start-up and established firms, government agencies, nonprofit research institutes, and leading research hospitals have played key roles in conducting and funding research, while venture capitalists and law firms have played essential parts as talent scouts, advisors, consultants, and financiers. Two factors are highly salient. One, all the necessary skills and organizational capabilities needed to compete in biotechnology are not readily found under a single roof. Two, in fields such as biotech, where knowledge is advancing rapidly and the sources of knowledge are widely dispersed, organizations enter into a wide array of alliances to gain access to different competencies and knowledge. Progress with the technology goes hand-in-hand with the evolution of the industry and its supporting institutions. The science, the organizations, and the associated institutions' practices are co-evolving. Universities are more attentive to the commercial development of research, DBFs are active participants in basic science inquiry and pharmaceuticals more keyed into developments at DBFs and universities.

Nevertheless, organizations vary in their abilities to access knowledge and skills located beyond their boundaries. Organizations develop very different profiles of collaboration, turning to partners for divergent combinations of skills, funding, experience, access, and status. Biotech firms have not supplanted pharmaceutical companies, and large pharmaceuticals have not absorbed the biotechnology field. Nor has the basic science component of the industry receded in its importance. Consequently, DBFs, research universities, pharmaceutical companies, research institutions, and leading medical centers are continually seeking partners who can help them stay abreast of, or in front of, this fast-moving field. But organizations vary considerably in their approaches to collaboration. Put differently, some organizations reap more from the network seeds they sow than do others. Despite the efforts of nearly every DBF to strengthen its collaborative capacity, not all of them cultivate similar profiles of relationships, nor are all able to harvest their networks to comparable advantage. Similarly, not every pharmaceutical firm is positioned comparably to exploit the latest breakthroughs in genomics, gene therapy, and a host of other novel methodologies for drug discovery. A key challenge, then, for both small biotechnology firms and large global pharmaceutical corporations is in learning from collaborations with external parties, and in constructing a portfolio of collaborators that provides access to both the emerging science and technology and the necessary organizational capabilities.

COLLABORATIVE PORTFOLIOS

The various key participants in the biotechnology and pharmaceutical industries pursue different avenues of collaboration. A cursory study of the portfolios of key firms reveals distinctive mixes of alliances for different business functions. For example, in biotech, Amgen, a Los Angeles-based firm founded in 1980, is often regarded as a bellwether for the industry. Amgen has extensive R&D and marketing collaborations with numerous small biotech companies, among them ARRIS, Envirogen, Glycomex, Guilford, Interneuron, Regeneron, and Zynaxis. These are relationships based on a division of labor in which the smaller firm develops promising technology with Amgen's financial and scientific assistance, and Amgen will market the eventual product. Amgen also holds several key licensing agreements with Sloan-Kettering Hospital (for a cell growth factor), the Ontario Cancer Institute (for knockout mice), and Rockefeller University (for an obesity gene). In contrast, Cambridge-based Biogen, founded in 1978 but with only 750 employees, adopted a strategy of licensing its initial research discoveries to such established firms as Abbott, Lilly, Pharmacia Upjohn, Merck, Organon Teknika, and Schering Plough. By 1996, Biogen's royalty stream had grown to $150 million annually. Biogen also outsourced the costly and time-consuming task of analyzing clinical trial data on its medicines in development to contract research organizations, but monitored the work with in-house experts.[14] Chiron, the largest biotech with more than 7500 employees, and 9 subsidiaries, is also partially owned by Novartis (49.9%) and Johnson and Johnson (4.6%). Chiron, founded in 1981, has the most extensive array of collaborations of any biotech with numerous R&D ties with smaller biotechs and universities, licensing agreements with large pharmaceutical and animal health companies, partnerships with larger biotechs, and manufacturing and marketing alliances with other large firms as well. Indeed, in a January, 1997 news release, Chiron reported that it now has more than 1,400 (informal) agreements with universities and research institutions and 64 (formal) collaborations with other companies. "This network is a core strength of Chiron," the release proclaims.

These different collaborative profiles reflect, in important respects, the mixed motives of strategy and exigency in the early years of building a company. Amgen works with younger, early-stage biotechs, but eschews close affiliations

---

[14] Lawrence M. Fisher, "Biogen's Triumph against the Odds," *Strategy and Business,* 8 (3rd Quarter 1997): 55–63.

with many established pharmaceuticals. Biogen licensed out some of its initial research discoveries, and the substantial royalties it takes in now fund the development, sales, and distribution of Avonex, its successful drug for multiple sclerosis. Chiron has a spider-webbed universe of affiliations with basic scientists in universities, and it maintains ongoing ties with diverse biotechs and health-care companies. The partial "parent" owner, Novartis of Switzerland, appears to use Chiron as its window into this rapidly developing field.

Similarly, in the pharmaceutical industry, divergent approaches to collaboration are pursued. By the accounting of Recombinant Capital, a San Francisco company that tracks high tech, the big pharmaceutical firms poured $4.5 billion into deals with biotech companies in 1996.[15] Their aim is to capitalize on promising technology and the skills of the nimbler small companies in doing more rapid development. But dominant firms pursue these aims in quite different ways. Industry giant Merck, for example, spreads its search efforts globally, working with research institutes in France, Canada, China, Japan, Costa Rica, and the United States, while pursuing research partnerships with but a few biotechs such as Affymetrix and Transcell to access new technologies. In addition, Merck has innumerable licensing agreements, as well as arrangements to do manufacturing, marketing, and sales for smaller companies. Eli Lilly, another big pharmaceutical player, but about two-thirds the size of Merck, has both more focused and more extensive collaborations. Pursuing a strategy of "discovery without walls," Lilly has several dozen research alliances with a wide variety of U.S. biotech firms, ranging from new startups to more established companies. In addition to these extensive external discovery efforts, Lilly also has licensing and joint sales and distribution agreements with biotechs, but the clear emphasis has been on the research side. The Swiss firm Hoffman LaRoche, one of the largest firms in the industry, has an even more focused approach, owning 66% of the stock in the U.S. biotech firm Genentech, in addition to multiple research, development, and marketing collaborations with Genentech. Roche counts Amgen, Affymetrix, and several other biotechs as partners also, but it utilizes Genentech as its primary talent scout to stay abreast of the field.

At a more micro level, however, these collaborative profiles have their origins in myriad small decisions, stemming from different purposes and initiated by different parties. At one of the larger U.S. pharmaceutical firms, I was involved in a multi-year internal executive development program. During this time, I had regular contact with senior managers on the science side, in the finance and strategy groups, and those in charge of the different therapeutic product lines. I used our conversations to informally trace the origins of the more than twenty R&D partnerships the firm has with various small biotechs. In following these different "stories," it became apparent that collaborations emerged from very different routes. Some were brought forward by business development staff who had "found" young biotechs in financial trouble and in need of cash. Thus,

[15] See Erick Schonfield, "Merck vs. the Biotech Industry: Which One Is More Potent?" *Fortune*, March 31, 1997, pp. 161–162.

promising technology could be "had" inexpensively. In other circumstances, however, breakthrough technologies triggered great interest throughout the pharmaceutical industry, and all the major players were part of the gold rush, bidding for the new discovery In still other cases, long-standing personal ties among scientists, sometimes forged decades earlier at universities, led to formal collaborations. Other partnerships were driven by a pressing need to fill out a product portfolio or to replenish the product pipeline in a particular therapeutic category. And still other connections' literally fell into their laps, as biotech firms approached the company with proposals that proved viable.

I use these examples of very different starting points not to suggest that the process of deciding which parties to collaborate with is random or haphazard, but to illustrate that there are, especially in a larger company, multiple inputs and opportunities and many decision makers involved. Except in the smallest companies, the same people rarely review all the relevant information and make decisions about whom to ally with and under what terms and for what period of time. Nor should such decisions necessarily be made by the same people or units. But what is necessary is the ability to negotiate two hurdles, the first leaping from information to knowledge, and the second jumping from individual-level learning and expertise to organizational-level learning and routines. In any technology-intensive field, information is abundant and accumulates rapidly. Long ago, Herbert Simon alerted us to the fact that, increasingly, attention is the scarcest commodity in organizations. As firms embark on different combinations of formal and informal collaborations and divergent mixes of external sourcing and internal production, the parties who are most closely involved with outsiders develop skills at relatiqnal contracting: How much of an agreement needs to be specified in a contract? How much should rest on a handshake or good faith? What role should the "entangling strings" of friendship or reputation play? What kinds of milestones or interventions are needed to insure a project stays on course?[16] In short, knowledge of how to collaborate means that information is filtered by a specific context· and an ongoing relationship, by experience and reflection, and by interpretation. When multiple participants are involved, and their availability varies, making knowledgeable decisions is a challenge.

But even more daunting is moving from individual learning (which is embodied in experienced personnel) to organization-level learning (in which the skills of relational contracting become embedded in organizational routines and procedures) without rendering those competencies lifeless and inert. As an illustration, Richard Di Marchi, Vice President for Endocrine Research at Eli Lilly and Company, remarks that one of the bigger challenges his company faces in managing research partnerships with small firms is in not treating them as "one-offs," that is, independent relationships pursued separately. On the other hand, it is ineffective to force all decisions about collaboration to go forward only after the decision has been vetted by a key committee, composed of staff from

16 See Ian Macneil, "Relational Contracting: What We Do and Do Not Know," *Wisconsin Law Review*, 3(1985): 483–526.

different business functions. Such a move can result in a needless delay, which is fatal in a fast-moving field, and can also dampen initiative. Another side-effect of formalizing the approval process is to force external relationships underground, into subterranean linkages, as savvy managers opt to pursue relationships without risking going through the rigamarole of formal approval. But covert efforts may run the risk that key intellectual property or process issues are not aired at the outset. The challenge, then, is to develop routines for cooperation that are widely shared, that apply across decisions, and allow for lessons to be transferred from project to project. In the biotechnology and pharmaceutical fields, firms vary enormously in their capacity to learn across projects.

LEARNING HOW AND WHAT TO LEARN

My claim that learning from collaboration is both a function of access to knowledge and possession of capabilities for utilizing and building on such knowledge is not a claim that individuals and organizations are exceedingly calculating or far-sighted. In making the argument that knowledge facilitates the acquisition of more knowledge, I am building on research that stresses that skills are embedded in the exercise of routines. The development of these routines is a key feature in explaining the variability of organizations' capacity for learning. Only by building these skills can knowledge be transferred from one project to another, from one unit to another, in a manner that allows insights gained from one set of experiences to shape subsequent activities.

Most firms in biotech and pharmaceuticals have key individuals who function as network managers, "marriage counselors," and honest brokers. These individuals provide the glue that sustains relationships between parties who have ample opportunities to question one another's intentions or efforts. The participants in a collaboration often learn at very different speeds, prompting one side to wonder if it is benefitting equally. Moreover, the wealthier party is sometimes regarded as a "sugar daddy," present only to write checks. So there are numerous situations where monitoring and interventions are needed to maintain balance in a collaboration. A critical task for the participants enmeshed in a web of many such relationships is to take lessons learned on one project and make them systemic, that is, portable across multiple relationships.

Finding solutions to the problem of learning how to learn is critical for both small and large firms. Biotech companies have created organizational capabilities well out of proportion to their relatively small size by building on relationships with external parties to gain access to resources, knowledge, and skills to support every organizational function from R&D to distribution. And given the huge sums that pharmaceuticals are pouring into biotech, these large firms have had to find methods to harmonize and coordinate their far-flung partnerships. The steps involved range widely, and it is probably too early to pronounce some efforts most efficacious. Clearly not all firms maneuver with equal ease, have comparable access, or utilize high-quality partners with similar results. But some methods do hold promise for facilitating learning.

An enormous amount of information and knowledge resides in the minds and electronic mail of key people, but this material is rarely organized in a fashion that allows for its transmission to others. Some firms build repositories, where contracts, milestone agreements, working papers, publications, press releases, and overheads are stored. These data banks are primarily useful for novices and new hires. A few firms have set up discussion databases in which archival material and reports are enlivened with notes and chat-room-like interactions about lessons learned. These more active sources, where key participants record their experiences as well as respond to others, are potentially quite valuable. Nevertheless they have, according to some informants, a somewhat sterile feel to them, like critiquing others' critiques of a performance, rather than engaging the performance itself. And, to many people, there simply is not sufficient time to join in these discussions. They are too busy with the press of daily activities.

Informal seminars on lessons learned from a partnership, particularly when staff from multiple functions are involved, are a good way to transmit experience across projects. Only limited effort needs to be made to organize such presentations, so they have the advantage of freshness and a hands-on feel.

Nevertheless, these seminars, unless performed on a more or less regular basis, are much more valuable in a smaller company than a larger one because the information diffuses more extensively. I have not personally encountered any case where participants from both sides of a collaboration made a joint presentation, although almost every time I suggest such an approach, I am met with a comment, "That would be interesting!" Talking about failures, shortcomings, and rough spots in a relationship would be equally as valuable as discussions of successes and lessons learned. But I have rarely seen presentations where such difficulties are openly discussed. To be sure, these conversations are often pursued, heatedly, but off-stage, again the closed nature of the discussion inhibits the transfer of information. Moreover, problematic points are often dismissed as idiosyncratic to a particular party and not felt to be generalizable. While there is, of course, truth to such claims, a large part of building a reputation as a preferred partner is learning how to broker unexpected disputes.

Many biotech and pharmaceutical firms turn to multi-functional teams to supervise collaborative activities, building on the popular idea of the heavyweight teams used in product development efforts. The more thoughtful teams opt to disseminate their discussions either through electronic posting of minutes of their meetings or by having different participants act as scribes to send out short summaries of meetings.

In all these activities, there is a persistent tension between those activities done informally and on an ad hoc basis and those efforts that are more formalized and structured. Clearly, there are tradeoffs with both approaches. The insight appreciated by only a minority of the firms that we have had contact with is that developing routines for the transmission of information and experience does not necessarily entail formalization. Information can be conveyed routinely through informal means. While formal repositories and powerful task forces can be useful, they are too often not a forum in which outside input is allowed. Building routines for regular contact without formalization allows for the possibility that participants not only contribute ideas, they will take lessons learned and spread them in unexpected and unobtrusive ways.

CONCLUSION

In innovation-driven fields, firms are engaged in learning races. These contests proceed on parallel tracks, one involving learning *from* collaborations, the other concerns learning *how* to collaborate. Both contests require the development of skills to facilitate the transfer of information and knowledge and their subsequent deployment in other situations. In some respects, the task of learning from outside parties is more difficult. But perhaps because of the importance of the task and/or its considerable expense, organizations in the biotechnology and pharmaceutical fields are rapidly developing the capability to collaborate with a diverse array of partners to speed the timely development of new medicines. Much less refined is the more mundane but difficult and vital task of transferring information and knowledge obtained from external parties throughout the organization. This is done in order that subsequent actions are informed by and strategic thinking based on, these experiences. A variety of efforts at learning are underway, ranging from electronic discussions to data depositories to seminars to regular meetings of heavyweight teams. All these activities reflect efforts to see that information becomes more widely diffused, and that with reflection and interpretation, becomes "thickened" into knowledge. But developing routines for knowledge dissemination is always a double-edged sword: informal mechanisms may preclude wide dissemination, while formal procedures can inhibit learning. The challenge is to develop regular venues for the informal transmission of information, such that the process itself becomes tied to knowledge seeking and creation.

Chapter 4

Growing Intellectual Capital at IBM: More than Technology

Don Cohen and Richard Azzarello[1]

By the middle of 1997, thousands of IBM Global Services practitioners could share technical materials, engagement experiences, industry information, proposals, and other valuable documents over the world-wide IBM Lotus Notes network using the firm's new Intellectual Capital Management System. In addition to submitting and retrieving intellectual materials, they can take part in issue-based online discussions and use author information accompanying submissions to contact each other directly. The system helps consultants in more than a hundred countries share the intellectual assets they create and bring their combined expertise to bear on client work. It is designed to increase both the speed and quality of their response to customer needs.

Intellectual assets are important to any company that makes innovative or technically complex products; they are central and intrinsic to service businesses, whose products *are* knowledge and expertise. Managing intellectual assets has become increasingly critical to IBM as its service sector, which generated $23 billion in revenue in 1996, continues to grow. For consulting groups and other services, giving value to customers means providing deep, appropriate, useful knowledge as rapidly as possible. No one expert or team can know everything the customer needs to know; nor can they independently develop new expertise fast enough to satisfy clients trying to reap the benefits of speed in their own businesses. Much of the knowledge they need and can build on already exists in the company, though. The size and breadth of IBM make it an engine of knowledge creation. Competitiveness, efficiency, and customer satisfaction depend on capturing that knowledge and quickly putting it to work wherever else in the company it may be needed.

As early as 1991, IBM Consulting Group founder Bob Howe recognized the potential benefits service providers could derive from a system for

---

[1] Reprinted with kind permission of the authors Don Cohen and Richard Azzarello.

exchanging intellectual material. To meet the need, he approved construction of a Lotus Notes network for 2500 consultants in IBM's Consulting Group. Not surprisingly, the familiar "If you build it, they will come" strategy proved faulty. Too few consultants came to the system; those who did found it hard to pick the gems out from the mass of less valuable documents. In August of 1994, Howe recognized that the system wasn't working and said, "We have to do this right to compete in the service business." He appointed Barbara Smith to head an effort to figure out how.

Smith and IBM consultant Rich Azzarello assembled an Intellectual Capital Management team of 15 respected professionals from IBM Consulting and Global Services to consider three questions:

- What's wrong with the current system?
- What is the right way to do intellectual capital management?
- What organizational and technical enablers do we need to do it right?

During the last three months of 1994, the team conducted over 200 internal interviews and studied intellectual capital management practices and initiatives of 16 other large service and technology firms to find answers that would help them define the context and essential components of a successful system. Joe Movizzo, who became general manager of the Consulting Group while the team was doing its assessment, believed that a clear conceptual framework and business model are essential for successfully developing and deploying a global knowledge-sharing system. He says, "they make the *idea* of intellectual capital management *actionable*."

THE ICM FRAMEWORK: A HOLISTIC APPROACH

The team concluded that effective management of intellectual capital depends on dealing simultaneously with a variety of human, organizational, and technical issues. Their belief in the importance of this kind of holistic approach is supported by Thomas Davenport in his recent book, *Information Ecology*. Davenport's ecological approach:

> . . . addresses all of a film's values and beliefs about information (culture); how people actually use information and what they do with it (behavior and work processes); the pitfalls that can interfere with information sharing (politics); and what information systems are already in place (yes, finally, technology).[2]

When the earlier collaborative system was built, virtually no work was done to develop processes or behaviors that would influence *how* and *why*

---

[2] Thomas H. Davenport, *Information Ecology* (New York: Oxford University Press, 1997), p. 4.

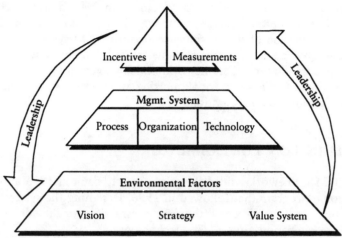

FIGURE 4.1 IBM's *Intellectual Capital Management Framework*

people would use it. For instance, no process had been established for evaluating content. People used what Smith calls "the big bucket approach," dumping in whatever they had on hand. Similarly, potential users did not get training and support to encourage them to use the system, and almost no attention was given to the underlying cultural issues that might promote or inhibit knowledge-sharing in the first place.

Synthesizing the best parts of the external efforts and their learning from internal interviews, the team constructed a framework that showed the relationship among what they concluded were the essential elements of a successful intellectual capital management strategy. It describes the range of issues involved in a holistic intellectual capital "ecology."

As defined by the framework, the management system itself is not just a technology system. The *processes* needed for managing intellectual capital and the *organization* in which and through which knowledge is shared are as much a part of the system as the *technology* that makes capturing and sharing intellectual capital possible. This three-part system sits on a "base" of environmental factors. To work successfully, it must operate in an environment (or culture) that provides a *vision* of company goals (so individuals understand what they are collectively trying to accomplish), and a set of *values* (such as trust and respect) that make them willing to help one another. The team found that IBM Global Services, like many organizations, tended to reward self-sufficiency, unique expertise, and directly billable work—all inhibitors of knowledge-sharing. Unless these norms change, even the most advanced collaborative technology will be ineffectual. The capstone of the framework consists of *incentives* and *measurements*, which influence cultural norms. Busy professionals sensibly spend most of their time on work that is rewarded; without the incentives of public recognition and some promise of financial benefit, they would be unlikely to give much effort to sharing intellectual capital. Measurements are important because both individual rewards and evaluation of the overall success of the ICM system must be based on consistent, convincing measures of value created. Finally, active participation of leadership is implicit in the framework: senior managers have direct responsibility for vision and values and for supporting an incentive system that rewards knowledge-sharing and collaboration.

BUILDING ON THE FRAMEWORK

The ICM framework guided the pilot project begun in 1995 and supports the operational program that followed in 1996. Designing the system, the ICM team gave balanced attention to it the three central components identified in the framework: organization, process, and technology.

To take advantage of organizational structures that favored knowledge exchange, they first deployed the system within existing competency groups communities of consultants who had already been drawn together by mutual interests and had experience sharing complementary expertise. Members of these groups regularly met to exchange ideas, so the ICM system electronically extended familiar activities. Organizationally and culturally, the groups provided a ready-made environment for knowledge-sharing.

The processes established by the team emphasized close collaboration with system users and a steady focus on business value. That emphasis and focus began during the assessment period, when team members asked potential users what kinds of information they most needed to do their work well—an obvious step sometimes ignored by system designers. When asked, "If your office were on fire, what five things would you take out with you?" those interviewed overwhelmingly named customer information, skills information (information on internal experts), proposals, lessons learned, and success stories. These needs are reflected in the basic document types that define system content.

The processes for working collaboratively with competency groups to build their networks are defined by a series of milestones. They include the selection and training of a core group leader within the competency, the development of a work plan and structure for organizing the group's intellectual material to make it most applicable to their particular work, building the databases, and launching the network. Processes are also in place to educate the competency groups and help them develop growth plans after the network is operating.

During the planing phase, the ICM team chose not to start by evaluating technologies. They wanted to define functionality first and then find technology to provide it, rather than let technology dictate how the system would work. As it happened, IBM's purchase of Lotus made Notes the choice, not only because it was now an IBM product but because the company saw advantages in using it for multiple purposes, including ICM. There were potential benefits to be derived from using a product that would be a company standard, among them that employees would more willingly use a familiar, multi-purpose tool than a specialized one. Because ICM was one of the first uses of Notes at IBM, the benefits were not seen at the beginning, but they are becoming evident as Notes use increases. From the beginning, the software's security features and easy database replication were important pluses. Its biggest drawback—isolation from Web technology—has been overcome by Domino, which allows Notes to link seamlessly to the Internet and has led to the development of the ICM AssetWeb.

CULTURE AND VISION

A joint study by IBM and the Economist Intelligence Unit of 345 companies around the world found wide agreement that the use of knowledge-sharing systems is often limited by cultural factors and that a belief in the value of learning and collaboration must be embedded in the culture for such systems to work effectively.[3] At IBM, one of the traditional barriers to collaboration has been the "expert trap"—the identification of important knowledge with an individual who believe that success and security depend on his keeping his special knowledge to himself and who may also believe that no one else has much to teach him.

The ICM team recognized early on that encouraging cultural change was part of their task. Working first with competency groups that were a knowledge-sharing subculture within IBM, they used success stories from those groups to begin to influence the wider culture. Because telling these stories is so important, the team includes a full-time communications person who details user experiences of time saved and work won and disseminates them via newsletters, online reports, and video.

Visible and vocal senior management support for knowledge-sharing also influences culture, and ICM has benefited from growing management commitment to collaboration and learning. The management vision of IBM as a learning organization that must have a shared understanding of its goal and speak with one voice is helping to redefine the culture. The new IBM headquarters, completed in 1997, with their open spaces and mobile computer technology, materially demonstrates a corporate belief in making knowledge-sharing the norm.

Cultural change requires effort and persistence. Movizzo says, "We went to a senior manager to demonstrate the system. He said, 'I don't have time.' We told him, 'We're going to show you the system.' We gave him a half-hour demo and he loved it." Michael Sinneck, who is responsible for establishing Systems Integration competency groups in the U.S. says managers must take the lead in making clear that using the ICM system is central to how work should be done. He

[3] Economist Intelligence Unit and the IBM Consulting Group, *The Learning Organization: Managing Knowledge for Business Success* (New York: Economist Intelligence Unit, 1996).

says, "For each proposal, managers should say, 'Did you look in ICM? Why not? Let's look together.' Management must be out front."

MEASUREMENT AND INCENTIVES

As with most knowledge-projects, the economic value of the ICM system cannot be calculated precisely. When Smith and Azzarello prepared a business case to gain funding for the pilot, they conservatively projected an overall 5% improvement in productivity, a 10% savings in proposal and work plan development, and other similar improvements. Their targets have been surpassed, but there is no clear way to show how much of the success of Global Services has been due to intellectual capital management and how much to other factors. At best, a series of mainly "soft" measures demonstrates that the system works and has value. Stephanie Pate, Senior Professional Financial Analyst, has used the following measures to prepare the executive summary on ICM system value:

- Internal customer satisfaction (based on user reports and anecdotes)
- Overall business value (anecdotal reports of time saved and work won)
- Overall business value of hard code assets (value can be attached to these assets and revenue from re-use calculated)
- Overall program vitality (based on number of users, number of documents, number of competency networks)

Pate says that executives will and should accept anecdotal evidence to some extent. "If your end customer is happy," Pate says, "and you can show a relation to ICM, you have been successful." In fact, the pressure to show a return on investment in precise numbers is decreasing as the system begins to be perceived as one of the tools people need to do business.

Pate believes that the quality of soft measures can be improved by gathering them in a more systematic way. Having some meaningful measures of system value contributes to learning how to improve it and provides a solid basis for rewards and incentives that will encourage use. Busy professionals give time and energy mainly to the core activities that clearly create value and earn recognition. Understanding this fact, the team successfully argued that performance evaluations and incentives for consultants and other service professionals should be changed to reward effort given to knowledge-sharing and learning. Since performance evaluation categories reflect the real values and expectations of an organization, these changes encourage new behaviors and signal a real change in organizational culture.

SIGNS OF SUCCESS

By the fall of 1997, 12,000 practitioners and 30 competency networks were part of the system, with rapid further growth expected. Stories of benefits abound. A workflow practice consulting group reported that it consistently cut proposal preparation time by two-thirds thanks to ICM, and the IT Architecture competency network reduced time spent creating deliverables by 40–60%. IBM's Canadian consulting team used material from the system to help win an engagement with a major Canadian bank that, since then, has generated more that $2.5 million in revenue. In perhaps the clearest demonstration of the value of sharing intellectual materials, the Enterprisewide Systems Management competency collaboratively developed a new methodology for defining and designing systems management processes. Competency leader John-Michael Helmbock gave major credit to the framework and the re-use of other intellectual capital for a 90% win rate (up from 50%), a 50% reduction in time spent preparing presentations and proposals, and a reduction of 10–15% in the cost of delivering results. These stories and others have led to a waiting list of groups that want to join the system.

SOME LESSONS LEARNED

The experience of developing and deploying the Intellectual Capital Management System has highlighted essential factors that determine the success of a knowledge-sharing initiative. In summary, these are the most important lessons the team and their management have learned.

A Holistic Approach

From early on, the ICM team recognized that developing methods for sharing knowledge and fostering a desire to share are as much a part of system design as the technology that makes sharing possible. The ICM framework, with its emphasis on the interdependence of culture, organization, people, processes, and technology, has helped the team maintain this broad focus and has guided the systematic approach necessary to develop a robust and broadly useful knowledge-management system. Movizzo believes that independent or ad hoc projects lack the structure, support, and breadth of vision needed to produce more than a local or temporary effect.

Pilots for Guidance

A pilot program is essential to prove the value of the concept and to learn from mistakes (and successes) on a small scale before introducing a system to the larger organization. To be meaningful, a pilot must be replicable and scalable.

Feedback

A process for collecting and evaluating feedback helps measure the value of the system and guide improvement. Developing and enhancing a complex system is an iterative process, with user response leading to changes, further response, and further changes.

Close Collaboration with System Users

From the beginning the ICM project has been characterized by close collaboration with users. The team continues to work closely with competency groups to tailor the system to their needs. Technical enhancements are based on user needs and user testing. Rather than "If you build it, they will come," the operating assumption has been "If you build it *with them,* they are much more likely to come." In fact, they are already there. Collaborative system design is the best way to meet users' needs and gives them a sense of involvement and ownership.

The Time Crunch

Despite the fact that the aim of knowledge-sharing is to achieve higher quality faster, allowing people enough time to share knowledge remains a critical difficulty in a highly competitive, cost-conscious economic environment. Michael Sinneck says, "Time pressure is problem one. The consultant in his hotel room at 1 AM isn't going to take time to put content in unless knowledge-sharing can be made central to how work is done."

A Business Focus

ICM is a central business concern, linked to significant business objectives and outcomes. The team has helped competency groups understand the business purposes ICM can serve, not just how it works. Thanks in part to this focus, the initiative ceased being paid for as a reengineering project and became an operational program in 1996, funded by the business units that benefit from it.

It's Not Free

An innovative knowledge system demands a substantial, sustained investment of money, time, effort, and commitment. Management must be willing to pay for necessary infrastructure and high-quality personnel. Projects involving cultural change and new technology will be met with skepticism and resistance which can only be countered by a committed project team and strong management support. Even the most systematic plan sometimes needs to be supported by what Movizzo called "appropriate terrorist activities." For instance, when budget staff wanted to cut the project's 1996 deployment budget as part of overall cost-reduction, the ICM team practiced a form of constructive insubordination because they believed the project would be seriously damaged by reduced funding. They refused to discuss cuts or attend meetings, and the project received full funding. The project is by no means exempt from financial accountability, however. Movizzo reviews measurements quarterly, tracking them against the original business case.

FUTURE DIRECTIONS

The Intellectual Capital Management System is not finished. It must continue to adapt to changing needs and absorb technological enhancements.

The recent addition of an issue-based discussion tool to the ICM software and the growing use of Lotus TeamRoom (a Notes application that provides a structured workspace for collaboration over distance) reflect a trend toward more online collaboration. Instead of mainly drawing on stockpiled intellectual material, users meet on line to develop new content together.

The team hopes to refine tools and techniques for gathering information about the value participants derive from the system. Currently, users can voluntarily enter their judgments of how easy the system was to use, and whether they found helpful material. Fuller information would provide more reliable evidence of the business value of the ICM system. Better user feedback will also guide and encourage to contributors of intellectual content.

ICM has been successful but more needs to be done before intellectual capital is widely and efficiently shared. Turning the ICM system into a standard working tool, like the telephone, depends on continuing to develop reliable and convenient technology, supportive corporate vision, values and incentives, management commitment, learning by success stories, and learning by example—that is, it continues to depend on a holistic approach to the cultural, organizational, political, and technical issues that affect the sharing of knowledge in organizations.

Chapter 5

Knowledge Workers and Radically New Technology

John J. Sviokla[1]
*Associate Professor of Business
Administration
Harvard Business School*

In a study of the predictors of success and failure in implementing technology, the author examines the introduction and use of profiling, an expert system intended to aid the insurance sales process at four insurance companies. Lutheran Brotherhood, National Mutual, Prudential, and Sun Alliance tried to get more than 5,000 field salespeople to implement Profiling. The study results indicate that in implementing a radically new technology, managers need to assemble "constellations" of actions, consider the political ramifications throughout the organization, manage the momentum of the project, and work to achieve economies of scale.

Information technology implementation in organizations has gone from automating back-office clerks to supporting the complex tasks of autonomous knowledge workers. The research I report here is not about new organizations or those transcending a deep crisis; rather, it concerns the push and pull of managers attempting to implement a new technology. It tells the story of companies trying to change the behavior of employed but fiercely independent "revenue producers" while, at the same time, trying not to drive away the best performers. The research investigates how different executives try to make the same people in the same roles work with a new tool.

My research was inspired by the notion that the work of salespeople (or lawyers or doctors) might be as radically transformed by technology as was the

[1] Reprinted from "Knowledge Workers and Radically New Technology" by John J. Sviokla, *Sloan Management Review*, Summer 1996, pp. 25–40, by permission of publisher. Copyright © 1996 by Sloan Management Review Association. All rights reserved.

work of tinsmiths, hoopers, and portrait painters when technology impinged on their lives and livelihood. Traditionally, the knowledge worker has had more autonomy than the laborer, thus challenging the manager who is attempting to "automate" knowledge work. However, as technology infringes on the domain of symbolic, abstract work, the interaction between user and tool becomes more complex. Although automating knowledge tasks has proved a noxious process, organization after organization has tried to gain more influence over knowledge workers. The promise of productivity in this domain is a powerful force, drawing entrepreneur and bureaucrat alike into new, more comprehensive attempts.

The increasing sophistication of the type and degree of information technology has heightened this tension. More often, computer technologies are not passive but active tools that manage the process of work. A doctor's notes on a patient, once a document of record, now are an interactive "protocol-driven data-capture device"—both supporting and constraining the doctor's activities. The salesperson's "pitchbook" is replaced by a multimedia offering, and the old order form is replaced by a configuration system based on laptop computers and their software. An aggressive form of software is expert systems, which specifically aim at codifying knowledge and creating a specific method to do a task. The challenge of getting people to use expert systems is an interesting example of the general problem of influencing knowledge workers' behavior with computer-based tools.

Creating a model that will predict the successful implementation of any new technology is almost as challenging as creating a general-purpose thinking machine. Neither has come to fruition. Despite the vast literature on technology implementation and the universal recognition that we have entered a "postindustrial" economy, there are only a few examples of systematic research on the implementation of new tools by knowledge professionals in a field setting.[2] There are singular case studies, of course, but with little cross-case analysis. Pentland's extensive study of the Internal Revenue Service professionals' use of laptop technology is one exception. Pentland studied laptop implementation in four districts, using interviews and a questionnaire survey of roughly 1,000 agents. He found radically different adoption; only two of the four districts had high usage.[3] The high-use districts were characterized by high quality training rumors that laptop use would be mandatory; and supportive attitudes toward the central automation office. The low-use districts did not exhibit these characteristics.

Thus practicing managers who are concerned with implementation are left with scant evidence from rather distant examples that they must then extrapolate

[2] For the pioneering work of Fritz Machlup in categorizing and articulating the nature of the knowledge economy, see: F. Machlup, *The Branches of Learning* (Princeton, New Jersey: Princeton University Press, 1982). Daniel Bell's work set the path for many to follow. See: D. Bell, *The Coming of Post-Industrial Society: A Venture in Social Forecasting* (New York: Basic Books, 1976).
[3] B. T. Pentland, personal conversation.

to their own situations. In this study, I try to add to the knowledge base by examining an expert system that helps field salespeople sell more insurance.

THE RESEARCH CHALLENGE

There is no theory that can predict the outcome of an implementation process. Markus and Robey, in an interesting synthesis of the implementation literature in the MIS field, characterize three categories of implementation: variance, process, and emergent.[4] *Variance* theories assume an invariant relationship between independent and dependent variables. These factors often include top management support, an effective champion, and training. Other researchers have focused on implementation processes, i.e., how people adjust to the technology during its implementation.[5] Some complex models incorporate both *process* and factor variables. Lucas et al. constructed a complex model of implementation with twenty-seven variables.[6] In what Markus and Robey call the *emergent* school, there is a more phenomenological argument in which the implementation process emerges, as do the important variables for analysis. These occur as the implementation process unfolds. Kling and Iacono thought through the variety and richness of the phenomenon of interest in an even more elaborate model.[7] Although informative, few if any of these theories have been tested for predictive validity.

Because there is no theory with predictive validity and because this research examines a new technology in a field setting, I designed a two-phase approach. In phase one, I did early case and field work to understand how early adopters used the technology and to qualify the most important independent and dependent variables. In phase two, I performed a cross-case analysis to investigate the relationships among these variables.

Phase One: Field Research

Knowledge-intensive tasks, by definition, cannot be generalized. Knowledge work is specific; indeed, the more knowledge intensive, the more specific it is. To fathom the complexities of an elaborate, abstract, and leading-edge tool

[4] M. L. Markus and D. Robey, "Information Technology and Organizational Change: Causal Structure in Theory and Research," *Management Science*, volume 34, May 1988, pp. 583–598.
[5] See M. L. Markus, and M. Keil, "If We Build It, They Will Come: Designing Information Systems That People Want to Use," *Sloan Management Review*, volume 35, Summer 1994, pp. 11–25.
[6] H. C. Lucas, M. J. Ginsberg, and R. L. Schultz, *Information Systems Implementation: Testing a Structural Model* (Norwood, New Jersey: Ablex Publishing Corporation, 1990).
[7] R. Kling and S. Iacono, "The Control of Information Systems Development after Implementation," *Communications of the ACM*, volume 27, 1984, pp. 1218–1226.

such as a large-scale expert system in the context of the fluid, idiosyncratic process of insurance sales, I needed to understand the technology itself, the insurance industry, and the insurance sales process. Following the suggestions of Bonoma and Cook and Campbell, I created an initial, in-depth case study to understand the basic industry dynamics, the products, and the technology.[8] I tried to understand the nature of the business, the competition, the products and services, the regulations, and the global insurance environment. Preliminary research into the use of the technology in a financial planning organization and early field research into the use of the Profiling expert system by potential and existing clients provided considerable insight. I also interviewed the technology developers and managers at the company that created the software, thus gaining intimate knowledge of the system and its purpose.[9]

Phase Two: Comparative Case Studies

Previous research has shown that environmental context can have a significant influence on the likelihood that an organization will adopt new technology.[10] The nature of the industry and the evolving patterns of product and process design have an important relationship to the nature of innovation, especially in information technology.[11] Company strategy shapes the nature of technology use as well.[12] All these different contextual factors—control variables in the study—influence the adoption of new technology. Within individual firms, the organization structure, distribution structure, compensation systems, and product and service mix are important variables: training, job roles, and potential career paths all interact with the adoption of a new, technology.[13]

---

[8] T. V. Bonoma, "Case Research in Marketing: Opportunities, Problems, and a Process," *Journal of Marketing Research*, volume 22, May 1985, pp. 199–208; and T. D. Cook and D. T. Campbell, "Validity," in *Quasi-Experimentation* (Chicago: Rand-McNally, 1977), pp. 37–94.

[9] See J. Sviokla, "PlanPower: The Financial Planning Expert System" (Boston: Harvard Business School, Case 186–293, 1986); and J. Sviokla, "Expert Systems and Their Impact on the Firm: The Effects of PlanPower Use on the Information Processing Capacity of the Financial Collaborative," *Journal of Management Information Systems*, volume 6, Winter 1989–1990, pp. 65–84.

[10] J. E. Etillie, "A Note on the Relationship between Managerial Charge Sector Firms," *R&D Management*, volume 13, October 1983, pp. 231–244.

[11] See J. McKenney, *Waves of Change: Business Evolution through Information Technology* (Boston: Harvard Business School Press, 1995).

[12] See L. Applegate, J. McKenney, and F. W. McFarlan, *Corporate Information Systems Management* (Homewood, Illinois: Irwin Publishers, 1996).

[13] For a comprehensive model of implementation factors, see: Lucas et al. (1990).

I designed the study to follow the implementation of the same technology in similar but distinct organizations.[14] More specifically, I chose companies in the insurance industry that had similar strategies and product and market emphases and were located in countries that had broadly similar regulatory and economic contexts.[15] Each company sold a fill line of life, disability, and insurance investment products (e.g., annuities and pension plans), and each had a direct salesforce that was the intended target user of the technology. Thus the control variables were company product, regulatory environment, organizational structure, distribution method, compensation systems, and role of the salesperson. The technology was the Profiling expert system, which I will describe in detail later.

After reviewing the vast literature on diffusion, I focused on four independent variables: (1) the role of the technology sponsor; (2) the role of the champion, (3) the design of the implementation, and (4) the rationale for the radical change.[16] (A technology sponsor is willing to support the technology's implementation. The champion is the active participant and leader of the implementation effort.) All four independent variables have been identified as integral components of achieving "fit" between the project and the overall organization. In a number of large-scale research projects on the implementation of computing in local government settings, researchers at the University of California at Irvine have shown that management rhetoric on technology has been central to successful implementation.[17] Walton, in a study of new IT in organizations, has noted

---

[14] In a seminal book on case research, Yin suggests that when trying to isolate specific causative variables, researchers should choose sites with control variables as similar as possible and independent variables with as much variance as possible, which he terms "case replication logic"; each case is a "test." See: R. K. Yin, *Case Study Research: Design and Methods* (Newbury Park, California: Sage Publications, 1989).

[15] For example, I had the opportunity to include a Japanese site in the study, but I refrained from including this site because the distribution of life insurance in Japan is much different from that in England, Australia, or the United States. In Japan, the tradition of door-to-door selling of life insurance—with frequent collection of premiums (mostly by women) still is a thriving distribution mechanism. I also had the opportunity to, but consciously avoided looking at, this same technology in the context of a direct sales insurance provider or in a large financial services firm that also rolled out the technology. 1 wanted to keep the basic industry, organizational, and individual context as comparable as possible.

[16] See D. Leonard-Barton, "Implementation as Mutual Adaptation of Technology and Organization," *Research Policy*, volume 17, October 1988, pp. 251–267; J. F. Rockart, "The Line Takes the Leadership—IS Management in a Wired Society," *Sloan Management Review*, volume 29, Summer 1988, pp. 57–64; and E. von Hippel, *The Sources of Innovation* (New York: Oxford University Press, 1988).

[17] J. L. King, V. Gubarani, K. Kraemer, F. W. McFarlan et al., "Institutional Factors in Information Technology Innovation," *Information Systems Research*, volume 5, June 1994, pp. 139–169.

the importance of how management frames the meaning of new technology.[18] Orlikowski, in a study of adoption of radically different CASE software for software developers, found that the successful projects made a conscious rhetorical link between the current task and the strategic organizational goals.[19]

In this study, I revisited the fundamental relationships among these important variables in an "apples to apples" comparison.

DATA GATHERING

Because Profiling is a batch system (i.e., it is centrally controlled, with Profiles coming in and out on a batch basis), it was possible to capture every single use of the technology.[20] I also collected data on individual sales performance, demographic background statistics, organizational statistics, and geographic statistics.[21] Next I describe the technology and the four companies and their similarities in order to identify the control variables. I then show the radical change that Profiling represented for selling insurance at all the organizations in the study Finally, I look at the four implementation variables and their impact on Profiling use at the companies.

[18] R. Walton, *Up and Running: Integrating Information Technology and the Organization* (Boston: Harvard Business School Press, 1989).

[19] W. Orlikowski, "CASE Tools as Organizational Change: Investigating Incremental and Radical Charges in Systems Development," *MIS Quarterly,* volume 17, September 1993, pp. 309–340.

[20] I encountered a number of significant methodological challenges when trying to assess the introduction of Profiling technology and its subsequent use and effect or sales. Perceived usage and end-user satisfaction, two often-used measures, have been severely criticized for their lack of reliability. See: N. P. Melone, "Theoretical Assessment of the User-Satisfaction Construct in Information Systems Research," *Management Science,* volume 36, January 1990, pp. 76–91. My study utilizes actual use statistics gathered from the information systems, down to each individual transaction as be measure of use. Many studies stop at satisfaction or have only a tenuous link to performance; this study, by contrast, uses product sales and commission data as sources of actual performance of individuals: the organizational metrics are the aggregation of the individual measurers.

[21] I conducted structured interviews with more than 100 salespeople, sales managers, and senior managers both before and after Profiling's implementation on the selling approach, the types of technology in current use, and Profiling's fit with current methods. I compiled a year-by-year comparative history of each firm's environmental situation and tracked the major internal organizational changes and business initiatives. In addition, I created a technology time line that documented the entire implementation effort at each organization in terms of important meetings, dates, and personnel changes. I constructed a comparative time line across each organization. And I regularly met with senior managers to review impressions and verify findings.

What Is Profiling?

In 1986, Applied Expert Systems of Cambridge, Massachusetts, created Profiling to perform comprehensive financial planning in cash management, risk management, income protection, general insurance (e.g., property or casualty), education funding, wills, credit management, investment planning, and retirement planning. Profiling also provides a net-worth restructuring statement to guide clients to a healthier financial balance sheet through asset diversification. Its primary market is couples, families, and individuals with incomes from $30,000 to $150,000, although the system's logic can accommodate significantly higher incomes.

Profiling uses an extensive questionnaire, a personal financial profile (the client's report), and an agent's report. On the questionnaire, the client assembles financial and personal data, including future goals like buying a new house or putting children through college. Profile then makes generic recommendations. At the same time, Profile uses computed text to prepare a plan seemingly written to the client's personal situation instead of "boilerplate" text with numbers inserted. The agent's report matches specific company products to the recommendations. (See Tables 5.1 and 5.2 for samples of a client's report and an agent's report that one company adopted.)

In short, with the data on the questionnaire, the expert financial planning logic of the system (with more than 2,000 rules) presents a comprehensive financial picture and reveals the client's insurance and investment needs. The client receives a document detailing the financial situation and pinpointing areas for improvement, plus a strategy for meeting future goals. The agent works from this document and the agents report.

Companies that implement Profiling hope that it will provide significant self-reinforcing benefits. Profiling can enable a clearer focus on the customer and create a total financial plan presenting the best products in an integrated manner. This, in turn, enables salespeople to sell more products on each sales call. Since customers with many products from the same company are much less likely to drop their coverage, Profiling can be important for retaining customers. The potential profitability implications of increased client retention are enormous.[22] In addition, the better compensated agents who resulted from this process are less likely to leave, thus helping to decrease turnover. Achieving these high expectations and promises, of course, necessitates radical changes to how products are sold and how agents are trained at each site.

[22] See F. F. Reichheld and W. E. Sasser, "Zero Defections: Quality Comes to Services," *Harvard Business Review,* volume 68, September–October 1990, pp. 105–112. This article articulates the significant financial implications of keeping retailing customers. See also: J. Sviokla and B. Shapiro, *Keeping Customers* (Boston: Harvard Business School Press, 1994).

TABLE 5.1 Sample Client's Report For Albert And Catherine Friendly

Case Management	Analysis of Future Income Needs in Today's Dollars		

Case Management

1. Monitor your spending so that you will be able to continue your savings to meet your goals.
2. Set up a cash reserve of $2,527 in a Statement Savings Account. Ensure that you have a line of credit for at least $5,055.

Special Case Need

3. Set aside $7,660 of your assets to buy a new car.

Special Case Need

4. Allocate $511 of annual increasing savings to fund your daughter's wedding.

Risk Management

5. Purchase at least $461,785 of life insurance on Albert's life in addition to his existing coverage to provide funds for high priority needs.
6. Also purchase at least $96,900 of life insurance on Catherine's life to provide funds for high priority needs.

Income Protection

7. Purchase an Income Protection policy for Albert with a weekly benefit of $790 for sickness or accident to age 65.

General Insurance

8. Review the cover for your primary residence. Ensure that the cover for all your home contents, personal property, and personal liability is adequate. Make sure you have an inflation rider on this policy.

Analysis of Future Income Needs in Today's Dollars

	Catherine with Children (8 years)	Catherine Alone (20 years)	Catherine during Retirement
Monthly Need	$3,438	$3,071	$3,071
Sources of Income: Catherine's Income	0	0	0
Survivor Benefits: Social Security	0	0	0
Total Income	0	0	0
Net Need	3,438	3,071	3,071
Capital Needed for Income*	282,406	340,720	135,534

Total Capital Needed for Income	$758,660
Total Capital Required	$461,785

*Assumptions: This Capital is invested at 11% with the monthly need inflated at 6% being drawn against the capital.

The above capital needs analysis indicates:

• If Albert died today, there would be adequate assets to cover immediate needs.

• There would be sufficient resources to provide Catherine with income during the time that your children will rely on her for support.

• There would be insufficient resources to provide Catherine with ongoing income after your children become independent.

TABLE 5.1 *Continued*

9. Review your car insurance to determine if your cover is adequate. Elect the highest excess with which you feel comfortable.

Education Funding

10. Set aside $5,113 of your assets and allocate $1,896 of your annual savings to partially fund the education of your children.

Wills

11. Have a will prepared for Catherine. Review Albert's will immediately.
12. Consider the execution of "Enduring Power of Attorney" documents.

Credit Management

13. Review your loan situation.

Meeting immediate cash needs after death is a high priority. Providing income during the period when your children are dependent on Catherine for support is another high priority. You have adequate capital to meet your two most pressing needs.

However, to also cover Catherine's estimated ongoing income needs after your children are no longer dependent, the total capital required becomes $461,785. The most cost-effective way (and often the only way) to generate this capital is through insurance.

Since the majority of Albert's life insurance is employer-provided, he should review his capital needs again in the event of a change in his financial, personal, or especially his work situation.

TABLE 5.2 Sample Agent's Report for Albert and Catherine Friendly

Initiating Agent Name: John Sample
Agent Name: Branch Direct
Agent Division: Branch Direct
Plan Date: 12/11/90

The clients have indicated their principal financial objective:
- To buy a car
- To fund daughter's wedding
- To fund children's education

Action Plan

Call Albert and Catherine to set up an appointment to present this plan. Let them know that someone else prepared this plan. You may disagree with some recommendations or have other ideas.

Client Summary

Albert Friendly
Age: 44
Computer Programmer

Catherine Friendly
Age: 37
Home Duties

TABLE 5.2 *Continued*

Home: 24/2001 Space Odyssey Drive
   Apollo Bay

Telephone: 052 381-2272 (home)

Dependents:
David, 10-year-old son; Kelly, 16-year-old daughter

Income $56,780	Annual Savings Capability $4,490
Assets $316,800	Effective Tax Rate 31%
Liabilities $75,700	Client Marginal Tax Rate 47%
Net Worth $241,100	

The Research Sites

- Lutheran Brotherhood, headquartered in Minneapolis, Minnesota, was established in 1917.[23] A fraternal organization, the company sells only to Lutherans and their families, a nationwide population of approximately 14.5 million people. Owned and operated for the benefit of its members, Lutheran Brotherhood boasts an uninterrupted history of dividend payments on its life insurance. In 1987, it issued $3.5 billion in new business with $20.9 billion of insurance in force, placing it in the top 5 percent by size of all U.S. life insurance companies. In 1989, the company estimated assets under management at $7.5 billion and about 1 million members.
- National Mutual, established in 1869, is the second largest insurance company in Australia, with offices in New Zealand, Great Britain, the United Stares, and elsewhere, although most of its market, especially in personal insurance, is in Australia.[24] With a premium income of $3.8 billion in 1990, National Mutual has an extensive field salesforce of 3,500 captive agents, 1,200 associate agents, and more than 100 specialty planners.
- Sun Alliance Insurance Group PLC is the oldest and largest personal insurer in Britain, with one of every five households holding one of its products.[25] Its two major distribution companies—Sun Alliance Life and Sun Alliance UK—cover the personal insurance market, and property and casualty for companies, respectively. In 1990, it had more than £10 billion under management, about 8,000 employees, 2,000 company representatives, and more than 9 million policy holders.

---

[23] J. Sviokla, "Lutheran Brotherhood and the FSNAR+ Pilot" (Boston: Harvard Business School, Case 190-163, 1990).
[24] J. Sviokla, "Profiling at National Mutual (A), (B), and (C)" (Boston: Harvard Business School, Cases 191-078, 191-101, and 191-102, 1991).
[25] J. Sviokla, "Sun Alliance Insurance Group, PLC" (Boston: Harvard Business School, Case 192-073, 1992).

• The Prudential Insurance Company was originally incorporated as the Widows and Orphans Friendly Society in 1873.[26] The company has four core businesses: insurance and investment for individuals, and asset management and employee benefits for institutions. Prudential is the largest insurer in the United States for both individual life premiums and the amount of insurance in force, and is divided into four major geographical areas. I studied the western region.

Similarities among Sites.

Each site has three critical functions: sales, underwriting, and investment. In life insurance companies, the underwriting, product design (on which the sales, underwriting, and investment areas collaborate), and investment activities are highly centralized to maximize control and concentrate expertise. (See Table 5.3 for similarities and differences among the companies.)

TABLE 5.3 Comparison of Insurance Companies

	Lutheran Brotherhood	*National Mutual*	*Sun Alliance*	*Prudential*
Typical Products	Ordinary and universal life, annuities, accident and disability, variable insurance products, mutual funds	Full line of life insurance, investment funds, financial planning	Life, home, accident, health, auto, investment funds	Ordinary, home, auto, group life, annuities, accident, health
Distribution	• 1,548 soliciting agents • Primary distribution through captive, direct agency force • 1989	• 3,500 sole agents • 1,200 associate agents • 50 investment advisers • Primary distribution through captive, direct agency force • 1990	• Tied agents, direct marketing, 52% of new business from directly controlled outlets; direct sales force of 1,100 • Agencies • 1990	• 27,000 full-time agents • 1990

[26] J. Sviokla, "Client Profiling: The Prudential Insurance Company of America" (Boston: Harvard Business School, Case 193–084, 1993).

TABLE 5.3 *Continued*

Compensation	• Small initial agent stipend • 100% commission • Overrides for general agents • Awards for outstanding sales performance	• Small initial agent stipend (e.g., $3,000 of income filed) • Low interest rate agency • Development loans for stronger agents	• Small initial agent stipend (e.g., $3,000 of income filed) • Low interest rate agency loans	• Small initial agent stipend (e.g., $3,000 of income filed)
New Agent Training	• Two to three weeks on product knowledge, sales skill training • Modest (e.g., one to two days) account knowledge	• Two to three weeks on product knowledge, sales skill training • Modest (e.g., one to two days) account knowledge	• Two to three weeks on product knowledge, sales skill training • Modest (e.g., one to two days) account knowledge	• Two to three weeks on product knowledge, sales skill training • Modest (e.g., one to two days) account knowledge
Ongoing Training	• Individual courses sometimes supported or subsidized • New product training (½ day to weeks)	• Individual courses sometimes supported or subsidized • New product training (½ days to weeks)	• Individual courses sometimes supported or subsidized • New product training (½ days to weeks)	• Individual courses sometimes supported or subsidized • New product training (½ days to weeks)
Organization Structure	• Central home office • Decentralized branch office and distribution structure	• Central home office • Decentralized branch office and distribution structure	• Central home office • Decentralized branch office and distribution structure	• Five "home offices" in five U.S. regions • Decentralized branch office structure within each region
Product Development	Home office	Home office	Home office	Home office
Hiring	Local sales staff	Local sales staff	Local sales staff	Local sales staff
Product Issuance	Centralized underwriter	Centralized underwriter	Centralized underwriter	Centralized underwriter

TABLE 5.3 *Continued*

Policy Administration	• Billing—home office • Client contract shared between agent and home office	• Billing—home office • Client contract shared between agent and home office	• Billing—home office • Client contract shared between agent and home office	• Billing—home office • Client contract shared between agent and home office
Systems	• Central MIS develops policy systems and other systems • Some third party purchased software	• Central MIS develops policy systems and other systems • Larger field offices • Some local systems development • Some third-party purchased software	• Central MIS develops policy systems and other systems	• Decentralized MIS structures systems in each regional home office
Regulation	By state	National with some state regulation	National	By state

Sources: Best's Insurance Reports—Life/Health 1990, Moody's Bank and Finance Manual 1990, volume 1, Reuters Textline database, ICC Online Ltd. databases.

Each company fields a geographically diverse salesforce with a central home office. At three sites, the home office is in one location; due to its size, Prudential has five home offices, which report to corporate headquarters in New Jersey. The types of products, especially life insurance, that each firm offers are similar, as are agent relationships with parent organizations. However, the amount of independence grew as agents became more successful. Very successful agents and large agencies often arranged special relationships with the patent company.

Compensation systems are also similar in the four firms. Each provides a small stipend at the outset of an agent's tenure, usually while she or he is in training, to encourage the individual to become self-supporting on commission income. All four firms are subject to government regulation. In the United Kingdom and Australia, regulation is at the national level. In the United States, the regulatory power is largely with the states, but the federal government heavily regulates the investment aspects. Finally salespeople across the organizations have similar training, job responsibilities, and potential career paths.

The Context for Insurance Companies

During the late 1970s and 1980s, deregulation hit many of the world's financial markets, including those in the United States, the United Kingdom, and Australia; managers, including those in the insurance industry, responded with many product innovations. At the same time, clients became more sophisticated as companies educated consumers about options and as various products became available. Hence, experienced and novice salespeople faced external pressures and an avalanche of internal demands on their knowledge, not to mention ongoing changes in tax laws and regulations. The insurance industry experienced what some termed "knowledge overload." Salespeople often compensated by focusing carefully on a well-defined market and mastering a few products.

During this same period, the cost of face-to-face selling time rose, with the typical personal sales call reaching $150 or more.[27] Competition from other distribution forms (e.g., direct mail) was also increasing, as were new distribution outlets like banks. The United Kingdom enacted legislation providing commission disclosure on life insurance products. Such factors, individually and together, pushed the managers of large life insurance companies to consider how their agents could provide more value-added services to justify the expense of a personal selling effort.

Adding to the cost pressure was the large field salesforce turnover, which, in this industry, ranges from 70 percent to 95 percent during a five-year period; high customer turnover often accompanies high agent turnover. Most life insurance contracts are heavily front-end loaded, with commissions paid to the agent early in the life of the contract; products typically do not become profitable until the third year, at which point commissions, underwriting costs, and initiation expenses are recovered in premium payments. Thus the profit implications of even small changes to product retention promise significant short- and long-term rewards.

The Selling Process

Based on previous research on the impacts of financial planning software in general, I judged that Profiling was likely to necessitate a radical change in the selling processes at all four companies.[28] (See Figure 5.1 for the companies minimal sales process with and without Profiling.)

[27] Estimate by senior sales managers at Lutheran Brotherhood.
[28] J. Sviokla, "Managing a Transformational Technology: A Field Study of the Introduction of Profiling" (Boston: Harvard Business School, Working Paper 93–059, 1993).

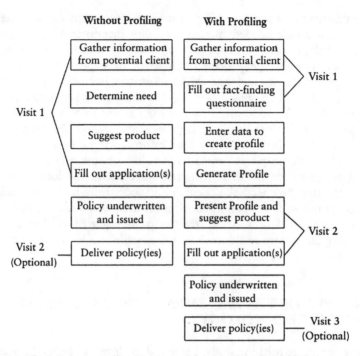

FIGURE 5.1 The Minimum Selling Process without and with Profiling

Without Profiling

In the selling process with a single-need approach to a new client, the agent's only required paperwork is to fill out the insurance application, which then typically goes to underwriting for pricing and approval. Underwriting, from a sales perspective, is frequently a source of unwanted delay; commissions are rarely paid at the time of application but are usually paid only on issued business.

With Profiling

In the sample companies, using Profile lengthened the sales process in two ways. First, it necessitated at least one and probably two more sales call on the customer. The agent needed to fill out the questionnaire; clients needed to provide information about previous life insurance policies, benefits packages from their jobs, banking and checking account information, and so on, to detail their financial situations. The Profiling system had only eleven required fields of data to make a plan, but the more complete the questionnaire, the more accurate the plan. Employees at the local sales office entered the questionnaire information into a computer. Every day the data was sent by phone to a central facility where the Profile was produced and mailed, along with the agent's report, back to the agent.

The underwriting process, which came next, frequently caused a delay. Profile plans often recommended buying disability insurance because people are much more likely, in the short run, to become disabled rather than to die. However, life insurance salespeople are often loath to suggest disability coverage because the premiums are high and the underwriting is much more involved.

Because of its comprehensiveness, Profiling also required considerable product knowledge. In addition, it changed the access to client information and salesperson activity. Before Profiling, both new and established agents often had proprietary access to their own client files. Information for underwriting product issuance, and billing purposes passed from field to home office, but the client's needs, habits, and even financial situation stayed with the local agent. Established agents often "owned" the clients and successfully took their business as they moved from one firm to another. After Profiling was implemented, however, all the detailed client data were fed straight to the home office. Hence, the company adopting the system could track its salespeople at a higher level of detail by looking at their Profiling activity.

ANALYSIS OF THE IMPLEMENTATION AND USE OF RADICAL TECHNOLOGY

In the second part of the study, I assessed the levels of technology use in the four companies and the impact of the four variables—the role of the champion, the role of the sponsor, the design of the implementation, and the rationale for the radical change. It is important to note that the technology had very different levels and patterns of use in these similar companies. From a research standpoint, I was fortunate to find such wide variance.

The successful organizations designed two very different implementations. Prudential completely changed the agent's role and job design. It folded the technology into that redesign and altered task and technology together, an approach I call *redesign*. Sun Alliance did not change the nature of the task, but rather, through concerted championship on the part of senior and local line management, achieved adoption by constant emphasis and management effort, an approach I call *focus*. The common characteristics in both companies were an office-by-office rollout strategy and a significant degree of implementation momentum.

Interestingly, failure (defined as lack of adoption) had similar aspects in the two firms that did not succeed in implementing Profile; both relied on the *caveat emptor* approach. Lutheran Brotherhood and National Mutual both had thorough approaches to the implementation process. Both firms began with lead users across the organization and then progressively widened availability of the technology to other participants. Experts in training, technology, and financial planning led the effort. As rational as this approach was—and as scientific as the pilot design attempted to be—both companies failed to achieve adoption.

TABLE 5.4 Three Implementation Strategies

Implementation Strategy	Sponsor	Champion	Implementation	Management Rationale
Redesign	CEO	Line manager	Pilot: Prove concept, redesign entire job Design: office-by-office rollout	Transform the sales channel, change selling method
Focused	Top management	Line manager	Pilot: Prove concept Design: office-by-office rollout	Transform to best financial planning firm, change selling method
Caveat emptor	CEO, president	Staff managers	Pilot: Test concept Design: Small number of users in many offices, widening availability of technology	More sales, more efficient

Overall, Sun Alliance and Prudential used a focused office-by-office approach, driven by senior line managers, to implement Profiling. National Mutual and Lutheran Brotherhood took the approach that the technology should be tested and made available on a wider and wider basis to the professionals. (See Table 5.4 for a comparison of the three implementation strategies.)

Different Levels of Use

At its zenith, National Mutual reached 642 Profiles in a single month, only to end Profiling completely in January 1992. Use at Lutheran Brotherhood peaked at 68 Profiles in September 1989 and steadily declined until the pilot was stopped in November 1989. In contrast, Sun Alliance had approximately 4,760 Profiles in November 1991, and Prudential, by January 1992, had 744 per month, with the numbers steadily increasing. (See Figure 5.2 for comparative use statistics.) At National Mutual, the number of agents who could use the technology was approximately 3,600; at Lutheran Brotherhood, 150; at Sun Alliance, 1,100; and at Prudential, 175. On an individual agent basis, the statistics are even more striking. Thus management at Sun Alliance considered that it had achieved a success implementation. Prudential also achieved solid success. At Lutheran Brotherhood and National Mutual, on the other hand, there was little

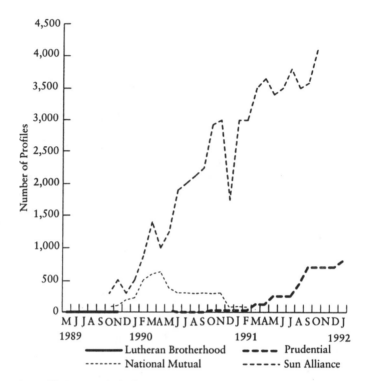

FIGURE 5.2 Profile Use per Month

adoption; both ended up dropping the technology altogether. Why were the levels of use so different?

Each site had its own constellation of the four variables: the champion, the sponsor, the design, and the rationale for the change. First I examine the redesign implementation at Prudential.

Prudential

The Profiling effort at Prudential was part of an overall strategy to redesign the selling process through the tied salesforce channel. (The agents were not independent but were tied to Prudential.) Senior sales management analyzed sales activity and discovered that a significant percentage of a sales-person's time was spent on nonsales and nonservice activities. This caused the salesforce to be less productive than management desired. To make the direct sales channel more productive, John Tymochko, one of two senior managers running the company's western region (which generates a significant percentage of the entire firm's premium income), led an overall strategy to redesign the salesperson's entire job, an initiative called Locally Deployed Agent (LDA).

The concept of the LDA was to give salespeople better administrative and technology support simultaneously. Prudential gave agents a budget for a full-time assistant to answer phones, make appointments, and perform other client servicing. The agents set up shop in storefront locations, where they literally hung out the Prudential shingle. The technology support had two major components: (1) the salesperson had a suite of office productivity tools such as call management, calendar software, and database management software to enable efficient marketing operations at the office and effective communications to the Prudential information systems; and (2) the internal Prudential systems were modified to make it easier to get product illustrations and client information from the company's central computer systems. Profiling was designed to give both local and remote support. The local office conducted Profiling and then shipped the Profiles to the salesperson (just as the other firms in the study did). In return for this additional support, Prudential expected the agents to be twice as productive in their sales quotas.

Prudential's pilot design called for an office-by-office rollout. The company rejected the idea of having a firmwide or regionwide initiative. Instead, it focused on one region at a time and worked to get the new form deeply accepted before moving to a new location (see Table 5.5). Local managers at each location supported the implementation process; Tymochko had selected them because of their willingness to redefine the sales process.

Prudential's CEO was the sponsor; the day-to-day champion was Tymochko, a line manager with significant responsibility for the sales region; the nature of the pilot was a focused redesign of the entire sales process, and the management rationale was to create an entirely new distribution mechanism— one that was more efficient than the traditional sales channel. This implementation strategy is "redesign" because several major factors in the salesperson's job changed. The nature of day-to-day activity was more focused on selling and less on administration. The access to technology and its character also changed to support the sales process more directly. Profiling, as a full-service tool, matched

TABLE 5.5 Prudential Training Class Date, Location, and Participation

Date	Location	Number of Agents
May 1990	Idaho transition	27
October 1990	New Idaho agents	7
January 1991	New Idaho agents	7
March 1991	Tucson transition	29
May 1991	New agents Tucson/Idaho	9
August 1991	New agents Tucson/Idaho	10
September 1991	Northern states transition	60
October 1991	New agents Tucson/Idaho	13

the strategy of providing a more service-oriented and complete relationship with the Prudential client.

Sun Alliance

Sun Alliance created an extremely targeted implementation approach that aimed for significant adoption by building up support in each local office. This approach is "focused" implementation because: (1) management assumes that the performance of the task needs changing, but the fundamental task does not need to be redesigned; (2) the technology will facilitate the change and aid in both enabling and stabilizing the new state of the task; and (3) the manager's role is to achieve sufficient use of the technology so a new pattern and new approach to selling is established.

At Sun Alliance, Paul Tebbutt, a senior line manager in sales, championed the Profiling implementation and was deeply involved in the overall training for its use. Although he was the marketing manager and, subsequently sales director, Tebbutt was known throughout the organization as a high-volume, high-quality salesman. He continued to sell insurance, even in his management role. As one agent put it, "Paul knew how to communicate with the salespeople because he had lived it himself." Tebbutt commented on the early challenges of implementation: "The first time through, we made a big mistake. We brought in one consultant from each branch and made him or her the Profiling expert. When these "experts" went back to the field, they did not have the support of their peers. They were alone. At the head office, we thought that the logic was right, therefore it should work. We did not have the champions of change in place."

Sun Alliance's focused approach succeeded because it introduced the technology as a way to help reinforce cultural change and transform tasks. For example, in the two-day training sessions for agents, one day was dedicated to Profiling and one to basic motivation and selling techniques, with Profiling as the key concept. Tebbutt led an effort to change Sun Alliance's mission statement to read: "We will be the best financial Profiling company in the U.K." Moreover, with the passage of the Financial Services Act (FSA) in the United Kingdom, senior managers wanted to ensure that their agents provided the best quality advice. Profiling adoption was not a "natural" consequence of the FSA, hut management seized on such external pressure to support introduction of the radical technology into the selling process.[29]

---

[29] In 1987, the passage of the Financial Services Act in Great Britain required any insurance agent to show "knowledge of the customer" and "best advice." For Sun Alliance, this meant filling out a fact-finding questionnaire for the client to sign or not. (The client also had the option of not sharing data; that exercised right would be noted on the form.) Most insurance organizations dealt with the regulation by having individual agents fill out a generic questionnaire that was then filed at the local sales office.

I could not easily identify the project sponsorship at Sun Alliance. The top management group described the initial introduction of the technology but in more than two dozen interviews with senior management, I could not find a single sponsor. While the managers saw Profiling as a group decision, its champion was clearly Tebbutt. The pilot design was focused; its purpose was to achieve penetrated adoption, not just trial. The management rationale was to completely change the nature of the relationship with the client from "policy sales" to "advice relationship."

Sun, however, did not change its compensation structure or administrative support. The Profiling effort was integrated into the existing management structure and systems. There were no changes to the fundamental job design as at Prudential or any additional budget for administrative or clerical support for the field agents. Sun managers simply pushed this way of doing business onto the existing roles and structure.

Other Explanations for Success.

A number of alternative hypotheses might explain the success at Sun and Prudential. Each organization's strong culture may have helped to reinforce the implementation process. This cultural effect could be at the country level (e.g., the English insurance industry is more likely to adopt Profiling due to its history of heavy consumer focus or regulation). Culture could also be an important variable at the company level (e.g., the employees at Sun Alliance might be more willing to follow management directions). Although we cannot measure culture in a way that can rule out these alternative explanations, there are some other indicators. First, the two successful implementations were in different countries, which lends credence to the claim that this is not an issue of culture. Second, within Sun Alliance, there was a second sales organization, the executive agency division (EAD), which also tried to implement Profiling. (See Figure 5.3 for a comparison of the two Sun divisions.)

Paul Tebbutt directed SAPLIS, one of the Sun Alliance divisions that adopted Profiling. However, he did not direct EAD, where little adoption occurred. EAD chose an implementation strategy similar to caveat emptor. There was no line leader; a staff person at EAD was responsible for the implementation. Profiling was available to anyone who wanted to use it, but there was no office-by-office focus on the product's rollout. The data from this division seems to support the idea that Profiling's success was not due to a specific cultural issue within Sun Alliance or to the Financial Services Act; otherwise, there would have been more adoption at EAD.

Explaining the Failure to Implement

At both organizations where Profiling did not succeed, the CEOs were the sponsors. At National Mutual, George Meier, chief executive of National Mutual

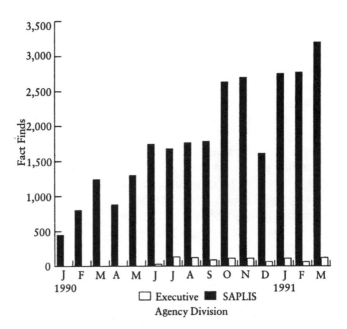

FIGURE 5.3 EAD versus SAPLIS: Total Monthly Fact Finds (January 1990–March 1991)

Group, sponsored the project. At Lutheran Brotherhood, President Bob Gandrud was the sponsor and paid for the project from special funds allocated to him for new initiatives. The head-office staff people championed the Profiling initiative; their main method of persuasion was a rational analysis that explained how the technology had helped other salespeople sell more. The champions' role was to make the technology available to a geographically dispersed group of representative agents simultaneously. They did not attack the method of selling directly.

When Lutheran Brotherhood and National Mutual managers designed the pilot, they drew on an existing implementation method similar to the way they introduced new products. In the decision to launch Profiling like a new product, senior managers did not consciously examine the implications of instituting a radical technology as if it were an incremental technology. They simply thought that if the technology itself had value, agents would use it. In addition, both organizations drew on previous implementation efforts as a model.

Thus, when new products were to be rolled out to the field salesforce, Lutheran Brotherhood's head office created the products, gave the agents introductory training, and encouraged them to use the products; this was the same approach they took with Profiling. Vicki Obenshain, the head office manager most involved with Profiling, had been in charge of the successful rollout of laptop computer support and the designer of a number of successful marketing initiatives.

At National Mutual, Neville Mears, the head-office manager in charge of introducing Profiling to the field sales agents, had more than twenty-five years with the firm and a track record of innovation in administrative support. Among his accomplishments was an innovation giving agents better access to the client information in the firm's various databases, an effort that earned him the managing director's Award for Excellence. The primary support group for the Profiling integration was a central head-office group. "Product consultants," who constantly pushed out or "sold" new products to the field, provided distribution.

Caveat Emptor Implementation

To understand the caveat emptor approach, we need to understand the nature of the implementation approach, the management rationale, and the championship. For instance, in the implementation of Profiling at Lutheran Brotherhood and National Mutual, the pilot design of the technology had significant, interrelated implications for subsequent management actions. The field salesforce's perception of the role of technology was particularly important because the company viewed agents as "independent" businesspeople. That independence was reflected in the organization's compensation systems and policies; for example, agents had to buy their own software and hardware. While they had a small stipend for office support, any additional support came from their own funds. In addition, project championship was embedded in the pilot design decision, so the champions were head-office staff people, not sales managers who were credible to the field sales agents and managers. Further, implementing Profiling as a new product rather than a new process further emphasized the agents' discretionary adoption. That is, the agents were not obliged to sell all the products available or to purchase all the sales technologies they were offered.

A number of connected factors constitute caveat emptor implementation. First, the individual (the agent) is the best judge of whether to adopt. Second, a small number of trials give the agent ample information to make that judgment. Third, the manager's role as implementer is to make the technology available for the agent to judge.

Lutheran Brotherhood and National Mutual used this approach to introduce new products and most other tools to their agents and implemented Profiling this way. Specifically, both companies constructed the pilots to ascertain a representative sample of agents. Lutheran Brotherhood chose six offices reflecting a wide range of markets to measure whether the technology would work in the broad market that the firm served. It also used two agencies as a control for overall economic factors. At one point in the pilot design, Obenshain and the vice president of sales discussed the choice of pilot offices, debating whether the pilot should concentrate only on "friendly" offices, i.e., where the local managers would actively push the technology. They determined, however, that this would overly bias the sample toward positive results, so they chose geographically dispersed offices in representative markets, with only a few agents experimenting with Profiling in each.

National Mutual employed a similar logic. For its pilot, it chose thirty-six agents from each of the seven states in the country. Internal analysis of pilot results suggested that the average sale increased from $1,400 to $2,900 (in Australian dollars), adding impetus to the idea that the technology would be efficient and that a laissez-faire implementation strategy would work.[30] Thus the extended pilot also strove to achieve the same singular penetration in a number of geographically dispersed offices; that is, one agent in each office was designated the Profiling agent. The company did not train or encourage other agents in that branch to use the tool.

This philosophy extended to National Mutual's "limited deployment" phase, in which it designated one Profiling agent in each of 150 branch offices. Given National Mutual's motivation and previous history of rolling out products to a wide selection of field agents, the caveat emptor strategy had mechanisms inherited from a management rationale created for product introductions.

Interestingly, by early 1990, when adoption volumes were lower than expected, the comments of National Mutual managers suggested that they were committed to transforming the sales process. The head of the agency remarked at that time: "We won't know for four more years if Profiling is a success or not. I won't entertain a review of the Profiling decision for at least three years. We are going to do Profiling because it is central to our strategy. Cultural change takes years, and we are going to have a go at it.[31]

Unfortunately, after another year of low adoption volumes, management support for the project waned, and, with the deepening of the worldwide recession, it ended in January 1992. Thus, even though the rhetoric of change and transformation was present, there was little direct line management involvement in the implementation.

IMPLICATIONS FOR MANAGING THE IMPLEMENTATION OF TECHNOLOGY

The implementation of Profiling provided a delightfully complex challenge to managers. On the one hand, the potential gains to the organization from implementing this new method of work were tremendous. The strategic implications for profitability, customer satisfaction, and agent retention were potentially lucrative; moreover, if well implemented, the organization could achieve significantly better information about its customers and their use of products. If well executed, a successful implementation of Profiling might give the adopting organization a significant competitive advantage. On the other hand, management faced the task of getting autonomous knowledge workers to change their behavior. Knowledge workers already have much more power and autonomy than clerical workers. By providing current revenue to the organization, they enhance

[30] An Australian dollar equals approximately US $0.80.
[31] Sviokla, "Profiling at National Mutual (B)," p. 2.

their power base even more. Implementing a new technology tool at the heart of their task process is difficult.

A Constellation of Actions

Faced with these challenges, the successful managers in this study took different approaches. Paul Tebbutt of Sun Alliance used strong leadership and a focused implementation approach. At Sun, managers simply pushed the technology into the organization, a sobering reminder of the power of impatient, credible line management. Prudential looked more comprehensively at the core assumptions and design of the task, started with a clean slate, and redesigned.

At a quick glance, these findings are not particularly striking. We have always known that leadership matters. What is interesting is that radical technological change may necessitate a constellation of actions by the manager to achieve success. To claim that there is only one solution is an overstatement of current understanding. Such hubris is potentially more damaging if it anchors the manager's planning and thinking in the incorrect assumption that there is one best way to implement a new technology. My data indicate that a better starting point is to acknowledge, a priori, that there may be a number of (or at least more than one) equally effective means to achieve the desired end state. More specifically, the research indicates that redesign and focus implementation strategies may substitute for each other. Very different processes may have equivalent outcomes. To begin with a frame of mind and analytic approach that precludes this isomorphism is to fundamentally misframe the task and hamper a manager's options.

The job of a manager is to think broadly about options and perhaps search for possible approaches, which may be surprisingly different. From this research, it seems that the strategizing must be done early in the implementation process, because once the first decisions are made, the implementation process takes on a life of its own, and the core design variables may be difficult or impossible to change. Just as the dominant design of manufacturing products and processes constrains the alternatives from supply through distribution, so does the path of new technology implementation rarely return to its roots and core assumptions.

A striking finding of the study is that the senior managers rarely thought of the different options as isolated activities but rather in patterns or constellations. Practically speaking this means that while the senior managers were figuring out what to do, they were also figuring out who should do it, what to expect, and how to do it.[32]

---

[32] Jeanette Lawrence documents how consider goals, means, and feasibility of decision options simultaneously. This is similar to the behavior we saw in the managers concerning implementation. See: J. Lawrence, "Expertise on the Bench: Modeling Magistrates Judicial Decision Making," in *The Nature of Expertise*, ed. M. Chi, R. Glaser, and M. Farr (Hillsdale, New Jersey: Lawrence Erlbaum Associates, Inc., 1988), pp. 229–259.

Political Ramifications

Managers were also trying to assess the nature of the potential political ramifications of implementing a new technology. Each managerial lever for change had significant constraints and meanings that were predominantly local. For example, events concerning technology can influence potential users' perceptions of the next technology, which often vary from firm to firm. Thus Profiling and the accompanying total-needs analysis embedded in its approach resembled Lutheran Brotherhood's earlier effort, "Financial Dimensions," which the head office brought to the field during the mid-1980s. Financial Dimensions was a selling approach emphasizing the customer's total needs, complete with a sales pitch and training system. Employees saw it as a failure. During the implementation of Profiling, some agents reported seeing it as another Financial Dimensions and immediately predicted failure. At Prudential, technology per se did not seem to have this negative reception.

The nature of the supporting organization also has an impact on implementation. For example, any selling system that the head office brings to the field has a very different flavor than one that field sales agents introduce. Behind the bland phrase "I'm from Corporate and I'm here to help you" lies the strong implication that the field organization is pitted against the head office, especially when administrative innovations are involved. Consequently who the owner is becomes tremendously important because it has nothing to do with the technology itself but everything to do with its reception. At Lutheran Brotherhood and National Mutual, the prime movers in the implementation process were from the head office; they were not senior line managers in sales. This too affected adoption of the technology. Even though there were sponsors at the top of the organization and the day-to-day champions were capable managers, the target audience for the technology did not identify with them. The "owner" of the innovation was a factor loaded into the value of the technology before it was even tried. The more successful managers seemed better at sensing these complexities and assembling the right constellation of people and resources. The less successful managers allowed a scattered approach and support that was not credible to the field personnel.

By the end of implementation at National Mutual, Profiling had become a symbol similar to Lutheran Brotherhood's Financial Dimensions. National Mutual's program manager, installed in late 1991, wanted to ensure that none of his efforts were labeled "son of Profiling." Other National Mutual managers used anti-Profiling positioning. One began a field salesforce meeting by announcing, "The first thing I want to say is that this idea has nothing to do with Profiling"

Momentum

In addition to their strong constellation of choices, the senior managers at Sun and Prudential consciously managed the momentum of the project. Tyre has discussed the windows of opportunity for changing manufacturing methods.[33] In implementations with radical organizational implications, the issue of momentum takes on even more significance because training and local management support has a half-life, and the novelty of a new tool soon wanes.

In this study, the two examples of success each exhibited a particular momentum. This variable has been implicitly dealt with in many implementation studies but rarely measured as an explicit management concern. While adoption rates have been carefully tracked and managed in consumer product consumption, project momentum is rarely if ever measured in research on software implementation for knowledge professionals.[34] But, in the design of the two successful efforts, managers concern was to create a sequence of events that would build momentum for implementation.

Many organizational theorists argue that radical change is best effected quickly. But if a manager faces a powerful cadre of knowledge workers, the swiftness and decisiveness of the implementation process can be constrained by the need to keep the implementees happy and employed. This implies a need to act swiftly and make a concerted effort to manage momentum over time. The more radical the software, the more important it is to manage organizational momentum.

Economies of Scale

What would cause a need for organizational momentum? What would make the caveat emptor process fail so miserably in the case of a tool that would help the end users? Why do the focus and redesign approaches work better? There may be economies of scale and scope in sales knowledge. If minimum efficient scale for a new method is not reached, it will fail after early experimentation. In the case of a complex sales tool, people's knowledge must be created and shared. If only one person uses such software as Profiling, the intellectual cost of "inventing" all this local knowledge might be too much to manage efficiently. This factor places a heavy load on sales personnel who are the sole users of the technology. By contrast, staying on top of the learning and the changing nature of a complex tool is easier if a substantial majority uses the tool.

Managers who intuitively understand these economies of scale may see their roles as champions to be less like scientists and more like change agents for rapid achievement of economies of scale in local knowledge. Implementing radical software seems to need a significant amount of organizational and

[33] M. J. Tyre and W. Orlikowski, "Windows of Opportunity: Temporal Patterns of Technological Adaptation in Organizations," *Organization Science*, volume 5, February 1994, pp. 98–118.
[34] For an interesting exception and specific discussion of the mechanisms of momentum, see: G. Moore, *Crossing the Chasm: Marketing and Selling Technology Products* (New York: Harper Business, 1991).

managerial effort to cause adoption. This also works in concert with a manager's concern to manage momentum. The more momentum, the faster you get to minimum efficient scale in the knowledge work.

The economies of scale may be even more challenging to achieve if they have delayed benefits. In many interviews, sales agents and managers reported that people took significant time becoming comfortable with Profiling. The process also delayed the payment of commissions, even though the commissions were expected to be higher. If the radical software technologies have delayed benefits, focus or redesign are important for sustaining or creating the knowledge necessary to use the tool practically. As managers move from automating the clerical tasks to supporting knowledge work, the issue of creating and managing economies of scale in knowledge work will become central to a firm's value-creating activities. When introducing technologies that are incremental and not radical, the concern about minimum efficient knowledge scale may not be as great. But minimum efficient scale of knowledge surely arises when radical software is involved.

CONCLUSION

There are a number of tasks for researchers. First, if the idea of implementation isomorphism is correct, they need to construct models that can accommodate non-obvious, isomorphic substitutions. One constellation of variables may have the functional equivalency of another set, but the nature of these trade-offs may not be immediately apparent. Traditional, single-form models do not identify these factors. Larger samples do not solve this specification problem, which may explain why there has been so little progress in creating implementation theory with any predictive validity.

Second, researchers need to create tools to measure momentum. In the change process, the speed and surety with which change moves forward has tremendous impact. This issue is especially acute if significant learning is needed to use the new software, because lack of momentum can turn into delays. Delay provides time to forget, and forgetting itself slows momentum.

Senior management must understand that a single solution is not the *only* solution. There is probably no optimal way to implement a technology. Successful implementation of radically new software in autonomous work necessitates significant motivation—perhaps beyond short-term individual economic benefit. Senior managers are personally responsible either to participate in the implementation process or to change the nature of the organization so that the new technology can be absorbed. The natural propensity when implementing technology to support autonomous professionals is to adopt a caveat emptor strategy, because it implicitly relies on independent judgment for the technology's acceptance and subsequent use. But radical software technologies also need concentrated action. Projects have life and momentum.[35] The managers of a project must assume a strategy of "diffuse or die." If the project does not grow, it will probably end.

[35] R. E. Walton, "The Diffusion of New Work Structures: Explaining Why Success Didn't Take," *Organizational Dynamics*, Winter 1975, pp. 3–22.

Chapter 6

Will the Internet Revolutionize Business Education and Research?

Blake Ives and Sirkka L. Jarvenpaa[1]

The international data highway will transform business education, although not necessarily its traditional supplier, the business school. Will the business school remain insulated from the knowledge revolution? Will it play a leadership role? Will it wither away? Two scenarios, one based on assumptions about education and the other on assumptions about research, are intended to help business schools and their stakeholders recognize the inevitability of change and envision what this new world might look like.

Blake Ives is Constantin Distinguished Professor of the management information sciences department at the Cox School of Business, Southern Methodist University, and a professor at the University College Dublin. Sirkka L. Jarvenpaa is an associate professor of information systems at the University of Texas at Austin.

Revolutions, whether the overthrow of governments or breakthroughs in technology, are usually visible. The knowledge revolution, though propelled by the twin engines of computer technology and communication technology; is a revolution of minds and ideas rather than of mass and energy. It is nearly invisible and easy to ignore, particularly by those who stand on the seemingly safe shoreline of tradition. This knowledge revolution threatens universities' advantage in

[1] Reprinted from "Will the Internet Revolutionize Business Education and Research?" by Blake Ives and Sirkka L. Jarvenpaa, *Sloan Management Review*, Spring 1996, pp. 33–41, by permission of publisher. Copyright © 1996 by Sloan Management Review Association. All right reserved.

knowledge creation and dissemination. Davis and Botkin paint a bleak picture of the role of schools:

> Business, more than government, is instituting the changes in education that are required for the emerging knowledge-based economy School systems, public and private, are lagging behind the transformation in learning that is evolving outside them, in the private sector at both work and play, with people of fall ages. Over the next few decades, the private sector will eclipse the public sector as our predominant educational institution.[2]

Private-sector intrusion is a real risk for business schools. Cable operators and telecommunications companies are aggressively developing virtual classrooms, often without university involvement.[3] Publishers and software houses are developing multimedia products that will substitute for, rather than complement, traditional classroom education. The business school's own faculty working independently or as consultants for other entities, represent another serious threat.[4] Already there is both an audio- and videotape market for high-profile lecturers, and one can imagine well-known professors marketing and delivering personalized courses from their homes, with or without an institutional affiliation. The new electronic infrastructure also allows the best-known institutions to establish a local electronic presence in new markets.

We now find centers for innovation in management education outside the business school. Bankers Trust is revolutionizing its training environment through collaborative technologies such as Lotus Notes that eliminate formalized training programs. Materials are on-line in the form of self-serve offerings and just-in-time education from office desktops. Motorola University uses personal, computer-based virtual reality (VR) technology to teach employees to run assembly lines. Preliminary studies show that the employees assigned to VR training learn faster and make fewer mistakes than those assigned to traditional training, at considerably lower cost.[5] Sometimes the innovations are in partnership with faculty or centers at a university. Andersen Consulting is working with Roger Schank, the director of Northwestern University's Institute for the Learning Sciences, on computer simulations that teach interpersonal and selling skills.[6]

---

[2] S. Davis and J. Botkin, "The Coming of Knowledge-Based Business," *Harvard Business Review,* volume 72, September–October 1994, p. 170.

[3] For example, Jones International Ltd. has a Mind Extension University cable that teaches more than 26 million households in the United States with degree programs from thirty universities (e.g., an MBA from Colorado State University). Bell Atlantic has also announced plans to build virtual campuses with universities. See: "Bell Atlantic Awarded Multimillion Dollar Contract to Build 'Virtual Campus'," PR Newswire, Financial News, 25 October 1994.

[4] "Media: A College Campus as Close as the Couch," *Business Weekly.* June 1994, p. 2.

[5] N. Adams. "Lessons from the Virtual World," *Training.* June 1995, pp. 45–48.

[6] S. S. Rao. "The Simulator Classroom," *Financial World* (17 January 1995), pp. 56–58.

Interest in company-based universities is also on the rise. Many U.S. companies have had such programs for decades (e.g., General Electric, Motorola, Disney). Sprint's University of Excellence offers some 750 courses; Motorola University lists 300. Motorola has even formed partnerships with accredited colleges to design work-related degree pmgrams.[7] Cemex, a large Mexican-based cement company with international operations, has traditionally sent executives to programs in the United States and the United Kingdom but is now considering its own university focused on Mexican management style. Japanese firms have long trained executives within their own corporate structure.[8] In-house programs provide tailored instruction at times and places convenient to the customer and individual participants.

Advancements in information and communications technology will drive additional major changes in business education. In this article, we highlight an emerging intellectual infrastructure for the knowledge revolution and explore the assumptions about education and research that this infrastructure challenges.[9] We then draw two scenarios to help us envision opportunities and barriers in business education. We describe two early prototype electronic learning forums. In conclusion, we discuss the barriers to progress and what is required to lower them. Although we focus on the business school, there are many of the same drivers and barriers in corporate education programs, training centers, and corporate R&D groups.

[7] B. S. Watson, "The New Training Edge," *Management Review,* May 1995, pp. 49–51.

[8] J. C. Linder and H.J. Smith, "The Complex Case of Management Education," *Harvard Business Review,* volume 70, September–October 1992, pp. 16–33.

[9] An effective learning environment depends on the student's experience, ability, effort, and learning style as well as the instructional goals, instructor skills, and the particular pedagogy and learning technology. See: D. E. Leidner and S. L. Jarvenpaa, "The Use of Information Technology to Enhance Management School Education: A Theoretical View," *MIS Quarterly,* volume 19, September 1995, pp. 265–291. Our focus here is on educational alternatives for master's and executive level audiences—adult learners. While there is no universally superior mode of learning, mature, motivated adult students learn best when they are in control of their learning and can reconstruct the material in their own terms and in the context of their own interests. See: J. W. Apps, *Mastering the Teaching of Adults* (Malabar, Florida: Krieger Publishing, 1991). Some learning models also stress the importance of learning in the context in which it will be used. See: M. O'Loughlin, "Rethinking Science Education: Beyond Piagetian Constructivism toward a Sociocultural Model of Teaching and Learning," *Journal of Research in Science Teaching,* volume 29, October 1992, pp. 791–820. An active, experience-based learning mode associated with the Internet fits well with adult learning. See: A. D. Yakimovicz and K.L Murphy, "Constructivism and Collaboration on the Internet: Case Study of a Graduate Class Experience, *Computers and Education,* volume 24, number 3, 1995, pp. 203–209.

A GLOBAL INFRASTRUCTURE

The emerging infrastructure will so fundamentally change the rules of supply and demand that a new economic order will result. During the past thirty months, a version of the U.S. National Information Infrastructure arrived in the guise of an ungainly, unreliable, and perhaps unmanageable World Wide Web.[10] The Web lets almost anyone, at a modest cost, publish information accessible to others anywhere in the world. Based on Internet protocols, this universal information repository allows grade school students to look at live pictures from the space shuttle or accompany a robot into a live volcano. From our offices in Texas and Dublin, we can examine the information technology plan of Singapore, build electronic enterprises with colleagues in Australia and Finland, or communicate with each other by Internet phone. Located behind security firewalls, companies can use public networks (the Internet and the Web) to provide a secure private communications infrastructure (an "intranet").[11]

Commercial interest in the Internet is high and continues to grow. In August 1994, the Commercial Sites Index had several hundred listings of businesses on the Web. Eighteen months later, there were more than 22,000; at its current growth rate, the list will double in about eight months. By February 1996, more than 360 banks had sites on the Web, with half located outside the United States. Internet Solutions estimated that, on 12 February 1996, there were more than 50 million people with some form of access to the Internet and more than 400,000 Web sites, a fourfold increase in just six months.[12]

To many, the Internet technologies resemble the personal computer revolution of the early 1980s, which transformed information management. But, unlike the personal computer, this technology arrives with a built-in distribution channel. Netscape Communications, a new entrant in the information technology industry, released, marketed, sold, and distributed its product, a user interface for the World Wide Web, in little more than a day—using as its prime distribution channel the very product it was replacing. Future "information appliances" will identify the software required to process a given piece of information—say, a spreadsheet—and retrieve it from the Net without human intervention. The existence of this hyperchannel for the distribution of knowledge-based products will have far-reaching consequences.[13]

---

[10] C. Anderson, "The Accidental Superhighway: A Survey of the Internet," *The Economist,* 1 July 1995, p. S3.

[11] "Enter the Intranet," *The Economist,* 13 January 1996, p. 66.

[12] Commercial Sites Index, Open Markets Inc. <http://www.directory.net>; RJE Communications Inc., "Directory of Banks," 12 February 1996 <http://www.bankweb.com/bankweb.html>; Internet Solutions, "Internet Statistics: Estimated," 12 February 1996, 6:11:40 (Pacific time) <http://www.netree.com/netbin/internetstats>.

[13] N. Gross, "Internet Lite: Who Needs a PC?" *Business Week,* 13 November 1995, pp. 52, 54.

Some predict that education on demand to homes, schools, and workplaces is going to be a vastly bigger business than entertainment on demand.[14] There are some early indicators. In the summer of 1994, an undergraduate at the University of Alabama offered a course about the Internet to Internet subscribers. Each day for six weeks, 62,000 students in 77 countries received a short Roadmap lecture or tutorial and assignments.[15] At Los Alamos National Laboratory is another harbinger of the new intellectual infrastructure. A physicist there maintains a database of working papers for scientists in high-energy physics and related fields. Each day, his system automatically fulfills 20,000 requests for preprints.[16]

SCENARIOS FOR A NEW INTELLECTUAL INFRASTRUCTURE

Harnessing the emerging electronic infrastructure will require that the business education establishment make radical changes. Implementing a radical change, in turn, requires a shared vision of the future of business education. A vision can ground the discussion and begin to reveal institutional obstacles. Scenario planning can help illuminate the uncertain path.[17]

Underlying Assumptions about Education

An important element of scenario planning is identifying the assumptions that will characterize the new environment:

- *Virtual Learning Communities.* Students' need to interact physically with each other and with a teacher will decrease as electronic spaces begin to supplant physical classrooms.[18] Among the advantages will be lowered costs (for travel and classrooms), greater convenience, security, and flexibility, and the ability to ignore time differences and geographic distance.[19] Students learning in virtual

---

[14] A. Reinhardt "New Ways to Learn," *Byte,* March 1995, pp. 50–71.
[15] Roadmap is an Internet tutorial delivered by daily e-mail messages in three different five-week offerings in summer and fall 1994. It was developed by Patrick Crispen, at the time a senior at the University of Alabama. It is available at <http://www/brandonu.ca/~ennsnr/Resources/Roadmap/Welcome.html>.
[16] G. Stix, "The Speed of Write," *Scientific American,* December 1994, pp. 106–111.
[17] P. J. H. Schoemaker, "Scenario Planning: A Tool for Strategic Thinking," *Sloan Management Review,* volume 36, Winter 1995. pp. 25–40.
[18] M. Scardamalia and C. Bereiter, "Technologies for Knowledge-Building Discourse," *Communications of the ACM,* volume 36, 5 May 1993, pp. 37–41.
[19] Reinhardt (1995). Several universities already offer virtual classroom courses via Internet based e-mail and computer conferencing supplemented with videoconferencing. A few are experimenting with Lotus Notes-based collaborative learning environments. Schools

communities will also have the advantage of being grouped by homogeneity of interests and intellect, while benefiting from heterogeneity of cultural background and previous experiences.

- *Pull Rather than Push.* Instructors will do less structuring of course content as students take greater control of their own education and as the need for personalized learning grows. In addition, an instructor's role as expert will shift to facilitator or coach.[20]

- *Lifelong Learning.* Where once schools provided a discrete, career-spanning set of concepts and tools, now they will build the skills and motivation for lifelong learning.[21]

- *Just-in-Time Rather than Just-in-Case Education.* Knowledge, according to Davis and Botkin, "is doubling about every seven years, and in technical fields in particular, half of what students learn in their first year of college is obsolete by the time they graduate."[22] Rather than providing education to students in advance— "just in case" they need it—schools will give them the skills to achieve education "just in time" to apply to the task at hand. Executive education will likely move fastest to the education-on-demand model.[23]

- *Demonstrated Skills versus Certification.* Certification will increasingly be pushed aside by demonstrated skills or work products. In knowledge-based industries, increasingly, work will be observable after the fact. Similarly skills will be readily tested through automated schemes, such as evaluating performance via simulation or virtual reality.

- *Nonuniversity Certification.* Even as certification becomes less important, it will no longer be the sole providence of universities or professional associations. For-profit organizations will increasingly provide certification in specific skill areas.

- *Global Disaggregation.* Education, like many other knowledge-based processes, will be disaggregated throughout the world.[24] Institutions or students will borrow or pay for components of education from global providers.

- *Global Collaboration.* Both students and faculty will work closely with peers worldwide. Faculty will have more opportunities to share materials; students will work with people of varying cultural backgrounds.[25]

- *Open Competition.* Students will be able to compare, almost first-hand, educational offerings across institutions in considerable detail. Already, in one of our

---

with virtual classroom courses for business or information systems courses include New York University, Pennsylvania State University, Drexel University, Mount Allison University in Canada, and Open University in the United Kingdom. The University of Phoenix offers a complete business program interactively on line.

[20] Leidner and Jarvenpaa (1995).

[21] A. Laszlo and K. Castro, "Technology and Values: Interactive Learning Environments for Future Generations," *Educational Technology,* March–April 1995, pp. 7–13.

[22] Davis and Botkin (1994), p. 170.

[23] Reinhardt (1995).

[24] U. M. Apte and R. O. Mason, "Global Disaggregation of Information-Intensive Services," *Management Science,* volume 41, July 1995, pp. 1250–1262.

[25] K. Knoll and S.L. Jarvenpaa, "Listening to Work in Distributed Global Teams," *Proceedings of Hawaii International Conference,* volume 4, 3–6 January 1995, pp. 92–101.

classes, parents or prospective employers can watch an individual student's progress and even participate in class.

- *Visual Rather than Textual.* Written language developed, not that long ago in human evolution, as an efficient alternative to drawing pictures. But our mental processes are much better equipped to deal with pictures and spatial relationships than with text or audio.[26] The emerging visual information systems will let us once again leverage our ability to process images.

- *Simulation.* Students will learn not by memorization but by doing, albeit in a simulated environment. Students at Carnegie-Mellon University and the MIT Sloan School use a simulation of a live trading room with links to real-time data feeds from Reuters to the stock, money, and options markets; the trading environment is linked to schools in Tokyo and Mexico City.[27]

- *University and Business Together.* A global highway will provide a low transaction-cost vehicle for linking students with mentors, project sponsors, or prospective employers. It will also enhance interaction between professors and practitioners.

- *Context and Concept.* Historically, theory and conceptual framework have come together with business applications only in assignment questions, examples in texts, case studies, visiting speakers, projects, and the like. In a hypertext world, students will be able to move directly between real-world application and conceptual underpinnings. For instance, an electronic business's payment scheme will provide links to information on the particular scheme and, from there, to its conceptual underpinnings.[28]

A Revolution in Learning

Although there is little debate about many of our assumptions, there has been slight progress toward a new vision for business education. Scenario planning can spur the emergence of such a vision.

One scenario is relatively easy to identify—the status quo. This scenario portrays incremental change within a traditional paradigm of classroom-based education, with no changes in the reward system. Some will enthusiastically defend that incremental model, which has served us adequately for decades. Time may vindicate them. But, based on our understanding of the technological and intellectual opportunities now available, the changing requirements of business customers, and some experimentation with new approaches, we believe strongly that "business as usual" is a recipe for failure and an open invitation to nontraditional competition.

Business schools must seek an alternative vision. Our scenario is not intended to be that vision but, rather, a stimulus for thought.

---

[26] Although the information processing rate is higher with visuals, the retention rate is lower than with audio.

[27] D. Barker, "Seven New Ways to Learn," *Byte*, March 1995, pp. 54–55.

[28] A. B. Whinston, "Reengineering Education," *Journal of Information Systems Education*, Fall 1994, pp. 126–133.

Tara Rogers, consultant for the World Wide Group, is currently on an airplane over the Atlantic ocean. With little notice, Rogers has been summoned to England. But, because of electronic communications, her travels have little adverse impact on her participation in an executive MBA program.

An hour before touchdown at Gatwick, Rogers is awakened by the plane's passenger comfort system. After freshening up, she begins work on a project for her executive MBA program. Course material, stored on the World Wide Web, is now accessible almost any time and place. Intelligent agents, built into her personal assistant computer and linked to the university server, remind her of upcoming course commitments. Classroom sessions are becoming less frequent; students prefer asynchronous electronic discussion over several days or participation in on-line tutorials. Also, there are no syllabi with detailed outlines for each classroom or virtual session. Rather, courses change as the students reveal problems, issues, and topics during discussions or competency tests and as new material becomes available. Exams are personalized for each student's learning objectives.

Video-conferencing allows Rogers to participate in classroom and discussion group sessions without being physically present. A tiny camera provides an image of her face to her classmates. As students speak in class, their images appear on a wall at the front of the classroom and on lap- top screens. Students can make their facial images available to any student in the class who wishes to establish a one-on-one connection. A keyboard permits students to send messages back and forth and to read their university mail or anything else encountered on the Net.

The powerful personal assistants that most students carry challenges traditional educational assumptions, but the outcomes are not always desirable. One of Rogers' s professors complained of undergraduates sending e-mail messages to friends during class, playing video games, disfiguring the professor's electronic image, and searching global databases for information to discredit the lecture. Once Rogers invited an executive to join the class by videoconference to reveal that the scheme described in a case, which the instructor endorsed with some enthusiasm, had later gone awry.

Students are not alone in their creative exploitation of this new technology. Faculty sometimes arrive at class in electronic form—from home, office, car, or conference site. There is no technical reason why an instructor can't run a class session from a golf cart, and Rogers knows one colleague who regularly participates from similar venues—with his camera "in for repairs." For most executive MBA students, however, the ability to participate without being physically on campus has been the program's key attraction.

Attending class electronically has forever changed the dynamics of the classroom. In Rogers's class, as many as half the students come to class electronically; two or three have never been seen in person after the first week. Electronic participation can be evaluated, but not as reliably as physical attendance. Participants can come late to the session, electronically, say a few words, and then leave unnoticed. Those not in attendance, theoretically at least, can go back later and look at the electronic archive, but without the ability to interact. In some urban universities with limited space, entire courses are conducted outside of the classroom walls.

Business cases have long fueled classroom discussions, but both the discussions and the cases have now taken on new forms. Professors around the world are able to distribute cases electronically at little cost to other professors. An e-mail message from Rogers's instructor reveals that he has just discovered a new case and is assigning it for the following week's class. Rogers pulls up the case from the university server and finds that it includes video segments of interviews with executives, marketing materials, current financial reports, and even an opportunity to use some tools and systems described in the case. The case also includes electronic links to databases about the company, links to competitors' Web pages, demonstrations of products, and so on. The Web sites included in these cases are constantly changing, so Rogers can, with a little extra effort, bring information to the discussion that the instructor very likely doesn't know before class. In preparing for case discussion, Rogers sometimes develops exhibits that she can call up to support her arguments.

"Air time," long a valued commodity in quality MBA classrooms, has become even more revered as the quality of student comments and evidence improves. That, coupled with the external resources that can now be brought into the classroom, reduces the instructors' own air time. Last year's class created electronic bulletin boards for some of the cases, often drawing on similar bulletin boards run by students at other schools. As the faculty member embellishes his summary points, Rogers or another student is annotating the handout and loading it on the server. Such bulletin boards, accessible throughout the world, include the kind of information that has previously been available only from the case teaching notes. Professors use this technology to discuss how they will use a case.

Rogers is pleased that "chalk and talk" classes, with their emphasis on one-way lecturing, are among the first casual-tics of the revolution in education. Rogers uses self-paced learning tutorials with built-in expert facilitators for such courses as statistics and introductory finance. Virtual reality modules let students fly through visual representations of data as statistical analyses are demonstrated.

The intelligent agent leads students to the appropriate statistic for a given problem and informs them if the data are appropriate, given the assumptions of the particular statistic. Rogers sometimes misses the human interaction but welcomes the opportunity to move at her own speed and to digress into interesting areas.

Among those competing in the education marketplace are the old textbook publishers, software houses, and a menagerie of movie and video game producers. Some materials used in Rogers's program are free, or nearly free, as professors provide cases and tutorial materials in exchange for visibility. For other materials, the original author (often a faculty member) is compensated based on the frequency of access.[29]

Rogers's firm gave her the opportunity to attend either a tailored in-house MBA program or, if accepted, one of the world's top ten executive MBA programs. Well-known business schools have expanded into distance learning, which has significantly decreased the demand for local graduate and executive education programs. A geographically fragmented industry has suddenly concentrated; advances in communications make it possible for businesses to reach out to the top ten executive educational programs rather than settle for the top thirty program in their own backyard. With the exception of short "in residence" periods, neither students nor faculty are required to leave their offices.

Underlying Assumptions about Research

The new intellectual infrastructure will also transform how we create and publish original knowledge and how we evaluate researchers. Again, it is difficult to predict the exact changes, but we see dramatic possibilities. Our second scenario is based on the education assumptions as well as the following assumptions:

- *An Open Process.* The peer review process will become more open. Journals will give authors access to information about manuscripts under review and allow them to assess the quality of individual reviewers much more readily.[30] Automated indexing systems will immediately bring articles to the attention of interested researchers, consultants, or executives. Colleagues' new publications will be available on acceptance. Reputations will be earned, or lost, more quickly. Journals will routinely publish data along with findings, thus fueling replication or reanalysis. Plagiarism will be easily detected.
- *Articles, not Journals.* Archival journal issues, usually a collection of unrelated articles, will become irrelevant as individual articles are published after they clear the reviewing and editing process. Journals will sell individual articles by access and by subscription.
- *Access Rather than Citations.* Citations to previous work, long an important, if faulty. element for evaluating scholarship will be challenged by direct access to the articles themselves. The number of universities, countries, companies, and even well-known individuals accessing or linking to an article may be a surrogate for quality, and sophisticated programs will be developed for analyzing them.
- *Living Scholarship.* Existing journals will face hard choice between replicating their current, paper-based archival scheme in electronic form or allowing

---

[29] "Carnegie-Mellon, Visa Plan to Offer Payment System for Data from Internet," *Wall Street Journal,* 15 February 1995, p. B6.
[30] One journal in the information systems field, *MIS Quarterly,* has already started to implement such capability. See: <http://www.misq.org/>. B. Ives, "MISQ Central: Creating a New Intellectual Infrastructure," *MIS Quarterly,* volume 18, September 1994, pp. xxxv–xxxix.

interactive links to other works within their publications. In the latter model, the works, which we describe here as "living documents," will perish as links grow stale. Mechanisms and rewards will ensure that publications are updated or retired to archival status.

- *Researcher as Maintainer.* Researchers will be responsible for maintaining research that they did years ago or for allowing it to deteriorate in quality. A researcher's vita will no longer be a historical record of past accomplishment, but a public interface to living scholarship.
- *Tracking and Longitudinal Traces.* While researchers have had limited data available—say, a customer's purchase decision—they will now have detailed data on, for instance, the steps that a customer takes in purchasing a product from a catalog. The massive amounts of transaction data available will be time stamped, thus permitting analysis over time. Longitudinal, process-oriented research will replace much of today's point-in-time, outcome-focused studies. Business research will be based on real-time or near real-time happenings.
- *Library as Distributor.* Research libraries once built collections that paralleled one another, then made them available to local users. In the future, they will be singular repositories for their local institutions' publications. Rather than being global collectors and local distributors, they will become local collectors and global distributors.

The following scenario illustrates many of our assumptions.

A Revolution in Knowledge Creation

While checking his morning e-mail, Professor Michael Smith is pleased to see a note, sent the previous afternoon, informing him that a journal has accepted the third revision of his "IT Outsourcing Revisited" article for publication. Another message from an indexing service informs him of a new paper of interest. He is amused to discover it is his own outsourcing article, published just a few hours earlier. He calls it up from the journal's Web site and scans the abstract. Because his university library is a subscriber to the journal, he can look at the article without paying for it. As an author, he is also authorized to examine the data reports on the number of people who have already looked at the article. He notices that there have already been ten accesses, including one from EDS and another from Nokia. He tracks down the EDS source and is gratified to see that his paper has been added to a "What's Hot in Outsourcing" index that EDS maintains for its consultants, customers, and prospective customers. Smith updates his on-line résumé, authorizing a link so that future viewers of his résumé can also look at the current access data.

Smith's next message is less inspiring—a disgruntled reader pointing out a problem in one of Smith's older pieces. In the past, journals were archived in research libraries, where they remained unchanged. But living Web documents are considerably more volatile. Simple errors, typographic and otherwise, can be quickly repaired before they are inaccurately cited. But links within the paper are not dependable. Links are to a single server with a unique address that, from time to time, changes. Worse, the server may cease operating or remove the material that is the source of the original citation. One of Smith's colleagues had based a major piece of research on a study later discredited for plagiarism and removed from a journal's server.

Smith feels at times like a 1980s maintenance programmer as he seeks to keep his links updated, his material current with recent thinking, and his online article logs an accurate reflection of all the updates. He has already allowed two papers to lapse into the archival "tombs" reserved for unmaintained papers, but they weigh heavily on his sense of professional responsibility.

Smith calls up the home page for the *MIS Quarterly* to check on the status of his most recent submission. Only one review has thus far been returned, but it is generally positive. The editor's log notes that an automated reminder was sent a few days before to the other two reviewers. Although he cannot determine the reviewers' identities, he can look at their past performance. He is disappointed to see that one has a history of slow turnarounds.

TWO ELECTRONIC LEARNING FORUMS

Alter raising assumptions and writing scenarios, our next step is to construct a prototype based on the assumptions and scenarios. During the past year, we have been involved in creating such prototypes. The initiatives, though still crude, provide an interesting perspective on the knowledge revolution.

ISWorld Net

ISWorld Net attempts to create a repository of learning resources and a new intellectual infrastructure.[31] It has a presence on the World Wide Web as well as on a listserv, ISWorld.[32] Most subscribers are information systems faculty. The discussion list is intended as a relatively low-volume (two or three messages a day), high-subscription communication channel. Another listserv, ISWNet, provides a higher-volume communication vehicle for 50 people who have thus far volunteered to help build ISWorld Net and another 120 who follow its activities. We anticipate adding channels for video-conferencing, synchronous and asynchronous bulletin boards, and lectures from distinguished speakers. The current ISWorld Net presence on the Web, though rudimentary, provides information on research areas, teaching and learning (e.g., an index of cases), and a repository of other information (e.g., a faculty directory).

The electronic commerce page, for instance, has its own discussion list of some 100 faculty; five editors assemble course syllabi, articles, case studies, and

---

[31] <http://www.isworld.org/isworld/future.html>.

[32] Listservs are electronic mailing lists permitting individuals to send messages to hundreds or even thousands of others with shared interests.

books. The page is "one-stop shopping" for faculty teaching an electronic commerce course. Students, who also use the page, help to structure it. Essentially the page is a distribution channel for teaching materials, as well as a meeting place for faculty and students. When a case is released for publication, it can be announced on the list immediately; participants can access it on the Web and, perhaps the next day benefit from an interview with the case writer broadcast over the list.

One assumption of ISWorld Net's supporters is that each participant will contribute. For instance, a professor in Nova Scotia maintains a page of links to various information systems departments; a professor in New Zealand maintains a file of discussion lists. To succeed, this approach requires that most of the responsibilities be small and easy to fulfill, and that individuals be held accountable.[33]

Global Virtual Teams

The second initiative focuses on virtual peer-to-peer learning. Since 1993, master's degree students worldwide who are studying global IT management have joined a prototype exercise on virtual teamwork.[34] The experiment is based on two premises: (1) that fast-paced learning occurs in teams, and (2) that the best way to learn virtual teaming and global networking skills is by working on a project that requires them. In 1993, 120 master's students from 15 universities learned skills for collaborating in globally dispersed, ad hoc teams. Teams consisted of students from different countries, sometimes separated by as much as 16 hours. Students learned first-hand the challenges of communicating with people in countries that have poor technological infrastructures. They developed comparative country analyses on information technology discussed global management cases, completed team project assignments on multinational companies, and developed proposals for starting new products or new businesses. Learning depended on the students' attitudes toward the new forum, their ability to socialize, their cultural sensitivity. and the depth of their previous experiences.

In 1995, the prototype was scaled up to include 250 master's students from 20 universities around the world. Each student was assigned to a three- to five-member global virtual team and was the only team member from his or her university. The members never met face to face. The teams, on average, had fourteen-hour time differences between the most geographically distant members. They communicated using e-mail and other Internet communication resources. The teams developed a business plan for an Internet-related business, including the financing and staffing requirements. Practitioners from Nokia, Sterling Information Systems, and Digital Equipment Corporation judged the proposals and

---

[33] B. Ives and R. Zmud, "ISWorld Net: Scholarly Infrastructure for Information Systems," *MIS Quarterly,* volume 18, December 1994, pp. liv–lvi.

[34] <http://uts.cc.utexas.edu/~bgac313/index.html>. See: Knoll and Jarvenpaa (1995).

picked the most innovative and thoroughly researched plan. The exercise demonstrated that students can learn in a virtual collaborative setting; many students were convinced that this was more effective than face-to-face learning teams.

In 1996, the two virtual organizations—ISWorld Net and the global teams—will be brought together. The assignment for students participating in the global teams exercise will be to create a module for ISWorld Net.

BARRIERS TO PROGRESS

It seems clear that nothing will protect the business school from being swept into the current of technologically driven change. In fact, as the examples and scenarios in this paper suggest, the soil is crumbling around us.

The promotion and tenure system itself is an almost insurmountable barrier to rapid change. In North America, candidates for tenure continue, as they have for decades, to be reviewed based on publication in archival scholarly journals that take three to five years to publish articles. While businesses constantly shorten cycles of product-introduction and production cycles, the gestation time for published business research, at least in one prominent journal, increased over three decades from thirteen to thirty-three months.[35] Faced with fast-paced change in their business environments, businesspeople naturally question the timeliness, if not the relevance, of research contributions.

Furthermore, within the business school at least, there is an assumption that research concerned with learning or pedagogy is, almost by definition, inferior work that must be relegated to second- or third-tier journals.[36] Similarly with few exceptions, teaching is judged by students watching the instructor in a classroom. Faculty teaching loads are based on teaching a class in a traditional setting. Resources for pedagogical development are in short supply, and innovations are almost invariably constrained by the prevailing paradigm of the traditional classroom.

Skeptics will argue, first, that our predictions are technology-centric and, second, that new media have done little to increase students' learning. We would respond that many of the skeptics' studies are flawed.[37] Some studies have

---

[35] B. Ives, "Cycle-Time Reduction for Disseminating Scholarly Research," *MIS Quarterly* volume 17, June 1993, pp. xxi–xxiv.

[36] Essentially true for interdisciplinary work and research on international business as well.

[37] Some explain that this is because teachers resort to the same traditional teaching methods in high-tech environments as they do in traditional classes. See, for example: D. E. Leidner and S. L. Jarvenpaa, "The Information Age Confronts Education: Case Studies on Electronic Classrooms," *Information Systems Research*, volume 4, March 1993, pp. 24–54; and Leidner and Jarvenpaa (1995). Others criticize early applications of technology as based on limited or faulty assumptions of learning, See: E. J. Ullmer,

found differences among students' receptiveness to new learning environments.[38] It is not yet clear what kinds of innovations in learning can have the greatest impact on the greatest number of learners.

Faculty reskilling is also a significant issue. To contribute to this revolution, one must participate in it. An emerging set of Internet tools will make such participation more likely and less frustrating. Once faculty are connected, the Web itself is a marvelous facilitator for reskilling.[39]

CONCLUSION

Many people find solace in the durability of the university. One of our deans enjoys pointing out that, of the sixty-six institutions from the fifteenth century that still exist, sixty-two are universities. But that durability may provide false security. The business school's journey into the turbulent waters of the knowledge age will be difficult. When the storm is over, the boat will still be there. But some of the sailors will be lost, perhaps run over by the speedboats of innovative and adaptive private-sector entrepreneurs.

Business schools—particularly nondegree executive programs—are vulnerable. Surviving institutions will likely have the strongest brand names, be able to provide both scale and scope, and have the most flexible faculty.[40] Institutions

"Media and Learning: Are There Two Kinds of Truth?," *Educational Technology Research & Development*, volume 42, number 1, 1994, pp. 21–32.

[38] Some feel that the new technology-based models make assumptions that may be unrealistic: that is, they may require curious students with lots of initiative and good social skills who can learn in interactive collaborative settings. See: Reinhardt (1995). High-ability students are known to benefit more from pull-based learning than low-ability students. See: R. C. Bovy, "Successful lnstructional Methods: Cognitive Information Processing Approach," *Educational Communication & Technology Journal*, Winter 1981, pp. 203–217. Research at the New Jersey Institute of Technology found that the virtual classroom was a more effective learning environment for mature, motivated students, but not for less motivated, less mature students. Students found the virtual classroom setting as convenient but also more demanding than the traditional classroom, because they had to take an active role in the learning process. The highest level of learning occurred in classes where both the traditional and virtual modes were used. See: S. R. Hiltz, "Collaborative Learning in a Virtual Classroom: Highlights of Findings," *Proceedings of the Conference Computer-Supported Cooperative Work*, 26–28 September 1988; and S. R. Hiltz, "Collaborative Learning: The Virtual Classroom Approach," *Technology Horizon Education Journal*, June 1990, pp. 59–65.

[39] W. Spitzer and K. Wedding, "LabNet: An Intentional Electronic Community for Professional Development," *Computers and Education*, volume 24, number 3, 1995, pp. 247–255.

[40] These economies of scale and scope are likely to be similar to what publishing houses have faced as the industry has moved into the electronic era. McGraw-Hill has been successful with its Primus electronic print-on-demand system for custom textbooks because it

should already be reexamining inflexible, outdated reward systems. The inflexibility of traditional universities, however, suggests that nontraditional educational suppliers may be best positioned to exploit the lucrative market for business education in an electronic world.

had enough material under its control to build a large database to support a program. Smaller college publishers cannot respond with similar offerings. For example, Elsevier eventually left the college text market after it determined it did not have sufficient critical mass to go into custom publishing. See: K. Hunter, "Issues and Experiments in Electronic Publishing and Dissemination,". *Information Technology and Libraries,* June 1994, pp. 127–132.

PART II

The Technical Enablers

Chapter 7
Designing Groupware Applications: A Work-Centered Design Approach[1]

Kate Ehrlich

Lotus Development Corp.

INTRODUCTION

Groupware is about group *work*. Group work is the work practice that evolves to get ordinary, daily work done. Group work includes the informal ad hoc communication that happens between people in adjoining offices or people in different countries and time zones. Group work happens in a context of personal, managerial and organizational imperatives that encourage people to share their work with others and reward them when they do.

The design of single user applications translates users' tasks and needs into a functional description which directs the overall design and development of the application. When delivered, most single user applications can be used "right out of the box"—aside from time spent learning the application. Groupware applications, designed to support group work, require a different methodology to understand the tacit, invisible aspects of work practices. Translation into cogent, explicit requirements is not straightforward but requires extensive ongoing collaboration between researchers and application developers to translate descriptions of group work into application features. The functional requirements govern the technical development of the application. But adoption of the application is just as likely to be determined by organizational and managerial preparedness as by the design and technical implementation of the application itself.

This chapter draws on recent research and practical examples to examine groupware applications from three perspectives:

---

[1] To appear: Beaudouin-Lafon (Ed). *Trends in CSCW*. Wiley and Sons. 1998.

- **Methodologies** for providing new product ideas or for extracting requirements from work practices
- Common themes that emerge in the design of many groupware applications
- Technical and social challenges in deploying an application

The chapter concludes with a case study of the design, development and deployment of an application to support coordination in distributed teams.

Definitions and Examples of Groupware Applications

Groupware, the applied side of CSCW (Computer Supported Cooperative Work), has been described by Cameron et al (95) in the Forrester report as:

> Technology that communicates and organizes unpredictable information, allowing dynamic groups to interact across time and space.

And by Bob Johansen of the Institute for the Future as:

> a generic term for specialized computer aids that are designed for the use of collaborative work groups. Typically, these groups are small, project-oriented teams that have important tasks and tight deadlines. Groupware can involve software, hardware, services and/or group process support (Johansen, 88, p. 1).

Groupware applications provide computer support for group work. At a general level, group work includes written and spoken communication, meetings, shared information, and coordinated work. Some group work occurs when people interact with each other at the same time (synchronously). Face-to-face meetings are an example of people working together at the same time and often in the same place. People can also work together at different times (asynchronously). When people leave messages in electronic mail, the communication occurs over a period of time.

Communication

Perhaps the most common type of group work is communication between individuals or groups. Groupware applications to support *synchronous* communication includes video conferencing, shared screens/applications, MediaSpaces, Chat. These application let people communicate with each other even though one person(s) is located at a different place than the other person(s), by using technology to link separate screens. For instance, when people communicate using video conferencing a camera pointed at one person's face can relay that image and any sounds to the screen of someone sitting at another computer. That other computer could be located down the hall, or in another city or country. In this way people who cannot be physically in the same place at the same time can still communicate with each other.

Applications to support *asynchronous* communication includes electronic mail, perhaps the most widely used groupware application Electronic mail lets people leave messages for one or more other people at any time to be read by that person any time and any place.

Other things can emerge from communication such as the development of virtual communities whose continued communication/articipation is then further supported by technology

Meetings

One of the most common work activities in most organizations are face-to-face meetings. While it might seem that this is one place where there are no barriers of time or place, there is still opportunity for applications to support work. Groupware applications to support meetings include software that captures and organizes ideas for brainstorming, summarization and reporting. This software is most often used in specially equipped rooms with computers embedded in desks. People attending one of these meetings can enter ideas, comments, votes into the computer at particular times during the meeting. The software might simply display the written ideas, let someone, usually a meeting facilitator group the ideas, or, the software might tally votes. All of which supports the work of the meeting in a way that goes beyond what the people in the meeting could do on their own.

Information Sharing

When people work together, there is often a need not only to communicate with others but to share information. Information is commonly shared by leaving an electronic document in a database where it can be read by anyone with access to that database. This is different than electronic mail where a document is sent to a particular person or sometimes a group of people. Groupware applications include discussion databases, bulletin boards and electronic news groups where documents and their responses are often grouped together under a single heading or keyword making it easier to follow the thread of a discussion.

Applications for publishing documents have sometimes also been called groupware. However, this labeling is somewhat controversial. This chapter takes the position, that an application can be considered groupware only when more than one person has the opportunity to create documents or other responses. Applications that let one person publish documents to a wide audience of readers are not good examples of groupware.

Coordinating Work Processes

In many operational settings, people coordinate their work over time making sure that decisions made by one person are acted upon before being passed on to the next person. Commonly referred to as workflow systems, these applications often embody features such as privacy control, sequencing, notification, and routing. Workflow systems may also include a decision support component as part of the overall process. Workflow systems are often thought of in the context of formal approval processes or large production settings. Systems designed to support coordination between people include project management, tracking systems, shared calendars. As defined here, workflow could also describe the kind of system used in medical settings where several people need to interact with the same data in handling administration of patient records. While not necessarily formally acknowledged as workflow or groupware, these kinds of applications meet the criteria of having multiple people interacting with the same application and hence the need on the part of the application developer to pay attention to issues of access, privacy and simultaneity of use.

Forrester (Brown et al, 97) gives this description of a groupware application built by a computer company to better manage projects:

> We are the professional services division of a major computer company. Time is our enemy. The longer a project goes, the worse things are. We're building a project management system that puts the project plan on the Internet for feedback, updates, notation, and comments from all team members, including customers. Before, one person managed the project with relatively static plans, but with this program, project management becomes much more dynamic and fluid.

Groupware Solutions

In addition to applications designed to solve particular problems, there are also efforts such as digital libraries, electronic commerce, knowledge management and distance learning, all of which include some degree of groupware within a larger context. It is often the case that the scale of these efforts requires a stronger "solution"-based approach in which technology is embedded within technical and professional services such as training and management consulting. These "solutions" are often distributed through consulting and other service organizations who are best suited to adapt the solution to the customers' needs and to handle the larger scale effort.

REQUIREMENTS

This chapter assumes a phased approach in the development of a new groupware application. In broad terms, the first phase, called *requirements,* concerns the translation of the users' needs into a functional specification from which a detailed design can be made. The second phase, called *design,* focuses on what gets built and how. The third phase, called *deployment,* attends to the details of introducing and rolling out the application to the customer or user.

In gathering requirements for the development of a new groupware application, the focus should be on understanding the invisible work and work practices (Nardi, 98; Suchman, 95) as well as the visible, and on understanding the physical and organizational context in which work is done. That work context is increasingly nontraditional—homes, airports, train stations, hotel rooms; anywhere where a laptop computer—or a fax or phone—can be carried and attached to a wide area network such as the Internet. If members of a group frequently work apart, both the technology and the culture of the group needs to accommodate a different style of interaction and coordination, as O'Hara-Devereaux and Johansen (94) emphasize:

> Global organizations cannot function without information technology But the technology itself is not the answer to the myriad problems of working across geographical and cultural boundaries. The ultimate answers to these problems remain in the realm of human and organizational relations. (p. 74)

It should be noted that the emphasis on groups, work, and work practices should not obscure the need for some level of task analysis within the application design. Workflow applications may have specific tasks embedded within them that are amenable to conventional task analysis methods. Similarly, applications originally designed for single users may be appropriated by the group. For example, spreadsheets, originally designed for individual use, were found to be part of an overall group collaboration (e.g. Nardi, 93), especially in sharing expertise and generating alternative scenarios. Groupware applications also need to be deliberate about the design of the user interface so that each person interacting with the application understands how to use the application as well as understanding the meaning of the work that is being supported by the technology. Designing for ease of use is as much a part of the design of groupware as it is for single user applications.

Work Practices

Before plunging into the methodological approaches toward collecting requirements, it is important to understand what is meant by work *practices* and how these might differ from what is thought of as work *processes* or routine work.

Most groups engage in some degree of routine work that appears predictable, is often thought to be tedious, may be time-consuming, and is often error-prone. Some organizations, such as insurance companies, make a business out of such routine work by, for instance, processing insurance claims. This would appear to be an area in which computer support could reduce the amount of uninteresting work that people do, reduce error rates, provide accurate, up-to-the-minute status information and save money. Because the work is routine, it should be relatively straightforward to write down the sequence of steps that make up these workflows.

However, it turns out that even in simple cases, the work is never simply "routine" (e.g. Muller et al, 95) even though the people doing it might describe it that way. When Suchman (83) studied accounting clerks, they described their jobs in a way that corresponded to the formal procedures. However, when Suchman observed these clerks, it was clear that they relied on informal, locally determined practices to get their work done. These practices were not written down anywhere nor where they part of any explicit training that the clerks received. Rather these practices were learned on the job.

If the application fails to support local work practices, people will either stop using the application or develop workarounds so that they can continue to work in a way that has evolved to be effective and efficient. People may also resist adoption if the application is perceived as compromising core skills and competencies. The two examples below, from a rich literature of work practice studies (e.g. Pycock & Bowers, 96; Star & Ruhleder, 94; Hughes et al, 92; Heath & Luff, 91), illuminate what can happen when systems are designed and delivered based on externally generated processes rather than the actual work practices.

Printing

Bowers et al (95), describe work done by a large printer with several offices around Britain. The organization used both traditional print technology, such as hot metal presses and offset lithography, as well as newer technologies, such as high-end photocopying and digital reprographics. From an outsider's point of view, printing might seem to be a well-known and somewhat routinized process that should be easily described in terms of the sequence of tasks and movement of materials. As such, the work of printers might be considered amenable to some level of automation through, for instance, a workflow application that would handle some of the administrative work by which jobs are categorized by type and assigned codes, customers, delivery dates and so forth. The application might further capture data about length of time and type pf materials, as well as control some of the more routine operations so that the operator had more time to handle other parts of the job.

From the point of view of the people doing the work, however, the operations and their sequence are anything but routinized. In fact, close inspection of the work reveals that the print operators evolved numerous small but significant modifications to the normative sequence of operations to ensure a smooth and efficient flow of work These practices included: prioritizing the work, anticipating the work, supporting each other's work, knowing the idiosyncrasies of the machines, identifying and allocating interruptible work. For instance, each print job, which often involved multiple processes and different people, was accompanied by a "docket" marking details of the job, such as materials required, cost code, and desired delivery date. This docket would get transferred with the print job from operator to operator. Operators were supposed to order these dockets in terms of delivery date and select the next print job with the earliest date. However, in practice the operators would ensure a smooth flow of work by sometimes juggling these jobs based on complexity of job, how long it would take and whether there were other time-consuming processes later on, as well as factoring in jobs remaining from the previous day. In fact, the digital reprographics technology used in the print industry meant that simply following date order would not utilize the equipment efficiently, requiring, for instance, frequent changes of paper type or size or long idle times following a short print job if the operator was busy with another part of the job.

The operators were very familiar with the competing demands on the equipment and other resources and had evolved practices which adapted the normative ordering to the situation enabling them to conduct their work smoothly and efficiently. Moreover, these variations on the explicit process were well understood by all the operators and the administrative staff and constituted, as it were, their shared and distributed cognition of the work.

This group had a contractual obligation to install and use a workflow application designed specifically for the print industry, although not necessarily for this particular group. The application was designed to automate many of the routine administrative tasks while also maintaining a record of time taken on a job, materials used, etc. Such information was useful in preparing reports and maintaining stock control. By contrast with the efficient smooth flow of work that had evolved in practice, the imposition of the workflow application disrupted the smooth flow of work by requiring that all print jobs be handled only in a normative fashion. For instance, the application required that no job could be started until an order form had been submitted. While this is the correct procedure, in practice, the operators would often jump the gun and begin the work in order to utilize the equipment effectively. The method of recording jobs and time failed to take into account that an operator could be doing multiple jobs at the same time. Using the system generally demanded extra time by everyone.

Because the operators had a contractual obligation to use the application, ignoring it and returning to the familiar method of working was not an option. Instead, they responded to the system by either developing work around, or, in extreme cases, reorganizing the work itself to adapt the work to the system. In either case, the overall work was done less efficiently

As Bowers et al (95) expressed,

> Workflow from within characterises the methods used on the shopfloor which emphasise the local and internal accomplishment of the ordering of work. Workers juggle their in-trays, jump the gun, glance across the shopfloor, listen to the sounds coming from machines, re-distribute the work in the here and now so that what to do next can be resolved. . . . In contrast, workflow from without seeks to order the work through methods other than those which the work itself provides.

When technology makes things worse, not better, there are various approaches to the redesign: a) features in the application should have more flexible mappings between processes and operators; b) redesign the application with greater emphasis on awareness and mutual monitoring; c) acknowledge real management practices and pressures to adopt technology and adapt some of the practices.

Trouble Ticketing System

A similar example of a well intentioned groupware application failing to embody the actual work practices comes from Sachs (95). She describes a system intended to improve the efficiency of assigning work to telephone company workers who are called in when there is a problem with a phone line. The system acts as a general dispatcher routing job tickets to the office nearest to the person to whom the work has been assigned. The job ticket gets recorded and is available for the worker to pick up. When one job is finished the worker picks up the next ticket in the stack. This dispatch function was one part of a larger system which also handled scheduling, work routing and record keeping.

While this method would seem to make sense and help increase the efficiency of getting information to the workers in a timely fashion, in practice it failed to acknowledge critically important informal. When a linesman picked up a ticket he/she would spend some time talking with the coworker. During the conversation, the linesman would pick up incidental information such as useful phone numbers, prior history as well as a more detailed explanation, of the actual problem. These valuable "invisible" transactions were getting lost by the application. Where some level of diagnosis is involved, it helps if the person fixing the problem can converse with the person who detected it (see also Ehrlich & Cash, 94, 98) What happened with the TTS system was that people reverted to their old habits and used the system after the fact to encode what happened rather than, as intended, to direct their work.

> While TTS was designed to make job performance more efficient, it has created the opposite effect: discouraging the training of new hands, breaking up the community of practice by eliminating troubleshooting conversations, and extending the time spent on a single job by segmenting coherent troubleshooting efforts into unconnected ticket-based tasks (p. 41).

Methodologies

Having emphasized the importance of studying groups at work, the question arises, what is the best method to use to study work practices and group behavior. The work is largely tacit, invisible and unarticulated, distributed across time and place and hence hard to observe, and involves multiple people.

This section outlines three methodologies commonly used to understand work practices and group behavior: Ethnography, Participatory Design, Action Research. Even a deep understanding of work practices does not automatically result in requirements for applications to support those practices. There is an additional and explicit step required to translate the results of empirical research into ideas for new applications. This step is explored in a discussion of "Applied

Ethnography" which describes how empirical results might be used to a) identify new product opportunities; b) evaluate existing technologies; c) provide input to design specifications.

It should be noted that groupware applications are frequently developed in direct consultation with the user. In cases where the application is built by a consulting group or an internal IS department, the close relationship with the customer often means that the customer's problem is known ahead of time. In these cases, the challenge for the application developers and designers is to elicit requirements from the customer that get at the root of what the problem *really* is, rather than what the customer says it is. Methods such as focus groups (e.g. Holtzblatt and Beyer, 93), brainstorming and scenarios (e.g. Carroll, 95) may be employed, along with an iterative development process using rapid prototyping techniques to elicit these requirements.

When a particular customer has not been identified ahead of time, as is the case with research projects and "shrink-wrapped" commercial applications that are not designed for a particular customer, then methods derived from research may be more appropriate. These methods can, of course, also be used in consulting and other settings. Three methods are described here which have been used by researchers and practitioners of CSCW and groupware.

Ethnography

Perhaps the most common methodology used in CSCW and groupware derives from ethnography as it was developed in anthropology, building on the recognition that work places are types of specialized cultures (see especially Blomberg, 93; Jordan, 96).

> As practiced by most ethnographers, developing an understanding of human behavior requires a period of field work where the ethnographer becomes immersed in the activities of the people studied. Typically, field work involves some combination of observation, informal interviewing, and participation in the ongoing events of the community. Through extensive contact with the people studied ethnographers develop a descriptive understanding of the observed behaviors. (Blomberg, p. 124).

By focusing on observation and the study of people at work in their normal work setting, ethnographic methods can uncover and articulate the tacit, invisible work practices.

> The ethnographic method through participant observation, pays attention to how actors construct their understandings with others through a set of shared practices (Bannon, 96, p. 14).

Asking people directly about their work won't reveal what is going on because even those who spend time reflecting on their own work—and they are in a minority—are too engaged in the work to be able to step back and explain the minutiae of what they do. However, some researchers have developed video-based observational and analysis methods in part to elicit post-hoc reflections from the users (e.g. Jordan and Henderson, 95).

Yet, as we saw in the examples from the print industry and the phone company, developers must pay attention to the minutiae of work practices in order to design and build an application that will be accepted, adopted and adapted by users to their work.

> The purpose of ethnography is to carry out the detailed observations of activities within their natural setting. The aim is to provide details of the routine practices through which work is accomplished, identifying the contingencies that can arise, how they are overcome and accommodated, how divisions of labor are actually achieved, how technology can hinder as well as support activities, and so on. (Blythin et al, p. 40)

Participatory Design

A complementary method is one in which the users and other stakeholders of the software are involved in the design from a very early stage and throughout the design and development process. Often referred to as Participatory Design (Schuler and Namioka, 93; special issue of CACM, 93), this approach emerged from work ·by labor unions and others in Scandinavia acting as advocates for workers and for workplace democracy (see Greenbaum and Kyng, 91 for review of work). A Participatory Design approach privileges the users in design decisions.

> The focus of participatory design (PD) is not only the improvement of the information system, but also the empowerment of workers so they can co-determine the development of the information system and of their workplace. (Clement and Van den Besselaar, 93, p. 29)

Action Research

There are a number of methods from social psychology and related social sciences which seek to understand groups and group behavior (see especially, McGrath, 84). Of these, Action Research, is distinguished for its emphasis not only on groups—especially teams—but for its desire to apply the results of the research to interventions that are designed to improve team performance (e.g. Argyris 78, 82).

A premise of Action Research is that organizations learn—and hence improve—by reflecting and reexamining the premises under which they are operating:

> The ultimate purpose of action science is to produce valid generalizations about how individuals and social systems, whether groups, intergroups, or organizations can (through their social agents) design and implement their

intentions in everyday life. The generalization should lead the users to understand reality and to construct and take action within it. (Argyris, 82, p. 469)

Action Research resembles ethnographic methods only in so far as both rely on observation and qualitative rather than quantitative descriptions. They diverge, in how the empirical results are used. Ethnographers prefer to take a neutral position on imposing any value judgment on what they observe; action researchers have it as a goal to change, for the better, the team's behavior and performance.

Historically, practitioners of Action Research have eschewed technology preferring direct personal interventions to achieve organizational change. However, there is no a priori reason why the understanding and insights from Action Research methods could not be applied to the design of technologies which reflect organizational practices. Indeed it is not uncommon for people engaged in adapting, advising on or building groupware applications to describe their work as Action Research. Action Research and Participatory Design differ in whether the application should support or challenge the current status quo. Participatory Design priviledges current users and current practices and seeks, by and large, to design applications to support and maintain those practices. Action Research enters into a study of a team with a belief in the value of bringing in interventions in order to assess patterns of activity.

Some potential points of synergy between these methodologies can be found in Snyder (98) who combines theories of organizational learning with ethnographic research to yield insights and potential new interventions to communities of practice. Orlikowski et al (95) discuss strategies for introducing technology into organizations.

Applied Ethnography

There has, unfortunately often been a disconnect between those who study work practices and those who develop groupware systems. On the one hand, research ethnographers have generally shied away from translating their empirical results into specific design recommendations lest their descriptive findings be misconstrued as being too prescriptive. On the other hand, developers have not delved into the details of the findings to extricate the implications for their particular application.

The gap between empirical results and application is due in part to the difficulty in translating from the specificity of the work environment being studied to the general and often unknown constraints and requirements of the application environment. Plowman et al (95) argue that the lack of translation from ethnographic studies to application design arises in part because the people who do the workplace research by and large do not also develop the applications. This, they argue, means that someone has to translate the results from the empirical to the technical domain—a problem compounded by the inherently descriptive nature of ethnographic findings.

Some, (e.g. Rogers & Bellotti 97) have taken the translation task to heart and arrived at various techniques such as creating a set of guiding questions, using video clips and photos, and highlighting breakdowns in the current process to convey the results of ethnographic studies to the development team. Others (e.g. Bentley et al, 92) acknowledge the philosophical differences between ethnographers and system developers. The ethnographers are able to influence the design by working closely with the development team and showing a willingness to be flexible.

When properly applied, insights and results of ethnographic studies can: a) identify new product opportunities, b) evaluate the use of existing technologies, and c) provide input to design specifications (Bly, 97). Examples of this "applied ethnography" can be found in the proceedings of conferences such as the biannual CSCW and European ECSCW conferences.

Identify New Product Opportunities

Ideas for new, innovative applications won't come exclusively from ethnographic studies (see Brown, 91 for extensive discussion on the source of ideas for innovative applications). However, ethnographic studies, because they focus so closely on the actual work being done, are well suited to generate insights into potential new software applications. When the result of an ethnographic study is used to identify new product opportunities, the group being studied is often different than the group targeted by the application. For instance:

1. In a study of a customer support organization, Ehrlich & Cash (94) observed that support analysts routinely shared references to previous cases and to printed or online material. Most of these references were shared as part of the normal dialog about a case. These and other observations of how people share recommendations led to the development of a collaborative filtering system for semi-automated personalized recommendations to online documents (Maltz & Ehrlich, 95). Using the application, a person who finds a document that he/she believes will be of interest to a colleague can forward an email link to the document along with a personal recommendation.

2. Nardi et al (98) report on the design of Apple Data Detectors, which are intelligent agents that analyze structured information and perform the appropriate operations. For instance, a user finding a meeting announcement could instruct the Detector to automatically add the announcement to a calendar. The development of this product emerged in part from observations made by Barreau & Nardi (95) who, in a study of how people organize their desktops, found that users often complained of not being able to act on structured information found in common documents. The development of the product was also informed by a detailed ethnographic study of reference librarians (Nardi and O'Day, 96) who acted as agents on behalf of users looking for information. The results of that study

translated into a design goal of having the software agent be unobtrusive and able to infer user needs.

Evaluation of Existing Technology

A variety of field methods can be used to evaluate how well existing applications are being incorporated into the work practice. If the application is not well suited to the setting, as we saw in the earlier example of the print shop, the failure will be readily apparent. Conversely, when technology has been successfully incorporated into the work practices, the application designer can consider extending the application or applying the application to other settings, but not without considering the consequences of transfer.

In a recent ethnographic study of nurse reviewers who worked on disability and workers compensation cases, Ehrlich & Cash (97) found that an administrative application with an embedded decision support component was well integrated into the nurse reviewers' work practice. They used the application to estimate the length of time that an injured worker should be away from work. The successful use by the nurse reviewers led to speculation that the application could be successfully deployed by physicians and physician assistants who were treating the patients. Although the physicians and nurse reviewers are linked in a type of extended enterprise, they nevertheless acted independently. The decisions made by the nurse reviewers were informed by their professional judgment and by their evolved work practices. Ehrlich and Cash argue that reallocating tasks to another part of an enterprise requires re-analysis of the overall context.

Lab rather than field methods can also be a useful way of evaluating applications, especially when the goal is to identify particular effects. For instance,

Mark et al (95) studied the effect of a hypermedia system, DOLPHIN, on the form, content and linkage amongst ideas created in a face-to-face meeting. Participants in the meeting were engaged in problem-solving exercises. Mark et al found that the people who used the application would group their ideas into networks rather than hierarchical structures and provide more elaboration for their ideas. Those people not using the application generated less elaborated ideas. Thus, the technology had a qualitative effect on problem-solving behavior of the people in the meeting.

Input to Design Specifications

New applications often follow a process in which an initial concept—generated from marketing requirements or from the vision of a small group of people—is modified and elaborated into a richer functional specification. Ethnography and other field methods, when used to study the intended user population, can provide input to these design requirements. The examples below provide a diverse set of cases where ethnography had a direct influence on design directions.

1. In a study of air traffic controllers Bentley et al (92) and Hughes et al (92) found that seemingly routine work was coordinated through a sophisticated use of flight "strips". These pieces of paper carry static information about expected and current flights along with instructions to the aircraft being controlled by the center. However, the controllers had evolved a practice of manually organizing the strips on a visible flight progress board. The physical ordering of the strips provided implicit, tacit cues to help the controllers dynamically coordinate and allocate their work. Based on these observations the ethnographers could direct the design of an automated system for controllers away from an automatic assignment of strips and toward maintaining elements of the manual method. The study highlights one of the critical roles of ethnography which is to articulate and demonstrate to developers that "manual intervention and manipulation of information may be essential implicit methods of communication and cooperation."

2. Blomberg and Suchman (93) offer brief descriptions of several studies done under the rubric of work-oriented design in which attention to the details of work is used to help guide the design of new applications. For instance, they studied the use of color and highlighting to distinguish the text annotations of different people on order forms as part of the coordination of activity across organizational boundaries. "By providing developers with visual representations of how the work of processing orders is supported by annotations, and by viewing videotapes of the people engaged in the work, we are exploring with developers and work practitioners how computationally active marks on paper might support this work."

3. In a different arena, Kukla et al (92) worked with Monsanto and Fisher Controls Inc. "to investigate and apply modern information technology" to Monsanto's integrated nylon facility in Pensacola Florida. The goal was to optimize the use of raw materials and energy through the facility. An ethnographic approach, comprising interviews, observations and detailed information on one sector of the plant was used to "construct models of events, conversations and processes within that area of the plant. These models were to be used as a basis for developing software tools for use within the plant." At the beginning, work was characterized as routine and repetitious. But based on ethnography, a number of less visible aspects of work were uncovered. These included: the ability of people working in the plant to do ad hoc juxtaposition of data screens (such as compare live process data to histograms or maintenance records); and, the importance of manual, not automated, collection of data (e.g. by sensors of machines) by people to get the richness of the environment (e.g. noises, smells, comments by people working near and with machines). These and other findings were translated into the design and development of specialized software for the process industry, linking realtime process data with desktop applications. The product, DEC@aGlance was marketed in 92.

4. Bly (88) and Tang (91) studied teams of people, working at distance, who need to work together to create drawings, designs and engage in general brainstorming. Ethnographic studies of people working together as well as people working apart led to many observations about such things as the use of gestures and marks to illustrate ideas, how control is passed from

one person to another and how drawing and talking are combined. These observations led to the development of a prototype (e.g. Minneman and Bly 91) for use in a research setting. That prototype subsequently influenced the development of products for synchronous shared collaboration from Sun Microsystems (e.g. ShowMe) and Xerox (e.g. LiveBoard).

5. Blythin et al (97) describe an ethnographic study at a bank of a service center which processed routine administrative details of accounts. Based on studying this group over time, the researchers uncovered limitations and problems imposed by the physical and organizational setting which impeded the effective arid smooth flow of work. For instance, there was a physical separation between some supervisors and their teams which reduced the opportunity for informal awareness of the progress of work. Based on these and other findings, the researchers made recommendations for changes in management practices and processes, to provide better review and oversight and changes in (physical and functional) office assignments. These changes helped increase the supervisor's awareness of the group's work.

6. Katzenberg and Piela (93) used work language analysis combined with ethnography to study and verify "work language" in the form of names that different groups of people use to label computer systems, such as "compile, instantiate, create, build." The results of the ethnographic study were a set of guidelines for the continued development of a technology used in engineering and economic forecasting to analyze desig alternatives.

Being able to use the results of ethnographic studies means that researchers and practitioners must be open to question their initial assumptions in the face of user data. For instance, in a field study of a distributed team, Bellotti & Bly (96) observed that members of the team were rarely at their desks but instead could be found in the hallways or working in labs. Although Bellotti & Bly went to the site to gather requirements for a computer-based application to support distance collaboration, it was apparent that such applications would not be used if it was only available from the computer. Instead, the researchers were able to recommend alternative solutions based on mobile computing devices.

Working Together

These examples also draw our attention to the most important part of the design process, which is the collaboration between the ethnographers and the application designers. The results of ethnographic studies do not stand on their own but must be interpreted by both the ethnographer and the application designer. Just handing a report of the ethnography to the designers is not sufficient. The two groups must work together as a team when the data are being collected and analyzed. It is also crucial that there be reciprocal appreciation and respect of others' viewpoints. The need to overcome different world views, cultures and perspectives is a recurring theme in these studies.

An especially good example of a successful collaboration comes from a study by Linde, Pea and others at IRL (Institute for Research on Learning) for the design of an interactive multimedia communication device (Goguen, 96;

Allen, 91; de Vet & Allen, 91). In a close examination of actual work sites, a multidisciplinary team of researchers representing application developers and ethnographers investigated the learning and work practices that emerged as new communication and computational technologies were integrated into ongoing activities. The design and development process was highly iterative. Outcomes of the studies would get translated into mock-ups which would be tested with users, modified and retested.

In one phase of this study, the ethnographers were videotaping a small group of graphic designers at work (Linde, 91). The graphic designers organized their ideas using folders. But what the ethnographers observed was that during group meetings the folders were placed on the table in a particular way. The placement—close to the owner or toward the middle—was a form of non verbal communication used to signal permission for others to talk. The ethnographers were able to point out this observation to the application designers who would not otherwise have been aware of the importance of the folders and their place-ment. Based on the ethnographers' analysis and their own observation, the appli-cation designers realized that the design of the software would need to include not just the ability to share folders but those folders would need to be marked as read only, private or open. This is a small example that was repeated many times in the course of the collaboration between the ethnographers and the application designers.

DESIGN

Part of the appeal of groupware lies in the promise of being able to eradi-cate barriers of time and place. Using technology, colleagues should be able to collaborate on projects whether their offices are next to each other or in separate countries, whether they work at the same at the same time or different times of the day. Applications that help bridge barriers of time and place include video conferencing, shared screens, media spaces, electronic mail, shared files/data-bases, shared authoring, and group calendaring systems. However, subtle social protocols influence the willingness of participants to communicate with others, the candor of their communication, the richness of information they are willing to impart, and the degree of their engagement in the process. If technology is going to mediate communication especially for people who lack opportunities for face-to-face meetings, it must support rather than ignore these protocols. Get-ting inside this notion of group *work* a few themes emerge:

- communication is generally ad hoc, **informal** and unplanned
- there is a need to be **aware** of others for communication and in coordinating work
- issues of sharing often hinge on subtle notions of **anonymity**

Informal Communication

Research on synchronous, informal communication emphasizes its importance and prevalence in most workplace settings (Kraut et al, 90; Whittaker et al, 94). These studies suggest that formal communication is used to coordinate routine tasks whereas brief, informal communication such as spontaneous hallway conversations can help to establish trust, promote social relationships and provide background information about the work environment. Moreover, these spontaneous conversations are more likely to occur amongst people who are physically located close to each other; as many as 91% of all conversations recorded in a particular study occurred among people on the same floor (Kraut et al, 90).

One type of video-based system, known as MediaSpaces, has been developed to provide visual access and opportunity for conversation to people who are not located in the same place (Fish et al, 90; Mantei et al, 91; Dourish & Bly, 92; Bly et al, 93; Fish et al, 93). These systems provide continuous visual access between sites through large video screens, often placed in public areas such as hallways or informal meeting places. However, despite their careful design, these systems cannot substitute for unmediated face-to-face conversations.

Awareness

Awareness, of the location and activity of other people, is a critical mechanism for regulating and coordinating our behavior with others. We use cues in the physical environment such as a colleagues' open door, the placement of a work-related document (Hughes et al, 92) or the level of participation in an on-line discussion to make decisions about whether to initiate a conversation, begin the next sequence of work or anticipate a meeting. The same social protocols still operate when the work is mediated through computer technology. Groupware applications designed to support coordinated work, need to find new ways to represent what were physical cues, so that even when online, people can be aware of the activity of their colleagues.

Awareness of others usually takes place when there is on-going or anticipated, direct, synchronous communication between people. But there is also a need to be aware of a general level of involvement and participation of a group over time. Both synchronous and asynchronous awareness are explored below.

Synchronous Awareness

The Montage desktop video conferencing system (e.g. Tang et al 94; Tang & Rua, 94) supports the kind of momentary, reciprocal glances that occur when one person peeks into another's office to see if that person can be interrupted. In Montage the person initiating the conversation selects the name of the person to be contacted, which causes the recipient to receive an auditory signal that a call is about to commence, followed by a gradual fade-in small video image of the caller. Either person can acknowledge the glance by pressing a button to open an audio channel followed by a 2-way audio-video connection. This mediated inter-ruption can get translated into a more extended interaction supported by the full desktop video conferencing system by pressing the Visit button. If the caller sees from the glance that the other person is not available, the caller can browse the person's calendar, send a short note or send an e-mail message. As in office-based social conventions, Montage users can set their system to display different levels of interruptibility. These range from "locked" which means no interruptions, to "out of the office" and "other," which lets the caller leave a message, to "do not disturb" which still lets the caller glance in to negotiate an interruption, to "available."

There are numerous other studies of awareness including those on aware-ness as a mechanism to support coordination (e.g. Dourish & Bly, 92) and social awareness (e.g. Tollmar et al, 96). Products to support awareness include "buddy lists" (e.g. Michalski, 97) which signal when someone from the list is on line and hence potentially available for an online "chat".

Asynchronous Awareness

We also develop awareness of the general work patterns of our colleagues based on cues left in public or semi-public places. If I want to schedule a meeting with my manager, I might ask his assistant about his availability or I might check online sources such as group calendars, e-mail or online discussions to pick up cues about upcoming meetings, trips and so forth. In the case of group calendars, availability of people's schedules is both a strength for scheduling meetings, and a source of noncompliance for those people who feel exposed (e.g. Grudin and Palen, 95).

Anonymity

In face-to-face communication, whether direct or mediated by computer technology, the contributors to the conversation are known and visible or audi-ble. However, when there is no visual component to the communication, as in the case of electronic mail and asynchronous communication in general, the technol-ogy can hide the identity of the sender or the recipient of the message. This fea-ture has interesting and often unexpected affects on the communication. For instance, people are much more likely to engage in antisocial behavior, such as "flaming" in electronic mail, where the sender's identity may be hidden by an obscure e-mail address and where the usual social protocols to discourage such behavior are absent. Sproull & Kiesler (93) argue that social norms are not well established in computer mediated communication in part because social cues, which are normally present in the physical environment are absent. For example, the physical appearance and dress code of someone we are about to meet clues us in to the level of formality expected.

On the other hand anonymity can have positive effects. Several researchers have observed that anonymity can reduce effects of power, status and attractiveness (e.g. Zuboff, 88; Turkle, 95) enabling people who might not have participated in social engagements due to lower status or power can do so when they are anonymous. Similarly, Sproull & Kiesler (93) report that junior members of an organization are much more likely to communicate with senior managers or executives using electronic mail than in a face-to-face meeting. As a classic cartoon in the New Yorker put it: "On the internet no-one knows you are a dog".

Similar effects of anonymity on people's social behavior in computer mediated settings have been observed with computer supported meetings (e.g. Nunamaker et al, 91). Computer supported meetings typically take place in rooms which have been specially configured with computers embedded into desks or tables (Mantei, 89). The software running on these computers support activities such as brainstorming by letting people freely enter their ideas. The software can then display the individual ideas or some aggregated version of those ideas on the individual terminals or on a large screen visible to all participants. These meetings are generally controlled by a trained facilitator who provides some degree of software support and training as well as handling the dynamics of the meeting itself.

The software portion of these systems can be easily configured to control when ideas get shared amongst the group and whether the ideas are marked with the name of the person who contributed them. Nunamaker and his colleagues have observed that in these kinds of settings, anonymity reduces the pressure to conform and reduces apprehension related to evaluation by one's peers. This, in turn, may encourage a more open, honest and freewheeling discussion. On the other hand, anonymity can increase free riding. If nobody's comments are attributed, there is no way of checking that everyone in the meeting is actually participating.

Application of Design Themes

Themes such as informal communication, awareness and anonymity rightly belong to the category we have described as *group work* in that these features are not readily apparent from a task focused view. Yet, the presence of these features in an application can materially affect *how* the application is used and *whether it* is used. The inclusion of these and other themes into the design of the application depends in part on the type of application. Using the division of applications laid out in the introduction, those that focus primarily on communication such as e-mail, video conferencing, media spaces and chat, may be designed around themes of informal communication and awareness. Applications designed to support meetings, on the other hand, need to pay attention to whether issues such as anonymity are needed in the design. In the case of applications that support information sharing, one of the main barriers to acceptance is the readiness of the organization in which the application is to be deployed. This topic will be addressed in the section on deployment and adoption of applications.

Customization

We may think of groupware applications such as those that support communication, meetings and information sharing as general purpose applications ready to be used by a wide range of users for a variety of purposes. This is true of individual "productivity applications" which are designed to be used out of the box with little or no customization. However, groupware applications are rarely ready to use "out of the box" but require some degree of customization. How much work is required depends in part on the type of application, whether it was developed for a particular customer and how the application is architected.

It is fair to say that while customization is not exclusive to groupware applications, in practice there is sufficient differences in work, culture and context from one customer to another that most groupware applications require some degree of customization. This is an important topic which has received little public discussion and hence is only covered briefly here and based largely on personal observations.

1. Content-based customization. This is a case where the application is merely a shell and doesn't really become useful until someone begins putting content in. Prime examples are discussion databases, news groups, e-mail etc. Examples from outside the realm of communication software include applications for distance learning where the instructor needs to add course material before the software is useful for the students. In all these examples, the customization is done by one or more end-users by supplying content. No specialized technical skill is required.

2. Setting external parameters. This is also end-user customization but is more intentional. Examples include TeamRoom (see description in section on case study) which is an application to support distributed team work through shared documents, etc. TeamRoom defines attributes such as document category and communication type whose values get set by the team. In this way, the team gets to customize the application to suit the way they intend to use it. A research group, for instance, may want to define categories for documents to represent different research projects while a product group may want to define documents in terms of product families. This is still end-user customization but this time it may involve an outside facilitator to guide the thinking of the group around the goals of the project, the group norms and expectations for the level of participation.

3. Setting internal parameters. This is where some degree of system administration or macro level programming comes in. For instance, in an internally developed system to support online reviewing of papers submitted to conferences, the level of customization from one conference to the next ranged from inputting a new set of reviewer names to rewriting parts of the interface to recoding the rules that govern who sees which papers and

at what stage of the reviewing process. Many of these changes reflected differences in the reviewing process and from one conference to another.

4. Totally customized solutions. Applications that match the particulars of an organization's work practices, processes and culture often require that a customized application be built either by someone within the organization or by engaging external consultants.

Some issues of customization are addressed by the available development tools and environments which may provide the pieces out of which the customization is done. One example is the use of templates out of which new solutions can be fashioned. In an article on the use of templates for building business applications, Hofman and Rockart (94) provide an example of a template developed by John Wiley, the publisher, to support internal business processes that allowed for customization by each business unit. This approach allowed them to share best practices, both applications as well as knowledge, aggregate data centrally, and "tailor the business process and system to local needs."

DEPLOYMENT AND ADOPTION OF THE APPLICATION

In addition to the challenges of building a good groupware application, there are significant challenges facing a developer who is trying to get the application adopted by an organization. Unlike single user applications which can often be purchased by an individual, groupware applications are, by definition, for groups of people. Hence, enough copies of the application need to be purchased and installed at about the same time for the application to be available to more than one person. Moreover, groupware applications often require a sophisticated technology infrastructure which may in turn require skilled technical staff for the system's administration. In addition to the financial cost of purchasing, installing and maintaining a groupware application, there are also organizational implications of deploying the application. These implications vary with the type of application. For instance, deploying a video conferencing system may require very little preparatory work within the group, assuming the application itself has been well designed and the infrastructure is in place. On the other hand, an application that depends on a high level of information sharing presumes an organization in which information sharing is already well established and rewarded. This section explores a few of the organizational and cultural barriers to successful deployment and adoption.

Organizational Preparedness

Technology can be introduced into organizations through a mandate imposed by senior management. This method has the advantage of ensuring continued financial and technical support through deployment and in helping disperse the technology through the organization to reach a critical mass of users (e.g. Markus and Connolly, 90). However, this method of adoption can leave end-users feeling that a decision was forced on them. For instance, Orlikowski (92) reports on the adoption by a large consulting company of groupware to support information sharing. Not only was the culture of the group one in which information sharing was not rewarded but the technology was introduced to the group without sufficient explanation or training, thus giving these end-users no real understanding or motivation for wanting to expend the extra effort to learn and use the technology. As a result, the technology was poorly adopted and only gained in acceptance over time and with considerable investment and push on the part of senior management, who retained strong conviction in the benefits of the technology.

Although an interesting side note is that the same technology was adopted more or less spontaneously by other groups in the same company where there had been no mandate by management.

Technology can also be introduced into an organization by someone within the organization seeing the potential of the technology. This method has the advantage of getting end-users involved early on. But it has the disadvantage of needing to get buy-in from senior management for continued support.

In a recent study, Grudin and Palen (95) examined the adoption of shared calendar applications in two large organizations They observed widely dispersed use of the application despite no clear mandate from senior management. They argued that

> The features . . . may attract a critical mass of users, after which technology-abetted social pressure by peers and others extends use (p. 277).

In at least one organization, the adoption was slow when the application was first introduced. Over time, what changed was a more consistent infrastructure that gave wider access to the application, improved functionality and ease of use and peer pressure. Once a critical mass of people begin using the application, there is strong peer pressure to bring others in line. Calendaring is an example of a groupware application that requires near universal adoption to be successful. Once someone uses the tool to schedule meetings with some colleagues, they will want to be able to use the tool to schedule meetings with other colleagues, and will apply pressure to those colleagues not yet using the application to begin to do so.

Incentives and Motivation

In a work setting, most people are persuaded to adopt a new technology by arguments that make it clear how that technology will improve their work. Such arguments may focus on the technology as enabling the person to do something that was previously very difficult or cumbersome to do. For instance, online discussions make it easier to share information with a number of colleagues simultaneously than it is to attend face-to-face meetings. This is especially true if colleagues are not all located in the same place or if it is hard to schedule a time when everyone can attend a meeting. New technology in general, especially groupware, will get adopted more easily if it fills a need rather than simply replaces an existing well understood, working process. For instance, video conferencing technologies got a major push during a recent oil crisis when it got harder and 'more expensive for people to travel. The need to communicate and collaborate with colleagues didn't go away, but reaching those people got harder.

Convincing end-users of the benefit of any new technology is challenging—especially so for groupware applications for which there may be no visible examples of use. For example, several years ago, Wang introduced a multimedia communication system which bundled together image capture, voice recording, electronic mail, pen annotation and high-resolution graphics (Francik, Rudman, Cooper and Levine, 91). The system was intended to be used to annotate and route documents through an organization However, when the system was introduced into client sites it failed, in part because neither end-users nor management were ready to risk new unproven methods of working despite being told of the benefits of the system.

Critical Mass

Groupware applications are principally designed to benefit and reward the group rather than the individual. But most people are not altruistic. They want some personal benefit from using the application. Getting enough early adopters to use a new system is especially challenging for applications which rely on a large number of people to be effective. Many collaborative filtering systems recommend selections (e.g. of video, music, Net News) based on a statistical aggregate of individual ratings (e.g. Hill et al, 95; Shardanand and Maes, 95; Resnick et al, 94; Goldberg et al, 92). When the database has been seeded with enough ratings, users can query it to learn which selections are recommended. But where is the incentive for the early adopters to add their ratings? Resnick et al (94) argue that some people are altruistic, while others may be motivated by external rewards such as money to be an early adopter. Reaching a critical mass also proved to be the key factor in a study which systematically compared adoption rates of two similar video telephone systems (Kraut et al, 94).

The potential asymmetry between those who contribute and those who get the benefit has been underscored by Grudin (90). He points out that group-enabled systems such as group calendars and shared project management applications, the beneficiary is often the person scheduling meetings or managing the project, rather than the people contributing the information about their schedules or time.

CASE STUDY: TEAMROOM

To illustrate many of the points in this chapter, this section presents a brief case study of the design, development and deployment of a particular groupware application. The application, called TeamRoom, was initially developed for use by internal task forces at Lotus (Cole, 96) to support discussion and coordination. It was then made available to outside customers as part of a consulting engagement, and is now sold as one of the family of Lotus/Domino applications.

Teams

Before building an application to support discussion and coordinating by members of a team, it is important to understand how teams work. At a very general level, teams of people work collectively and collaboratively to:

- make decisions
- share information
- coordinate actions

Teams will be high performing, to the degree that they engage in these activities in a deliberate and persuasive manner to produce something of value to the organization such as a tangible product, a process or a service. There is a large amount written about teams and team performance, which will not be addressed here. As Katzenbach and Smith (93) expressed recently:

> Real teams are deeply committed to their purpose, goals, and approach. High-performance team members are also very committed to one another. (p. 9)

However, there is increased pressure on teams to deliver more value in less time with few resources. Moreover, teams are often "ad hoc" (e.g. Finholt et al, 90); formed "just in time" to solve a particular problem and then disbanded. And, members of the team may be dispersed throughout the organization as well as separately located due to travel or residence. Team members often come from different cultures in terms of professional training, background, tenure with the company, or nationality.

Technology cannot eliminate these barriers on time and place. However, in conjunction with judicious training, technology can help make the team, once formed, more effective and efficient. People working together need: shared context, shared language and shared objectives. They also need a "workplace" in which the majority of work will get done and where shared discussions as well as private conversations can take place. It is not the place of technology to help create the team, but rather, to support the team once it has formed. (An important and debatable question is whether the application is only as effective as the team or whether a well designed application can overcome limitations in the group dynamics.)

Requirements

TeamRoom was developed in response to a request from one of the senior vice-presidents at Lotus for an application that could support the work of internal task forces. Although all the people on a task force worked for the same company, they came from different parts of the organization and also traveled frequently. This meant that face-to-face meetings occurred only occasionally, necessitating the need to have a place to post documents, have discussions, plan meetings and share ideas. The development team was composed of people from development, design, internal information systems, Human Resources/Organizational Development, as well as the main customer and a representative group of users. Detailed user requirements and functional specifications were arrived at through discussions within this team and by exposing early prototypes to the users.

Design Features

Instead of having team members go to one application to retrieve shared documents, another for group e-mail and a third application for coordination, TeamRoom provides a single "place" for these activities by integrating all three functions in a single application.

TeamRoom builds on the Lotus Notes model of a threaded discussion database where messages can be posted and read by anyone who has access to the database. Documents can be entered to start a topic or as a response to an existing topic. In TeamRoom documents are keyed by communication type as well as by category. Common communication types include: discussion, action request, meeting announcement and reference document, and are used to signal the intent and type of communication. For instance, a discussion document signals that the author wants other people to respond, whereas a reference document may require little or no further discussion. These different document types reinforce and simplify communication. Documents can be viewed by topic, communication type and author as well as by date, so that a user can quickly see which documents have been added recently.

One of the distinguishing characteristics of TeamRoom is its embodiment in the software, of the communication norms of a group. The translation of norms to features is handled through the *process* of having the group define its goals, mission, categories and communication types, and the *mechanism* of having these instantiated in the software by completing information about the team on a "Mission Page". This information includes: categories, communication types, participants and events. Once entered, this information becomes available to the team in the form of keyword lists, which a user selects when composing a document, and visible categories, which users see when viewing documents. Documents can also be automatically archived, which reduces the problem of information overload. The Mission Page is the place where the team records details of their processes and norms; such things as when to post documents to particular people rather than have the document default to be seen by everyone; and the meaning and intent of the different communication types and categories. Teams who have spent time filling out the mission page have found the information there to be invaluable as a source of group memory and an excellent vehicle for new members to get oriented. TeamRoom, especially the Mission Page, becomes a *work* space for *group* memory.

Relation to Design Themes

An earlier section of this chapter, identified three main group work themes: informal communication, awareness of others, and anonymity. Many of these themes can be seen in TeamRoom.

TeamRoom differs from both e-mail and discussion databases in that it is a place where all work—not just discussions—gets posted. Making each person's work visible to the rest of the team contributes to an awareness of other people's level of contribution and, the current status of their work. By looking across the different categories, it is easy to see which documents are still in process and which are completed. An index view also shows the number of documents per authors or communication type. An author view shows documents by type, which provides a view into whether a person is mostly commenting on other people's work or contributing their own.

TeamRoom supports informal communication by supporting loosely structured discussions. But it doesn't really support ad hoc informal communication since it is designed for teams that are not co-located (see under Lessons Learned at the end of this section).

TeamRoom does not let people participate anonymously, but it does support private, as well as public discussions, and personal as well as shared workspaces. When a document is posted in TeamRoom, the author is required to specify only the communication type and the document type. The author can optionally mark a document as private to be seen only by people who the author lists in the To: field. The To: field is also used to designate people who need to pay particular attention to a document, even if that document can be seen by the rest of the team. TeamRoom constructs personal workspaces for each member of the team, based on documents for which the person is listed in the To: or cc: field or documents that the member has authored. In this way, TeamRoom supports personalized as well as shared views.

Relation to Deployment

When it comes time to deploy the groupware application, organizational preparedness, incentive and motivation, and critical mass are some of the factors which influence the ultimate adoption of the application.

TeamRoom addresses issues of organizational preparedness by accompanying the introduction of the technology with a facilitated meeting during which the members of the team go through the exercise of deciding on their mission, communication and work styles as a team. In this way, all members of the team can participate in setting the goals. The mission and the technology can be seen as being in service of the core work of the team.

One of the ways in which TeamRoom addresses the problem of critical mass—that is making sure that there is enough activity to promote more activity—is by having a facilitator as one of the designated roles in the TeamRoom. This person, who is also a team member, monitors traffic in the TeamRoom and encourages participation if the discussion and postings are getting reduced.

Lessons Learned

TeamRoom has been deployed in a wide range of companies and settings. Based on informal feedback there are several themes that emerge that are critical success factors: 1) strong leadership; 2) a distributed team who need TR to overcome barriers of time and place and for whom face-to-face meetings are often scheduled, rather than ad hoc; 3) a well defined team. Below are examples where these factors were absent.

Strong leadership. Strong leadership is needed, especially early on, to get people to submit postings. For some teams, collaboration and sharing was a new way of working and if the team leader didn't demonstrate and lead by example, the team generally did not take to it. This was lacking at one company where it seems the team leader set the tone/behaviour for the group. In a few cases, the workers still took to the tool, seeing its value and needing the communication that it provided.

Geographically distributed team. TeamRoom is a good alternative to voice or video conferences for teams whose members are far apart. Especially for complex projects, TeamRoom becomes an information repository to facilitate analysis. However, there can sometimes be delays in replicating TR to the different sites for these distributed teams. On the other hand, when team members were co-located, TR was just another thing to have to worry about and it wasn't used.

Well-defined team. A well-defined team has a common mission and a shared context, language and objectives. Team membership is limited and definable. Well-defined teams are not about longevity; a team could be just forming or be together for a long time. One team that used TeamRoom that wasn't really a team, but just a department, failed in their use because there was no real team mission, team norms, or team deliverables. In this case, TR served as a place to communicate meeting agendas and some marketing announcements. TR is a mirror on the team. If the team is chaotic, then so it will appear in TR and people's experience with the tool will be frustrating. A well-organized team takes a lot of work.

SUMMARY

This chapter takes the position that where single user applications are about *tasks;* groupware applications are about *work*. Tasks are generally explicit, observable, concrete. Work is generally tacit, invisible and amorphous. Work is about people, habits and culture.

Generating a product concept and design specifications for a groupware application demands a methodology that can capture these invisible work practices. The methods, derived from social and management sciences, that are most commonly used in groupware or CSCW (Computer Supported Cooperative Work) are often descriptive rather than prescriptive, leaving it up to the design team to fashion requirements, functions and architecture themselves. A multidisciplinary team is essential for the design and development of groupware applications.

Getting inside the notion of group "work," a few themes emerge—communication is generally ad hoc, informal and unplanned. There is a need to be aware of others for communication and in coordinating work. Issues of sharing hinge on subtle notions of anonymity, which play out in different ways.

Finally, deploying a groupware application is perhaps the most difficult step in process. First, the application itself will need some level of customization to fit in each customer's work context. Second, groupware applications are rarely ready to go "out of the box"·but need to be accompanied by some measure of training in organizational behavior to ensure a fit between the tool and organizational processes. Factors such as motivation, incentives and critical mass are potential show-stoppers when it comes to rolling out the application to the entire group.

The notion of work and translating it into an application is put into perspective by describing a Lotus Notes application that was designed to provide a "place" on line to support discussion and coordination of work amongst members of a distributed team.

Groupware and CSCW are still in their infancy compared with more established practices in the development of single user applications. Yet, technological developments such as the world wide web seem to lead to more need for groupware applications where people spread across the globe, across the country, or just across the street can use technology to coordinate their work and communication with each other.

Acknowledgments

There are many people who have contributed to this chapter through discussions, especially those enlightening me on various methodological issues. For their time and patience in talking with me about methodology, I extend my appreciation to: Barbara Katzenberg, Charlotte Linde, Bonnie Nardi, Roy Pea, and Lee Sproull. My colleagues at Lotus Institute, especially Barbara Kivowitz,

Linda Carotenuto, and Nicol Rupolo helped me understand many of the nuances and tacit features of TeamRoom. I extend a special thanks to my colleague Debra Cash with whom I have had many engaging and heated conversations and who took the time to read and comment on several drafts of this paper. Thanks are due to Paul Cole, Sal Mazzotta and especially an anonymous reviewer who read and commented on an earlier version of this paper.

REFERENCES

Allen, C. (1993). The reciprocal evolution of technology, work practice and basic research. In D. Schuler and A. Namioka (Eds.) *Participatory Design: Perspectives on System Design*, Hillsdale, NJ: Lawrence Erlbaum Associates.

Argyris, C. (1982). *Reasoning, learning and action: Individual and organizational*. San Francisco: Jossey-Bass.

Argyris, C. and Schon, D. (1978) *Organizational learning*. Boston: Addison-Wesley.

Bannon, L (1996). Ethnography and design. In D. Shapiro, M. Tauber and R. Traunmuller (Eds.) *The Design of Computer Supported Cooperative Work and Groupware Systems*. Amsterdam: Elsevier Science, 13–16.

Barreau, D. and Nardi, B. (1995). Finding and reminding: File organization from the desktop. *SIGCHI Bulletin*, July 1995.

Bellotti, V. and Bly, S. (1996). Walking away from the desktop computer: Distributed collaboration and mobility in a product design team. In *Proceedings of the Conference on Computer Supported Work; CSCW '96 (Boston, MA)*, 209–219. New York: ACM Press.

Bentley, R., Hughes, J. A., Randall, D., Rodden, T., Sawyer, P., Shapiro, D., and Sommerville, I. (1992). Ethnographically-informed systems designs for air traffic control. In *Proceedings of the Conference on Computer Supported Work; CSCW '92 (Toronto, Canada)*, 123–129. New York: ACM Press, pp. 123–129.

Blomberg, J., Giacomi, J., Mosher, A. and Swenton-Wall, P. (1993). Ethnographic field methods and their relation to design. In D. Schuler and A. Namioka (Eds.) *Participatory Design: Perspectives on System Design*, Hillsdale, NJ: Lawrence Erlbaum Associates, 123–154.

Blomberg, J., McLaughlin, D. and Suchman, L. (1993). Work-oriented design at Xerox. *CACM*, vol. 36, no. 4, June, p. 91.

Bly, S. (1988). A use of drawing surfaces in different collaborative settings. In *Proceedings of the Confrrence on Computer Supported Work; CSCW '88*, New York: ACM Press, pp. 250–256.

Bly, S. (1997). Field work: Is it product work? *Interactions, January–February*, 25–30.

Bly, S., Harrison, S., and Irwin, S. (1993). Media spaces: Bringing people together in a video, audio and computing environment. *CACM*, 36(1), January, 28–45.

Blythin, S., Rouncefield, M. and Hughes, J. A. (1997). Ethnography in the commercial world. *Interactions, May–June*, 38–47.

Bowers, J., Button, G. and Sharrock, W. (1995). Workflow from within and without: Technology and cooperative work on the print industry shopfloor. In H. Marmolin, Y.

Sundblad, K. Schmidt (1995) (Eds.) *Proceedings of the Fourth European Conference on Computer-Supported Cooperative Work; ECSCW '95 (Stockholm, Sweden)*, Dordrecht: Kluwer Academic, 51–66.

Brown, J. S. (1991). Research that reinvents the corporation. *Harvard Business Review* Jan/Feb, 330.

Brown, E. G., Dolberg, S. Boehm, E. W. and Massey, C. (1997). Beyond groupware. *Forrester Report: Software Strategies*, vol. 8, no. 4, July 1997.

Cameron, B., DePalma, D. A., O'Herron, R. and Smith, N. (1995). Where does groupware fit? *The Forrester Report: Software Strategies*, vol. 6, no. 3 June 1995.

Carroll, J. M. (1995). Introduction: The scenario perspective on system development. In J. M. Carroll (Ed.) (1995). *Scenario-Based Design: Envisioning work and technology in system development*. New York: John Wiley and Sons.

Cole, P. and Johnson, E. C. (1996). Lotus development: TeamRoom—A collaborative workspace for cross-functional teams. In P. Lloyd and R. Whitehead (Eds.) *Transforming organizations through groupware: Lotus Notes in action*. New York: Springer-Verlag, Berlin.

Clement, A. and Van den Besselaar, P. (1993). A retrospective look at PD projects. *CACM*, vol. 36, no. 4, 29–37.

de Vet, J. and Allen, C. (1991). Picasso system design rationale. IRL Technical Report, November 1991.

Dourish, P and Bly, S. (1992). Portholes: Supporting awareness in a distributed work group. In *Proceedings of Human Factors in Computing Systems, CHI '92 (Monterey, CA)*, 541–547. New York: ACM Press.

Ehrlich, K. and Cash, D. (1994). Turning information into knowledge: Information finding as a collaborative activity. In *Proceedings of the Conference on Digital Libraries* (College Station, TX), 119–125.

Ehrlich, K. and Cash, D. (1997). Communication and coordination in workers compensation cases: Implications for extended enterprises. Internal Report.

Ehrlich, K. and Cash, D. (1998). The invisible world of intermediaries: A cautionary tale. *Computer Supported Cooperative Work: An International Journal*. In Press.

Finholt, T., Sproull, L. and Kiesler, S. (1990). Communication and performance in ad hoc task groups. In J. Galegher, R. E. Kraut, C. Egido (Eds.) *Intellectual Teamwork: Social and Technological Foundations of Cooperative Work*. Hillsdale, NJ: Lawrence Erlbaum. 291–326.

Fish, R., Kraut, R. E. and Chalfonte, B. (1990). The videowindow system in informal communication. In *Proceedings of the Conference on Computer Supported Work CSCW '90 (Los Angeles, CA)*, 1–12. New York: ACM Press.

Fish, R., Kraut, R. E., Root, R. and Rice, R. (1993). Video as a technology for informal communication. *CACM*, 36(1), January, 48–61.

Francik, B., Rudman, S. E., Cooper, D., Levine, S. (1991). Putting innovation to work: Adoption strategies for multimedia communication systems. *CACM* vol. 34, (12), Dec., 53–63.

Goguen, J. and Linde, C. (1996). Techniques for Requirements Elicitation. In R. Thayer and M. Dorman (Eds.) *Software Requirements Engineering, Second Edition.* IEEE Computer Society.

Goldberg, D., Oki, B., Nichols, D., Terry, D. B. (1992). Using Collaborative Filtering to Weave an Information Tapestry. *CACM* Vol. 35; (12), *December,* 61–70.

Greenbaum, J. and Kyng, M. (Eds.). (1991). Design at work: Cooperative design of computer systems. Hillsdale, NJ: Erlbaum.

Grudin, J. (1990). Groupware and cooperative work: Problems and prospects. In B. Laurel (Ed.) *The Art of Human Computer Interface Design.* Addison-Wesley.

Grudin, J. and Palen, L. (1995). "Why groupware succeeds: Discretion or mandate?" In *Proceedings of the Fourth European Conference on Computer-Supported Cooperative Work, ECSCW '95 (Stockholm, Sweden),* 263–278. Dordrecht: Kluwer Academic.

Heath, C. and Luff, P. (1991). Collaborative activity and technological design: Task coordination in London Underground control rooms. In *Proceedings of the Second European Conference on Computer Supported Cooperative Work; ECSCW '91* (Amsterdam), Kluwer Academic Publishers.

Hill, W., Stead, L., Rosenstein, M. and Furnas, G. (1995). Recommending and evaluating choices in a virtual community of use. In *Proceedings Human Factors in Computing Systems, CHI '95, (Denver; CO),* Addison-Wesley, pp. 194–201.

Hofman, J. D. and Rockart, J. F. (1994). Application templates: Faster, better and cheaper systems. *Sloan Management Review*/Fall 1994. pp. 49–60

Holtzblatt, K. and Beyer, H. (1993). Making customer-centered design work for teams. *Communications of the ACM* vol. 36, no. 10, 93–103.

Hughes, J. A., Randall, D. and Shapiro, D. (1992). Faltering from ethnography to design. In *Proceedings of the Conference on Computer Supported Cooperative Work; CSCW '92 (Toronto, Canada),* New York: ACM Press, 115–122.

Johansen, R. (1988). *Groupware: Computer support for business teams.* New York: The Free Press.

Jordan, B. (1996). Ethnographic workplace studies and CSCW. In D. Shapiro, M. Tauber and R. Traunmuller (Eds.) *The Design of Computer Supported Cooperative Work and Groupware Systems.* Amsterdam: Elsevier Science, 17–42.

Jordan, B. and Henderson, A. (1995). Interaction analysis: Foundations and practice. *J Learn. Sci* 4, 1, 39–102.

Katzenbach, J. R. and Smith, D. K. (1993). The Wisdom of Teams: Creating the High-Performance Organization. Boston, Mass: Harvard Business School Press.

Katzenberg, B. and Piela, P. (1993). Work language analysis and the naming problem. *CACM,* vol. 36, no. 4, pp. 86–92.

Kraut, R. E., Fish, R. S., Rot, R. W. and Chalfonte, B. L. (1990). Informal communication in organizations: Form, function and technology. Reprinted in R. M. Baecker (Ed.) *Readings in Groupware and Computer-Supported Cooperative Work.* Morgan Kaufmann. 287–314.

Kraut, R. E., Cool, C., Rice, R. E., and Fish, R. S. (1994). Life and death of new technology: Task, utility and social influences on the use of a communication medium. In R. Furuta and C. Neuwirtn (Eds.) *Proceedings of Conference on Computer*

Supported Cooperative Work, CSCW '94 (Chapel Hill, North Carolina), 13–21. New York: ACM Press.

Kukla, C., Clemens, E.A., Morse, R.S. and Cash, D. (1992). Designing Effective Systems: A Tool Approach. In Paul Adler and Terry Winograd, (Eds.) *Usability: Turning Technologies into Tools*, New York: Oxford University Press. 41–65.

Linde, C. (1991). What's Next?: The Social and Technological Management of Meetings. *Pragmatics* Vol. 1, no. 3.

Maltz, D. and Ehrlich, K. (1995). Pointing the Way: Active Collaborative Filtering. In *Proceedings of Human Factors in Computing Systems, CHI '95 (Denver, CO)*, New York: ACM Press, 202–209.

Mantei, M. (1939). Observations of executives using a computerized supported meeting environment. Reprinted in R.M. Baecker (Ed.) *Readings in Groupware and Computer-Supported Cooperative Work*. Morgan Kaufmann. 695–708.

Mantei, M. M., Baecker, R. M., Sellen, A. J., Buxton, W. A. S., Milligan, T. and Wellman, B. (1991). Experiences in the use of a media space. In *Proceedings of Human Factors in Computing Systems, CHI '91 (New Orleans, LA)*, 203–208. New York: ACM Press.

Mark, G., Haake, J. M., and Streitz, N. A. (1995). The use of hypermedia in group problem solving: An evaluation of the DOLPHIN electronic meeting room environment. In *Proceedings of the Fourth European Conference on Computer-Supported Cooperative Work, ECSCW '95 (Stockholm, Sweden)*, 197–213. Dordrecht: Kiuwer Academic.

Markus, M. L. and Connolly, T. (1990). "Why CSCW applications fail: Problems in the adoption of interdependent work tools." In *Proceedings of Conference on Computer Supported Cooperative Work, CSCW '90*, 371–330. New York: ACM.

McGrath, J. E. (1984). *Groups: Interaction and Performance*. Prentice-Hall.

Michalski, J. (1997). Conversation on the Net. *Release 1.0 newsletter*, January.

Minneman, S. L. and Bly, S. (1991). Managing a trois: A study of multi-user drawing tool in distributed design work. In *Proceedings of Human Factors in Computing Systems, CHI '91 (New Orleans, LA)*, 217–224. New York: ACM Press.

Muller, M. J., Carr, R., Ashworth, C., Diekmann, B., Wharton, C., Eickstaedt, C. and Clonts, J. (1995). Telephone operators as knowledge workers: Consultants who meet customer needs. In *Proceedings of Human Factors in Computing Systems, CHI '95 (Denver, CO)*, 130–137. New York: ACM Press.

Nardi, B. (1993). *A small matter of programming: Perspectives on End User Computing*. Cambridge, MA: MIT Press.

Nardi, B. (1998). A web on the wind: The structure of invisible work. Special issue of *CSCW*, 1998.

Nardi, B. and O'Day, V. (1996). Intelligent agents: What we learned at the library. *Libri* 46, 3, 59–88 (September 1996).

Nardi, B., Miller, J. R. and Wright, D. J. (1998). Collaborative, programmable intelligent agents. CACM, in press.

Nunamaker, J. F., Dennis, A. R., Valacich, J. S., Vogel, D. R. and George, J. F. (1991). Electronic Meeting Systems to Support Group Work. In *CACM*, 34(7), July, 40–61.

O'Hara-Devereaux, M. and Johansen, R. (1994). *Global Work: Bridging distance, culture and time*. San Francisco: Jossey-Bass.

Orlikowski, W. J. (1992). Learning from Notes: Organizational issues in groupware implementation. In J. Turner & R. Kraut (Eds.) *Proceedings of the Conference on Computer Supported Cooperative Work, CSCW '92 (Toronto, Canada)*, New York: ACM Press, 362–369.

Orlikowski, W. J. and Hofinan, J. D. (1997). An improvisational model of change management: The case of groupware technologies. *Sloan Management Review*/Winter, vol. 38, no. 2.

Plowman, L., Rogers, Y. and Ramage, M. (1995). What are workplace studies for? In H. Marmolin, Y. Sundblad, K. Schmidt (1995) (Eds.) *Proceedings of the Fourth European Conference on Computer-Supported Cooperative Work, ECSCW '95 (Stockholm, Sweden)*, 309–324. Dordrecht: Kluwer Academic.

Pycock, J. and Bowers, J. (1996). Getting others to get it right: An ethnography of design work in the fashion industry. In *Proceedings of Conference on Computer Supported Cooperative Work, CSCW '96 (Boston, MA)*, New York: ACM Press. 219–228.

Resnick, P., Iacovou, N., Suchak, M., Bergstrom, P., and Riedl, J. (1994). GroupLens: An open architecture for collaborative filtering of Netnews. In *Proceedings of Conference on Computer Supported Cooperative Work, CSCW '94 (Chapel Hill, North Carolina)*, 175–186. New York: ACM Press.

Rogers, Y. and Bellotti, V. (1997). Grounding blue-sky research: How can ethnography help? *Interactions,* May–June, 58–63.

Sachs, P. (1995). Transforming work: Collaboration, learning and design. *CACM,* vol. 38, no. 9 (Sept.), 36–44.

Schuler, D. and Namioka, A. (1993). *Participatory Design: Principles and Practices,* Hillsdale, NJ: Lawrence Erlbaum.

Shardanand, U. and Maes, P. (1995). Social Information Filtering: Algorithms for Automating "Word of Mouth". In *Proceedings Human Factors in Computing Systems, CHI95 (Denver CO)*, New York: ACM Press, pp. 210–217.

Snyder, W. M. (1998). Communities of practice: Combining organizational learning and strategy insights to create a bridge to the 21st century. *Organization Development and Change.*

Sproull, L. and Kiesler, S. (1993). *Connections: New ways of working in the networked organization.* Cambridge, MA: MIT Press.

Star, S. L. and Ruhleder, K. (1994). Steps towards an ecology of infrastructure: Complex problems in design and access for large-scale collaborative systems. In *Proceedings of Conference on Computer Supported Cooperative Work; CSCW '94 (Chapel Hill North Carolina)*, 253–264. New York: ACM Press.

Suchman, L. (1983). Office procedures as practical action: models of work and system design. *ACM Transactions on Office Information Systems,* Vol. 1, No. 4, pp. 320–328.

Suchman, L. (1995). Making work visible. *CACM;* vol. 38, no. 9 (Sept), 56–64.

Tang, J. C. (1991). Findings from observational studies of collaborative work. *International Journal of Man-Machine Studies* 34,2 143–160.

Tang, J. C., Isaacs, E. A. and Rua, M. (1994). Supporting Distributed Groups with a Montage of Lightweight Interactions. In R. Furuta and C. Neuwirth (Eds) *Proceedings of Conference on Computer Supported Cooperative Work (Chapel Hill North Carolina)*, New York: ACM Press, 23–34.

Tang, J. C. & Rua, M. (1994). Montage: Providing teleproximity for distributed groups. In *Proceedings of Human Factors in Computing Systems, CHI '94 (Boston, MA)*, New York: ACM Press, 37–43.

Tollmar, K., Sandor, O. and Schomer, A. (1996). Supporting social awareness@work: Design and experience. In *Proceedings of Conference on Computer Supported Cooperative Work, CSCW '96 (Boston, MA)*, 298–307. New York: ACM Press.

Turkle, S. (1995). Life on the screen: Identity in the age of the internet. New York: Simon and Schuster.

Whittaker, S., Frohlich, D. and Daly-Jones, O. (1994). Informal workplace communication: What is it like and how might we support it? In *Proceedings of Human Factors in Computing Systems, CHI '94 (Boston, MA)*, New York: ACM Press, 131–137.

Zuboff, S. (1988). *In the Age of the Smart Machine*. New York: Basic Books.

Chapter 8

Social Context and Interaction in Ongoing Computer-Supported Management Groups[1]

Michael H. Zack

Northeastern University, 214 Hayden Hall, Boston, MA 02115, (617) 373-4734, mzack@nuhub.neu.edu

James L. McKenney

Harvard Business School, Baker Library West, Boston, MA 02163

Abstract—Electronic communication has been proposed as a key technology enabling new organization forms and structures, work designs, and task processes. This view assumes that organization structure and form can be defined in terms of communication linkages among organizational units. Communication is a social process, however. Therefore, to better understand the potential for these technologies to enable fundamental organizational change, we must understand how existing structures and social contexts influence patterns of organizational communication.

This research examined the use of electronic messaging by ongoing management groups performing a cooperative task. By means of an in-depth multimethod field study of the editorial group of two daily newspapers, it examined the influence of the groups' social context on the patterns of face-to-face and computer-mediated communication. The results show

---

[1] Reprinted with permission.

that different groups using the same functional structure and performing the same task with identical communication technologies, but operating within different social contexts appropriated the communication technology differently and in a way that was consistent with and reinforcing to their existing social structure. This finding suggests that researchers must, at the very least, explicitly take into account social context when studying the effects of introducing technologies which may alter group interaction. Additionally, researchers should look to social context as an important explanatory construct to be explicitly varied and investigated with regard to effects and outcomes of these technologies. The findings also suggest that managers must diagnose and explicitly manage the social context of the workplace prior to implementing technologies whose intent is to restructure the patterns of interaction and information exchange in support of new organizational forms.

INTRODUCTION

Electronic communication has been proposed as a key technology enabling new organization forms and structures, work designs, and task processes (Benjamin and Scott Morton 1988, Finholt and Sproull 1990, Hammer 1990, Hammer and Mangurian 1987, Konsynski 1993, Malone, Yates and Benjamin 1987, Sproull and Kiesler 1991, Venkatraman 1994). These new forms include, for example, cross-functional and interorganizational teams, executive teams, networked organizations, and virtual corporations (Baker 1991, Davidow and Malone 1992, Drucker 1988, Jarillo 1988, Miles and Snow 1986, Nadler et al 1992, Thorelli 1986). An underlying assumption is that organization structure and form can be defined in terms of communication linkages among a set of organizational units, be they individuals, departments or entire organizations. By enabling new forms or channels of communication, we enable new forms of organization. To better understand the potential for these technologies to enable fundamental organizational change, however, we must understand how existing structures and social contexts influence the adoption and adaptation of these communication technologies.

Research on computer-mediated communication (CMC) suggests that CMC can increase the range, capacity, and speed of organizational communication (cf., reviews by Culnan and Markus 1987, Kerr and Hiltz 1982, Rice and Bair 1984, Sproull and Kiesler 1991, Steinfield 1986, Williams 1977). This research, however, has assumed almost exclusively a technological imperative for predicting and explaining the organizational impacts of CMC (Markus and Robey 1988). That is, the research is framed by the belief that given an appropriate design, once the technology is implemented communication processes and patterns will ultimately change in desired and intended ways. This assumption is so embedded that the potential influence of organizational culture or social context on patterns of CMC is rarely examined. Whether or not CMC will improve or even influence organizational performance, however, may depend on the particular social circumstances under which these electronic media are employed (Fulk and Boyd 1991, Kling and Saachi 1982, Poole and DeSanctis 1990, Rice et al 1990, Schmitz and Fulk 1991).

Markus and Robey (1988) framed the issue in terms of researchers' assumptions about causal agency. They proposed three perspectives: the technological imperative, the organizational imperative, and the emergent imperative. The technological imperative suggests that change to an organization is caused by implementing some external technology, and traditionally this has been the view adopted by implementation and impacts studies. The organizational imperative assumes that people act rationally and purposefully to accomplish their objectives. Regarding CMC, this view suggests that users' task-based information processing needs influence their usage patterns leading to rational and objective media choices (Fulk and Boyd 1991) as suggested by information processing theories such as Daft and Lengel (1986). The emergent imperative, in contrast, views change as emerging from the interaction of individuals, events, technology, and the organization. This view is consistent with "web models" (Kling and Saachi 1982) and other socially-oriented approaches to studying CMC.

Only a small amount of CMC research has observed ongoing work groups in natural settings where history, routine, norms, social relationships, and deeply shared interpretive and behavioral context may play a large role in determining interaction patterns and choice of communication mode[2] (e.g., McKenney, Zack, and Doherty 1992, Reder and Schwab 1989, 1990, Trevino, Lengel and Daft 1987, Zack 1991). However, communication is inherently a social act (Goffman 1967, Pearce 1976, Sigman 1987). Therefore any study of technologies having the potential to directly influence or alter communication patterns and processes must examine social interactions within their natural context (Hackman 1985, Schegloff 1987), and attempts to understand this phenomenon using social theories of communication should benefit from studying complete, intact social groups.

The research being reported here examined the use of electronic messaging (EM) and face-to-face communication (FTF) in two *ongoing* management groups performing a cooperative task. Ongoing means that the groups had an established culture and set of routines; and held an expectation of continuing to work together for the foreseeable future. By means of an in-depth multi-method field study of the managing editorial groups of two daily newspapers, we explored the relationship between social context and the interaction patterns within each group, and how these interaction patterns related to communication and performance effectiveness. We observed a variance across groups in social context, with one group displaying cooperation among its members and the other, conflict.

---

[2] *Communication mode* refers to the combination of communication channel and medium. In this study, we focused on the modes electronic messaging (electronic channel, textual medium) and face-to-face (interpersonal channel, multi-sensual medium).

This enabled us to compare observations across groups, strengthening the validity of our findings.

Information- and knowledge-based service organizations have been cited as potential models for new organizational forms. Therefore, understanding the use of communication technologies in this context may provide useful insight into how other types of organizations might gainfully employ these technologies to support new forms of organization.

SOCIAL INFLUENCES ON THE USE OF COMMUNICATION TECHNOLOGY

Individuals are embedded within social systems which influence their behaviors (Radcliffe-Brown 1940). Communication is socially and culturally situated and thus similarly influenced (Pearce 1976). However, an important theme emerging from reviews of the CMC and computer-supported cooperative work literature is that this research, with few exceptions (e.g., Fulk 1993, Rice and Aydin 1991, Rice et al 1990, Schmitz and Fulk 1991), has not adequately taken into account social influences on technology use and outcomes (Fulk and Boyd 1991, Fulk et al 1987, Kling and Saachi 1982, Kling 1991). The bulk of the CMC and group decision support system literature, reflecting the technological imperative, generally assumes that the impact, effect, or use of CMC will be influenced by the task, technology, or functional structure of the group or organization (Fulk and Boyd 1991, Kraemer and King 1988, Pinsoneault and Kraemer 1989, Sproull and Kiesler 1991, Steinfield 1986).

To redress the focus of past research, we adopted a social network perspective (Tichy et al 1979). This perspective proposes that a group's *social structure* is influenced by its *social context*. Social structure, a fundamental construct of social network research, refers to patterning in social relations (Freeman 1989, White, Boorman and Brieger 1976, Radcliffe-Brown 1940). Communication researchers specifically consider social structure to represent *patterns of interaction* (i.e., who communicates with whom about what) (Jablin et al 1987). These interaction patterns tend to persist over time, and therefore can be thought of as representing structure (Hammer 1979, Schwartz and Jacobson 1977). We defined interaction as the communication between or among group members. Social structure, then, was the overall pattern of interaction within the group.

Social structure is influenced by what we are calling *social context* (Pettigrew 1985) and is similar to what Barley (1990) referred to as social institution. Social context includes the culture, distribution of power, and the social norms, habits, practices, expectations and preferences held by a group regarding its present and past interaction.

Structuration theory similarly accounts for the influence of social context on social structure (Giddens 1979, Ranson, Hinnings and Greenwood 1980). The theory is entirely compatible with the social network perspective (Banks and Riley 1993) and, while not yet extensively tested within the CMC field, appears to offer promise in enhancing our understanding of CMC (e.g., Yates and Orlikowski 1992). Structuration theory adds a dynamic perspective by focusing on how social context constrains interaction and how interaction, in turn defines and redefines social context.[3] Social context is considered both the medium and outcome of interaction, therefore understanding interaction at any point in time requires taking the current and historical social context into account. Interaction patterns emerge, then, from the particular balance between the propensity to derive psychological comfort from existing routine and the propensity for social innovation. Kling (1991), in this spirit, proposed that

> The ways in which CSCW systems restructure social relationships at work, if at all, depend on preexisting patterns of authority, obligation, and coopera- tion, and an organization's openness to change.

Poole et al (1985), building on Giddens (1979), developed Adaptive Struc- turation Theory (AST) for examining group decision making. AST has been applied to the study of computer-supported group decision making processes (Gopal, Bostrom and Chin 1993, Poole and DeSanctis 1990, Poole, Holmes and DeSanctis 1991), and Fulk and Boyd (1991) proposed that AST might similarly offer a useful foundation for CMC research. Use of the technology is conceptual- ized as a socially constructed process in which the technology is "appropriated" by a group to reinforce, adapt or reproduce a set of interaction rules and prac- tices (Poole and DeSanctis 1990, Poole, Holmes and DeSanctis 1991). Appropri- ation of the technology thus becomes part of the interaction behaviors comprising social structure and, like the interaction the technology supports, influences and is influenced by the existing social context. Therefore, the particu- lar way group members choose to use the technology mediates the impact of the technology on the group.

> No matter what features are designed into a system, users mediate technolog- ical effects, adapting systems to their needs, resisting them, or refusing to use them at all (Poole and DeSanctis 1990, p. 177).

Rather than looking at how groups appropriate the particular structuring mechanisms embedded in group decision support systems, we examined elec- tronic messaging (EM)—a form of communication technology which

---

[3] While network theory is concerned with the relationship between social context and social structure, structuration theory focuses primarily on what we are calling social con- text, yet which they call social structure. Social structure in structuration theory refers to the rules and resources used in interaction, similar to our definition of social context, which result in "regularized relations of interdependence" (Poole et al. 1985), similar to our definition of social structure. To avoid confusion, we will continue to use the terms social context and social structure consistent with the network perspective described earlier.

technologically imposes no boundaries or constraints on patterns of interaction.[4] Poole and DeSanctis (1990) posited that lower-structure communication technologies such as EM provided a greater opportunity for variation in how a group would appropriate the technology. In our case, appropriation would reflect the influence of social context on the patterns of EM and FTF interaction and how those constraints on interaction are socially rather than technologically imposed.

Appropriation manifests at the individual and dyadic level in how EM users employ messaging system features such as distribution (one-to-one or one-to many) and timing (synchronous or asynchronous exchange). Appropriation also applies to choosing from among several communication modes, for example, based on the extent to which richness or interactivity is required (Zack 1993). However, consistent with the social network perspective, the influence of social context on the appropriation of EM at the *network* level is best reflected in how group members employ the technology to support interaction among themselves, and that is the approach we adopted.

While structuration theory makes provisions for both stability and change in social context, stability appears to dominate real work groups, and this is the aspect we emphasized. Groups and individuals require some degree of organizational routine, order, and steady-state to function properly. Stability is sought as a means to avoid anxiety and to make sense of the world (Schein 1985). Our approach assumed that organizations move through periods of relative stability punctuated by discontinuous interventions (e.g., implementing a new technology) which ultimately settle again into a state of stability. These interventions initiate rounds of social and technological adaptation (Leonard-Barton 1988), ultimately leading to some particular appropriation of the technology within some (possibly new) social context. The outcome may range from the technology imposing a new social context (e.g., Barley 1990), to the social context constraining the appropriation of the technology (e.g., Orlikowski 1992).

Communication technologies, unlike traditional production technologies, are explicitly used to support interaction and have been designed and implemented explicitly to enable changes to interaction patterns. These technologies therefore are especially subject to the constraints of the existing social context, and accounting for these constraints is important when studying CMC. Evidence of the constraints of social context on computer-supported interaction is beginning to accumulate (e.g., Norland 1992, Orlikowski 1992, Stone 1992), and calls are being made for social and cultural explanations of the institutional inertia inhibiting the intended effectiveness of CMC (Perrin 1991).

Poole et al (1985) similarly posited that the key to understanding group behavior lay in recognizing the "essential continuity of institutions and

---

[4] While electronic messaging can place technological constraints on interaction at the micro level, for example by regulating the ability to send graphics as well as text, it typically poses no constraints at the network level of interaction. That is, typically there are no design constraints preventing anyone from connecting to anyone else having access to the mail system.

negotiated activity." (p. 96). Actors must cope with historical precedent in the form of preexisting social context as these existing contexts constrain later ones and perpetuate themselves through their influence on patterns of interaction (Poole et al 1985). Guetzkow and Simon (1955) found that imposed interaction patterns could restrict a group's ability to properly communicate to organize and to create an efficient strategy for performing its task. Thus to the extent that existing social context constrains the interaction comprising social structure, it might in turn constrain a group from creating a more "ideal" structure under new circumstances (new task, technology, etc.), even if *that new technology itself* could enable new forms of communication.

Poole et al (1985) further posited that features of the actors' knowledge condition their actions. Tacit knowledge of how to participate in group interactions results in actors overlooking interaction choices not part of their accustomed or "legitimate" repertoire. Even talking about this knowledge is constrained by it and may limit the group only to justifying its existing practices. Therefore, we would expect that media choices and communication links would be constrained by each individual's existing socially constructed "how to's" for interaction with other individuals in the group.

Structuration theory suggests, then, that absent some significant discontinuity or external intervention, CMC technology will be appropriated in a manner that reinforces the existing social context (Kraft 1987, Poole and DeSanctis 1990). The theory further suggests that there is no particular reason, per se, to expect that the use of EM would expand the communication network or alter the patterns of communication (as assumed by the technological and organizational imperatives) beyond those which the group might consider appropriate to the existing social context of the group.[5] Studying this proposition requires comparing groups whose task, functional structure and technology (per the technological imperative) and perceptions and preferences regarding the technology (per the organizational imperative) are similar, yet whose social context is not.

This discussion leads to the following proposition:

PROPOSITION 1: *Groups with similar tasks, functional structures, electronic messaging systems and perceptions, preferences and practices regarding those messaging systems, but different social contexts will exhibit different patterns of FTF and EM interaction and those patterns of interaction will reflect each group's particular social context.*

Social information processing theory (SIP) has offered one approach to accounting for social influences on media use (Fulk 1993, Fulk et al. 1987). SIP

---

[5] This is not to say that EM could not expand or alter communication networks, but rather those new patterns of communication would be expected to be considered socially legitimate by the group. We would not expect those who for socially-based reasons *chose* not communicate with one another before the availability of CMC to want to communicate merely because a new communication mode was now available. Our thesis is that existing research has not sufficiently examined the influences of social context on CMC.

theory posits that significant others in an individual's social field (e.g., superiors or coworkers) influence that individual's attitudes and behaviors. Fulk and Boyd (1991), based on SIP, proposed that work groups are important sources of social support and regular interaction. They reasoned, therefore, if social influences were more important than task influences on media use, one should observe similar patterns of individual media use within work groups regardless of the task's communication characteristics, and different patterns of media use across groups. While we are proposing a different conception of social influence at the group level of analysis, the outcome should be similar, namely group-level patterns of EM and FTF interaction that are more similar within than across groups.

Theories that do not account for social context should predict organizations having the same task, functional structure, and CMC technology, yet possibly different social contexts, to exhibit equivalent patterns of interaction. Our framework, in contrast, suggests that groups with different social contexts would exhibit different patterns of interaction and that the patterned use of communication modes (in this case FTF or EM) would be expected to vary more across than within different social fields (Fulk and Boyd 1991, Fulk et al 1987), leading to the following proposition:

PROPOSITION 2: *For groups with similar tasks, functional structures, electronic messaging systems and perceptions, preferences and practices regarding those messaging systems, but different social contexts, patterns of FTF and EM interaction will be more similar within groups than patterns of FTF or EM interaction across groups.*

Bavelas and associates initiated a stream of experimental research studying the impact of patterns of interaction (represented as communication networks) on task-group processes and outcomes (e.g., Bavelas 1950, Bonacich 1987, Freeman et al 1980, Guetzkow and Simon 1955, Leavitt 1951). Much of the network-task research (e.g., Shaw 1959) focused on examining the effects of communication networks which restrict communication opportunities, versus those which were more open and connected (Guetzkow 1965). The central finding of this research was that the communication requirements of a particular task determined the most appropriate communication network for the group, thus group performance depended on the fit of its interaction patterns to the task (Glanzer and Glaser 1961). For example, groups whose members had access to required information were able to solve group problems more quickly (Gilchrist, Shaw and Walker 1954), and structures which got information to where needed when needed improved group performance (Roby and Lanzetta 1956). An extensive review by Guetzkow (1965, p. 568) concluded that "there is clear demonstration of effects in the laboratory of the interrelations between communications and task upon performance."

Tushman (1977), studying seven departments of the R&D laboratory of a large corporation, provided real-world evidence that for high-performing units, communication structure, measured as the degree of centralization of the communication network, was contingent on the communication requirements of the units' work. The less routine and more complex the work, the more decentralized (connected) the communication network. David et al (1989) found similar results with banks. O'Reilly and Roberts (1977) extended this line of research by examining the mediating influence of communication effectiveness (measured as communication accuracy and communication opennesss) on the relationship between patterns of interaction and group effectiveness, using data from three real-world task groups. They found that communication effectiveness was significantly related to group interaction patterns measured as vertical and horizontal differentiation, connectedness, degree of two-way interaction, and average rank (hierarchical level) of group members. The communication effectiveness measures were, in turn, significantly related to group effectiveness. Additional field evidence for the relationship between appropriate interaction patterns and effective group performance has been provided by the group decision support system research (e.g., Jarvenpaa, Rao and Huber 1988, Poole, Holmes and DeSanctis 1991) and by Hackman's (1990) research on effective work groups.

We adopted group communication effectiveness as a means to link interaction patterns to outcome effectiveness (Farace, Taylor and Stewart 1978). Given our expectation that groups performing the same task yet having different social contexts will exhibit different patterns of interaction, we would further expect those groups, therefore, to exhibit different levels of communication and performance effectiveness, leading to the following proposition:

PROPOSITION 3: *Groups with similar tasks, functional structures, electronic messaging systems and perceptions, preferences and practices regarding those messaging systems, but different interaction patterns will exhibit different levels of communication and performance effectiveness.*

In summary, we adopted a research framework proposing that the social context of the group influences its social structure, as reflected in its patterns of FTF and EM interaction, leading to more or less effective communication and group performance. Our goal was to show that the use of EM and FTF as described by the groups' interaction patterns was consistent with each group's social context and, in turn, influenced the groups' communication and performance effectiveness.

Blalock (1969) proposed that theoretical models or frameworks be restated in more operational terms using measurable "indicators." This operational theory links the concepts of the literature to the actual research performed. Figure 8.1 illustrates our theoretical research framework comprising the constructs social context, social structure, communication effectiveness and performance effectiveness, and a related framework comprising a less abstract set of constructs linking the theoretical framework to the indicators actually measured. The following describes our operationalization of the theoretical constructs.

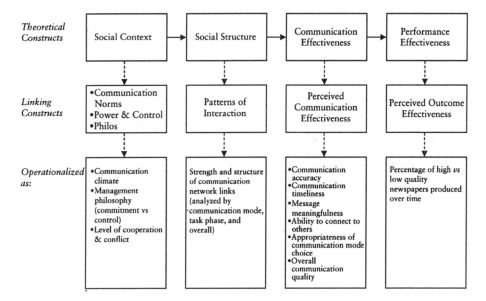

FIGURE 8.1 Research Framework

Social Context

Structuration theory proposes three modalities by which social context influences interaction: interpretive schemes for meaningful communication, facilities for the application of power, and normative schemes for the legitimization of action (Poole et al 1985). Therefore, interaction cannot be studied without also considering the norms and power structures within which it is situated and how those influences have shaped the structuring of interaction itself (Riley 1983). The social network research, while similarly focusing on how power and control are related to interaction (Burt 1980, Freeman 1989), has also focused on "philos" (Krackhardt 1992), the level of comraderie, respect, attraction, and general spirit of cooperation among social actors. We therefore included communication norms, power and control, and philos as important descriptors of social context.

We used *communication climate* to represent the normative influences on communication. The extent to which information is shared is positively related to the strength of perceived norms supportive of information sharing (Dewhirst 1971), and perceived communication openness is strongly related to group structure (David, Pearce, and Randolph 1989, O'Reilly and Roberts 1977). Communication climate, therefore, potentially is an important contextual influence on interaction. We used *management philosophy* to capture the influence of power and control on group interaction. Poole and DeSanctis (1990) proposed that the appropriation process depended on the behavior of the group leader, particularly the leader's willingness to act in a manner consistent with the intended spirit of the technology. Walton and Hackman (1986) proposed a framework for group leadership which could be usefully applied here. They defined two leadership strategies: control and commitment. Under a control strategy management's positional authority is emphasized in controlling the group via top-down communication and coordination. Under a commitment strategy, on the other hand, authority is derived more from competence and experience than position; coordination and control are handled through shared philosophy and goals and lateral group interaction. We used *philos* to denote the level of cooperation or conflict within each group.·

Social Structure

For purposes of measurement and representation, the interaction patterns comprising social structure can be viewed as a *network* of relations (Radcliffe-Brown 1940). Social networks, a formalism representing relations as nodes and links, have been used extensively as a means for measuring or describing social structure (cf., Bevalas 1950, Burt 1980, Freeman 1989, Leavitt 1951, Tichy et al 1979). Nodes represent the social units or actors (e.g., individuals, organizations, etc.) and the links, their relations. In our case, the social units comprising the network were the individual group members. The links were represented by group members' exchange of information. The network, then, represented the overall interaction patterns of the group. The particular network measures taken were the strength (in terms of overall interaction frequency), and the structure (in terms of the degree of hierarchy and lateral connectivity in each group).

Communication Effectiveness

We measured the perceived quality of communication in terms of accuracy, timeliness, meaningfulness, coordination, ability to communicate with whomever needed, frequency of miscommunication, appropriateness of communication mode choices, and overall quality of communication (Driver and Streufert 1969, O'Reilly and Roberts 1977, Steiner 1972).

Outcome Effectiveness

We proposed that effective communication was needed for producing a high quality newspaper. Because of complex and emergent interactions among people, events, the task, and the technology, effective groups might occasionally perform ineffectively, and ineffective groups might occasionally perform effectively, but over time we would expect effectively communicating groups to produce a high quality newspaper more frequently than ineffective groups. That suggested measuring outcome effectiveness as a frequency over time of newspaper quality at different levels. We measured via the questionnaire the overall effectiveness of the group in terms of the perceived quality of the news section. The editors indicated the percent of time they felt the news section was unacceptable, average, good, and great. We then summed the two lower and the two upper categories into a "good" and "bad" percentage for clarity and ease of cross-organizational comparison.

RESEARCH SITES

We studied the managing editorial group of two daily morning newspapers, one medium-sized (referred to as *The Statewide Times*) and the other large (referred to as *The Regional News*).[6] Both organizations were part of the same parent corporation. Each group comprised the senior and middle-level newsroom managers responsible for producing the "hard" news section of the newspaper. *The Statewide Time's* editorial group had fifteen members, and *The Regional New's* fourteen.

The task process was essentially the same at both organizations. Stories were written, transmitted, edited, and the process managed using EM together with FTF. While managers had written memo and telephone readily available, memos played little or no observed role in the day-to-day production of either paper and were reserved solely for infrequent, formal administrative communication among the top executives. Telephone accounted for just over 5% of the observed communication events at *Statewide* and less than 4% at *Regional*, almost all for communicating to others outside the newsroom and where no alternative existed (e.g., to a reporter on location or a call received from an outside party). Therefore the study focused on EM and FTF. Both groups conducted daily scheduled meetings to coordinate efforts and to negotiate newspaper content and story placement, and communicated on an ad hoc basis throughout the publishing cycle using both EM and FTF.

Researchers often make favorable assumptions about social context which may have little grounding in reality. According to Kling (1991),

> Many CSCW [computer-supported coopertive work] articles impede our understanding of the likely use and impact of CSCW since they rely on concepts with strong positive connotations such as "cooperation," "collaboration," and images of convivial possibilities to characterize workplace relationships, while understating the levels of conflict, control, and coercion—also common in professional workplaces.

The prediction of social theories that communication technology usage patterns will differ across groups, implies the need to compare groups differing only along their social dimensions. However, evidence supporting this proposition is scarce because of the difficulty in identifying truly equivalent groups with similar

---

[6] Pseudonyms.

tasks and media options but different norms or social context (Fulk et al 1987). We measured contextual similarities to validate comparability of groups, and we believe that our groups met the criteria for examining this proposition. All of the contextual factors except social context were essentially the same for both groups, enabling us to explicitly examine the relationship of social context to interaction patterns and performance effectiveness.

Not only did our study explicitly address social context, but purposely compared cooperative and conflicted groups to introduce a meaningful variance in that construct. Senior management of the parent corporation nominated for our study the two (of approximately 30) of their newspaper organizations which, in their opinion, exhibited the greatest contrast in social context. We were introduced to the executive editors and then negotiated our entry directly with each newspaper.

As our goal was to better understand whether or not social context constrained the ultimate appropriation of the technology at a point where relative stability had been reestablished, we purposely sought out stable groups who had been using the technology for a period long enough for it to have become embedded in the routines of the group. We made our observations of each group during periods in which no major discontinuities or interventions occurred. Our repeated observations of the daily work cycle provided further evidence of stability during our data collection period.

METHODS

We employed the case-study approach whereby the primary unit of analysis was the site itself (Yin 1984). That is, data, both quantitative and qualitative, were collected and analyzed on a site-by-site basis, rather than pooled, to identify convergent findings about that site. Data can be categorized as qualitative or quantitative and as objective or subjective (relative to the respondent), defining four categories. Our data collection methods addressed each category, enhancing the reliability of our findings (Jick 1979).

We used questionnaires (quantitative/subjective) to measure group members' perceptions of all constructs including perceived strength of communication ties by communication mode and phase of the task process. We computed within-group mean responses from the questionnaire data and ran two-tailed t-tests to establish significance or lack thereof in the differences between group means. We were comparing small populations, therefore achieving significant differences could be difficult. Given our small population and our use of multiple methods to validate our findings, we felt comfortable considering differences of $p \leq 0.10$ to be "significant" and $p \leq 0.125$ to be "moderately significant".

The questionnaire was administered to the entire, although small, population of each group. To enhance its validity, it was developed and tested at a pilot site prior to its administration in the research sites reported on in this study. The

TABLE 8.1 Reliability Coefficients for Multiple-Item Measures

Table	Construct	α
7	Communication climate	0.75
10	Communication Effectiveness	
	Phase 1	0.89
	Phase 2	0.77
	Phase 3	0.88
	cross-shift phase 1	0.91
	cross-shift phase 2	0.88
	cross-shift phase 3	0.86

questionnaire was developed after interviewing 23 senior editors at the pilot site, was reviewed by several editors and then revised by us prior to being administered to the pilot group. After administration to the pilot group, we conducted follow-up interviews to identify ambiguous or problematic questions. We then analyzed the data to identify anomalous results. We conducted additional follow-up interviews to understand the anomalies, and further revised the questionnaire. Threats to reliability and validity were reduced by items (e.g., tenure) being of a low level of abstraction and close to the phenomenon (Kerlinger 1986), focused on behavior (e.g., communication mode usage), focused on measuring cross-site differences rather than absolute amounts, and exhibiting small within-site variances among group members. We used multi-item scales to measure communication constructs (viz., communication climate and communication effectiveness), and the alpha reliability coefficients are presented in Table 8.1. In an attempt to keep our questionnaire to a reasonable length, we employed single-item measures for the remaining constructs, precluding our establishing their reliability individually. However, to enhance validity, we still measured many of the constructs using multiple items. While those items addressed different subconstructs and were not designed to covary for the purposes of establishing reliability, it was still possible to combine them by construct and compute reliability coefficients (Table 8.2). In this context, the reliability coefficients for these measures might therefore be somewhat lower than for true multi-items scales. The reader is cautioned to interpret the reliabilities within this context. Also, several measures (Table 8.5: Preference for FTF vs EM, Table 8.8: All three items addressing management philosophy, and Table 8.10: Frequency of communication breakdown and cross-shift coordination) did not lend themselves to combination with other items, and the reader is cautioned to interpret these measures accordingly.

We used interviews (qualitative/subjective) to identify, frame, discuss and corroborate the constructs. We used observation (qualitative/objective) to corroborate media choice rules, communication climate, communication quality, overall communication density and management style and to obtain the message

TABLE 8.2 Reliability Coefficients for Composites of Single-Item Measures

Table	Composite Construct	Subconstructs	α
3	FTF Perceptions	FTF Reachability FTF Meaningfulness FTF Restrictiveness FTF Efficiency	0.50
3	EM Perceptions	EM Reachability EM Meaningfulness EM Restrictiveness EM Efficiency	0.81
4	Appropriateness of Use	Composite score, by communication mode, of the appropriateness of using that mode in four different real-world scenarios.	
	FTF		0.64
	EM		0.55
	Notes		0.72
	Telephone		0.68
	Memo		0.84
4	Rules of Use	Various tacit rules of use derived from interviews and observation.	
	FTF		0.76
	EM		0.63
	EM (Regarding Reliability)		0.43
	FTF (Regarding Richness)		0.87
	EM (Regarding Richness)		0.64
10	Extent of communication Breakdowns	Extent of in-shift breakdowns. Extent of cross-shift breakdowns.	0.65

content of FTF exchanges. We captured electronic messages (qualitative/objective) to obtain the content of EM. We used electronic message capture and structured observation of FTF communication (quantitative/objective) to describe and measure the links among group members.

The particular case design used was the multiple site replication with embedded units of analysis (Yin 1984). Replicating our study in two sites differing on the key construct of interest (i.e., social context) yet similar with regard to those constructs representing competing sources of explanation enabled us to enhance the validity of the findings (George and McKeown 1985).

While the case site represented the primary unit of analysis, other lower-level units of analysis were employed within each site. Yin (1984) referred to these secondary units as embedded units of analysis. Rogers (1986) proposed the information exchange relationship (or interaction event [Fulk and Boyd 1991, Goffman 1967, Sigman 1987]), rather than the individual, as the appropriate unit of analysis for CMC research. We used the interaction event as an embedded unit of analysis within each case site, providing the data for performing a network analysis of each group's interaction patterns.

Network analysis is central to the field of structural inquiry (Monge and Eisenberg 1987) and represents the appropriate method for guiding data collection and analysis of groups when the focus is on patterns of interaction over time (O'Reilly and Roberts 1977, Tichy 1980). Network analysis has been used in several CMC studies (Eveland and Bikson 1987, Rice and Aydin 1991, Rice and Love 1987, Rice et al 1990), and others have called for its use with CMC research (Fulk and Boyd 1991, Rice 1990). The network paradigm is ideal for examining a socially based view of communication technologies in that it refocuses attention away from individuals as independent users of the technology to a view of users as an interconnected set of interdependent relationships embedded within organizational and social systems (Contractor and Eisenbert 1989).

Interview and general observation notes were transcribed and sorted according to our research framework. Communication events recorded during structured observation, and electronic messages captured from the electronic messaging system, were entered to a database and coded to identify the parties to the communication, the direction (from/to), the time, the mode, a summary of the content of the interaction, and the purpose of the message. Content analysis of the interactions was based on an ethnographic interpretation informed by our extended time spent in the field. We treated our interpretations as hypotheses regarding the social context of the group and its relationship to social structure, and validated our interpretations against those of the editors during follow-up interviews.

At *The Statewide Times*, 18 interviews were conducted with all but one member of the management group and with several non-group managers. The publishing process was observed (usually shadowing a central actor) for 62 hours, distributed throughout the twenty-four hour publishing cycle.[7] Four news meetings were attended. Electronic mail messages sent during each observation period were obtained directly from most of the editors at the end of the observation, and electronic messages corresponding to two days of observation were obtained directly from the editorial computer system. After conducting all interviews and observations, a questionnaire was administered; and completed questionnaires were received from the 14 of 15 editors for a response rate of 93%.

At *The Regional News*, nineteen interviews were conducted with all but two members of the management group and with several non-group managers. All phases of the publishing process were observed during a total of 100 hours of observation. Again, particular editors were shadowed during most observations.

---

[7]   The task process at both newspapers exhibited three phases: planning, decision-making, and execution. These phases were initially developed as a result of a literature review and interviews and observations at a pilot site. They were confirmed for both research sites via interview and observation. At *Regional*, the planning phase was observed four times, the decision-making phase eleven times, and the execution phase seven times. At *Statewide*, the planning phase was observed five times, the decision-making phase seven times and the production phase four times. During each observation, a central actor was shadowed, and the time, mode, participants, and content of all observed interactions were recorded. An ongoing record of the context of exchange was also kept.

Ten news meetings were attended. Electronic messages were obtained directly from participants at the end of each observation period. The questionnaire, modified slightly to reflect the particular process and jargon at this site, was administered to the fourteen managers. Twelve questionnaires (85%) were returned.

In the following sections we first establish the similarity between groups regarding functional structure, task process, electronic messaging technology, and group member perceptions regarding that technology. We then establish their dissimilarities in social context. Next we present the resulting differences in their patterns of interaction, consistent with their social context (Proposition 1). We show how the patterns of interaction were more similar across modes within groups than within modes across groups (Proposition 2). Finally, we link interaction patterns to performance (Proposition 3).

CONTEXTUAL SIMILARITIES BETWEEN GROUPS

This section establishes the similarities between the groups. In addition to controlling for the functional structure, task process, and technology as suggested by the technological imperative, we also controlled for influences on communication mode choice as suggested by the organizational imperative.

Functional Structure

Functional structure refers to the organization and assignment of occupational roles and responsibilities. Both groups used essentially the same functional structure comprised of senior managers, reporting editors, news editors, and copy editors. Senior management in both groups comprised an executive editor (EE) and a managing editor (ME). The EE managed the editorial division, set the tone of the paper, influenced editorial content, and might become involved with major stories. The ME reported to the EE and was responsible for the day-to-day news gathering and editing operations. The ME made or was involved with most of the decisions on newsroom administration and editorial policy, and guided or monitored the day-to-day selection of stories to run on page one, the primary daily news decision. Reporting editors were responsible for assigning reporters, helping them to craft their stories, and monitoring their progress against deadline. Reporting editors in both groups were coordinated by an Associate Managing Editor (AME) for Reporting. News desk editors managed and coordinated the content of the news section, reviewing all copy to run in that section and deciding which stories would run on page one, which would run inside the news section, and would not run in the section at all. News desk editors determined story placement and specified final story length. The news desk in both groups was coordinated by an AME/News. The copy desk was responsible for giving stories a more detailed editing for grammar, spelling and factual accuracy. They wrote headlines and trimmed stories to fit the length specified by the news desk.

Senior copy editors, called slots, assigned stories to particular copy editors and reviewed their work.

Task Process

Both groups performed essentially an identical task: creating the first ("news") section of the daily newspaper. The daily publishing process at both papers could be broken into three phases: Planning, decision making, and execution/production (Figure 8.2). From about 9 a.m. to 3 p.m. (Phase 1), reporting and coverage plans were being made and stories assigned and reported. Reporting desks were creating news "budgets"—a list of stories with estimated length to be offered to the news desk that evening—based on preliminary conversations with reporters and on intuition. Between 3 p.m. and 7 p.m. (Phase 2), several hours before the actual stories were filed, a preliminary decision about what would run where was made based on the news budget. This decision was formally made at a daily news meeting (4 p.m. at *Statewide*, 5 p.m. at *Regional*) attended by representatives of all four functions, however, the decision was affected by interactions occurring before and after the news meeting. Based on

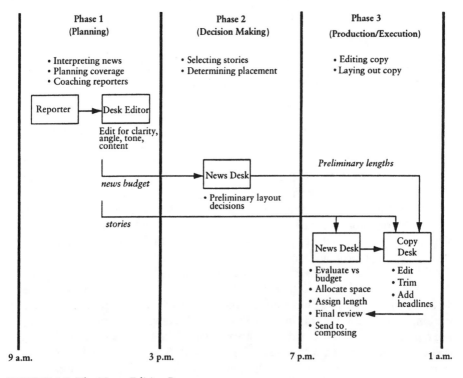

FIGURE 8.2 The News Editing Process

the budget and the preliminary placement decisions, the news desk allocated space for each budgeted story and communicated that to the copy desk. Phase 2 was especially important as this represented the transition from the day shift to the night shift and the hand-off from the planners to the producers. Communication and coordination between the day reporting editors and the night production and layout editors was essential to producing an effective news section. From about 7 p.m. to 1 a.m. (Phase 3), late stories were filed and sent from reporting desks to the copy desk for final editing and trimming to the budgeted length assigned by the news desk. News editors monitored stories for revaluation possibly resulting in changes to the placement decisions. The reporting editors left midway through phase 3, once all major stories were filed and edited. The news desk spent the next few hours laying out each of several editions while making changes as stories changed or new stories were filed. The copy desk edited its backlog of stories, writing headlines, and responding to changes in the budgeted length of stories it was editing. Once a story was edited and headlined by the copy desk, the news desk would do a final read then send the story to composing for paste up and plating.

Technology

Both sites used an identical group authoring and messaging computer system. *Statewide* had been using the system for four years and *Regional* for six years. Both sites appeared to have reached an equilibrium point in the mutual adaptation of the organization and the technology (Leonard-Barton 1988). All group members were well accustomed to the technology and knowledgeable about its features.

Communication Mode Perceptions

Adopting the argument that media characteristics are perceived rather than objective or determined (Fulk et al. 1987) and thus sociocognitively influenced, different media perceptions between the two groups might account for differences in their communication patterns and outcomes. Questionnaire data (Table 8.3) showed no significant differences in how both groups perceived most characteristics of FTF and EM, the exception being that *Statewide* significantly perceived FTF to be somewhat more efficient than did *Regional*.

Communication Mode Usage Rules and Practices

Social context, comprising rules for behavior (Poole et al. 1985), also may govern the rules for utilizing communication modes. Tacit, informal rules for

TABLE 8.3 Communication Mode Perceptions

	Statewide		Regional			2-tail
	Ave	SD	Ave	SD	Diff.	p
Reachability: Confidence (1 = high, 5 = low) that message will reach those it needs to via						
• FTF	1.57	0.65	1.43	0.51	0.14	0.523
• EM	2.23	0.83	2.14	0.77	0.09	0.779
Confidence (1 = high, 5 = low) that message will be understood when using						
• FTF	1.50	0.52	1.57	0.65	0.07	0.750
• EM	2.38	0.87	2.21	0.80	0.17	0.602
Restrictiveness: extent to which you feel restricted (1 = high, 5 = low) when using						
• FTF	4.29	0.61	4.50	0.86	0.12	0.453
• EM	2.92	1.44	3.71	1.14	0.79	0.129
Efficiency: extent to which mode is an efficient means for communication (reverse scored) (1 = high, 5 = low)						
• FTF	3.43	1.02	4.21	0.98	0.79	0.047
• EM	3.77	0.73	3.86	0.86	0.09	0.776

TABLE 8.4 Communication Mode Usage Rules and Practices

	Statewide		Regional			2-tail
	Ave	SD	Ave	SD	Diff.	p
Appropriateness of using for 4 scenarios (1 = high, 5 = low)						
FTF	2.36	0.69	2.33	1.07	0.03	0.920
EM	1.43	0.48	1.33	0.57	0.10	0.629
telephone	2.89	0.81	3.12	1.05	0.23	0.554
text file annotations	3.41	0.61	3.60	1.11	0.19	0.602
written memo	3.98	0.75	4.35	1.13	0.37	0.350
Overall extent to which subjects agreed with a stated set of rules for using FTF (based on interactivity required, proximity, perceived reliability, richness required, and social presence required (1 = high, 5 = low)	1.58	0.41	1.39	0.48	0.19	0.270

TABLE 8.4 *Continued*

	Statewide		Regional			2-tail p
	Ave	SD	Ave	SD	Diff.	
Overall extent to which subjects agreed with a stated set of rules for using EM (based on speed required, asynchroneity required, interactivity required, and directedness of search required (1 = high, 5 = low)	1.91	0.41	1.79	0.53	0.13	0.493
Extent of agreement on rules specifically regarding EM use and perceived reliability (e.g., Never use EM for important or urgent messages) (1 = high, 5 = low)	2.50	0.50	2.14	0.69	0.36	0.135
Extent of agreement on rules specifically regarding FTF richness, interactivity and social presence (e.g., use FTF in situations requiring lots of back-and-forth exchange, to create a common understanding, to influence the other person) (1 = high, 5 = low)	1.54	0.47	1.34	0.54	0.20	0.315
Extent of agreement on rules specifically regarding EM richness, interactivity and social presence (e.g., use EM in situations requiring only simple or no response, use EM when parties share common knowledge of topic, use EM to avoid personal contact) (1 = high, 5 = low)	2.03	0.44	1.81	0.62	0.22	0.300

using EM and FTF were derived from interview and observation data and verified by questionnaire (Table 8.4). The extent to which the editors agreed with these rules, averaged by communication mode, was strong over all (confirming the rules) and showed no significant difference between groups. This finding held for subsets of the rules specifically addressing reliability and richness. Additionally, to confirm our findings and insure comparability between groups, four real-world scenarios requiring a communication mode choice were presented to the editors. For each scenario they were asked to evaluate the appropriateness of five communication modes (FTF, EM, telephone, annotations embedded in text files, and written memos). The average evaluation across the four scenarios for each mode showed no significant difference between the groups. Both groups rated EM as the most appropriate communication mode, followed by FTF. Telephone

TABLE 8.5 Communication Mode Preference

	FTF vs. EM	
	Ave	SD
Statewide	2.16	1.41
Regional	1.79	0.96
Difference	0.36	
2-tail p	0.441	
(1 = strongly prefer FTF, 3 = neutral, 5 = Strongly prefer EM)		

received a neutral evaluation while annotated files and memos were considered inappropriate over all. Thus both groups appeared to have the same strong propensity at the micro-interaction level to use EM and FTF in similar common situations, when considered apart from the macro social context.

Individual Preferences Regarding Communication Modes

Regardless of a group's rules and norms, individuals may have particular preferences for one communication mode or another. Questionnaire responses (Table 8.5) showed no significant difference in the average communication mode preferences of the two groups.

Tenure

The average tenure of the groups was not significantly different (Table 8.6).

Summary

The groups were remarkably similar in many ways. They comprised editors of similar tenure using identical technologies performing the same task using the same functional structure to perform the same process. They similarly perceived characteristics of FTF and EM communication modes, and shared the same basic rules for choosing between communication modes. Despite these similarities, the groups differed significantly in social context as described in the following section.

TABLE 8.6 Tenure

	Statewide		Regional			2-tail
	Ave	SD	Ave	SD	Diff.	p
Years in current job	4.62	5.05	5.19	4.96	0.57	0.765
Years at paper	11.93	8.34	13.94	8.35	2.01	0.530
Years in industry	18.93	9.42	20.79	8.98	1.86	0.598

CONTEXTUAL DIFFERENCES BETWEEN GROUPS

This section describes the key differences between groups regarding social context, namely communication climate, management philosophy, and group *philos*.

Communication Climate

Questionnaire items addressing openness of communication and information sharing (Table 8.7) showed significant differences between the groups, with *Regional* the more open of the two. *Regional* clearly embraced open communication while *Statewide's* response was more moderate. This difference was clearly observed by us, as indicated by a much greater amount of frank and open exchange of views at *Regional* than at *Statewide*.

Management Philosophy

Questionnaire data (Table 8.8) showed no significant difference in the extent to which both groups tended to follow the formal hierarchy, however they differed significantly in their ability to transcend that structure when needed.

TABLE 8.7 Communication Climate

	Statewide		Regional			2-tail
	Ave	SD	Ave	SD	Diff.	p
Information sharing is encouraged among the group. (1 = strongly agree, 5 = strongly disagree)	2.36	1.01	1.79	0.89	0.57	0.125
We share information openly among group members. (1 = strongly agree, 5 = strongly disagree)	2.64	0.84	2.07	0.73	0.57	0.066

TABLE 8.8 Management Philosophy

	Statewide		Regional			2-tail
	Ave	SD	Ave	SD	Diff	p
We follow a strict and formal hierarchy for managing and controlling our work. (1 = strongly agree, 5 = strongly disagree)	2.86	0.87	3.07	1.14	0.21	0.581
We let whomever has the knowledge and expertise direct the task, regardless of formal position. (1 = strongly agree, 5 = strongly disagree)	3.93	0.48	2.86	1.10	1.07	0.004
The group operates in a highly flexible and fluid manner. (1 = strongly agree, 5 = strongly disagree)	2.50	1.01	1.79	0.70	0.71	0.051

This aspect (viz., knowledge vs hierarchy, and flexibility) showed the largest and most significant differences between groups among contextual differences questionnaire items.

Regional's editorial group tended to let those with the relevant knowledge concerning the task at hand override the formal hierarchy to a large extent, whereas this usually did not occur at *Statewide*. At *Regional* individual knowledge and expertise were highly respected and relied on, while the editors at *Statewide* experienced a much lower level of mutual respect. *Regional* was able to operate hierarchically where needed, yet was flexible enough to transcend that structure. *Statewide* usually was not, regardless of the particular circumstances. Thus, while both organizations routinely operated in a hierarchical and structured fashion, *Regional* maintained the flexibility to transcend the formal hierarchy where needed, supported by a climate conducive to open and frank communication. *Statewide* was more rooted to its structure within an environment less conducive to the open sharing of information.

We observed the *Regional* ME routinely delegating important news decisions to the news, reporting and copy editors. For example, the ME had little involvement in determining the content of page one, but rather delegated this decision to the news desk in consultation with the other two functions. This was corroborated during our interviews.

Statewide showed a marked contrast. The ME inserted himself into most of the day-to-day news decisions regarding the news process. While the news editor had formal responsibility for the page one decision, we observed him being directed and overridden by the ME on a regular basis. The news meeting, formally hosted by the news desk, typically became an opportunity for the ME to take over the meeting, query each person regarding their budget and then impose his view of page one on the news editors. They regularly deferred to him, anticipating that he would make the decision anyway. We observed several instances where the news editor would seek the approval of the ME for very routine matters before making a change to the paper.

Philos and Cooperation

The reporting desks (the "artists") and the news and copy desks ("production") operated under different goals, perspectives, and time constraints. Producing a high quality newspaper required effective coordination and communication between those who reported the news and those who determined what stories would actually run each day. At both papers, as with most newspapers, there was a natural difference in orientation between these subgroups. However, this schism ran deeper at *Statewide* than at *Regional*, particularly between the news desk and the reporting desks. The group at *Regional* exhibited a high level of philos, while the group at *Statewide* exhibited little philos and a moderate amount of hostility among the functional subgroups.

According to the AME/Reporting at *Statewide*,

> We tried something a couple of months ago, we call a "group grope." And I got several reporters together first thing in the morning and we said to ourselves "What's the best thing we can do tomorrow that will knock the readers' socks off?" And we had one reporter in the group who agreed that no matter what idea we came up with he would take that story and produce it for tomorrow, and we would hope it would be a page one story—the best story in the paper. And we did it for about 2 weeks. And every story we did, the news desk buried. And the reporters were just outraged; "Don't they know what we're trying to do? Why don't they come to this meeting if they're committed to this process too?" And I said, "Well, I agree with you." [AME/Reporting–*Statewide*]

Another *Statewide* reporting editor expressed a low opinion of the news editor.

> The news editor, whom I think is a real dink, by the way, shouldn't be anywhere *near* a newspaper. [Suburban Editor–*Statewide*]

The news desk often complained about finding out about reporting desk changes too late in the cycle to take appropriate action. The reporting editors countered that it was the news desk's attitude and an unwillingness to deal with the constraints of the process that was at fault.

> If we know early in the day that we've got some potentially swapable stories, we'll try to tell [the news editors], but we really don't know until later. That's one of the hard parts. You kind of have to, in my opinion, change attitudes, rather than try to fight this every day on a story-by-story basis. [Suburban Editor–*Statewide*]

We observed the *Statewide* AME/Reporting querying a news desk editor to find out why several of their stories did not get in the paper. The news editor described the stories she had accepted, showing him the layout and implying that her stories were better and more important given the limited space.

AME/Reporting:	Can any of these stories be reduced to briefs?
Asst news editor:	What really needs to get in?
AME/Reporting:	Trim the hell out of them [the stories he wants to get in].
AME/News:	(overhearing) Why are you bringing this up now? We're 2 hours from closeout. Send them over the right length.
AME/Reporting:	I'd like a lot more short stories in more often.
AME/News:	Start that at *your* end.
AME/Reporting:	I can't monitor that. I raise the issues at the [news] meeting.

On another occasion, the ME, bothered by a good story having been dropped from the paper, was trying to impose more interaction between the reporting and news desks.

News Editor:	I was in a time crunch and had no time to think about this stuff by the time I got it. I need to see the stuff before 8 p.m. to give it special treatment.
ME:	Help [the reporting editors] to conceptualize it.
News Editor:	For special layouts, I need to get the copy with enough time—for example by 4 or 5 p.m., not 8 p.m.
ME:	Often that's not possible. You should be doing *conceptualization* at that hour. Put more effort into the front end so that when it arrives late and its wrong you can slap wrists.

The ME then had a similar discussion with the AME/Reporting. The AME/Reporting rebutted that the story in question "just didn't work" and they had to make changes on deadline.

ME:	You need to communicate to [the News Editor] when you make a change, either face-to-face or with a[n electronic] message rather than just dropping it off on him.
AME/Reporting:	We are figuring out what happened while they are at dinner. When they come back, we're in the crunch.
ME:	Send a message or tape it on their screen to alert them "We need to talk when you get back."

AME/Reporting: OK. We can do that.

ME: (exasperated) Areas do it and then shove it over and don't care how it looks or don't think about it.

It was clear in this case that even though the reporting editors *could* simply have sent an EM, they never even considered that option (cf., Guetzkow and Simon 1955), and that neither the reporting nor the news editors were predisposed to consider communicating with the other.

The sports editor, who fancied himself an impartial observer, offered his perspective developed from having worked at seven newspapers during his career.

> There are more turf battles here than elsewhere. They hurt us day in and out. Everyone wants to protect their turf including the page-one layout guy [news editor]. He guards that with a vengeance. The A section overall is pretty good, but it has the potential to be much better, if there were less rules and if it were not [the news desk's] job to rain on everyone's party each day, somehow.

The level of philos at *Regional* presented a clear contrast. Although *Regional's* group members frequently negotiated their differing views and opinions, we never observed any instances of acrimony, personal argument, or hostile intent. In fact, we observed a large amount of bantering, story telling, and joking among the editors representing all functions, and especially between the reporting desks and the news desk. At *Regional*, the reporting desks and news desk each were highly respectful of the others views and decisions.

> The news desk has a lot of overlap of responsibility with [the reporting desks] and lots of participation. More likely we will over-discuss something rather than miss something. Sometimes there are too many people involved in deciding page-one heads [headlines] and stories. But having too many people involved is almost never a problem. It improves the heads and stories and tone. It is usually better to get more viewpoints. [Associate News Editor–*Regional*]

According to the AME/Reporting, the news desk limited as much as possible the amount of changes they (the news desk) made to stories "so as not to surprise the reporting desks, create any error of fact or interpretation, and just out of courtesy." We observed many instances of one desk deferring to the opinion of the other and making an effort to cooperate. For example, a primary goal of each desk editor was to get their reporters' stories into the paper and especially onto page one. However, given a fixed amount of space, this often meant dropping or shortening major stories and was a potential source of hostility between the reporting desks and the news desk, as observed at *Statewide*. However, at *Regional* we observed a much higher level of cooperation. On one night of heavy news and little available space, we observed the national editor volunteering to cut a major story to allow the news editor to run additional stories from other desks. We also observed instances where the news desk volunteered to assist the copy desk when the workload became heavy. Relations between the reporting desks and the copy and news desks were so positive, that the reporting editors (who usually left midway into phase three) informally gave their proxy on most news decisions to the copy slots and news editors, who stayed until the end of the cycle.

> The night associate news editor is my alter ego after I leave." [National Editor–*Regional*]

> We consider the slots to be "deputy desk editors." [Foreign Editor–*Regional*]

> The [associate news editor] and the slots are the representatives of the [reporting] desks at night. [AME/News–*Regional*]

The level of cooperation was reflected in the day-to-day interactions of the editors. For example, at *Regional*, the night editor and reporting desk editors made it a habit to walk around the newsroom to have conversations with each other and the various reporting desks, news desk and copy desk many times during the evening to nurture and maintain a shared context and vision of the night's paper, space issues, news events, and coordination of production and deadlines.

> People maintain personal ties with each other. There is lots of informal chat with other editors when walking around. It keeps us coordinated. It's like an informal news meeting. [AME/Metro–*Regional*]

Walking around rarely occurred at *Statewide* other than to announce the page-one decision or if an editor happened to encounter another editor, for example, on the way to the snack room. As another example, at *Regional*, editors representing all four functions would usually congregate around the television to view the evening news headlines and to exchange their reactions. At *Statewide*, this opportunity to interact was replaced by a junior reporter viewing the news, typing a summary of the headlines, and broadcasting it to the editors via EM.

These findings were corroborated by our structured observation of communication events. A comparison of the messages exchanged via lateral cross-function links (reporting–news, reporting–copy, news–copy), especially during phase 2 when coordination among the functions was most important, revealed a much greater level of cooperation at *Regional* than at *Statewide*.

Summary

The groups differed significantly in social context. *Regional* provided a flexible, cooperative, decentralized, participatory climate supportive of open communication among the editorial functions. *Statewide,* in contrast, provided a hierarchical, fractional, relatively uncooperative climate that employed centralized decision-making and did not encourage open exchange of communication among the editorial functions.

COMMUNICATION PATTERNS AND STRUCTURES

Proposition 1 suggested that groups having different social contexts would appropriate EM differently, as reflected by different patterns of interaction. Specifically, we expected the groups to differ regarding the overall strength and structure of the prominent integrating ties among occupational roles, consistent with their respective social contexts. Proposition 2 suggested that interaction patterns would be more similar within groups across communication modes than within modes across groups, requiring us to analyze interaction patterns by communication mode. Having observed different communication requirements for the three different task phases, we compared interaction patterns by task phase as well as communication mode to see if our findings held at this greater level of detail.

We drived the social structure of interaction from the sociometric questionnaire data.[8] Editors were presented with a list of all group members and asked to indicate by task phase and communication mode (EM and FTF) the frequency of interaction (less than once per day, more than once per day but less than once per hour, or at least once per hour). We created six adjacency matrices, one for each task phase and communication mode.[9] The matrices were made symmetric, as we were primarily interested in the existence and strength of links rather than their directionality. However, this did not significantly influence the analysis, as the data showed almost no unreciprocated links. We assigned values to the links using an exponential function. If both editors forming a link reported high frequency the link was scored 8. If one reported high and the other medium it was

---

[8] Network analysis was performed using UCINET 3.0 (MacEvoy and Freeman 1987).
[9] An adjacency matrix is one whose columns and rows list all nodes (i.e., people) in the network (i.e., the group). Each cell represents a relation *from* the row *to* the column, and the value of each cell is a measure of the strength of the link between the group members represented by that cell. Consequently, adjacency matrices are often called "who-to-whom" matrices. Thus the value in cell (1,2) of the matrix represents the strength of the link from person 1 to person 2 and is usually interpreted as 1's perception of 1's relationship to 2. In a symmetric matrix, the strength of the link is the same in both directions, and one half of the matrix mirrors the other. The density of the matrix is the percent of possible ties actually made (i.e., the percent of cells with nonzero values) and is a measure of group connectivity or cohesiveness. Rows and columns are often sorted (e.g., by placing next to each other in the matrix all those who in some way are similar). The new matrix can then be divided into meaningful submatrices of "blocks" by assigning all those considered sufficiently similar to the same block. The density of these submatrix blocks then can be computed and compared.

scored a 4. Both low (or one high and the other none) was scored 2. One low and the other none was scored 1, and if neither reported a link it was scored 0. These values were used in aggregating matrices by communication mode and task phase and in developing useful cutoff points for dropping low-frequency links to clarify the analysis.[10]

The network data were analyzed and groups compared by creating submatrix blocks ("blockmodels") based on occupational role and analyzing their density patterns. Blockmodels are a representational means of data reduction applied to social networks (Faust and Wasserman 1992, White et al 1976). They are constructed by clustering members of a social network according to some measure of social distance or similarity (Burt 1980) and then rearranging the adjacency matrix or matrices so that members of the same cluster are placed next to one another in the matrix. Each cluster forms a submatrix block which can be analyzed in terms of its own within-cluster tie density (the proportion of actual links to maximum possible links among members of the block) or between block densities (the proportion of actual to possible links between members of different blocks). These densities provide a measure of tie strength or communication activity within and between blocks. Blockmodels can be thought of as hypotheses

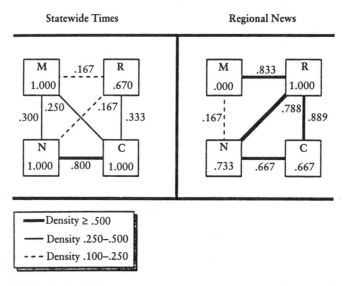

FIGURE 8.3a Overall Social Structure

---

[10] Thus, the maximum tie strength within any phase/mode matrix was 8. The maximum tie strength for matrices combining both communication modes for a particular phase was 16 (2x8). The maximum tie strength for matrices combining all three phases for a particular communication mode was 24 (3x8). The maximum tie strength for matrices combining all modes and phases was 48 (6x8).

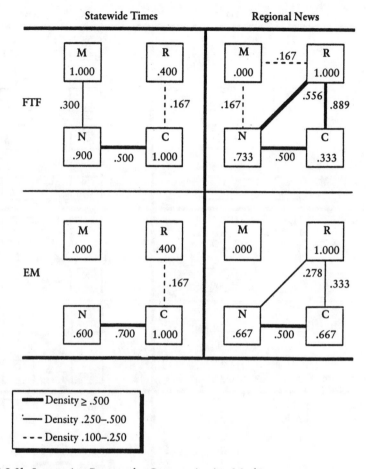

FIGURE 8.3b Interaction Patterns by Communication Mode

(White et al 1976) or assumptions. Based on prior fieldwork within this context, we assumed that coordination and communication among the editorial functions in the group was required for effective performance. To reflect this assumption and to create directly comparable representations of the groups' interaction patterns, we used the blocking technique to cluster the groups by occupational role (Barley 1990, Rice and Aydin 1991). Thus each blockmodel comprised blocks representing the four primary occupational roles of the newsroom: senior management (M), reporting editors (R), copy desk slots (C), and news desk editors (N). Figure 8.3 illustrates these blockmodels with their corresponding tie densities superimposed on the links (between-block tie densities) and nodes

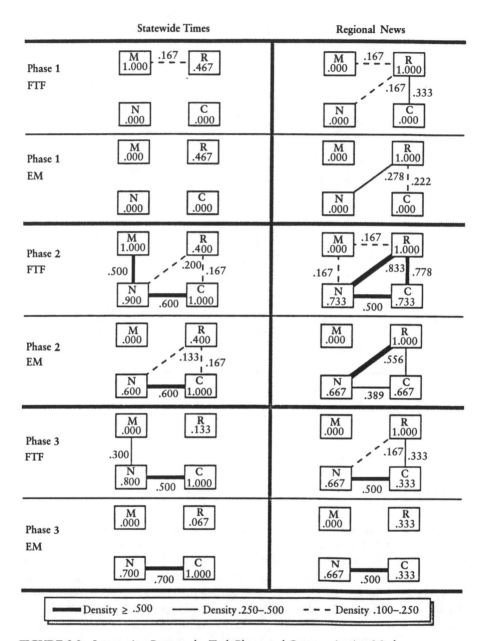

FIGURE 8.3c Interaction Patterns by Task Phase and Communication Mode

TABLE 8.9 Network Densities

		Block Image Network Density		
Phase	Comm. Mode	Statewide	Regional	Ratio
1	FTF	0.095	0.110	1.16
	EM	0.067	0.110	1.64
2	FTF	0.352	0.538	1.53
	EM	0.238	0.385	1.62
3	FTF	0.219	0.330	1.51
	EM	0.162	0.231	1.43
ALL	FTF	0.222	0.326	1.47
	EM	0.156	0.242	1.55
	ALL	0.189	0.284	1.51

(within-block tie densities).[11] Figure 8.3a compares the interactions aggregated across all task phases and communication modes, providing a picture of the overall social structure of the two groups. Figure 8.3b compares the groups by communication mode, with all task phases combined. Figure 8.3c shows interaction by communication mode and task phase.

Strength of Ties

We expected *Regional*, having the more collaborative social context, to exhibit stronger ties among the editorial functions, and in fact the links between blocks were stronger at *Regional*. The *Regional* group was more strongly connected overall (Figure 8.3a) and regardless of communication mode (Figure 8.3b) or task phase (Figure 8.3c). The overall connectedness of the two groups could be further compared (Table 8.9) by comparing the overall densities of the phase/mode matrices show in Figure 8.3c. Except for task phase 1, where the networks for both groups were sparse and the network density of *Regional* was only 16% greater than that of *Statewide*, the remaining phase-by-mode network densities showed *Regional* with network densities ranging from 43% to 64% greater than *Statewide*, indicating a much greater tie strength overall at *Regional* regardless of task phase or communication mode. Compared by communication mode across all task phases, the average FTF density was 47% greater and the average EM density was 55% greater at *Regional* than at *Statewide*.

---

[11] Blockmodes were constructed using binary matrices dichotomized to highlight the primary interaction patterns of the groups.

Structure of Ties

We expected *Regional* to exhibit a more integrated and less control-oriented structure than *Statewide*, again consistent with their respective social contexts. Regarding the overall structure (Figure 8.3a), *Statewide* senior management was most strongly tied to the news desk, reflecting senior management's control over news decisions, while *Regional* management showed a strong tie to the reporting desk, reflecting participatory consultation during the planning phase. Senior management was clearly more involved with the news desk and its news decisions at *Statewide* than at *Regional*, reflecting the control philosophy of the *Statewide* ME *vs.* the delegated decision making approach of the *Regional* senior management.

The *Statewide* network exhibited a weak senior management-news-copy (M-N-C) triangle with reporting tied into the group primarily via the copy desk, functionally the weakest of the three potential points of linkage and representative of the sequential flow of news copy (Figure 8.2). Linking via the copy desk enabled reporting to influence the process only after-the-fact (final editing), while linking to the news or management blocks would have provided more leverage by enabling them to influence outcomes during the earlier planning or decision-making stages. The primary link was between the news and copy desks (the production desks) who were only weakly tied to the rest of the group (the "artists" and planners). In contrast, the pattern at *Regional* showed a strong reporting-news-copy (R-N-C) triangle with senior management tied into the group primarily via reporting, a functionally strong link. The strong reporting-news-copy triangle showed the extent to which all three functions collaborated in producing the paper.

Regardless of communication mode (Figure 8.3b), reporting at *Statewide* was relatively disconnected from the other functions, while at *Regional* the three functional groups remained strongly tied.

Examined by communication mode and task phase (Figure 8.3c), during task phase 1 (planning), *Statewide* showed an almost completely functionally disconnected group while at *Regional*, the cross-block links were much stronger, regardless of communication mode. For example, the second strongest cross-block link among all groups and modes during task phase 1 was the reporting-to-news link via EM at *Regional*. *Regional's* reporting editors were sending electronic messages to the news desk in preparation for the evening's production, and EM was being used to transcend time and space to coordinate these functions. While EM *enabled Statewide* to constitute this link, it did not occur.

During task phase 2 (decision-making/transition) a difference between groups in their use of hierarchy was apparent. At *Statewide*, senior management was strongly tied into the news decision-making structure via FTF. The news and copy desks were strongly tied to each other via both communication modes, while reporting was only weakly linked via either communication mode. At *Regional*, the reporting, news, and copy functions were strongly linked via both modes as they collaborated to make the news decisions. Senior management was kept weakly in the loop via FTF ties with reporting and news for status updates once or twice each evening.

During task phase 3 (production/execution) senior management at *Statewide* continued to interact with the news desk via FTF, directing news decisions, and the news and copy desks continued their multiplex (EM and FTF) link in support of production, while reporting was essentially disconnected at this point. At *Regional*, reporting continued to be tied into the process, weakly to the news desk and moderately strongly to the copy desk. Similar to *Statewide*, the copy and news desks were strongly tied by both modes at this time.

These findings were corroborated by our structured observation of communication events. We sorted our notes describing the observed interactions by task phase, communication mode, and the six possible role-block linkages. These data showed essentially the same structural patterns as the analysis of sociometric questionnaire data. The message content of our task phase 2 and 3 observations in particular found that senior management at Statewide was much more directive and control-oriented, while at *Regional* the senior management was more "hands-off", delegating decisions and allowing the other three functions to coordinate among themselves. Interaction was more intense and cooperative within and among the functions at *Regional* than at *Statewide*.

Similarity of Ties

Comparing the groups by communication mode (all task phases combined) (Figure 8.3b), the pattern of EM interaction resembled the pattern of FTF interaction in both groups, and was almost identical when senior managers (who made relatively little use of EM overall) were disregarded. Examined by communication mode and task phase (Figure 8.3c), again except for the senior managers, EM patterns continued to reflect the strongest FTF links in each task phase for both sites. Additionally, ties were more similar within group than across group within mode.

Summary

In support of Proposition 1, our network analysis of the interaction patterns of both groups clearly showed that a) the functional subgroups at *Regional* were much more integrated and connected, b) the density of connections and level of communication involvement was much greater at *Regional*, and c) that *Regional* was a much more lateral organization, while *Statewide* was much more hierarchical and less integrated or interconnected. These finding were consistent with the social context of the groups and held regardless of the communication mode. In support of Proposition 2, the patterns of EM communication were highly similar to FTF within both groups and dissimilar within communication mode between the groups.

PERFORMANCE EFFECTIVENESS

Proposition 3 was that outcome effectiveness would depend on the effectiveness of communication within each group and would differ between groups having similar functional structures, task processes and communication technologies, but different interaction patterns.

Communication Effectiveness

Based on questionnaire responses (Table 8.10), perceived communication by task phase and overall was rated significantly more effective at *Regional*. The largest difference was specifically for cross-shift communication. The phase 1 to

TABLE 8.10 Communication Effectiveness

	Statewide		Regional			2-tail
	Ave	*SD*	*Ave*	*SD*	*Diff.*	*p*
Communication Effectiveness by Phase (1= high quality, effective, 5 = low quality, not effective)						
PHASE 1	2.78	0.75	2.03	0.54	0.75	0.42
PHASE 2	2.57	0.60	2.12	0.47	0.45	0.049
PHASE 3	2.75	0.82	2.02	0.37	0.73	0.014
Between-shift Communication Effectiveness (1 = high quality, effective, 5·= low quality, not effective)						
PHASE 1	2.84	0.81	1.82	0.55	1.02	0.014
PHASE 2	2.93	0.67	2.50	0.85	0.43	0.187
PHASE 3	2.94	0.69	2.56	0.80	0.38	0.285
Overall Communication Effectiveness overall communication patterns are effective; overall communication detracts from quality of work (reverse scored) (1 = effective, 5 = not effective)						
	2.71	0.80	1.92	0.51	0.79	0.005
Miscommunication						
Extent of within-shift communication breakdowns (1 = large extent, 5 = small extent)						
	3.07	0.83	3.57	0.94	0.50	0.147
Extent of between-shift communication breakdowns (1 = large extent, 5 = small extent)						
	2.36	0.84	2.93	1.00	0.57	0.114

TABLE 8.10 *Continued*

	Statewide		Regional			2-tail
	Ave	SD	Ave	SD	Diff.	p
Frequency of communication breakdowns (1 = almost never, 2 = 1 / months, 3 = 1 / week, 4 = 1 / day, 5 = > 1 / day	3.79	0.70	2.86	1.10	0.93	0.014
Coordination (1 = high coordination, 5 = low coordination)						
PHASE 1	2.48	0.56	1.79	0.43	0.69	0.012
PHASE 2	2.67	0.47	2.15	0.62	0.52	0.035
PHASE 3	2.56	0.39	2.22	0.75	0.34	0.246
Extent to which activities and tasks between or across shifts are well-timed (and coordinated (1 = large extent, 5 = not at all)	3.14	0.36	2.61	1.00	0.53	0.078

2 cross-shift communication, primarily the communication of the morning news plans from the reporting editors to the production (news and copy) editors who would eventually execute them, and, again, a key link to producing a successful paper, was rated much less effective at *Statewide*. Cross-shift communication during the other two phases showed smaller, non-significant differences. Information tended to be more factual, focused and logistics-oriented at these points in the process and its exchange was more routine. *Regional* also perceived a significantly lower extent of communication breakdowns across shifts and lower frequency of breakdowns overall than *Statewide*. While both groups received favorable coordination scores, over all, *Regional* was perceived to be significantly better coordinated during the planning and decision making phases (one and two) and when coordinating across shifts.

These findings were corroborated by the structured observation data, especially during the phase 2 cross-shift transition, and by interview data where many of the *Statewide* editors volunteered that day-to-day communication was not effective, while most of the editors at *Regional* felt that day-to-day communication was generally effective.

Outcome Effectiveness

Regional had a higher rate of good or great papers than did *Statewide*, as expected (Table 8.11). *Statewide* was good or great a bit over half the time, while

TABLE 8.11 Outcome Effectiveness

| | Statewide | | Regional | | 2-tail |
News Section Quality	Ave	SD	Ave	SD	p
% Good or great	55.2	17.6	71.2	25.3	0.72
% Unacceptable or average	44.8	17.6	28.8	25.3	0.72

Regional was considered good or great over two-thirds of the time. These results were corroborated by our interview data, and the rank order of quality and effectiveness reflected the opinions and beliefs of the parent corporation, enhancing validity of the findings.

DISCUSSION

Our research examined the relationship between social context and patterns of FTF and EM interaction in two similar ongoing management groups. It is the only published field study we know of that examined simultaneously both FTF and EM communication patterns, and their content as well as structure.

News editing, the task context of this study, would appear to be an ideal situation for CMC technology to flourish. The work is rapidly paced and communication intensive, uncertainty concerning breaking news is high, interaction is intense, the group must respond quickly to changing events, and coordination is crucial. In this sense, the newsroom is potentially an appropriate model for new organizational forms supporting knowledge-based teamwork.

Technological and organizational imperatives regarding information technology suggest that EM, implemented in groups as similar as the editorial groups reported on here, should exhibit similar patterns of use; namely an integrated, lateral, and responsive network for information exchange. However, the evidence presented here showed that two similar groups can have very different patterns of EM use depending on the social context within which that EM interaction takes place.

Kling (1991) called for a more substantial shift from "technological utopianism to social realism", by engaging in *in-situ* research with real groups, especially in less "euphoric" circumstances than connoted by the terms cooperation and collaboration and which include control and hierarchy as a viable elements. In our study, *Statewide* was clearly managed under a control strategy and held a climate that was less conducive to open sharing of information, while *Regional* operated under a commitment strategy and a climate generally supportive of information sharing, providing a clear and useful social comparison.

Adopting the perspective of adaptive structuration theory (Poole et al 1985), we proposed that the groups' appropriation of EM would reflect the social context of each group (Poole and DeSanctis 1990). This would be reflected by observing different patterns of EM and FTF for each group, and by observing a greater similarity of interaction within group across communication mode than within communication mode across group. Further, we proposed that group outcomes would be mediated by the groups' interaction patterns and, given the same task requirements but different patterns of interaction, we would expect the communication and outcome effectiveness of the groups to differ.

Our findings strongly supported these propositions. The two groups were extremely similar on many measures of context, but differed sharply regarding cooperation, communication openness, and management philosophy. *Regional*, a cooperative, open, participatory group integrated their use of EM into a responsive and tightly connected interaction network enabling effective communication and coordination. *Regional* exhibited little vertical or lateral constraint on interaction. They enjoyed a much more participatory climate, and senior executives delegated almost all of the day-to-day decision making responsibility regarding reporting and production to those functions themselves. Laterally, the functions at *Regional* enjoyed a culture of trust, collaboration and information sharing and by working together and communicating to enact a shared context concerning each day's news, developed a shared worldview as well. *Statewide*, in contrast, was a much less cooperative and more fractionalized group operating under a hierarchical control philosophy. Their social context constrained them from appropriating either EM or FTF to form the communication links necessary for effective and coordinated action. *Statewide's* interaction was organizationally constrained both vertically and laterally. Vertically, they were under the leadership of an autocratic management with a centralized decision-making philosophy and a hierarchical culture. Laterally, they were socially constrained by a culture of low trust and a history of conflict between functions. Those functions held very different worldviews and employed no means to reconcile them. Ultimately *Regional* produced a higher quality newspaper than did *Statewide*.

Although we were able to describe a scenario for the effective use of EM applied to one particular cooperative group task, we did not expect those particular findings to generalize much beyond that context. Our primary intent was neither to identify particular conditions for success or failure of EM nor to propose any normative or prescriptive measures for making effective use of EM, but rather to raise awareness that social context counts when implementing technologies that support group interaction. The social context of every organization is in some ways unique and that uniqueness makes a difference to technology-related outcomes. While any set of initial conditions within either group could have given rise to a very different set of outcomes, our sites provided an opportunity to show clearly that the existing social context must be reckoned with, as it represents the vehicle by which the group adopts and adapts new communication technologies. We must take into account the unique social conditions within which groups operate to better understand the way in which technologies like EM, GDSSs, and groupware will be appropriated by the group. The impact of CMC technology on group outcomes is mediated by social context and related interaction patterns. Social context influences how a communication technology is appropriated (Poole and DeSanctis 1990), directly influencing the group's interaction patterns via that technology and in turn influencing the group's performance. We believe these results are quite useful, given the small amount of research on this topic (Poole, Holmes, and DeSanctis 1991).

Our findings also suggested that communication effectiveness operates on the micro and macro levels of interaction, and both must be dealt with for successfully employing CMC or other technologies affecting interaction. Producing meaningful messages between particular individuals at the micro-level of interaction says nothing about the use of EM and communication effectiveness at the macro level of interaction and the appropriateness of the resulting communication network. Although the group might understand how to employ EM to render particular micro-interactions meaningful, and although establishing new communication links might be easier or more convenient using EM, those potential links might not, in actuality, be realized. First, as we observed at *Statewide*, communicators are limited by their learned repertoire of interactions. Recall the situation where *Statewide's* AME/Reporting never even considered sending an EM to the news desk to alert them to an important change in a story, even though that communication link was "obviously" crucial to the effective performance of the group and simple to perform. Second, basic economics tells us that a transaction requires the ability *and* the willingness to transact on the part of both parties. EM provides the ability but the social context provides the willingness, therefore media choices may not be objectively determined by task requirements, per the organizational imperative. We observed many cases at *Statewide* where even though a potential link might be salient, it would not be made because the communicators plainly did not want to interact with each other, either for political, personal or normative reasons.

This finding has important methodological implications. Findings at one level do not necessarily generalize to the next level. Ignoring the levels problem invites misleading and confounded interpretation of results. For example, our context-free, micro-level questionnaire items regarding rules for using communication modes showed no intergroup differences, yet the study clearly revealed significant macro-level differences regarding EM and FTF. Therefore, if we relied only on context-free questionnaires at the micro-level, our results would be misleading unless interpretations were strictly contained to the micro-level. Network data collection and analysis offers a useful means to bridging these levels when investigating interaction (Fulk and Boyd 1991, Rice 1990).

The two levels influence each other as well. For example, Zack (1994) found that, at the micro-interaction level, shared interpretive context was required for the effective coordination of meaning (Pearce 1976) using EM. But in particular (macro) social contexts, communicators may not *want* to be understood. We observed *Statewide* editors intentionally choosing EM because they knew that their message would be sufficiently equivocal to enable them to be duplicitous yet appear not to be. Secondly, the macro social context influences who controls the cognitive frameworks and premises used for interpreting micro-level interactions. At *Regional*, interpretation and context building was a collaborative and consensual process. At *Statewide*, the ME was attempting to impose his vision and worldview on others, while the reporting and production functions were attempting to defend and impose their own perspectives on each other. These findings suggest that both micro- and macro-interaction levels must be investigated when studying information technologies, and that we not bound our studies, a priori, by level of analysis, but by the phenomenon we are investigating.

Despite the obvious benefits of doing extensive in-depth case analysis, our study had its limitations. We looked at a snapshot in time, and did not identify the way in which the structuration and appropriation processes unfolded within each group over time. We did not do a pre/post study of an implementation but merely provided evidence that different communication structures and appropriations of communication technology can emerge in apparently similar groups employing identical technologies and tasks. Our lack of explicit time-sequenced measures limits our ability to identify strict causal relationships. In traditional experimental research, groups would be formed, tasks assigned and other treatments applied, the process set in motion, and measures taken or observations made in the appropriate time-sequence. Rather than studying many groups performing a one-time task, we studied two ongoing groups performing the same task over and over. In our case, it was not possible to say where the process began. It was in motion when we arrived and continued after we left. In cases like this, we can only take "averages" of the groups' behavior and see how these constructs relate. This is especially true for struturation research. In our case, we do not know what events "caused" the social context of each group. All we can say is that each group's social context appears to be reflected in their patterns of interaction. We believe that longitudinal research is essential to expanding what we know about structuration and technology appropriation. Future research might also focus on different tasks, technologies, genders, and cultures—any dimension which might influence or be influenced by the social context of the group.

Our findings suggest a responsibility for CMC technology researchers to explicitly assess, describe, and, if applicable, control for the social context within which they collect their data. For example, questionnaires should include items addressing social, political, and communication climate. Beyond that we would call for researchers to consider social context as a key construct to be explicitly examined and varied. To this end, information technology researchers may benefit from cross-disciplinary research teams comprising, for example, technologists, sociologists, organizational behavioralists, and anthropologists.

Our findings have implications for the groups and organizations employing the technology as well. Groups with shared history, culture, and social context must explicitly acknowledge, describe and diagnose their existing social context and patterns of interaction related to that context before attempting a direct intervention on those patterns as occasioned by EM or other groupware technologies. The most difficult part of implementing groupware or other technologies to support new organizational forms effectively will be the implementation of social interventions (i.e., to culture, norms, interaction habits and practices, and leadership style) to align the social context with the technological and organizational intentions.

While implementation of communication technologies must be viewed as a social as well as organizational and technological intervention, social context is rarely addressed when implementing these technologies. Organizations should diagnose their existing social context to determine if the spirit of the technology (Poole and DeSanctis 1990) fits the social context of the group. Requirements analyses should focus on social and interactional requirements and constraints as well as technical flows of information. Training should be modified or expanded beyond the traditional approach focusing on the technology and task, to including socially-oriented training such as team-building exercises. This suggests an entirely new skill set for technology implementers and trainers. Additionally, technology development and implementation projects, similar to research teams, should have sociologists, social psychologists and organizational development specialists as central members to benchmark existing social context and to design appropriate interventions.

We believe that the strategic advantages associated with these technologies will not derive from having the technical skills to evaluate and implement these technologies, or even from being the first mover (especially if the social climate for appropriation is not favorable), but rather will come from having the appropriate social context, norms, politics, reward systems, and leadership to take advantage of electronic communications technologies for enabling new organizational forms. As organizations attempt to adopt new forms, especially those which cross functions, departments, and traditional organizational boundaries, social context will become even more important and influential.

REFERENCES

Baker, Wayne E., "The Network Organization in Theory and Practice", Chapter 15 in N. Nohria and R. G. Eccles (eds.), *Networks and Organizations: Structure, Form, and Action*, Cambridge, MA: Harvard Business School Press, 1991, pp. 397–429.

Banks, S. P. and P. Riley, "Structuration Theory as an Ontology for Communication Research," *Communication Yearbook* 16, 1993, pp. 167–196.

Barley, S. R. "The Alignment of Technology and Structure through Roles and Networks," *Administrative Science Quarterly*, Vol. 35, 1990, pp. 61–103.

Bavelas, A., "Communication Patterns in Task-Oriented Groups," *Journal of the Acoustical Society of America*, Vol. 22, 1950, pp. 725–730.

Benjamin, Robert I. and Michael S. Scott Morton, "Information Technology, Integration, and Organization Change," *Interfaces*, Vol. 18, No. 3, May–June, 1988, pp. 86–98.

Blalock, Hubert M., Jr., *Theory Construction: From Verbal to Mathematical Formulations*, Prentice-Hall, Englewood Cliffs, N. J., 1969.

Bonacich, Phillip, "Communication Networks and Collective Action," *Social Networks*, Vol. 9, 1987, pp. 389–396.

Burt, R. S., "Models of Network Structure," *Annual Review of Sociology*, Vol. 6, 1980, pp. 79–141.

Contractor, Noshir S. and Eric M. Eisenberg, "Communication Networks and New Media in Organizations," Chapter 7 in *Organizations and Communication Technology*, Janet Fulk, Charles Steinfield (eds.), Newbury Park, CA: Sage Publications, 1990, pp. 143–171.

Culnan, M. J., and M. L. Markus, "Information Technologies", Chapter 13 in *Handbook of Organizational Communication: An Interdisciplinary Perspective*, Frederic M. Jablin, Linda L. Putnam, Karlene H. Roberts, and Lyman W. Porter (eds.), Sage, 1987, pp. 420–443.

Daft, R. L. and R. H. Lengel, "Organizational Information Requirements, Media Richness and Structural Design," *Management Science*, Vol. 32, No. 5, May, 1986, pp. 554–571.

David, F. R., J. A. Pearce II, and W. A. Randolph, "Linking Technology and Structure to Enhance Group Performance," *Journal of Applied Psychology*, Vol. 74, No. 2, 1989, pp. 233–241.

Davidow, William H. and Michael S. Malone, *The Virutal Corporation*, New York: Harper Collins Publishers, 1992.

Dewhirst, H. D., "Influence of Perceived Information Sharing Norms on Communication Channel Utilization," *Academy of Management Journal*, Sept. 1971, pp. 305–315.

Driver, M. J. and S. Streufert, "Integrative Complexity: An Approach to Individuals and Groups as Information-processing Systems," *Administrative Science Quarterly*, Vol. 14, No. 2, 1969, pp. 272–285.

Drucker, P. F., "The Coming of the New Organization," *Harvard Business Review*, Jan.–Feb., 1988, pp. 45–53.

Eveland, J. D. and T. K. Bikson, "Evolving Electronic Communication Networks: An Empirical Assessment," *Office: Technology and People*, Vol. 3, 1987, pp. 103–128.

Farace, Richard V., James A. Taylor, and John P. Stewart, "Criteria for Evaluation of Organizational Communication Effectiveness: Review and Synthesis," *Communication Yearbook* 2, 1978, pp. 271–292.

Faust, K. and S. Wasserman, "Blockmodels: Interpretation and Evaluation," *Social Networks*, Vol. 14, 1992, pp. 5–61.

Finholt, Tom and Lee S. Sproull, "Electronic Groups at Work," *Organization Science*, Vol. 1, No. 1, 1990, pp. 41–64.

Freeman, L. C., "Social Networks and the Structure Experiment," Chapter 1 in Research *Methods in Social Network Analysis*, L. C. Freeman et al (eds), Fairfax, VA: George Mason University Press, 1989.

Freeman, L. C., D. Roeder, and R. R. Mulholland, "Centrality in Social Networks: II Experimental Results," *Social Networks*, Vol. 2, 1980, pp. 119–141.

Fulk, J., "Social Construction of Communication Technology," *Academy of Management Journal*, Vol. 36, No. 5, 1993, pp. 921–950.

Fulk, J. and B. Boyd, "Emerging Theories of Communication in Organizations," *Journal of Management*, Vol. 17, 1991, pp. 407–446.

Fulk, J., C. W. Steinfield, J. Schmitz, and J. G. Power, "A Social Information Processing Model of Media Use in Organizations," *Communication Research*, Vol. 14, No. 5, October, 1987, pp. 529–552.

George, A. L. and T. J. McKeown, "Case Studies and Theories of Organizational Decision Making," *Advances in Information Processing in Organizations*, Vol. 2, JAI Press, 1985, pp. 21–58.

Giddens, A., *Central Problems in Social Theory*, Berkeley, CA: University of California Press, 1979.

Gilchrist, J. C., M. E. Shaw, and L. C. Walker, "Some Effcts of Unequal Distribution of Information in a Wheel Group Structure," *Journal of Abnormal Social Psychology*, Vol. 49, 1954, pp. 554–556.

Glanzer, M. and R. Glaser, "Techniques for the Study of Group Structure and Behavior: II. Empirical Studies of the Effects of Structure in Small Groups", *Psychological Bulletin*, Vol. 58, 1961, pp. 1–27.

Goffman, E., *Interaction Ritual*, New York: Pantheon, 1967.

Gopal, A., R. P. Bostrom, and W. W. Chin, "Applying Adaptive Structuration Theory to Investigate the Process of Group Support Systems Use," *Journal of Management Information Systems*, Vol. 9, No. 3, Winter 1992–1993, pp. 45–69.

Guetzkow, H., "Communications in Organizations," Chapter 12 in J. G. March (ed.), *Handbook of Organizations*, Chicago, IL: Rand McNally, 1965, pp. 534–573.

Guetzkow, H. and H. A. Simon, "The Impact of Certain Communication Nets Upon Organization and Performance in Task-Oriented Groups," *Management Science*, Vol. 1, 1955, pp. 233–250.

Hackman, J. R., (Ed.), *Groups That Work (and Those That Don't): Creating Conditions for Effective Teamwork*, San Francisco, CA: Jossey-Bass, 1990.

Hackman, J. R., "Doing Research That Makes a Difference", in *Doing Research That is Useful for Theory and Practice*, E. E. Lawler, A. M. Mohrman, S. A. Mohrman, G. E. Ledford, and T. G. Cummings (eds.), San Francisco, CA: Jossey-Bass, 1985, pp. 126–149.

Hammer, M., "Predictability of Social Connections over Time", *Social Networks*, Vol. 2, 1979/80, pp. 165–180.

Hammer, M., "Reengineering Work: Don't Automate, Obliterate", *Harvard Business Review*, Vol. 90, No. 4, July–August, 1990, pp. 104–112.

Hammer, M. and G. E. Mangurian, "The Changing Value of Communications Technology," *Sloan Management Review*, Winter 1987, pp. 65–71.

Jablin, F. M., L. L. Putnam, K. H. Roberts, and L. W. Porter, "Structure: Patterns of Organizational Relationships," in *Handbook of Organizational Communication*, F. M. Jablin et al (eds.), Newbury Park, CA: Sage Publications, 1987, pp. 297–303.

Jarillo, J. C., "On Strategic Networks," *Strategic Management Journal*, Vol. 9, 1988, pp. 31–41.

Jarvenpaa, Sirka L., V. Srinivasan Rao, and George P. Huber, "Computer Support for Meetings of Groups Working on Unstructured Problems: A Field Experiment," *MIS Quarterly*, December, 1988, pp. 645–665.

Jick, Todd D., "Mixing Qualitative and Quantitative Methods: Triangulation in Action," *Administrative Science Quarterly*, Vol. 24, December, 1979, pp. 602–611.

Kerlinger, F. N., *Foundations of Behavioral Research*, third edition, New York: Holt, Rinehart and Winton, 1986.

Kerr, E. B. and S. R. Hiltz, *Computer-Mediated Communication Systems*, San Diego, CA: Academic Press, 1982.

Kling, R. "Cooperation, Coordination and Control in Computer-Supported Work," *Communications of the ACM*, Vol. 34, No. 12, December 1991, pp. 83–88.

Kling, R. and W. Saachi, "The Web of Computing: Computer Technology as Social Organization," *Advances in Computers*, Vol. 21, San Diego, CA: Academic Press, 1982, pp. 1–90.

Konsynski, B. R., "Strategic Control in the Extended Enterprise," *IBM Systems Journal*, Vol. 32, No. 1, 1993, pp. 111–142.

Krackhardt, D., "The Strength of Strong Ties: The Importance of *Philos* in Organizations," in *Networks and Organizations*, N. Nohria and R. Eccles, (eds), Cambridge, MA: Harvard Business School Press, December, 1992, pp. 216–239.

Kraft, Philip "Computers and the Automation of Work," Chapter 6 in *Technology and the Transformation of White-Collar Work*, Robert E. Kraut (ed.), Hillsdale, CA: Lawrence Earlbaum Associates, Publishers, 1987, pp. 99–111.

Kraemer, K. L. and King, J. L., "Computer-Based Systems for Cooperative Work and Group Decision Making," *ACM Computing Surveys*, Vol. 20, No. 2, June 1988, pp. 115–146.

Leavitt, H. J., "Some Effects of Certain Communication Patterns on Group Performance," *Journal of Abnormal and Social Psychology*, Vol. 46, 1951, pp. 38–50.

Leonard-Barton, D., "Implementation as Mutual Adaptation of Technology and Organization", *Research Policy*, Vol. 17, 1988, p. 251–267.

MacEvoy, B. and L. Freeman, *UCINET Version 3.0*, Irvine, CA: *Mathematical Social Science Group, School of Social Sciences, University of California*, 1987.

Malone, T. M., J. Yates, and R. I. Benjamin, "Electronic Markets and Electronic Hierarchies," *Communications of the ACM*, Vol. 30, No. 6, June, 1987, pp. 484–497.

Markus, M. Lynne and Daniel Robey, "Information Technology and Organizational Change: Causal Structure in Theory and Research," *Management Science*, Vol. 34, No. 5, May, 1988, pp. 583–598.

McKenney, J. L, M. H. Zack, and V. S. Doherty, "Complementary Communication Media: A Comparison of Electronic Mail and Face-to-Face Communication in a Programming Team," in *Networks and Organizations*, N. Nohria and R. Eccles, (eds), Cambridge, MA: Harvard Business School Press, December, 1992, pp. 262–287.

Miles, R. E. and C. C. Snow, "Organizations: New Concepts for New Forms," *California Management Review*, Vol. 28, No. 3, Spring, 1986, pp. 62–73.

Monge, P. R. and E. M. Eisenberg, "Emergent Communication Networks," in *Handbook of Organizational Communication*, F. M. Jablin et al (eds.), Newbury Park, CA: Sage Publications, 1987, pp. 305–342.

Nadler, David A., Marc S. Gerstein, Robert B. Shaw and Associates, *Organizational Architecture: Designs for Changing Organizations*, San Francisco, CA: Jossey-Bass Publishers, 1992.

Norland, Kenneth E., "Lotus Notes Implementation Factors," *GroupWare* '92, David D. Coleman (ed.), San Mateo, CA: Morgan Kaufmann Publishers, 1992, pp. 312–314.

O'Reilly, C. A., III, and K. H. Roberts, "Task Group Structure, Communication, and Effectiveness in Three Organizations," *Journal of Applied Psychology*, Vol. 62, No. 6, 1977, pp. 674–681.

Orlikowski, Wanda J., "LEARNING FROM NOTES: Organizational Issues in Groupware Implementation," *Proceedings of the AMC 1992 Conference on Computer-Supported Cooperative Work*, J. Tuner and R, Kraut (eds.), Toronto: ACM Press, October 31–November 4, 1992, pp. 362–369.

Pearce, W. B., "The Coordinated Management of Meaning: A Rules-Based Theory of Interpersonal Communication," in *Explorations in Interpersonal Communication*, G. R. Miller (ed.), Beverly Hills, CA: Sage Publications, 1976, pp. 17–35.

Perrin, C. "Electronic Social Fields in Bureaucracies," *Communications of the ACM*, Vol. 34, No. 12, December 1991, pp. 75–82.

Pettigrew, A. M., "Contextualist Research and the Study of Organisational Change Processes," in *Research Methods in Information Systems*, E. Mumford et al. (eds.), New York: Elsevier Science Publishers, 1985, pp. 53–78.

Pinsonneault, A. and K. L. Kraemer, "The Impact of Technological Support on Groups: An Assessment of the Empirical Research," *Decision Support Systems*, Vol. 5, 1989, pp. 197–216.

Poole, M. S., M. Holmes, and G. DeSanctis, "Conflict Management in a Computer-Supported Meeting Environment," *Management Science*, Vol. 37, No. 8, August, 1991, pp. 926–953.

Poole, M. S. and G. DeSanctis, "Understanding the Use of Group Decision Support Systems: The Theory of Adaptive Structuration," Chapter 8 in *Organizations and Communication Technology*, Janet Fulk, Charles Steinfield (eds.), Newbury Park, CA: Sage Publications, 1990, pp. 173–193.

Poole, M. S, D. R. Seibold, R. D. McPhee, "Group Decision-Making as a Structuration Process," *Quarterly Journal of Speech*, Vol. 71, 1985, pp. 74–102.

Radcliffe-Brown, A. R., "On Social Structure," *Journal of the Royal Anthropological Society of Great Britain and Ireland*, Vol. 70, 1940, pp. 1–12.

Ranson, S., B. Hinings, and R. Greenwood, "The Structuring of Organization Structures," *Administrative Science Quarterly*, Vol. 25, March, 1980, pp. 1–17.

Reder, S. and R. C. Schwab, "The Communicative Economy of the Workgroup: Multi-Channel Genres of Communication," *Office: Technology and People*, Vol. 4, No. 3, 1989, pp. 177–198.

Reder, S. and R. C. Schwab, "The Temporal Structure of Cooperative Activity," *Proceedings of the Conference on Computer-Supported Cooperative Work*, October, 1990, pp. 303–316.

Rice, R. E., "Computer-mediated Communication System Network Data: Theoretical Concerns and Empirical Examples," *International Journal of Man-machine Studies*, Vol. 32, 1990, pp. 627–647.

Rice, R. E. and C. Aydin, "Attitudes toward New Organizational Technology: Network Proximity as a Mechanism for Social Information Processing," *Administrative Science Quarterly*, Vol. 36, 1991, pp. 219–244.

Rice, R. E. and J. H. Bair, "New Organizational Media and Productivity," Chapter 8 in *The New Media*, R. E. Rice (Ed.), Newbury Park, CA: Sage Publications, 1984.

Rice, R. E., A. Grant, J. Schmitz, J. Torobin, "Individual and Network Influences on the Adoption and Perceived Outcomes of Electronic Messaging," *Social Networks*, Vol. 12, No. 1, March 1990, pp. 27–55.

Rice, R. E. and G. Love, "Electronic Emotion: Socioemotional Content in a Computer-Mediated Communication Network," *Communication Research*, Vol. 14, No. 1, February, 1987, pp. 85–108.

Riley, P., "A Structurationist Account of Political Culture," *Administrative Science Quarterly*, Vol. 28, 1983, pp. 414–437.

Roby, T. B. and J. T. Lanzetta, "Work Group Structure, Communication, and Group Performance," *Sociometry*, Vol. 19, 1956, pp. 105–113.

Rogers, E. M., *Communication Technology: The New Media in Society*, New York: The Free Press, 1986.

Schegloff. E. A., "Between Macro and Micro: Contexts and Other Connections," in J. C. Alexander, B. Giesan, R. Munch, and N. J. Smalser (eds), *The Micro-Macro Link*, Berkeley, CA: University of California Press, 1987, pp. 207–234.

Schein, E. H., *Organizational Culture and Leadership*, San Francisco, CA: Jossey-Bass, Inc., 1985.

Schmitz, J. and J. Fulk, "Organizational Colleagues, Media Richness, and Electronic Mail," *Communication Research*, Vol. 18, No. 4, August 1991, pp. 487–523.

Schwartz, D. F. and E. Jacobson, "Organizational Communication Network Analysis: The Liaison Communication Role," *Organization Behavior and Human Performance*, Vol. 18, 1977, pp. 158–174.

Shaw, M. E., "Acceptance of Authority, Group Structure and the Effectiveness of Small Groups," *Journal of Personality*, Vol. 27, 1959, pp. 196–210.

Sigman, S. J., *A Perspective on Social Communication*, New York: Lexington Books, 1987.

Sproull, Lee and Sara Kiesler, *Connections: New Ways of Working in the Networked World*, Cambridge, Massachusetts: The MIT Press, 1991.

Steiner, *Group Process and Productivity*, San Diego: Academic Press, 1972.

Steinfield, C. W., "Computer-Mediated Communication Systems," Chapter 6 in *Annual Review of Information Science and Technology*, Vol. 21, Martha E. Williams (ed.), 1986, pp. 167–202.

Stone, David, "Groupware in the Global Enterprise," *GroupWare '92*, David D. Coleman (ed.), San Mateo, CA: Morgan Kaufmann Publishers, 1992, pp. 312–314.

Thorelli, H. B., "Networks: Between Markets and Hierarchies," *Strategic Management Journal*, Vol. 7, 1986, pp. 37–51.

Tichy, N. M., "Networks in Organizations," Chapter 10 in *Handbook of Organization Design*, Paul G. Nystrom and W. Starbuck (eds.), London: Oxford U. Press, 1980, pp. 225–247.

Tichy, N. M., M. L. Tushman, and C. Fombrun, "Social Network Analysis for Organizations," *Academy of Management Review*, Vol. 4, 1979, pp. 507–519.

Trevino, L. K., R. H. Lengel, R. L. Daft, "Media Symbolism and Media Choice in Organizations: A Symbolic Interactionist Perspective," *Communication Research*, Vol. 14, 1987, pp. 553–574.

Tushman, M. L., "Work Characteristics and Subunit Communication Structure: A Contingency Analysis," *Administrative Science Quarterly*, Vol. 24, March, 1979, pp. 82–97.

Venkatraman, N., "IT-Enabled Business Transformation: From Automation to Business Scope Redefinition," *Sloan Management Review*, Vol. 35, No. 2, Winter, 1994, p. 73.

Walton, R. E. and J. R. Hackman, "Groups Under Contrasting Management Strategies," in *Designing Effective Work Groups*, P. S. Goodman (ed.), San Francisco, CA: Jossey Bass, 1986, pp. 168–201.

White, H. C., S. A. Boorman and R. L. Breiger, "Social Structure from Multiple Networks. I. Blockmodels of Roles and Positions," *American Journal of Sociology*, Vol. 81, No. 4, January 1976, pp. 730–780.

Williams, E., "Experimental Comparisons of Face-to-Face and Mediated Communication: A Review," *Psychological Bulletin*, Vol. 84, No. 5, 1977, pp. 963–976.

Yates, J. and W. J. Orlikowski, "Genres of Organizational Communication: A Structurational Approach to Studying Communication and Media," *Academy of Management Review*, Vol. 17, No. 2, 1992, pp. 299–326.

Yin, R. K., *Case Study Research: Design and Methods*, Newbury Park, CA: Sage Publications, 1984.

Zack, M. H., "Shared Context and Communication Effectiveness in a Computer-Supported Work Group," *Information & Management*, Vol. 26, No. 4, April, 1994, pp. 231–241.

Zack, M. H., "Interactivity and Communication Mode Choice in Ongoing Management Groups," *Information Systems Research*, Vol. 4, No. 3, September, 1993, pp. 207–239.

Zack, M. H., "Some Antecedents and Consequences of Computer-Mediated Communications Use in an Ongoing Management Group: A Field Study," *Proceedings of the Twelfth International Conference on Information Systems*, December, 1991, pp. 213–227.

PART III

The Effects in Organizations

Chapter 9

A Theory of the Effects of Advanced Information Technologies on Organizational Design, Intelligence, and Decision Making

George P. Huber[1]
University of Texas

This article sets forth a theory of the effects that computer-assisted communication and decision-aiding technologies have on organizational design, intelligence, and decision making. Several components of the theory are controversial and in need of critical empirical investigation. The article focuses on those technology-prompted changes in organizational design that affect the quality and timeliness of intelligence and decision making, as contrasted with those that affect the production of goods and services.

This article draws on the work of organizational researchers, communication researchers, and information systems researchers to set forth, in the form of a set of propositions, a theory concerning the effects that *advanced information technologies* have on organizational design, intelligence, and decision making. The motivations for such an article are four.

One motivation concerns the need to reinvestigate and possibly revise certain components of organization theory. A large part of what is known about the factors affecting organizational processes, structures, and performance was developed when the nature and mix of communication technologies were relatively constant, both across time and across organizations of the same general type. In contrast, the capabilities and forms of communication technologies have begun to vary, and they are likely to vary a great deal in the future. For example, communication technology (or communication medium) is now a variable whose traditionally relatively constant range (from face-to-face at one extreme to unaddressed broadcast documents at the other, cf. Daft & Lengel, 1984, 1988) is being expanded by organizations to include *computer-assisted communication technologies* (e.g., electronic mail, image transmission devices, computer conferencing, and videoconferencing) that facilitate access to people inside and outside the organization with an ease that previously was not possible. Also, more sophisticated and more user-friendly forms of *computer-assisted decision-aiding technologies* (e.g., expert systems, decision-support systems, on-line management information systems, and external information retrieval systems) are in the late stages of development or early stages of implementation. Consequently, as the uses, capabilities, and forms of communication and decision-aiding technologies increase in their range, researchers must reassess what is known about the effects of these technologies because what is known may change. "That is, new media impacts may condition or falsify hypothesized relationships developed by past research" (Williams & Rice, 1983, p. 208). Thus, one motivation for setting forth propositions concerning the impact of advanced information technologies is to encourage investigation and debate on what the nature of organizational design, intelligence, and decision making might be when these technologies became more sophisticated and more widely used.

The second motivation is to take a step toward creating a theory of the effects that advanced information technologies have on organizations. *Advanced information technologies* are devices (a) that transmit, manipulate, analyze, or exploit information; (b) in which a digital computer processes information integral to the user's communication or decision task; and (c) that have either made their appearance since 1970 or exist in a form that aids in communication or decision tasks to a significantly greater degree than did pre-1971 forms. (For expanded discussion of the term *advanced information technologies,* see Culnan and Markus, 1987; Gibson and Jockson, 1987; Johansen, 1988; Rice and Associates, 1984; and Strassman, 1985a.) The need for such a theory has been exemplified in a review by Culnan and Markus (1987) and in a special issue of *Communication Research* (Steinfield & Fulk, 1987). In that special issue, the guest editors noted that, although there are many empirical findings concerning the effects of advanced information technologies on organizations, "there has been little synthesis, integration, and development of theoretical explanations [and] that it is time for theory development and theory-guided research" (Steinfield & Fulk, 1987, p. 479).

Together, the propositions in this article comprise a theory such as that called far by Steinfield and Fulk, but like any theory, it is limited. It includes as dependent variables only (a) characteristics of organizational intelligence and decision making, such as timeliness, and (b) aspects of organization design associated with intelligence and decision making, such as the size of decision units. Further, within this still rather large set of dependent variables, the theory includes only those (a) that seem to be significantly affected by advanced information technology, (b) that are of interest to organization scientists or administrators, or (c) whose variance seems to have increased with the advent of advanced information technologies. The dependent variables included in the theory are shown in Table 9.1. Variables that are not included in the theory, but whose omission is briefly discussed, include horizontal integration, specialization, standardization, formalization, and the distribution of influence on organizational decisions.

As independent variables the theory includes only (a) the use of computer-assisted communication technologies and (b) the use of computer-assisted decision-aiding technologies. The theory does not encompass the use of computer-assisted production technologies or the use of transaction-enacting technologies such as computerized billing systems. (For ideas concerning the effects of advanced information technologies, broadly defined to include computer assisted automation, on a broader set of organizational attributes, see Child, 1984, 1988; Gibson & Jackson, 1987; Strassman 1985a; Zuboff, 1984.) Finally, the theory does not explicitly address use of advanced information technologies for

TABLE 9.1 Dependent Variables Included in the Theory (and the numbers of the propositions related to them)

Design Variables (Subunit Level)	Design Variables (Organizational Level)	Design Variables (Organizational Memory)	Performance Variables
Participation in decision making (1)	Centralization of decision making (4,5)	Development and use of computer-resident data bases (8)	Effectiveness of environmental scanning (10)
Size and heterogeneity of decision units (2)	Number of organizational levels involved in authorization (6)	Development and use of computer-resident in-house expert systems (9)	Quality and timeliness of organizational intelligence (11)
Frequency and duration of meetings (3)	Number of nodes in the information-processing network (7)		Quality of decisions (12)
			Speed of decision making (13,14)

impression-management purposes such as those described by Sabatier (1978) and Feldman and March (1981).

The third motivation far integrating the work of organizational research-ers, communication researchers, and information systems researchers is to help researchers in each of these fields became more aware of the existence, content, and relevance of the work done by researchers in other fields. Without such awareness, the efficiency of the research establishment is less, opportunities for synergy are lost, and progress in theory development is inhibited.

The fourth and last motivation is of practical, administrative importance. Advanced information technologies are becoming a pervasive aspect of organiza-tions, but their relatively recent appearance and rapidly changing nature virtually guarantee that administrators and their advisors will not have experience as a guide in anticipating and planning for the impacts they may have. In the absence of experience, the value of theory is considerable.

It is important to note that the theory described here is not based on a great deal of directly applicable empirical research. There are two reasons far this. The first is that the components of organization theory that were drawn upon in developing the propositions were not validated under conditions in which deci-sion and communication systems were computer assisted; consequently, they may not be valid for organizations that presently use a good deal of advanced information technology. The second reason is that many of the empirical studies that were drawn upon inductively in developing the propositions pertain to forms of technology that are not necessarily representative of the more sophisti-cated forms now in use or expected to be in use in the more distant future. (See Hofer, 1970; Pfeffer, 1978; Rice, 1980; Robey, 1977; Whisler, 1970, for brief reviews of same of these early studies, and Olson and Lucas, 1982, for some thoughtful speculations concerning the effects of advanced information technolo-gies an a variety of organizational attributes and behaviors.) Thus, most proposi-tions about the organization-level effects of advanced information technology must be viewed with same caution, whether derived from mature, but possibly outdated, organization theory or from recent, but perhaps soon-to-be outdated, empirical findings.

The above cautions notwithstanding, the propositions set forth are sup-portable to the degree necessary to be responsive to the motivations just noted, especially if the qualifications attendant to each proposition are seriously consid-ered by users. In any case, these propositions can serve as a basis for the develop-ment of specific hypotheses.

NATURE OF ADVANCED INFORMATION TECHNOLOGIES

What are the critical characteristics of advanced information technologies that might cause these technologies to have effects on organizational design, intelligence, and decision making different from the effects of more traditional technologies?

For purposes of discussion, characteristics of information technologies will be divided into two groups. *Basic characteristics* are related to data storage capacity, transmission capacity, and processing capacity. Advanced information technologies, largely as a result of their digital computer component, usually provide higher levels of these basic characteristics (Culnan & Markus, 1987, p. 420; Rice & Associates, 1984, p. 34). [No distinction is made in this definition or in this paper between data (stimuli and symbols) and information (data conveying meaning as a result of reducing uncertainty).]

Characteristics of the second group I will call *properties*. Although the above basic dimensions are relevant to users, often it is the multidimensional configuration of the levels characterizing a particular technology that is most relevant far a particular task. Some authorities have considered these configurations when comparing advanced information technologies with traditional information technologies, and have made generalizations about the resultant properties of advanced information systems. Because these properties cause the use of advanced information systems to have effects such as those noted in this paper, some of these generalizations are reviewed here. (See Culnan & Markus, 1987; Rice & Associates, 1984, especially chapter 2, for discussions of how these properties follow from the levels that the technologies attain on the basic dimensions.)

In the context of *communication,* these properties include those that facilitate the ability of the individual or organization (a) to communicate more easily and less expensively across time and geographic location (Rice & Bair, 1984), (b) to communicate more rapidly and with greater precisian to targeted groups (e.g., Culnan & Markus, 1987; Sproull & Kiesler, 1986), (c) to record and index more reliably and inexpensively the content and nature of communication events, and (d) to more selectively control access and participation in a communication event or network (Culnan & Markus, 1987; Rice, 1984).

In the context of *decision aiding,* the properties include those that facilitate the ability of the individual or organization (a) to store and retrieve large amounts of information more quickly and inexpensively; (b) to more rapidly and selectively access information created outside the organization; (c) to more rapidly and accurately combine and reconfigure information so as to create new information (as in the development of forecasting models or financial analyses); (d) to more compactly store and quickly use the judgment and decision models developed in the minds of experts, or in the mind of the decision maker, and stored as expert systems or decision models; and (e) to more reliably and inexpensively record and retrieve information about the content and nature of organizational transactions. (Discussions of these properties of computer-assisted decision-aiding technologies, richer in detail than space allows here, are contained in Sprague & McNurlin, 1986; Sprague & Watson, 1986; Zmud, 1983.)

MISTAKEN IMPRESSIONS

It may be helpful to draw upon the above discussion of the basic characteristics and properties of information technologies to dispel some occasionally held, but mistaken, impressions. One such mistaken impression is that advanced information technologies are universally inferior or superior to traditional technologies. This impression is erroneous because the properties just delineated may be less important than other properties possessed by a more traditional technology. In addition, particular uses of the advanced technologies may have undesirable side effects (cf., Culnan & Markus, 1987; Markus, 1984; Zuboff, 1984). Further, traditional technologies often score higher with respect to acceptability, ease of use, and richness (cf., Culnan & Markus, 1987; Fulk, Steinfield, Schmitz, & Power, 1987; Trevina, Lengel, & Daft, 1987), or have scores that overlap on these properties with the scores of advanced information technologies. For these reasons, use of advanced information technologies will not eliminate use of traditional technologies. However, when the properties of advanced information technologies are useful for enhancing individual or organizational effectiveness, and when retarding forces such as those just noted are not patent, it is reasonable to believe that organizations will use the advanced technologies.

The availability of the advanced information technologies increases the communicating or decision-aiding options for the potential user, and thus in the long run, unless the selected technology is inappropriately employed, the effect is to increase the quality (broadly defined) of the user's communication or decision-making processes. Presumably, through experience or observation, organizational members learn which communication or decision-aiding technology is most likely to achieve their purpose, and then adapt it. Field studies, which will be cited later, verify this belief.

In a related vein, it is a mistake to view advanced information technologies solely as substitutes for traditional technologies. To the contrary, advanced information technologies are frequently used more as supplements and complements to traditional technologies, rather than as substitutes. For example, electronic mail is often used to confirm with text what was said in a phone conversation or to set up face-to-face appointments, and image transmission devices are often used to make available drawings that will be discussed after all the parties have had a chance to study them. Of course, people do substitute computer-assisted media for traditional media when it seems efficacious to do so. Overall, the effect of availability of user-friendly computer-assisted communication technology is to increase the range of options for the communicator. Presumably, through experience or observation, organizational members learn to choose communication technologies wisely. Evidence, which will be cited, indicates that this presumption is correct. An analogous discussion applies to computer-assisted decision-aiding technologies, but limits of space force its omission.

A final mistaken impression is that, although advanced information technologies may lead to rational outcomes (such as information that is more accurate and comprehensive or decisions that are more timely) in organizations characterized by strong adherence to a norm of economic rationality, these out-comes are unlikely in more highly politicized or power-driven organizations. In the absence of scientific evidence with which to develop the required contingency theory, three observations are offered. The first is that the external environments of many organizations are sufficiently competitive that, in order to survive, the organizations must adapt and properly use rationality-enhancing communication and decision-aiding technologies. If organizational politics interferes with such adaption or use, the marketplace or parent organization intervenes until univer-sal conformance is achieved. Thus, in their time, the telegraph became a perva-sive technology in railroads, the calculator in brokerage houses, and the radio in armies. In the organizations that survived, those managers whose proprietary inclinations caused them not to use the technologies to further organizational goals (such as timely delivery of freight, accurate and comprehensive information for investors, or effective coordination in battle) were evidently converted or purged. In essence, super-ordinates or organizations require subordinates or sub-units to help them compete effectively or otherwise satisfy environmental demands, and if rational use of technology is necessary, it occurs in the long run, whatever the proprietary inclinations of the subordinates or subunits.

The second observation is that highly politicized or power-driven organiza-tions also have highly competitive internal environments, and in such environ-ments it is necessary for managers to maximize their own competitive effectiveness by appearing to satisfy the goals of resource controllers on an issue-by-issue basis. In these environments, technical or financial analyses are widely used to persuade the resource controllers that the manager's proposals best sat-isfy the resource controller's goals (Burgelman, 1982; Kelley, 1976; Shukla, 1982). Thus, even in organizations where power plays a significant role in resource allocation, so also do "the numbers" (cf. Gerwin, 1979; Pfeffer & Moore, 1980; Sabatier, 1978; Shukla, 1982). Managers who do not employ the most appropriate technologies in developing and selling analyses are at a compet-itive disadvantage; they must adapt or lose out.

The third observation is that, in almost all organizations, effective fulfill-ment of organizational responsibilities contributes to the development and main-tenance of a manager's reputation. Thus, aside from whatever a manager might do to negatively or positively affect the quality or timeliness of the design, intelli-gence, or decision making of superordinate units, he or she is likely to employ any communication or decision-aiding technologies that can contribute to his or her personal effectiveness or the effectiveness of his or her own unit (cf. Daft, Lengel, & Trevino, 1987).

Together, these observations suggest that even though power and politics influence organizational design, intelligence, and decision making, so too do information technologies; *for advancement of their own interests, organizational participants will use advanced information technologies in ways that increase their effectiveness in fulfilling organizational goals.* This fundamental assump-tion underlies many of the propositions included in the theory and seems to be validated in the studies referenced.

THE PROPOSITIONS

The propositions are grouped for expositional purposes into four sections. The propositions in the first three sections portray the effects of advanced information technologies on organizational design, that is, the effects on (a) subunit structure and process, (b) organizational structure and process, and (c) organizational memory. Although these effects will most often result from evolved practices rather than from prior managerial intentions, I expect that in the future, as administrators and their advisors learn about whatever functional effects of advanced information technologies on organizational design and performance may accrue, more and more of the effects will be the outcomes of intentions. In the short run, however, many managers will probably continue to introduce advanced information systems in order to reduce the number of personnel, to increase managerial efficiency, or to imitate other managers. After the systems are implemented for these purposes, these managers or other organizational participants will sometimes see that the systems can accomplish other purposes and will adjust the organization's design to facilitate accomplishment of these purposes (e.g., by extending the scope of responsibility of an organizational unit that now has easier access to a broader range of information).

The propositions of the fourth section set forth the effects of advanced information technology on organizational intelligence and decision making. Some of these effects are direct and some occur indirectly through changes in design. [Organizational intelligence is the output or product of an organization's efforts to acquire, process, and interpret information external to the organization (cf. Porter, 1980; Sammon, Kurland, & Spitalnic, 1984; & Wilensky, 1967). It is an input to the organization's decision makers.]

Each of these four sections contains specific suggestions concerning research that would seem to be useful for examining the validity and domains of particular propositions. The last section of the paper contains more general recommendations for researchers in the areas of organization science and information systems.

EFFECTS AT THE SUBUNIT LEVEL

The focus in this section is on those aspects of organizational design that ultimately affect organizational intelligence and decision making. For example, aspects of structure that affect the accuracy of communications or the timeliness of decisions are considered. The first three propositions of the section deal with variables generally thought of in the context of organizational subunits. The remaining six propositions deal with variables more associated with the design of the organization as a whole. (This distinction is made solely for expository purposes—the categorizations are not intended to have theoretical merit.)

Participation in Decision Making

In many organizational decisions, technical and political considerations suggest that the development, evaluation, or selection of alternatives would benefit from exchanges of information among a moderate to large number of experts or partisans. But communicating takes time and effort, and so the variety and number of participants is often narrower than post hoc analyses determine to be appropriate. Assuming that the time and effort involved in communicating are critical determinants of the number of individuals who become involved, *what is the effect of computer-assisted communication technology on the breadth of participation in decision making?*

Because computer-assisted communication technologies can greatly reduce the effort required for those individuals who are separated in time or physical proximity to exchange information (cf. Hiltz & Turoff, 1978; Culnan & Markus, 1987; "Special Report," 1988), it is probable that more people would serve as sources of information. Thus, we have the story where

> a product developer sent a message to distribution lists that reach thousands of people asking for suggestions about how to add a particular new product feature. Within two weeks, he had received over 150 messages in reply, cutting across geographical, departmental, divisional, and hierarchical boundaries, almost all from people the product developer did not know. (Sproull & Keisler, 1986, p. 1510)

And, of course, teleconferencing and other similar computer-assisted communication systems are useful for sharing information (Johansen, 1984, 1988; Rice, 1984).

In contrast, authorities have argued that computer-assisted communication technologies do not enable decision makers to obtain "soft" information (Mintzberg, 1975), "rich" information (Daft et al., 1987), the "meaning" of information (Weick, 1985), or information about sensitive matters. To the extent that this argument is correct, it would preclude the use of computer-assisted communication technologies where the need for such information is paramount. However, the circumstances where the arguments of these authorities are salient may be fewer than first thought. For example, the argument that computer-assisted technologies provide fewer cues than does face-to-face communication is valid, but it misses the fact that managers and other professionals usually choose the communication medium that fits the communication task (Daft et al., 1987; Rice & Case, 1983; Trevino et al., 1987). Thus, computer-assisted communication technology might still be used to exchange factual or technical information, whereas other media are used to elaborate on this information or to exchange other types of information.

The issue is not one of the technologies driving out the use of richer media, but rather of the technologies enabling communications that otherwise would be unlikely to occur. For example, Foster and Flynn (1984), Sproull and Keisler (1986), and others (Palme, 1981; Rice & Case, 1983) reported that the availability of electronic mail caused organizational participants to increase the overall amount of their communication; there was not a one-for-one trade-off between media. Overall, the preponderance of arguments and the available empirical evidence suggest that:

> Proposition 1: Use of computer-assisted communication technologies leads to a larger number and variety of people participating as information sources in the making of a decision.

There will be exceptions to the relationship explicated in this and all propositions. A proposition states that across a large number of cases, ceteris paribus, there will be a tendency for the stated relationship to be observed. Extensive testing of hypotheses derived from the proposition will, eventually, identify any *systematic* exceptions to the relationship.

Further research is needed, of course, to determine (a) if the increase in participation is of practical significance; (b) if the increase in participation leads to higher quality decisions or better acceptance of decisions; (c) if the information includes "hard" information, soft information, or both; and (d) if the decision process becomes more effective. (For reviews of the effects that computer-assisted communication technologies have on group behaviors, see Johansen, 1984, 1988; Rice, 1984. For a review of the behavioral effects of teleconferencing in particular, see Svenning and Ruchinskas, 1984.)

It is important to note that although organizational members tend to use the technologies that communicate their messages with timeliness and veracity (Trevino et al., 1987), they also consider the social acceptance of the technology (Fulk et al., 1987), the ease of use (Huber, 1982), and other attributes (Culnan & Markus, 1987).

Size and Heterogeneity of Decision Units

In many situations, organizational subunits are responsible for developing, recommending, or selecting a proposal for action. Thus, aside from the many individuals who might participate in this process, there is usually one individual or one group of individuals who is formally accountable for the decision. Such an individual or group is referred to as a *decision unit* (Duncan, 1974).

What is the effect of computer-assisted communication technology on the size and heterogeneity of decision units? To answer this question, note that small groups provide more satisfying experiences for their members (Jewell & Reitz, 1981; Kowitz & Knutson, 1980), and that small groups are less costly in terms of human resources. Also note that homogeneous groups provide more satisfying experiences and, if they have the necessary expertise, accomplish decision-related tasks more quickly (Jewell & Reitz, 1981; Kowitz & Knutson, 1980). Finally, note that the discussion associated with Proposition 1 suggests that computer-assisted communication technologies can help decision units to become relatively smaller and more homogeneous by obtaining information beyond that obtainable using traditional communication media; both experts and constituency representatives can often make their knowledge and concerns available through electronic mail, teleconferencing, or videoconferencing. Cost considerations suggest that organizations will seek such efficiencies in their use of human capital. For example:

> You cannot afford to have an expert in very rare kidney disease on your team, just in case you might need him or her someday. . . . The technology allows you to have experts available electronically. (Strassman, 1985b, pp. 22, 27)

What is the effect of computer-assisted decision-support technology, as *contrasted with communication technology, on the size and heterogeneity of decision units?* Sometimes experts can be replaced by expert systems and information keepers can be replaced by management information systems. To the extent that a decision unit can properly use the expert system for resolving same uncertainties, the expert need not be a member of the decision unit; therefore, the unit's size and heterogeneity will be decreased.

Research is needed, of course, to determine if these changes occur. They may not. For example, it may be that organizational aspirations will rise and information technologies will be used to acquire additional diverse information, information whose acquisition and interpretation will require approximately the same size face-to-face decision-group membership as is presently found. If the group's task involves less the acquisition of information than it does the routine processing of information, then the increase in the unit manager's span of control that is facilitated by increased internal communication capability may lead to an overall increase in unit size. It will be interesting to see if future studies can ascertain the net effect of the conflicting forces under various conditions. However, it seems that there are many situations where the increasing efficacy of the technologies and the need for efficient use of human resources will make valid the following:

> Proposition 2: Use of computer-assisted communication and decision-support technologies leads to decreases in the number and variety of members comprising the traditional face-to-face decision unit.

Thus, although Proposition 1 suggests that the total number and variety of *participants serving as information sources* are likely to increase with use of computer-assisted communication technologies, Proposition 2 suggests that the number and variety of *members within the traditional face-to-face decision unit* will decrease with use of either computer-assisted communication or decision-support technologies.

It was noted earlier that people consider multiple criteria when selecting communication media. Similarly, it is important to recognize that even though organizational members tend to choose decision aids and decision procedures that facilitate the making of timely and technically satisfactory decisions (Lee, McCosh, & Migliarese, 1988; Sabatier, 1978), they also consider other criteria when making this choice (Feldman & March, 1981; Sabatier, 1978).

Meetings

Research confirms the everyday observation that completing an organizational decision process often takes months or years (Mintzberg, Raisinghani, & Théorêt, 1976; Witte, 1972). Meetings are often used to speed up decision processes by creating situations where rate of decision-related information exchange among the key participants is generally higher than that which occurs outside of meetings. Meetings, whether ad hoc processes or co-joined with more permanent structures, such as standing committees, are an important component of organizational decision processes and occupy a good deal of the time of managers and other professionals.

What is or what will be the effect of computer-assisted communication and decision-support technologies on the time absorbed by meetings? Some arguments and evidence suggest these technologies will result in fewer meetings with no loss of progress in the overall organizational decision-making effort. For example, many times discussion is halted and another meeting scheduled because needed information is missing. On-line management information systems or other query-answering technologies, including expert systems, may be able to provide the information, avoiding the need to schedule a subsequent meeting. Also, electronic mail and other computer-assisted communication media sometimes can be used to access soft information that can be obtained only by querying people. Further, decision-support systems can sometimes be used within meetings to conduct analyses that provide new information with which to resolve disagreements about the significance of effects of different assumptions, and thereby allow progress to continue rather than forcing adjournment until subsequent staff work can clarify the effects and another meeting can be scheduled.

Reflection suggests that each of the technologies just mentioned as facilitating the completion of meetings can sometimes lead to the cancellation of meetings. That is, with the added communication and computing capabilities, organizational members can occasionally accomplish the task of the meeting before the meeting takes place. Finally, it seems that because group-decision support systems enhance information exchange, they contribute to the effectiveness of the meeting and, thus, may enable groups to complete their tasks with fewer meetings (Benbasat & Konsynski, 1988; Johansen, 1988).

In contrast, if managers and others involved in making organizational decisions believe that use of the technologies will result in more effective meetings, the availability of the technologies may encourage them to have more decision-related meetings than they would otherwise. In addition, electronic mail, decision support systems, and other information-sharing and generating technologies may facilitate mini-meetings. This might preempt the need for the larger, formal meetings, but the result might be more meetings in total. The outcome of the increase in technologically supported mini-meetings versus the decrease in traditional meetings is a matter for future empirical investigation. However, because such mini-meetings are likely to be shorter, and in view of the several preceding arguments, it seems reasonable to believe that on balance and across time:

> Proposition 3: Use of computer-assisted communication and decision support technologies results in less of the organization's time being absorbed by decision-related meetings.

It is important to note that, because computer-assisted communication technologies facilitate participation in meetings by persons remote in time or geography, more people may ultimately participate in a meeting (see Kerr & Hiltz, 1982, and the discussion surrounding Proposition 1). In contrast, the mini-meetings that sometimes preempt the larger, formal meetings will typically involve fewer people. Because the net effects of these two phenomena are likely to be highly variable, no proposition is offered with *person-hours as* the dependent variable.

Validation of Proposition 3 would be a significant step in documenting the effect that computer-assisted technology has on organizational processes. It would be desirable to test this proposition for each technology separately. This may not always be possible, however, because many technologically progressive organizations will have a variety of technologies in place. (For a review of the effects of advanced information technologies on the overhead costs and benefits of technologically supported meetings, such as document preparation and meeting summaries, see Rice and Bair, 1984.)

EFFECTS AT THE ORGANIZATIONAL LEVEL

Centralization of Decision Making

By enabling top managers to obtain local information quickly and accurately, management information systems reduce ignorance and help the managers to make decisions that they, otherwise, may have been unwilling to make (Blau, Falbe, McKinley, & Tracey, 1976; Child & Partridge, 1982; Dawson & McLoughlin, 1986). Motivations for top managers to make decisions that address local, lower level problems might include lack of confidence in subordinates (Vroom & Yetton, 1973), desire to reduce stress (Bourgeois, McAllister, & Mitchell, 1978), need for achievement (Miller & Droge, 1986), or concern that information about the organization's overall situation or about its policies be appropriately utilized (Huber & McDaniel, 1986). Thus, it seems likely that, on occasion, management information systems would cause decisions to be made at hierarchically higher organizational levels than if these systems were not available (cf. Carter, 1984). The opportunity to obtain contextual clarification with electronic mail and other computer-assisted communication technologies would amplify this tendency.

Conversely, electronic bulletin boards enable lower- and middle-level managers to stay better informed about the organization's overall situation and about the nature of the organization's current problems, policies, and priorities (cf. Fulk & Dutton, 1984) and, consequently, permit decisions made by these managers to be more globally optimal, rather than more parochial and suboptimal, as observed by Dawson and McLoughlin (1986). Further, computer-assisted communication technologies allow lower-level units to clarify information in a more timely manner. Thus, on same occasions it seems that computer-assisted communication technologies would cause decisions to be made at organizational levels lower than if such technologies were not available. Motivations that lead top managers to permit this practice include the desire to decrease the time for organizational units to respond to problems or the desire to provide autonomy for subordinates. Some evidence suggests that this downward shift in decision making occurs—after observing the implementation of networked personal computers in the General Motors' Environmental Activities Staff, Foster and Flynn (1984, pp. 231–232) concluded that "from the former hierarchy of position power there is developing instead a hierarchy of competency. . . . Power and resources now flow increasingly to the obvious centers of competence instead of to the traditional hierarchical loci."

Therefore, *is the net effect of the use of computer-assisted communication and decision-support technologies to increase centralization or to decrease it?* Perhaps this is the wrong question. Together, the arguments in the previous two paragraphs suggest that computer-assisted and decision-support communication technologies, when used to provide most organizational levels with information that was formerly known to only one or a few levels, enable organizations to allow decision making to occur across a greater range of hierarchical levels without suffering as much of a loss in decision quality or timeliness, as would be the case if the technologies were not available. Which hierarchical level would actually make a particular decision would depend on the inclination and availability of the relevant decision makers at the various levels (Cohen, March, & Olsen, 1972) or other idiosyncratic factors, as noted by Fayol (1949/ 1916) and Duncan (1973). Thus, given that the technologies can reduce the one-to-one correspondence between certain organizational levels and certain types of information, it is likely that:

> Proposition 4: For a given organization, use of computer-assisted communication and decision-support technologies leads to a more uniform distribution, across .organizational levels, of the probability that a particular organizational level will make a particular decision.

Corollaries to Proposition 4 are:

Proposition 4a: For a highly centralized organization, use of computer-assisted communication and decision-support technologies leads to more decentralization.

and

Proposition 4b: For a highly decentralized organization, use of computer-assisted communication and decision-support technologies leads to more centralization.

Propositions 4, 4a, and 4b follow from the arguments presented, but are not directly based on empirical studies. It may be that the forces implied in the arguments are weak relative to those that influence traditional practices. For example, advanced information technologies enable centralized organizations to become even more centralized without incurring quite the loss in responsiveness that would occur without their presence. Similarly, they enable decentralized organizations to operate in an even more decentralized manner. I believe that, on balance, the arguments preceding Propositions 4, 4a, and 4b will be the more predictive, but empirical studies may prove this judgment to be incorrect. Certainly, the propositions require empirical study.

It is important to emphasize that by increasing the hierarchical range across which a particular type of decision may be made without a corresponding loss in decision quality or timeliness, computer-assisted communication and decision-support technologies allow other decision-location considerations to be applied without prohibitive costs. Such considerations include political matters; adherence to organizational traditions, norms, or culture; and the preferred style of top managers. Because the relative influence of these considerations will vary from organization to organization it seems that:

Proposition 5: For a population of organizations, broadened use of computer-assisted communication and decision-support technologies leads to a greater variation across organizations in the levels at which a particular type of decision is mode.

Number of Organizational Levels Involved in Authorization

Consider the common situation where at least some conclusions of lower-level units about what actions should be taken must be authorized by higher-level units before being acted upon, and these are forwarded upward as proposals. In their study of the approval process for a research and development budget, Shumway and his associates (1975) found that the organizational design caused seven hierarchical levels to be involved in the proposal authorization process. Because each hierarchical level requires time to process a proposal in addition to the time required to render its judgments, the more levels involved, the longer the process takes. Each corresponding increment in the duration of the approval process can, in turn, adversely affect both the timeliness of the authorized action and the enthusiasm with which the proposers carry out the action once it is authorized.

Why then do organizations commonly involve several levels in authorizations? Frequently, the answer is that each level in the hierarchy has knowledge or decision-specific information that qualifies it to apply criteria or decision rules that less well-informed lower-level units cannot apply (cf. Meyer & Goes, 1988). For example, each higher level in an organization tends to know more about organizationwide issues, needs, and resources, and more about the nature of currently competing demands for resources, than does its subordinate units. The greater the amount of such information needed, the greater the number of hierarchical levels that will be involved in the authorization process. (In some respects this is the basis for vertical differentiation.)

What is the likely effect of communication and decision-support technologies on the number of hierarchical levels involved in authorizing a particular decision? It seems that the technologies will cause a decrease in the number of hierarchical levels involved in authorizing a proposal because technologies such as management information systems, expert systems, electronic mail, and electronic bulletin boards make information more widely available. In some cases organizational levels can obtain information that was previously unavailable and, thus, they can apply criteria or decision rules that they previously were not qualified to apply. Consequently, because the technologies facilitate the vertical distribution of information and knowledge (understanding about how to use information), there is more commonality (less extreme differentiation) of information and knowledge across organizational levels. Therefore, except when information technologies are allowed to create a problem of information overload, a given organizational level is more likely to be qualified to apply more criteria and decision rules than it could without the technologies. Assuming that use of the technologies does not somehow cause the number of decision rules to increase greatly, it follows that:

> Proposition 6: Use of computer-assisted communication or decision-support technologies reduces the number of organizational levels involved in authorizing proposed organizational actions.

Possible support for Proposition 6 is found in the observations of managers that use of information technology is associated with a decrease in the number of organizational levels ("Special Report," 1983a, 1983b; "Special Report," 1984). The link between these observations and Proposition 6 is questionable, however, since the observed decreases could follow from decreases in the number of employees. Apparently few systematic studies have examined the relationship between the use of information technology and the number of organizational levels involved in decision authorization. This is unfortunate, because more sophisticated studies may find that the two variables (i.e., the increases in the use of advanced information technology and the reductions in the number of levels) are less causally related *to* each other than they are related to other variables (e.g., attempts to reduce direct labor costs). Thus, such studies may find that observed correlations between the use of advanced information technology and reduction in the number of middle-level managers or organizational levels have much less to do with the seeking of improved decision processes than they have to do with general reductions in the size of organizations when robots replace blue-collar workers and when computers replace clerical workers (cf. Child, 1984).

Number of Nodes in the Information-Processing Network

Decision-making individuals and units obtain much of the information used to identify and deal with decision situations through an information-processing network. The outer boundaries of the network are the sensor units that identify relevant information from either inside or outside the organization. (Examples of sensing units include market analysts, quality control personnel, radar operators, and accountants.) These units serve as information sources, and in many situations they pass on their observations in the form of messages to intermediate units closer to the ultimate user, the decision-making unit. Quite often these intermediate units are at hierarchical levels between the sensor unit and the decision-making unit.

The recipients of the sensor unit's message process the message and pass it on to a unit that is closer still to the decision-making unit. The information processing performed by such intermediate units ranges from straightforward relaying to elaborate interpreting. For a variety of reasons the number of such units—the number of nodes on the network path connecting the sensor unit to the decision unit—may be greater than warranted. "Most managerial levels don't do anything. They are only relays" (Drucker, 1987, p. 61).

Besides the unnecessary costs implied in Drucker's observation, each information-handling unit in the network path tends to contribute distortions and delays, as detailed by Huber (1982). For these reasons, top managers sometimes attempt to reduce the role and number of such units and to use computer-assisted technologies as alternative means for obtaining the information ("Special Report," 1983a, 1983b; "Special Report," 1984). This reduces the workload used to justify the existence of these intermediate units and levels. Computers sometimes can be used to merge, summarize, filter, and even interpret information, thus eliminating clerical workers, managers, and the organizational units of which they are a part. These observations suggest that use of computer-assisted information processing and communication technologies would lead to the elimination of human nodes in the information processing network.

There is, however, a contrary argument. Elimination of intermediate nodes in the network results in an information overload on the decision unit. When the processing functions performed by intermediate information-processing units cannot be as efficiently or effectively performed with technology or changed practices, such as those suggested by Huber (1984) and Hiltz and Turoff (1985), the units will be retained. *So, do the aforementioned technologies actually decrease the number of nodes in the organization's information-processing network?*

Informal surveys ("Special Report," 1983a, 1983b; "Special Report," 1984) have found correlations between the use of computer-assisted communication technology and decreases in the number of managers. However, as mentioned previously, these surveys did not determine the cause of the correlation, and it may be the result of concomitant reductions in the overall number of employees. Certainly, there is a need for more sophisticated, in-depth studies to determine the nature of the cause-effect links between the use of computer-assisted technology and the number of nodes in the information-processing network. On balance, however, it seems that in some instances reductions would take place. Thus,

> Proposition 7: Use of computer-assisted information processing and communication technologies leads to fewer intermediate human nodes within the organizational information-processing network.

(Note that Proposition 7 deals with the number of intermediate nodes, Proposition 1 deals with the number of information sources, and Proposition 2 deals with the number of members in the traditional face-to-face unit.) If the network processes information across hierarchical levels, then a corollary of Proposition 7 is:

> Proposition 7a: Use of computer-assisted information processing and communication technologies reduces the number of organizational levels involved in processing messages.

The last two propositions of this section deal with the design of the organization's memory. Designing the organization's memory is a novel idea to organizational scientists, but will become more familiar as organizational learning becomes a more mature area of study and as top management increases its emphasis on intellectual capital.

EFFECTS ON ORGANIZATIONAL MEMORY

In their discussion of information search routines in organizational decision making, Mintzberg and his colleagues (1976) distinguished between an organization's memory search and the active or passive search of its environment. *Memory search* refers to "the scanning of the organization's existing memory, human or paper" (or, today, computer-resident) (Mintzberg, Raisinghani, & Théorêt, 1976, p. 255).

Everyday experience and some research suggest that the human components of organizational memories are less than satisfactory. For example, research shows that forecasts about the time necessary to complete organizational tasks are quite erroneous, even when such tasks have been carried out in the organization on many occasions. Kidd (1970), Abernathy (1971), and Souder (1972) studied the judgments of project completion times made by managers, and found them to be woefully inaccurate, even though the managers had a good deal of experience with similar projects. Given what is known about the many factors contributing to inaccurate learning and incomplete recall (Nisbett & Ross, 1980; Kahneman, Slovic, & Tversky, 1982) and to motivational distortions in sharing information (Huber, 1982), it is not at all surprising that the human components of organization memories are less than satisfactory.

The problem of poor memory is, however, much more complex than simple considerations of the deficiencies of humans as repositories of organizational information and knowledge might suggest. Everyday observations make clear (a) that personnel turnover creates great losses of the human components of an organization's memory; (b) that nonanticipation of future needs for certain information results in great amounts of information not being stored or if stored not being easily retrieved; and (c) that information is often not shared by organizational members. For at least these reasons, organizational information and knowledge frequently are less available to decision makers than they would wish.

What are the effects of computer-assisted communication and decision-support technologies on the nature and quality of organizational memory? One answer to this question follows from the fact that more and more organizational activities are conducted or monitored using computer-assisted technology. For instance, it is possible to obtain and maintain information about the times necessary to carry out many organizational activities just as readily as it is to obtain and maintain information about the financial expenditures necessary to carry out the activities (e.g., times necessary to fabricate certain products, to receive shipments, to recruit or train employees, or to deliver services). With sufficient foresight such information can be readily indexed and retrieved through computer technology (Johansen, 1988). Although much organizational knowledge is computer-resident at some point, its users often do not recognize its potential usefulness for future decision making.

Another type of useful computer-resident information is information that is exchanged across the organizational boundaries. In the future, smart indexing (cf. Johansen, 1988) or artificial intelligence will facilitate retrieval of this transaction information and will result in computer-resident organizational memories with certain properties, such as completeness, that are superior to the human components of organizational memories. Ongoing increases in the friendliness and capability of computer-based information retrieval systems suggest that today and even more so in the future:

Proposition 8: Availability of computer-based activity and transaction-monitoring technologies leads to more frequent development and use of computer-resident data bases as components of organizational memories.

Research is needed to understand what incentives are necessary for those organizational members whose actions produce the data to share it or to maintain its quality.

Since much of what an organization learns through experience is stored in the minds of its members, many organizations nurture members who are expert with respect to an intellectual task such as (a) diagnosing quality problems or equipment malfunctions; (b) learning the identities of extraorganizational experts, influence peddlers, resource providers, or other useful nonmembers; and (c) locating information or resources that cannot be located using official, standard sources. As the processes for eliciting knowledge, building expert systems (Welbank, 1983), and validating information (O'Leary, 1988) become standardized, organizations are creating computer-based expert systems using the knowledge of their own experts (Rae & Lingaraj, 1988; Rauch-Hindin, 1988; Waterman, 1986). These expert systems have properties such as accessibility, reliability, and "own-ability," that are both superior to humans and useful as components of organizational memories. Thus, even though expert systems have properties that are inferior to human experts, it seems reasonable to believe that:

Proposition 9: Availability of more robust and user-friendly procedures for constructing expert systems leads to more frequent development and use of in-house expert systems as components of organizational memories.

How do experts react when asked to articulate knowledge and, perhaps, their secrets, so that these can be incorporated into software that might diminish their importance? How do local managers react in such a situation when their influence and status, which are derived from this information or knowledge, is lessened by giving others the ready access to expert systems possessing much of this local information or knowledge? What incentives are appropriate and effective for motivating experts to explicate their knowledge so that it can be used without their future involvement? These are questions in need of investigation.

Propositions 8 and 9 suggest that certain advanced information technologies increase the range of memory components for an organization, just as other advanced information technologies increase the range of media with which the organization can communicate its information and knowledge.

EFFECTS ON OTHER DESIGN VARIABLES

Before leaving this discussion of organizational design variables, it seems useful to comment on the effects of advanced information technologies on some design variables that have not yet been explicitly mentioned: (a) horizontal integration, (b) formalization, (c) standardization, and (d) specialization. *Horizontal integration,* important as it is, requires little additional comment. Since it refers to the use of communication structures and processes for facilitating joint decision making among multiple units or individuals, the effects are the same as these discussed in Prepositions 1, 2, and 3, and, as will be seen, in Proposition 14.

Formalization is used to ensure adherence to standards, especially when behavioral norms cannot be counted on to provide the desired behavior. Thus, early in the adoption of any new technology, because the required norms have not had time to develop and to take hold, the level of formalization is often high. (Of course, very early in adoption, standards might not exist, so control might not be exercised through either norms or formalization.) As the new technology becomes familiar and "ages," it seems reasonable to believe that the degree of formalization associated with it approaches the degree of formalization associated with the technology being replaced. Consequently, the long-term effect of new technology on formalization might be nil. Although advanced information technology greatly facilitates the recording and retrieval of information about organizational events and activities and, thus, makes control of behaviors and processes through formalization more viable, the use of advanced information technology for closely controlling intelligence development and decision making has not been reported in the literature, to my knowledge. This may be due to the frequent need for initiative and non-routine activities by those engaged in these processes (cf. Wilensky, 1967). (For a discussion of the use of advanced information technology for controlling other behaviors and processes in organizations, *see* Zuboff, 1984.)

Standardization is the reduction of variability in organizational processes. As noted earlier, advanced information technologies have greatly increased the range of communication and decision procedures. If organizational members can use discretion when choosing which information technology to use (and such discretion seems commonplace), the variation of technologies will increase, and standardization will decrease: This is so apparent that no proposition is needed.

With regard to *specialization,* advanced information technology can either lead to the addition of job categories (e.g., computer programmer) or the deletion of job categories (e.g., bookkeeper), and, therefore, will affect the degree of specialization within the organization. However, such specialities support, make operational, or become part of technologies. The increase or decrease in the variety of support personnel has little or no impact on intelligence or decision making, independent of the technologies. For this reason, *specialization* was not discussed as a design variable that affects organizational intelligence and decision making.

Propositions 1 through 9 describe the effects that advanced information technologies have on those aspects of organizational design that, ultimately, influence organizational intelligence and decision making. The next section deals with more direct effects of the technologies on organizational intelligence and decision making and, ultimately, on organizational performance in these areas.

Of course the development of organizational intelligence and the making of decisions are organizational processes inextricably intertwined with an organization's design. The present conceptual separation of these processes from design is primarily for expository purposes.

EFFECTS ON ORGANIZATIONAL INTELLIGENCE AND DECISION MAKING

This section sets forth two propositions dealing with information acquisition and then three propositions concerned with decision making and decision authorization.

Environmental Scanning and Organizational Intelligence

To some degree, all organizations scan their external and internal environments for information about problems or opportunities. Yet sometimes managers do not learn about problems or opportunities in time to act with maximum effectiveness. In many cases the alerting message is delayed as it moves through the sequential nodes in the communication network. In other instances incumbents of adjacent nodes in the communication network have difficulty connecting across time, as in "telephone tag." *What is the effect of advanced information technologies on these impediments? What is the effect on information acquisition overall?* With regard to these questions, recall that the reasoning surrounding Proposition 7 suggested that the use of computer-assisted information processing and communications technologies leads to rifle-shooting of messages and ultimately to fewer intermediary nodes in the information processing network. This idea, in combination with the fact that the probability and duration of message delay and the probability and extent of message distortion are both positively related to the number of sequential links in the communication chain connecting the receiver to the information source, suggests that use of computer-assisted information processing and communication technologies would facilitate rapid and accurate identification of problems and opportunities.

A contrary line of reasoning exists, however. Since an important role of many information network nodes is to screen, package, and interpret messages, the use of advanced information technologies and the consequent elimination of nodes can result in an overload of irrelevant, poorly packaged, or uninterpretable messages. One study indicated that this danger may not be as serious as it appears. Hiltz and Turoff (1985) found that social norms and management practices tend to develop to reduce the problem to a level below what might be imagined. It is likely that computer-assisted technologies will be used to enhance information retrieval, especially from lower organizational levels and outside sources. Thus, on balance:

Proposition 10: Use of computer-assisted information processing and communication technologies leads to more rapid and more accurate identification of problems and opportunities.

Use of these technologies can aid not only in the identification of problems and opportunities, but also in a wide variety of more focused probes and data acquisitions for the purpose of analysis. Recalling Mintzberg et al.'s (1976) *active search,* and Mintzberg's (1975) notion that managers require timely information, consider that computer-assisted information systems can bring facts to the organization's decision makers almost immediately after the facts occur (e.g., checkout scanners and commodities market data).

Together, technologically advanced systems for the acquisition of external information and the development of computer-enhanced organizational memories enable organizations to increase the range of information sources that the producers and users of organizational intelligence can draw upon. Thus, in summary:

Proposition 11: Use of computer-assisted information storage and acquisition technologies leads to organizational intelligence that is more accurate, comprehensive, timely, and available.

This proposition is based on the assumption that the external information sources are accurate, comprehensive, timely, and available. Otherwise, garbage in, garbage out.

A matter of some interest is how inclined information users are to employ accessible sources, rather than those with the highest quality information (cf. Culnan, 1983; O'Reilly, 1982). How computer-assisted communications and information acquisition systems affect the trade-off between perceived accessibility and perceived quality, and the resultant information-seeking behavior, is an issue much in need of investigation.

Decision Making and Decision Authorization

It is reasonable to believe that the quality of an organizational decision is largely a consequence of both the quality of the organizational intelligence (as implied in Proposition 11) and the quality of the decision-making processes. Further, the discussion associated with Propositions 1 and 3 (and perhaps other of the propositions related to organizational design) strongly suggests that, by facilitating the sharing of information, computer-assisted communication technologies increase the quality of decision making, and that by aiding in the analysis of information within decision units, computer-assisted decision-aiding technologies increase the quality of decision making. Thus, in helping with Propositions 1, 3, and 11:

Proposition 12: Use of computer-assisted communication and decision-support technologies leads to higher quality decisions.

Because reducing the number of levels involved in authorizing an action will reduce the number of times the proposal must be handled (activities of a logistical, rather than a judgmental nature), it seems likely that:

Proposition 13: Use of computer-assisted communication and decision-support technologies reduces the time required to authorize proposed organizational actions.

Authorization as a particular step in the decision-making process has received little attention from organizational scientists (for exceptions, see Carter, 1971; Gerwin, 1979), and the time required for organizations to authorize action also has received little attention (for exceptions, see Mintzberg et al., 1976; Shumway et al., 1975). These topics are worthy candidates for study in general, and the potential effects of information technology seem to be especially in need of examination, given their probable importance and the total absence of systematic research on their effect on decision authorization.

Once a problem or opportunity has been identified, several types of activities are undertaken that might be more effective if undertaken using advanced information technology. For example, management information systems and electronic mail might enable decision makers to immediately obtain the information they seek when deciding what to do about problems and opportunities (see Proposition 11). Decision-support systems might enable decision makers or their assistants to analyze this information quickly (at least for some types of problems). Electronic mail and video- or teleconferencing might help decision makers obtain clarification and consensus without the delays imposed by the temporary nonavailability, in terms of physical presence, of key participants (see Proposition 1). Finally, forms of advanced information technology might reduce the time required to authorize proposed organizational actions (see Proposition 13). These facts suggest that:

Proposition 14: Use of computer-assisted communication and decision-support technologies reduces the time required to make decisions.

Available evidence supports this proposition:

For instance, managers in the Digital Equipment Corporation reported that electronic mail increased the speed of their decision making and saved them about seven hours a week (Crawford, 1982). Managers at Manufacturers Hanover Trust reported that electronic mail saved them about three hours a week, mostly by eliminating unreturned phone calls and internal correspondence (Nyce & Groppa, 1983). (Sproull & Keisler, 1988, p. 1492)

However, studies employing casual self-report data need to be supplemented with more systematic studies, such as some of those noted by Rice and Bair (1984). Sophisticated studies may find that the actual reduction in time is marginal, and that the net benefit may be offset to some extent by the losses in decision quality that may follow from a reduction in the time spent cogitating, as noted by Weick (1985).

TOWARD A CONCEPTUAL THEORY

Extensive organizational use of advanced information technologies is too new, and systematic investigation of their use is too limited, for a theory of their effects to have evolved and received general acceptance. As a result, the propositions set forth here were not derived from a generally accepied theory. Instead, they were pieced together from organizational communication and information systems research, extrapolating only when it seemed reasonable.

A *theory* may be defined as a set of related propositions that specify relationships among variables (cf. Blalock, 1969, p. 2; Kerlinger, 1986, p. 9). The set of propositions set forth in this article, related to one another (at the very least) through their possessing a common independent variable, advanced information technology, passes this definitional test of a theory. Yet, more is expected from a theory, such as a framework that integrates the propositions.

If other connecting relationships can be found to link them, perhaps the propositions of this paper can serve as building blocks for the development of a less atomistic, more conceptual theory. The result would, of course, be quite tentative, in that the propositions require additional substantiation and in that any one author's connective framework must be subjected to review, critique, and discussion across an extended period before gaining general acceptance. As a step in the development of a conceptual theory of the effects of advanced information technologies, the following concepts and constructs are offered. The constructs summarize and the concepts connect ideas that were mentioned previously but served a different purpose at the time.

Concept 1: Advanced information technologies have properties different from more traditional information technologies. *Availability of advanced information technologies* (Construct A) extends the range of communication and decision-making options from which potential users can choose. On occasion a technology will be chosen for use, and when chosen wisely-such that the chosen technology's properties better fit the user's task-use of the technology leads to improved task performance. This reinforcement in turn leads to more frequent *use of advanced information technology* (Construct B).

Concept 2: Use of *advanced information technologies* (Construct B) leads to more available and more quickly retrieved information, including external information, internal information, and previously encountered information, and thus leads to *increased information accessibility* (Construct C). Concept 2 follows from Propositions 1, 4, and 7 through 11.

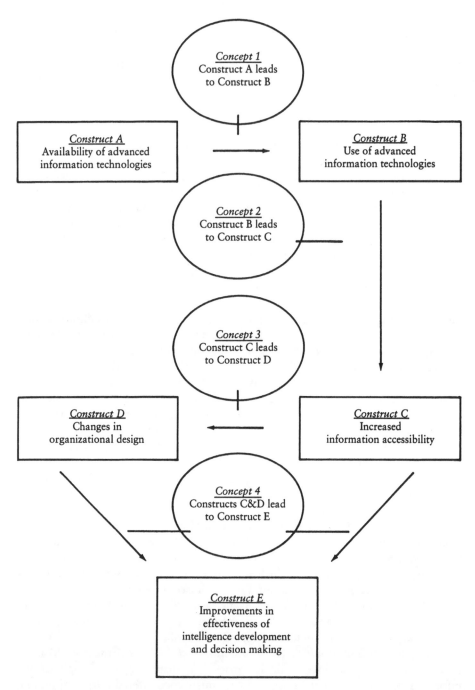

FIGURE 9.1 Conceptual theory of the effects of advanced information technologies on organizational design intelligence, and decision making.

Concept 3: *Increased information accessibility* (Construct C) leads to the *changes in organizational design* (Construct D). Concept 3 follows from Propositions 1 through 7.

Concept 4: *Increased information accessibility* (Construct C), and those *changes in organizational design* (Construct D) that increase the speed and effectiveness with which information can be converted into intelligence or intelligence into decisions, lead to organizational intelligence being more accurate, comprehensive, timely, and available and to decisions being of higher quality and more timely, decisions that lead to improvements in *effectiveness of intelligence development and decision making* (Construct E). Concept 4 follows from Propositions 11 through 14.

These constructs and concepts are summarized in Figure 9.1.

SUMMARY AND RECOMMENDATIONS

In the form of propositions and their corollaries, this article sets forth a theory concerning the effects that computer-assisted communication and decision-aiding technologies have on organizational design, intelligence, and decision making. Subsequently, the propositions were connected with constructs and concepts, and from these a more conceptual theory was developed.

Some boundaries on the original theory (here called *the theory)* were delineated early in the paper. The theory is, nevertheless, a candidate for elaboration and expansion. For example, it was not possible, within the space available, to extend the scope of the theory to include propositions having to do with the effects of advanced information technologies on the distribution of influence in organizational decision making (see Zmud, in press). Examination of some relevant literature makes clear that numerous propositions would be necessary because (a) the technologies may vary in their usefulness for generating the particular types of information used by decision participants having different sources of influence, (b) the technologies may vary in their usefulness for enhancing the image or status of participants having different organizational roles, and (c) the technologies may vary in their usefulness to different types of participants as aids in the building of decision-determining coalitions. Certainly, the theory is a candidate for elaboration and expansion, just as it is a candidate for empirical testing and consequent revision.

The process used to generate the propositions comprising the theory included drawing on components of established organization theory and an findings from communication and information systems research. Specific suggestions were made, with respect to many of the propositions, about matters in need of empirical investigation. In addition to these specific suggestions, three somewhat more global recommendations are in order. The first is directed to any researchers exploring the effects of advanced information technologies. In this article, different forms of advanced information technology were discussed by name (e.g., electronic mail) yet the propositions were stated in general terms. This latter fact should not obscure the need to specify more precisely the particular technology of interest when developing hypotheses to be tested empirically. As more is learned about the effects of computer-assisted communication and decision-support technologies, it may be found that even subtle differences count (cf. the discussion by Markus & Robey, 1988). Even if this is not so, as researchers communicate about these matters among themselves and with administrators, it behooves them to be clear and precise about what it is that they are discussing.

The second suggestion, directed to organizational researchers, is to believe (a) that information technology fits within the domain of organization theory and (b) that it will have a significant effect on organizational design, intelligence, and decision making. Organization researchers, in general (there are always welcome exceptions), may not believe that these technologies fit within the domain of organization theory. This would be an erroneous belief. Organization theory has always been concerned with the processes of communication, coordination, and control and, as is apparent from the research of communication and information systems researchers (Culnan & Markus, 1987; Rice & Associates, 1984), the nature and effectiveness of these processes are changed when advanced information technologies are employed. Organizational researchers also may not have recognized that organizational designs are, at any point in time, constrained by the capability of the available communication technologies. Two of the infrequent exceptions to this important observation are cited by Cul nan and Markus (1987):

> Chandler (1977) for example, argues that the ability of the telegraph to facilitate coordination enabled the emergence of the large, centralized railroad firms that became the prototype of the modern industrial organization. Pool (1983) credits the telephone with the now traditional physical separation of management headquarters from field operations, and in particular with the development of the modern office skyscraper as the locus of administrative business activity. (p. 421)

Also, Huber and McDaniel (1986) state that:

> Without telephones corporations could not have become as large as they have; without radios military units would be constrained to structures and tactics different from those they now use; without computers the processes for managing airline travel would be different from what they are. Any significant advance in information technology seems to lead eventually to recognition and implementation of new organizational design options, options that were not previously feasible, perhaps not even envisioned. (p. 221)

Since information technologies affect processes that are central to organization theory, and since they also affect the potential nature of organization design (a principal application of organization theory), a corollary of this second global recommendation is added: Organizational researchers should study advanced information technology as (a) an intervention or jolt in the life of an organization that may have unanticipated consequences with respect to evolved organizational design, (b) a variable that can be used to enhance the quality (broadly defined) and timeliness of organizational intelligence and decision making, and (c) a variable that enables organizations to be designed differently than has heretofore been possible. (A review of recent discussions of emerging organizational and interorganizational forms [Borys & Jemison, 1989; Luke, Begun, & Pointer, 1989; Miles & Snow, 1986; Nadler & Tushman, 1987] suggests that use of computer-assisted communication technologies can enhance the usefulness of such designs, requiring, as many will, communication among dispersed parties.)

The third global research recommendation is directed toward information systems researchers. It is straightforward. As is easily inferred by observing organizational practices, much information technology is intended to increase directly the efficiency with which goods and services are produced, for example, by replacing workers with computers or robots. But organizational effectiveness and efficiency are greatly determined by the quality and timeliness of organizational intelligence and decision making, and these, in turn, are directly affected by computer-assisted communication and decision-aiding technologies and are also indirectly affected through the impact of the technologies on organizational design. Therefore, it is likely that administrators will ask information systems researchers to help anticipate the effects of the technologies. In addition, builders and users of computer-assisted communication and decision-aiding technologies generally do not explicitly consider the effects that the technologies might have on organizational design, intelligence, or decision making. Thus, information systems researchers should arm themselves with the appropriate knowledge by increasing the amount of their research directed toward studying the effects that advanced information technologies have on organizational design, intelligence, and decision processes and outcomes.

REFERENCES

Abernathy, W. M. (1971) Subjective estimates and scheduling decisions. *Management Science*, 18, 80–88.

Benbasat, I., & Konsynska, B. (1988) Introduction to special section on GDSS, *Management Information Systems Quarterly*, 12, 588–590.

Blau, P. M., Falbe, C. M., Mckinley, W., & Tracey, P. K. (1978) Technology and organization in manufacturing. *Administrative Science Quarterly*, 21, 20–40.

Blalock, H. M., Jr. (1969) *Theory construction: From verbal to mathematical formulations*. Englewood Cliffs, NJ: Prentice-Hall.

Borys, B., & Jemison, C. (1989) Hybrid arrangements as strategic alliances: Theoretical issues in organizational combinations. *Academy* of Management *Review*, 14, 234–249.

Bourgeois, L. J. III, McAllister, D. W., & Mitchell, T. H. (1978) The effects of different organizational environments upon decision and organizational structure. *Academy of Management Journal*, 21, 508–514.

Burgelman, R. A. (1982) A process model of internal corporate venturing in the diversified major firm. *Administrative Science Quarterly,* 28, 223–244.

Carter, E. E. (1971) The behavioral theory of the firm and top-level corporate decisions. *Administrative Science Quarterly,* 16, 413–428.

Carter, N. M. (1984) Computerization as a predominate technology: Its influence on the structure of newspaper organizations. *Academy of Management Journal,* 27, 247–270.

Chandler, A. D., Jr. (1977) *The visible hand: The managerial revolution in American business.* Cambridge, MA: Harvard University Press.

Child, J. (1984) New technology and developments in management organization. *OMEGA,* 12, 211–223,

Child, J. (1988) Information technology, organization, and response to strategic challenges. *California Management Review,* 30(1), 33–50.

Child, J., & Partridge, B. (1982) *Lost managers: Supervisors in industry and society.* Cambridge, MA: Cambridge University Press.

Cohen, M. D., March, J. G., & Olsen, J. P. (1972) A garbage can model of organizational choice. *Administrative Science Quarterly,* 17, 1–25.

Crawford, A. B., Jr. (1982) Corporate electronic mail—A communication-intensive application of information technology. *Management Information Systems Quarterly,* 8, 1–14.

Culnan, M. J. (1983) Environmental scanning: The effects of task complexity and source accessibility on information gathering behavior. *Decision Sciences,* 14, 194–206.

Culnan, M. J., & Markus, L. (1987) Information technologies: Electronic media and intraorganizational communication, In F. M. Jablin, L. L. Putnam, K. H. Roberts, & L. W. Porter (Eds.), *Handbook of organizational communication* (pp. 420–444). Beverly Hills, CA: Sage.

Dolt, R. L., & Lengel, R. H. (1984) Information richness: A new approach to managerial information processing and organizational design. In B. M. Staw & L. L. Cummings (Eds.), *Research in organizational behavior* (pp. 191–233). Greenwich, CT: JAI Press.

Daft, R. L., & Lengel, R. H. (1986) Organizational information requirements, media richness, and structural design. *Management Science,* 32, 554–571.

Daft, R. L., Lengel, R. H., & Trevino, L. K. (1987) Message equivocality, media selection and manager performance: Implications for information systems. *Management Information Systems Quarterly,* 11, 355–368.

Dawson, P., & McLoughlin, I, (1986) Computer technology and the redefinition of supervision. *Journal of Management Studies,* 23, 116–132.

Drucker, P, (1987, September 28) Advice from the Dr. Spock of business. *Business Week,* pp. 61–65.

Duncan, R. B. (1973) Multiple decision-making structures in adopting to environmental uncertainty. *Human Relations,* 26, 273–291.

Duncan, R. B. (1974) Modifications in decision structure in adopting to the environment: Some implications for organizational learning. *Decision Sciences,* 5, 705–725.

Fayol, H. (1949/1916) *General and industrial management* [Constance Storrs, trans.]. London: Pitman.

Feldman, M., & March, J. (1981) Information in organizations as signal and symbol. *Administrative Science Quarterly*, 26, 171–186.

Foster, L. W., & Flynn, D. M. (1984) Management information technology: Its effects on organizational form and function. *Management Information Systems Quarterly*, 8, 229–236.

Fulk, J., & Dutton, W. (1984) Videoconferencing as an organizational information system: Assessing the role of electronic meetings. *Systems, Objectives, and Solutions*, 4, 105–118.

Fulk, J., Steinfield, C. W., Schmitz, J., & Power, J. G. (1987) A social information processing model of media use in organizations. *Communication Research*, 14, 529–552.

Gerwin, D. (1979) Towards a theory of public budgetary decision making. *Administrative Science Quarterly*, 14, 33–46.

Gibson, C. F., & Jackson, B. B. (1987) *The information imperative*. Lexington, MA: Heath.

Hiltz, S. R., & Turoff, M. (1978) *The network nation: Human communication via computer*. Reading, MA: Addison-Wesley.

Hiltz, S. R., & Turoff, M. (1985) Structuring computer-mediated communication systems to avoid information overload. *Communications of the ACM*, 28, 680–689.

Hofer, C. W. (1970) Emerging EDP patterns. *Harvard Business Review*, 48(2), 16–31, 168–171.

Huber, G. (1982) Organizational information systems: Determinants of their performance and behavior. *Management Science*, 28, 135–155.

Huber, G. (1984) The nature and design of post-industrial organizations. *Management Science*, 30, 928–951.

Huber, G. (1988) Effects of decision and communication technologies on organizational decision processes and structures. In R. M. Lee, A. McCosh, & P. Migliarese (Eds.), *Organizational decision support systems* (pp. 317–333). Amsterdam: North-Holland.

Huber, G., & McDaniel, R. (1986) Exploiting information technology to design more effective organizations. In M. Jarke (Ed.), *Managers, micros, and mainframes* (pp. 221–236). New York: Wiley.

Jewell, L. N., & Reitz, H. J. (1981) *Group effectiveness in organizations*. Glenview, IL: Scott, Foresman.

Johansen, R. (1884) *Teleconferencing and beyond*. New York: McGraw-Hill.

Johansen, R. (1988) *Groupwave: Computer support for business teams*, New York: Free Press.

Kahneman, D., Slovic, P., & Tversky, A. (Eds.) (1982) *Judgment under uncertainty: Heuristics and biases*. Cambridge, England: Cambridge University Press.

Kelley, G. (1976) Seducing the elites: The politics of decision making and innovation in organizational networks. *Academy of Management Review*, 1, 66–74.

Kerlinger, F. N. (1986) *Foundations of behavioral research*. New York: Holt, Rinehart & Winston.

Kerr, E. B., & Hiltz, S. R. (1982) *Computer-mediated communication systems: Status and evaluation*. New York: Academic Press.

Kidd, J. S. (1970) The utilization of subjective probabilities in production planning. *Acta Psychologica*. 34, 338–347.

Kowitz, A. C., & Knutson, T. J. (1980) *Decision making in small groups: The search for alternatives.* Boston, MA: Allyn & Bacon.

Lee, R. M., McCosh, A., & Migliarese, P. (1988) *Organizational decision support systems.* Amsterdam: North-Holland.

Luke, R. D., Begun, J. W., & Pointer, D. D. (1989) Quasi firms: Strategic interorganizational forms in the health care industry. *Academy of Management Review*, 14, 9–19.

Markus, M. L. (1984). *Systems in organizations: Bugs and features,* Marshfield, MA: Pitman.

Markus, M. L., & Robey, D. (1988) Information technology and organizational change: Conceptions of causality in theory and research. *Management Science*, 34, 583–598.

Meyer, A. D., & Goes, J. B. (1988) Organizational assimilation of innovations: A multi-level contextual analysis, *Academy of Management Journal*, 31, 897–923.

Miles, R., & Snow, C. (1986) Organizations: New concepts for new forms, *California Management Review*, 28(3), 62–73.

Miller, D., & Droge, C. (1986) Psychological and traditional determinants of structure, *Administrative Science Quarterly*, 31, 539–560.

Mintzberg, H. (1975) The manager's job: Folklore and fact, *Harvard Business Review*, 53(4), 49–61,

Mintzberg, H., Raisinghani, D., & Théorêt, A. (1976) The structure of "unstructured" decision processes. *Administrative Science Quarterly*, 21, 246–275.

Nadler, D., & Tushman, M. L. (1987) *Strategic organization design.* Glenview, IL: Scott, Foresman.

Nisbett, R., & Ross, R. L. (1980) *Human inference: Strategies and shortcomings of social judgment,* Englewood Cliffs, NJ: Prentice-Hall.

Nyce, H. E., & Groppa, R. (1983) Electronic mail at MHT. *Management Technology*, 1, 65–72.

O'Leary, D. E. (1988) Methods of validating expert systems, *Interfaces*, 18(61), 72–79.

Olson, M., & Lucas, H. C. (1982) The impact of office automation on the organization: Some implications for research and practice, *Communications of the ACM*, 25, 838–847,

O'Reilly, C. A. (1882) Variations in decision makers' use of information sources: The impact of quality and accessibility of information, *Academy of Management Journal*, 25, 756–771.

Palme, J. (1981) *Experience with the use of the COM computerized conferencing system.* Stockholm, Sweden: Forsvarets Forskningsanstalt.

Pfeffer, J. (1978) *Organizational design.* Arlington Heights, IL: AHM.

Pfeffer, J., & Moore, W. L. (1980) Power in university budgeting: A replication and extension. *Administrative Science Quarterly*, 19, 135–151.

Pool, I. de Sola (1983) *Forecasting the telephone: A retrospective assessment.* Norwood, NJ: Ablex.

Porter, M. E. (1980) *Competitive strategy: Techniques for analyzing industries and competitors.* New York: Free Press,

Rao, H. R., & Lingaraj, B. P. (1888) Expert systems in production and operations management: Classification and prospects. *Interfaces,* 18(6), 80–81.

Rauch-Hindin, W. B. (1988) *A guide to commercial artificial intelligence.* New York: Prentice-Hall,

Rice, R. E. (1980) The impacts of computer-mediated organizational and interpersonnel communication, In M. Williams (Ed.), *Annual review of information science and technology* (Vol. 15, pp. 221–249). White Plains, NY: Knowledge Industry Publications,

Rice, R. E. (1984) Mediated group communication. In R. E. Rice & Associates (Eds.), *The new media* (pp. 129–154). Beverly Hills, CA: Sage.

Rice, R. E., & Associates, (1984) *The new media.* Beverly Hills, CA: Sage.

Rice, R. E., & Bair, J. R. H. (1984) New organizational media and productivity. In R. E. Rice & Associates (Eds.), *The new media* (pp. 185–216). Beverly Hills, CA: Sage.

Rice, R. E., & Case, D. (1983) Electronic message systems in the university: A description of use and utility. *Journal of Communication,* 33, 131–152.

Robey, D. (1977) Computers and management structure, *Human Relations,* 30, 963–976.

Sabatier, P. (1978) The acquisition and utilization of technical information by administrative agencies, *Administrative* Science *Quarterly,* 23, 396–417.

Sammon, W..L., Kurland, M. A., & Spitalnic, R. (1984) *Business competitor intelligence: Methods for collecting, organizing, and using information,* New York: Wiley.

Shukla, R. K. (1982) Influence of power bases in organizational decision making: A contingency model. *Decision Sciences,* 13, 450–470.

Shumway, C. R., Maher, P. M., Baker, M. R., Souder, W. E., Rubenstein, A. H., & Gallant, A. H. (1975) Diffuse decision making in hierarchical organizations: An empirical examination. *Management Science,* 21, 697–707.

Souder, W. E. (1972) A scaring methodology for assessing the suitability of management science models. *Management Science,* 18, B526–B543,

Special Report: A new era for management. (1983a, April 25) *Business Week,* pp. 50–64.

Special Report: How computers remake the manager's job. (1983b, April 25) *Business Week,* pp. 68–76.

Special Report: Office automation. (1984, October 8) *Business Week,* pp. 118–142.

Special Report: The portable executive. (1988, October 10) *Business Week,* pp. 102–112.

Sprague, R. H., & McNurlin, B. C. (1986) *Information systems management in practice.* Englewood Cliffs, NJ: Prentice-Hall,

Sprague, R. H., & Watson, H. J. (1986) *Decision support systems: Putting theory into practice.* Englewood Cliffs, NJ: Prentice-Hall.

Sproull, L., & Keisler, S. (1986) Reducing social context cues: Electronic mail in organizational communication. *Management Science,* 32, 1492–1512.

Steinfield, C. W., & Fulk, J. (1987) On the role of theory in research on information technologies in organizations: An introduction to the special issue. *Communication Research,* 14, 479–480.

Strassman, P. (1985a) *Information payoff: The transformation of work in the electronic age.* New York: Free Press.

Strassman, P. (1985b) Conversation with Paul Strassman. *Organizational Dynamics,* 14(2), 19–34.

Svenning, L., & Ruchinskas, J. (1984) Organizational teleconferencing. In R. E. Rice & Associates (Eds.), *The new media* (pp. 217–248). Beverly Hills, CA: Sage.

Trevino, L. K., Lengel, R., & Daft, R. L. (1987) Media symbolism, media richness, and media choice in organization: A symbolic interactionist perspective. *Communication Research,* 14, 553–574.

Vroom, V. H., & Yetton, P. W. (1973) *Leadership and decision-making.* Pittsburgh: University of Pittsburgh.

Waterman, D. A. (1986) *A guide to expert systems.* Reading, MA: Addison-Wesley.

Weick, K. E. (1985) Cosmos vs. chaos: Sense and nonsense in electronic contexts. *Organizational Dynamics,* 14(2), 50–64.

Welbank, M. (1983) *A review of knowledge acquisition techniques for expert systems.* Ipswich, England: Martlesham Consultancy Services.

Whisler, T. (1970) *Impact of computers on organizations.* New York: Praeger.

Wilensky, H. L. (1967) *Organizational intelligence.* New York: Basic Books.

Williams, F., & Rice, R. E. (1983) Communication research and the new media technologies. In R. N. Bostrom (Ed.) *Communication yearbook 7* (pp. 200–225). Beverly Hills, CA: Sage.

Witte, E. (1972) Field research on complex decision-making processes—The phase theorem. *International Studies of Management & Organization,* 2, 156–182.

Zmud, R. W. (1983) *Information systems in organizations.* Glenview, IL: Scott, Foresman.

Zmud, R. W. (in press) Opportunities for manipulating information through new technology. In J. Fulk & C. Steinfield (Eds.), *Perspectives on organizations and new information technology.* Beverly Hills, CA: Sage.

Zuboff, S, (1984) *In the age of the smart machine.* New York: Basic Books.

George P. Huber is the Fondren Foundation Centennial Chaired Professor of Business at the University of Texas at Austin. Correspondence concerning this article can be sent to him at the Department of Management, CBA 4.202, University of Texas, Austin, TX 78712.

I am indebted to Janice Beyer, Richard Daft, John Huber, Reuben McDaniel, Chet Miller, Ronald Rice, and Robert Zmud for their helpful suggestions on earlier versions of this paper and to Reuben McDaniel for his earlier contributions to my thinking on this subject.

This research was largely supported by the U.S. Army Research Institute for the Behavioral and Social Sciences.

This paper draws upon and expands upon Huber (1988).

Chapter 10

Organizing Knowledge[1]

John Seely Brown and Paul Duguid[*]

The firm, taken for granted in the conventional economy, appears to have a doubtful future in the information economy. The new technologies that are helping to define this new economy are simultaneously battering the venerable institutions of the old economy—the press, broadcast media, universities, even governments and nations are all under threat. Enthusiasts suggest that no formal organization need or should come between the empowered individual and Marshall McLuhan's amorphous "global village." So it's not surprising to hear that cyberspace has served notice on the firm that its future, at best, may only be virtual.

Many such predictions favor a "transaction cost" view of the firm. Transaction costs are portrayed as the glue that holds an organization together, and many of these are thought to derive from inefficiencies in communication. Thus, it is easy to conclude that the new communications technologies might drive transaction costs so low that hierarchical firms will dissolve into markets of self-organizing individuals.[2]

[1] Copyright © 1998 by The Regents of the University of California, Reprinted from the *California Management Review*, Vol. 40, No. 3. By permission of The Regents.
[*] The authors are grateful for help generously provided by Robert Cole, Susan Haviland, Richard Kade, Johan de Kleer, Bruce Kogut, Kristina Lee, Teresa da Silva Lopes, Ikujiro Nonaka, J.-C. Spender, Sim Sitkin, Participants in the first Berkeley Knowledge Forum, September 1997.
[2] The classic statement on transaction costs is R.H. Coase, "The Nature of the Firm," *Economica* (1937), pp. 386–405. For more recent explorations, see, for example, Oliver Williamson and Sidney G. Winter, eds., *The Nature of the Firm: Origins, Evolution, and Development* (New York, NY: Oxford University Press, 1993). For relations between technology and transaction costs, see, for example, Thomas W. Malone, JoAnne Yates, and Robert Benjamin, "Electronic Markets and Electronic Hierarchies," *Communications of the ACM* (1987), pp. 484–497 or Claudio U. Ciborra, *Teams, Markets, and Systems: Business Innovation and Information Technology* (New York, NY: Cambridge University Press, 1993). For variants of arguments about "the fading boundaries of the firm," see vol. 152 of *Journal of Institutional and Theoretical Economics* (1966). It is interesting to note that Williamson has retreated a little from the totalizing view of transaction costs

Recently, however, through the work of Ikujiro Nonaka and others, a "knowledge-based" view of the firm has risen to counter the transaction-cost approach. Knowledge-based arguments suggest that organizational knowledge provides a synergistic advantage not replicable in the marketplace. Thus its knowledge, not its transaction costs, holds an organization together.[3] The knowledge-based view provides vital insight into why firms exist (and will continue to exist) and thus why organizational knowledge is a critical part of what firms do.

While knowledge is often thought to be the property of individuals, a great deal of knowledge is both produced and held collectively. Such knowledge is readily generated when people work together in the tightly knit groups known as "communities of practice."[4] As such work and such communities are a common feature of organizations, organizational knowledge is inevitably heavily social in character. Because of its social origin, this sort of knowledge is not frictionless. Beyond communities, locally developed knowledge is difficult to organize. The hard work of organizing knowledge is a critical aspect of what firms and other organizations do.

There are those who see the organization as primarily the unintended consequence of individuals acting in isolation and who believe that an organization's

reflected in many of these works and acknowledged the "complementary perspectives" that an understanding of "embeddedness" contributes. See Oliver Williamson, *"Transaction Cost Economics: How It Works; Where It is Headed,"* Business and Public Policy Working Paper, BPP 67, University of California, Institute of Management, Innovation, and Organization, Berkeley, CA, October 1997.

[3]   See, for example, Ikujiro Nonaka and Hiotaka Takeuchi, *The Knowledge-Creating Company: How Japanese Companies Create the Dynamics of Innovation* (New York, NY: Oxford University Press, 1995); Bruce Kogut and Udo Zander, "What Firms Do? Coordination, Identity, and Learning," *Organization Science,* 7/5 (1996): 502–518; R. M. Grant, "Toward a Knowledge-Based Theory of the Firm," *Strategic Management Journal,* 17 (1996): 109–122; J.-C, Spender, "Making Knowledge the Basis of a Dynamic Theory of the Firm," *Strategic Management Journal,* 17 (1966): 45–62; Dorothy Leonard-Barton, *Wellsprings of Knowledge: Building and Sustaining the Sources of Innovation* (Cambridge, MA: Harvard Business School Press, 1995). For a dissenting voice, see Nicolai J. Foss, "Knowledge-Based Approaches to the Theory of the Firm: Some Critical Comments," *Organization Science,* 7/5 (1996): 470–476. It might be argued that knowledge production simply imposes another transaction cost, so the knowledge-based view is merely part of the transaction cost argument. We argue, however, that some important knowledge is only produced through social, nonmarket relations. Thus the transaction cost for individuals in market relations would be infinite. To embrace infinite transaction costs as part of the transaction cost argument trivializes the very important contribution of transaction cost analysis to understanding organizations.

[4]   For "communities of practice" see Jean Lave and Etienne Wenger, *Situated Learning: Legitimate Peripheral Participation* (New York, NY: Cambridge University Press, 1993); John Seely Brown and Paul Duguid "Organizational Learning and Communities of Practice: Towards a Unified View of Working, Learning, and Innovation," *Organization Science,* 2 (1991): 40–57.

central challenge is to discover knowledge. Once found, such arguments tend to assume, knowledge should travel easily. However, organizations are often replete with knowledge (and also deeply embedded in larger fields or "ecologies" of knowledge). The critical challenge, from this perspective, is to make this knowledge cohere.[5]

It is easy to assume that knowledge-based arguments apply only to what are recognized as "knowledge" firms. These are firms (in software or biotechnology, for example) whose market value far outstrips their conventional assets and rests instead on intellectual capital. The transaction-cost view, it might seem, still applies to every other form of organization. This, however, is not the case. All firms are in essence knowledge organizations. Their ability to outperform the marketplace rests on the continuous generation and synthesis of collective, organizational knowledge.[6] For all organizations, the cultivation of this knowledge—often an implicit, unreflecting cultivation—is the essence of developing a core competency to maintain the organization and resist its dissolution.

The organizational knowledge that constitutes "core competency" is more than "know-what," explicit knowledge which may be shared by several. A core competency requires the more elusive "know-how"—the particular ability to put know-what into practice.[7] While these two work together they circulate separately. Know-what circulates with relative ease. Consequently, of course, it is often hard to protect. (Hence the current crisis in intellectual property laws.) Know-how, by contrast, embedded in work practice (usually *collective* work

[5] It might be possible to reach such a conclusion from Mark Casson, *Information and Organization: A New Perspective on the Theory of the Firm* (Oxford: Clarendon Press, 1997). It is important, however, not to elide information, Casson's main topic, and knowledge, though we do not expand on this problem here. See John Seely Brown and Paul Duguid, "The Knowledge Continuum," in preparation.

[6] See, for example, Leonard-Barton's portrayal of the "learning organization" and her example of Chaparral Steel. Leonard-Barton, op. cit.

[7] The distinction between know-what and know-how and the notion of "dispositional knowledge" comes from Gilbert Ryle, *The Concept of Mind* (London: Hutchinson, 1954). Know-how may appear to be little more than so-called "physical" skills, such as catching a ball or riding a bicycle. It is much more, however. For any student to "know" Newton's second law in any meaningful way requires having the skill to deploy the law in an analysis of colliding objects. This sort of knowledge, a disposition as well as a possession, emerges when called upon. It is evident, for instance, in such complex skills as talking, writing, and thinking or in negotiating with clients, overseeing employees, controlling production processes, developing strategy, conducting scientific experiments, fixing complex machines, cooking a meal, or writing computer programs. For the importance of dispositional knowledge, see S. Noam Cook and John Seely Brown, "Bridging Epistemologies: The Generative Dance between Organizational Knowledge and Organizational Knowing," *Organization Science* (forthcoming).

practice) is *suigeneris* and thus relatively easy to protect.[8] Conversely, however, it can be hard to spread, coordinate, benchmark, or change.

The recent vogue for knowledge management must encompass not simply protecting intellectual property in canonical knowledge organizations, but fostering this more complex form of organizational capital. In practice, this sort of fostering is very much what good managers do, but as knowledge production becomes more critical, they will need to do it more reflectively.

ENDS OF ORGANIZATION

Self-Organizing Systems

Disintermediation, demassification, and disaggregation have become the watchwords of cyberspace. New technologies are apparently breaking collectives down into individual units. (Indeed, it sometimes seems that the only large aggregates needed for the "third wave" will be very long words.) Any form of coherence and coordination beyond the individual, it is predicted, will be the effect be self-organizing systems.[9]

Undoubtedly, in the hands of prominent economists like Kenneth Arrow or Friedrich Hayek, analysis of self-organizing "catallaxies" has helped reveal the very real limits of formal organization.[10] In particular they have helped show the folly of planning economies or ignoring markets. They do not, however, necessarily reject planning or nonmarket behavior on a more local scale. Nor do they prove, as some would have us believe, that deliberate organization is somehow vicious, unnatural, and anti-market. As Hayek himself noted, within spontaneous catallaxies, goal-oriented organizational planning is important.

Curiously, many who argue for self organization often sound less like economists than entomologists: bees, ants, and termites (as well as bats and other small mammals) provide much of the self-organizing case. In a related vein, others draw examples from "artificial life," whose systems are themselves usually modeled on insect- and animal-like behavior.[11] While these provide forceful

---

[8] As the CEO of Chaparral Steel told Leonard-Barton, "He can tour competitors through the plant, show them almost 'everything and we will be giving away nothing because they can't take it home with them.'" Leonard-Barton. op. cit., p. 7.

[9] See, for example, George Gilder, *Life After Television* (New York, NY: W.W. Norton, 1994) for disintermediation; Alvin Toffler, *The Third Wave* (New York, NY: Morrow, 1980) for demassification; Nicholas Negroponte, *Being Digital* (New York, NY: Alfred A. Knopf, 1996) for disaggregation.

[10] Friedrich Hayek, *The Fatal Conceit: The Errors of Socialism* (Chicago, IL: University of Chicago Press, 1988). See, also, Friedrich Hayek, "The Use of Knowledge in Society," *American Economic Review,* 35 (September 1945): 519–30; Kenneth J. Arrow, *The Limits of Organization* (New York, NY: W.W. Norton, 1974).

[11] See, for example, Kevin Kelly, *Out of Control: The New Biology of Machines, Social Systems, and the Economic World* (New York, NY: Addison-Wesley, 1994) for bees; Andy

models, it's important to notice their limits. Humans and insects show many intriguing similarities, but these should not mask some important differences.

In particular, most champions of complex adaptive systems, particularly those of artificial life, overlook the importance to human behavior of deliberate social organization. It is well known that humans distinguish themselves from most other life forms by the increasingly sophisticated technologies they design. It is less often noted that they also distinguish themselves by designing sophisticated social institutions. To pursue the analogies from entomology or artificial life much further, we would need to know what might happen if bugs decided to form a committee or pass a law or artificial agents organized a strike or joined a firm.

Ants moving across a beach, for example, do exhibit elaborate, collective patterns that emerge as each individual adjusts to the environment. In this way, they reflect important aspects of human behavior—of, for example, the uncoordinated synchronicity of sunbathers on the same beach seeking the sun or trying to keep the blown sand out of their sandwiches. But, unlike the sunbathers, ants don't construct coastal highways to reach the beach; or beachfront supermarkets to provide food; or farms to supply the supermarket; or coastal commissions to limit highway building, supermarkets, and farming; or supreme courts to rule on the infringement on constitutionally protected private property rights of coastal commissions; or, indeed, constitutions or property rights at all.

Thus, while ants easily fall victim to diminishing provisions of their local ecology, humans do not. By organizing collectively, people have learned to produce more food out of the same areas of land, to extend known energy resources and search for new ones, to establish new regions for human endeavor, and to design the very technologies that are now paradoxically invoked as the end of organization. In all such cases, organization has helped to foster and focus humanity's most valuable resource: its infinitely renewable knowledge base.[12]

But perhaps most significantly of all, humanity has relied on organization not merely to harness advantage, but to ward off disasters produced by the downside of self-organizing behavior. For example, establishing and continually adjusting socially acknowledged property rights have limited the "tragedy of the commons." Establishing certain trading regulations has prevented markets from spontaneously imploding. Such institutional constraints help channel self-organizing behavior and knowledge production in productive rather than destructive directions. This ability may be one of humanity's greatest assets.

It is easy to cite the undeniable power of spontaneous organization as a way to damn formal organization. However, it makes no more sense to demonize

Clark, *Being There: Putting Brain, Body, and World Together Again* (Cambridge, MA: MIT Press, 1997) for termites; Richard Dawkins, *The Blind Watchmaker* (New York, NY: W.W. Norton, 1986) and Sherry Turkle, *Life On the Screen: Identity in the Age of the Internet* (New York, NY: Simon & Schuster, 1996) for artificial life.

[12] See Douglass C. North, *Structure and Change in Economic History* (New York, NY: W.W. Norton, 1981).

institutions than it does to demonize self-organizing systems. Rather, each must be deployed to restrain the other's worst excesses. That challenge is profoundly difficult, facing as it must the complex, reflexive feedback loops that social institutions create. These make human organization quite different from that of other species (and consequently make social sciences different from natural sciences).

Institutions and Technology

If institutions are endemic to human society, then it seems a mistake to set them in opposition to technologies or economies as some of the cybergurus do. Indeed, a glance back to the last great period of technological innovation suggests the importance of institutions. The end of the nineteenth century gave us the telegraph, the train, the car, the telephone, the airplane, the cinema, and much more. Yet it has been argued that the incredible creative energies of the nineteenth century are evident less in industry, engineering, or the arts than in the new kinds of social institutions that developed (among which are the limited liability corporation, the research university, and the union).[13] Moreover, Nobel economist Douglass North suggests that it was the absence of suitable institutions that caused the century-long lag between the dawn of industrial revolution and the late-nineteenth century's dramatic technological and economic expansion. Similarly, business historian Alfred Chandler claims that half of this expansion resulted from organizational, not technological innovation.[14]

So, while the changing economy may indeed be suffering from the drag of "second wave" institutions, as Alvin Toffler suggests, it doesn't necessarily follow (as Toffler's wired disciples often seem to think) that therefore the third wave will not need institutions at all. One clue to today's "productivity paradox" (which notes that the increasing investment in new technology is not yet showing up in increased national productivity) may well be that society is still struggling to develop third-wave institutions adequate for a new economy.[15]

If nothing else, these examples suggest a complex relationship between organizations and technologies which crude juxtaposition of new technologies and old institutions oversimplifies. It is often pointed out that the arrival of printing technology in the West profoundly destabilized the Catholic church, the dominant institution of its day. But even here, the direction was not simply against institutions. Printing allowed other institutions, the university in particular (and, in some arguments, the modern state) to flourish. And today, while

[13] Raymond Williams, *The Long Revolution* (New York, NY: Columbia University Press, 1961).
[14] Douglass C. North, *Institutions, Institutional Change, and Economic Performance* (New York, NY: Cambridge University Press, 1990): Alfred D. Chandler, *The Visible Hand: The Managerial Revolution in American Business* (Cambridge, MA: Harvard University Press, 1977).
[15] Though for a qualified view of this argument, see Daniel E. Sichel, *The Computer Revolution: An Economic Perspective* (Washington, DC: Brookings Institutions Press, 1997).

communications technologies have dispersed power and control in some sectors, leading to disaggregation and empowerment, in others they have clearly led to centralization and concentration. Francis Fukuyama points, for instance, to the extraordinary success of firms like Wal-Mart and Benetton, both of which have used technology to centralize decision making and disempower their peripheries. In other sectors (communication in particular) the trend has also been towards concentration.

More generally, the relationship between improving technologies and shrinking organizations has not been linear. The telegraph, typewriter, and telephone—which launched the communications revolution—allowed the growth and spread of the giant firms of industrial capitalism as well as the proliferation of small businesses.[16] Similarly, today the emergence of small, adaptable firms may not point in any simple way to market disaggregation. Research into small firms and start-ups highlights the concept of the "embedded firm."[17] These arguments indicate that many important relations between firms, let alone *within* firms, are not ultimately self-organizing, market relations. Increasingly, they reflect complex interorganizational networks. Even where interfirm relations are extremely competitive, cross-sector cooperation and agreements are often highly significant. In the cutthroat world of silicon chip manufacture, for example, firms continuously cross-license one another's patents and even engage in joint research through SEMATECH, a supraorganizational body. The classic antithesis between hierarchy (the firm) and market—even when hedged with the notion of "hybrids"—seems inadequate to describe what is going on. To understand them, we need better insight into what organizations do, and how knowledge plays an important part.

ORGANIZATIONAL ADVANTAGE

The firm has a future because it provides an important means of knowledge generation. In particular, it gives rise to types of knowledge not supported in a marketplace of individuals linked only by market relations. It also plays an

[16] Francis Fukuyama, "Social Networks and Digital Networks," in preparation. For an analysis of the complex relationship between communications technology and institutions see the classic study Harold Innis, *The Bias of Communication* (Toronto: University of Toronto Press, 1951).

[17] See Mark Granovetter "Economic Action and Social Structure: The Problem of Embeddedness," *American Journal of Sociology,* 91(1985): 481–510; Gordon Walker, Bruce Kogut, and Weijian Shan, "Social Capital, Structural Holes and the Formation of an Industry Network," *Organization Science,* 8 (1997): 109–112; Martin Kenney and Urs von Burg, "Bringing Technology Back In: Explaining the Divergence between Silicon Valley and Route 128," in preparation; AnnaLee Saxenian, *Regional Advantage: Culture and Competition in Silicon Valley and Route 128* (Cambridge, MA: Harvard University Press, 1996); Gernot Grabher, *The Embedded Firm: On the Socioeconomics of Industrial Networks* (London: Routledge, 1993).

important role in the development and circulation of complex knowledge in society—circulation that is too readily assumed to be friction free.

Know-How and the Community of Practice

Knowledge is usually thought of as the possession of individuals. Something people carry around in their heads and pass between each other. Know-what is to a significant degree like this. Know-how is different.

Know-how embraces the ability to put know-what into practice. It is a disposition, brought out in practice. Thus, know-how is critical in making knowledge actionable and operational. A valuable manager, for example, is not simply one who knows in the abstract how to act in certain circumstances, but who in practice can recognize the circumstances and acts appropriately when they come along. That disposition only reveals itself when those circumstances occur.

Such dispositional knowledge is not only revealed in practice. It is also created out of practice. That is, know-how is to a great extent the product of experience and the tacit insights experience provides. A friend and lawyer once told us that law school—with its research, writing, and moot courts—prepared her for almost everything she encountered in her work. It did not, however, prepare her for what she did most: answer the phone. That ability—the ability to deal in real time with critical situations, demanding clients, and irrevocable commitments, putting the knowledge she had acquired in school to effective use in practice—she was only able to acquire in practice itself. Her own and her colleagues' ongoing practice has created an invaluable reservoir of dispositional knowledge, which she calls on (and improves) all the time.

Experience at work creates its own knowledge. And as most work is a collective, cooperative venture, so most dispositional knowledge is intriguingly collective—less held by individuals than shared by work groups. This view of knowledge as a social property stands at odds with the pervasive ideas of knowledge as individual. Yet synergistic potential of certain people working in unison—a Gilbert and Sullivan, a Merchant and Ivory, a Young and Rice, or a Pippin and Jordan—is widely acknowledged. In less-exalted work places, too, the ability of certain groups to outstrip their individual potential when working together is a common feature.

Shared know-how can turn up quite unexpectedly. Julian Orr, a colleague at Xerox, studied the firm's "Tech Reps," the technicians who service machines on site. These technicians work most of the time in relative isolation, alone at a customer's office. And they carry with them extensive documentation about the machines they work with. They would seem to be the last people to have collective dispositional knowledge. Yet Orr revealed that despite the individualist character of their work and the large geographical areas they often have to cover, Tech Reps take great pains to spend time with one another at lunch or over coffee. Here they continuously swap "war stories" about malfunctioning machines that outstripped the documentation. In the process of telling and analyzing such stories, the reps both feed into and draw on the group's collective knowledge.[18]

Orr describes an extraordinary scene in which one technician brought in another to help tackle a machine that had defied all standard diagnostic procedures. Like two jazz players involved in an extended, improvisational riff, they spent an afternoon picking up each other's half-finished sentences and partial insights while taking turns to run the machine and watch it crash until finally and indivisibly they reached a coherent account of why the machine didn't work. They tested the theory. It proved right. And the machine was fixed.

This case and Orr's study as a whole suggest that, even for apparently individual workers armed with extensive know-what, collective know-how can be highly significant. More generally it supports the notion that collective practice leads to forms of collective knowledge, shared sensemaking, and distributed understanding that doesn't reduce to the content of individual heads.

A group across which such know-how and sensemaking are shared—the group which needs to work together for its dispositional know-how to be put into practice—has been called a "community of practice." In the course of their ongoing practice, the members of such a group will develop into a de facto community. (Often, the community, like the knowledge, is implicit. Communities of practice do not necessarily think of themselves as a community in the conventional sense. Equally, conventional communities are not necessarily communities of practice.) Through practice, a community of practice develops a shared understanding of what it does, of how to do it, and how it relates to other communities and their practices—in all, a "world view." This changing understanding comprises the community's collective knowledge base. The processes of developing the knowledge and the community are significantly interdependent: the practice develops the understanding, which can reciprocally change the practice and extend the community. In this context, knowledge and practice are intricately involved. (For a related argument, see Nonaka's celebrated "Knowledge Creation Spiral.")[19]

This picture of knowledge embedded in practice and communities does not dismiss the idea of personal, private knowledge. What people have by virtue of membership in a community of practice, however, is not so much personal, modular knowledge as shared, partial knowledge.[20] Individual and collective knowledge in this context bear on one another much like the parts of individual

[18] Julian E. Orr, *Talking About Machines: An Ethnography of a Modern Job* (Ithaca, NY: ILR Press, 1996).

[19] Nonaka and Takeuchi, op. cit., p. 72; Ikujiro Nonaka and Noboru Konno, "The Concept of '*Ba*': Building a Foundation for Knowledge Creation," *California Management Review*, 40/3 (Spring 1998).

[20] For views of personal knowledge, see M. Polanyi, *The Tacit Dimension: The Terry Lectures,* (Garden City, NJ: Doubleday, 1966); Ludwig Wittgenstein, *Philosophical Investigations,* G.E.M. Anscombe, trans. (New York, NY: Macmillan, 1953); David *Bloor,*

performers to a complete musical score, the lines of each actor to a movie script, or the roles of team members to the overall performance of a team and a game. Each player may know his or her part. But on its own, that part doesn't make much sense. Alone it is significantly incomplete: it requires the ensemble to make sense of it.[21]

Communities of Practice and Organizations

If in many situations, work and knowledge do not readily decompose into the possession of individuals but remain stubbornly group properties, then markets themselves do not readily reduce to homo economicus, the idealized individual. Nonmarket organization (the community of practice) may be a salient factor of market activity.

Does this suggest that, if nonmarket organization is needed at all, it is only at the level of community of practice? that everything else can be done in the market? On the contrary, most formal organizations are not single communities of practice, but, rather, hybrid groups of overlapping and interdependent communities. Such hybrid collectives represent another level in the complex process of knowledge creation. Intercommunal relationships allow the organization to develop collective, coherent, synergistic organizational knowledge out of the potentially separate, independent contributions of the individual communities. The outcome is what we think of as organizational knowledge, embracing not just organizational know-what but also organizational know-how.

Cross-community organization is important because it helps to overcome some of the problems communities of practice create for themselves. For instance, as Dorothy Leonard-Barton points out, isolated communities can get stuck in ruts, turning core competencies into core rigidities. When they do, they need external stimuli to propel them forward.[22]

Communities of practice, while powerful sources of knowledge, can easily be blinkered by the limitations of their own world view. In a study of technological innovation, for example, Raghu Garud and Michael A. Rappa show how even the most sophisticated of knowledge workers can fail to recognize quite damning evidence.[23] New knowledge often requires new forms of evaluation, and when the two are produced together, knowledge, belief, and evaluation may

---

Wittgenstein: A Social Theory of Knowledge (New York, NY: Columbia University Press, 1983); Thomas Nagel, The Last Word (New York, NY: New York University Press, 1997).

[21] For a discussion of collective sensemaking, see Karl Weick, Sensemaking in Organizations (Beverly Hills, CA: Sage Books, 1995); Karl Weick and K. Roberts, "Collective Mind in Organizations," Administrative Science Quarterly, 38/3 (September 1993): 357–381.

[22] Leonard-Barton, op. cit., especially chapter 2.

[23] Raghu Garud and Michael A. Rappa, "A Socio-Cognitive Model of Technology Evolution: The Case of Cochlear Implants," Organization Science, 5 (1994): 344–362.

only reinforce one another, while evaluation independent of that belief appears irrelevant.

Garud and Rappa's study explores this self-deluding/self-reinforcing social behavior in highly technological communities, where counterevidence is usually assumed to be easily capable of overwhelming belief. Obviously, such problematic interdependence between belief and evaluation is even more likely in areas where what counts as evidence is less clear cut and where beliefs, hunches, predictions, and intimations are all there is to go on—which, of course, is the case in most areas of human behavior.

Markets offer one very powerful way to punish self-deluding/self-reinforcing behavior or core rigidities once these have set in.[24] Such punishment tends, however, to be severe, drastic, and reserved for organizations as a whole. Organizations present an alternative antidote, which works more readily at the community level and is both more incremental and less destructive. By yoking diverse communities—with different belief systems and distinct evaluative practices—together into cohesive hybrids, organizations as a whole challenge the limits of each community's belief. This process generates knowledge through what Hirshhorn calls the "productive tension" or Leonard-Barton "creative abrasion," forcing particular communities beyond their own limits and their own evaluative criteria.[25]

Thus while markets punish those who produce bad ideas (or fail to produce at all), organizations work to produce beneficial knowledge out of social (rather than market) relations. The productive side of organizational tension, drawing on the experience of people throughout an organization, produces knowledge that requires systemic, not individual explanation. It adds value to the organization as a whole (and redeems those otherwise intractable battles between designers and engineers, sales and marketing, or accounting and almost any other division).

As most people know from experience, cross-divisional synthesis is itself an achievement. But organizations must reach beyond synthesis to synergy. In so doing, they both draw on and continuously create their unique organizational know-how—their ability to do what their competitors cannot. For this they must produce true, coherent organizational knowledge (which is quite distinct from an organization's knowledge—the scattered, uncoordinated insights of each

---

[24] Garud and Rappa argue that in such cases, markets are actually quite inefficient means to challenge the interdependence of belief and evaluation—in part because markets, too, rely on evaluations provided by the blinkered technologies. Garud and Rappa, op. cit., p. 358.

[25] Larry Hirschhorn, *Reworking Authority: Leading and Following in the Post-Modern Organization* (Cambridge, MA: MIT Press, 1997); Leonard-Barton attributes "creative abrasion" to Gerald Hirshberg of Nissan Design International. Leonard-Barton, op. cit., p. 63. See also Karl Jaspers, *The Idea of the University*, H. Reiche and T. Vanderschmidt, trans, (Boston, MA: Beacon Press, 1959) for the notion of "creative tension."

individual in its community of practice). Organizations that fail to achieve this particular synthesis are most likely to fall prey to market alternatives.

DIVISIONS OF LABOR AND DIVISIONS OF KNOWLEDGE

Search and Retrieval

In many ways the relationship between communities of practice and organizations presents a parallel to that between individuals and communities of practice. Yet there are important differences in the way knowledge moves in each relationship.

Organizing knowledge across hybrid communities is the essential activity of organizational management. It is also difficult, though why is not often appreciated. Certainly, most managers will acknowledge that getting knowledge to move around organizations can be difficult. In general, however, such problems are reduced to issues of information flow. If, as the saying goes, organizations don't always know what they know, the solution is seen to lie primarily in better techniques for search and retrieval. Given the opportunity, information appears to flow readily. Hence the belief that technology, which can shift information efficiently, can render organizations, which shift it inefficiently, obsolete. A great deal of hope (and money) is thus being placed on the value of Intranets. Intranets are indeed valuable, but social knowledge suggests that there is more to consider both with regards to search and retrieval.

The distribution of knowledge in an organization, or in society as a whole, reflects the social division of labor. As Adam Smith insightfully explained, the division of labor is a great source of dynamism and efficiency.

Specialized groups are capable of producing highly specialized knowledge. The tasks undertaken by communities of practice develop particular, local, and highly specialized knowledge within the community.

From the organizational standpoint, however, this knowledge is as divided as the labor that produced it. Moreover, what separates divided knowledge is not only its explicit content but the implicit shared practices and know-how that help produce it. In particular, as Garud and Rappa's example suggests, communities develop their own distinct criteria for what counts as evidence and what provides "warrants"—the endorsements for knowledge that encourage people to rely on it and hence make it actionable. (Warrants are particularly important in situations in which people confront increasing amounts of information, ideas, and beliefs; warrants show people what to attend to and what to avoid.) The locally embedded nature of these practices and warrants can make knowledge extremely "sticky," to use Eric von Hippel's apt term.[26]

---

[26] Eric Von Hippel, "'Sticky Information' and the Locus of Problem Solving: Implications for Innovation," *Management Science*, 40 (1994): 429–439.

If the division of labor produces the division of knowledge, then it would seem reasonable to conclude that the market, used to coordinate the division of labor, would serve to coordinate the division of knowledge. But markets work best with commodities, and this "sticky" knowledge isn't easily commodified. Within communities, producing, warranting, and propagating knowledge are almost indivisible. Between communities, as these get teased apart, division becomes prominent and problematic. Hence, the knowledge produced doesn't readily turn into something with exchange value or use value elsewhere. It takes organizational work to develop local knowledge for broader use. Development of knowledge in the organization is a process somewhat analogous to the way a film production company takes a story idea and, stage by stage, develops it into a movie.

Thus, ideas of "retrieving" locally developed knowledge for use elsewhere doesn't address the whole issue. Furthermore, organizations, while they may help get beyond "retrieval," present problems with the antecedent problem of search.

Organizational Blindness

Organizations, as economists have long realized, offer an alternative to markets. Instead of synchronizing goods and labor through markets, they do it through hierarchy. This allows them to overcome some of the stickiness arising from the indivisibility of know-how and practice. Nonetheless, in the organization of knowledge, hierarchical relations unfortunately introduce their own weaknesses. Hierarchical divisions of labor often distinguish thinkers from doers, mental from manual labor, strategy (the knowledge required at the top of a hierarchy) from tactics (the knowledge used at the bottom). Above all, a mental-manual division predisposes organizations to ignore a central asset, the value of the know-how created throughout all its parts.

For example, the Xerox service technicians develop highly insightful knowledge about the situated use (and misuse) of the complex machines they service. As such machines encounter a wide range of locations (some hot, some cold, some dry, some humid) and an inexhaustible range of uses (and abuses), the possible combinations make it impossible to calculate and anticipate all behaviors and problems that might arise. Knowledge about these only emerges in practice. Yet mental-manual divisions tend to make this knowledge invisible to the organization as a whole.

In an analysis of the importance (and anomalous position) of technologists in the modern work place, Stephen Barley has argued forcefully that the knowledge potential in the practice of such front-line employees must eventually force organizations to reconsider the division of labor and the possible loci of knowledge production. As Henry Chesebrough and David Teece point out, "some competencies may be on the factory floor, some in the R&D labs, some in the executive suits." The key to organizational knowledge is to weave it all together. Successful organizational synthesis of knowledge requires discovering knowledge as it emerges in practice. That can't be done if when and where to look are predetermined ex ante.[27]

BEYOND SEARCH AND RETRIEVAL

Within and Between

Bringing this knowledge into view is only a first step, however. Restricted search paths alone are not the problem, significant though these may be. Organizations that set out to identify useful knowledge often underestimate the challenge of making that knowledge useful elsewhere. Robert Cole's study of Hewlett-Packard's approach to quality, for example, shows how the firm successfully pursued "best practices" throughout the corporation. The search, however, assumed that, once these practices were identified, the knowledge (and practice) would spread to where it was needed. In the end, HP was quite successful in identifying the practices. It was not, however, so successful in moving them.[28]

Some knowledge moves quite easily. People assume that it is explicit knowledge that moves easily and tacit knowledge that moves with difficulty.[29] It is, rather, socially embedded knowledge that "sticks," because it is deeply rooted in practice. Within communities, practice helps to generate knowledge and evince collective know-how. The warranting mechanisms—the standards of judgment whereby people distinguish what is worthwhile and valid from what is not—inhere in the knowledge. Consequently, trying to move the knowledge without the practice involves moving the know-what without the know-how.

Due to its social origins, knowledge moves differently *within* communities than it does *between* them. Within communities, knowledge is continuously embedded in practice and thus circulates easily. Members of a community implicitly share a sense of what practice is and what the standards for judgment are, and this supports the spread of knowledge. Without this sharing, the community disintegrates.

Between communities, however, where by definition practice is no longer shared, the know-how, know-what, and warrants embedded in practice must separate out for knowledge to circulate. These divisions becomes prominent and problematic. Different communities of practice have different standards, different ideas of what is significant, different priorities, and different evaluating

---

[27] Stephen R. Barley, "Technicians in the Workplace: Ethnographic Evidence for Bringing Work into Organization Studies," *Administrative Science Quarterly,* 41 (1966): 401–444; Henry W. Chesbrough and David J. Teece, "When is Virtual Virtuous? Organizing for Innovation," *Harvard Business Review,* 74/1(1996): 65–73.

[28] Robert Cole, *The Quest for Quality Improvement: How American Business Met the Challenge* (New York, NY: Oxford University Press, forthcoming).

[29] Polanyi, op. cit.

criteria. What looks like a best practice in California may not turn out to be the best practice in Singapore (as HP found out).

The divisions between communities tend to encourage local innovation, as Adam Smith recognized, but they also encourage isolation. Anyone who has spent some time on a university campus knows how knowledge-based boundaries can isolate highly productive communities from one another. That it is very hard to get sociologists and mathematicians to learn from one another is obvious. What is sometimes less clear is that biochemists can't always share insights with chemists, economic historians with historians, economists with the business school, and so forth. Different precepts and different attitudes, shaped by practice, make interchange between quite similar subjects remarkably difficult, and thus they invisibly pressure disciplines to work among themselves rather than to engage in cross-disciplinary research. Over time, disciplines increasingly divide rather than combine.

On the campus, however, work across different communities has been relatively unimportant. In the past, few have expected a campus as a whole to produce synthesized, collective insight. Physicists work on physics problems; historians on history problems; and except when they come to blows over the history of physics the two, like most other departments, lead predominantly independent lives.

Firms, by contrast, cannot afford to work this way. When they get to the point they are so loosely connected that there is no synthesis or synergy of what is produced in their various communities—when, as Teece and colleagues argue, there is no "coherence"—then a firm has indeed lost its edge over the market. The firm then needs either to work towards synergy or divest until it achieves coherence.[30] Indeed, firms are valuable exactly to the extent that, unlike universities, they make communities of practice that expand their vision and achieve collective coherence. Consequently, the problematic *between* relationship is a critical organizational feature—and one that demands significant organizational investment.

It is a mistake to equate knowledge and information and to assume that difficulties can be overcome with information technologies. New knowledge is continuously being produced and developed in the different communities of practice throughout an organization. The challenge occurs in evaluating it and moving it. New knowledge is not capable of the sorts of friction-free movement usually attributed to information. Moreover, because moving knowledge between communities and synthesizing it takes a great deal of work, deciding what to invest time and effort in as well as determining what to act upon is a critical task for management.

---

[30] David Teece, Richard Rumelt, Giovanni Dosi and Sidney Winter, "Understanding Corporate Coherence: Theory and Evidence," *Journal of Economic Behavior and Organization,* 23/1(1994): 1–30.

STICKINESS AND LEAKINESS

The "leakiness" of knowledge out of—and into—organizations, however, presents an interesting contrast to its internal stickiness.[31] Knowledge often travels more easily between organizations than it does within then. For while the division of labor erects boundaries within firms, it also produces extended communities that lie across the external boundaries of firms. Moving knowledge among groups with similar practices and overlapping memberships can thus sometimes be relatively easy compared to the difficulty of moving it among heterogeneous groups within a firm. Similar practice in a common field can allow ideas to flow. Indeed, it's often harder to stop ideas spreading than to spread them.

A study of interorganizational work by Kristen Kreiner and Majken Schultz suggests that the tendency of knowledge to spread easily reflects not suitable technology, but suitable social contexts. They show how many of the disciplinary links between business and academia are informal. They argue that the informal relations between firms and universities are more extensive and probably more significant than the formal ones. Informal relations dominate simply because they are easier, building on established social links. Formal interfirm relations, by contrast, can require tricky intrafirm negotiations between quite diverse communities (senior management, lawyers, and so forth).

Studies of biotechnology support this view. A study by Walter Powell reveals biotechnologists working extensively across the boundaries of organizations. Some articles in this field have more than one hundred authors from different (and different types of) institutions.[32] Their extensive collaboration undoubtedly relies on communications technologies. But these are available to researchers in other fields where such collaboration does not occur. Biotechnology is distinct in that being a relatively young, emerging field, its researchers are significantly linked through personal connections. The field is not as tight as a local community of practice, but nonetheless relations are dense enough and practices sufficiently similar to help knowledge spread. While a field is small and relatively unfragmented, practitioners have a lot in common: their training, their institutional backgrounds, their interests, and in particular the warrants with which they evaluate what is important from what is not.[33]

People connected this way can rely on complex networks of overlapping communities, common backgrounds, and personal relationships to help evaluate

---

[31] For the notion of leakiness, see R. M. Grant and J.-C. Spender, "Knowledge and the Firm: Overview," *Strategic Management Journal,* 17 (1996): 5–9.

[32] Walter W. Powell, "Inter-Organizational Collaboration in the Biotechnology Industry," *Journal of Institutional and Theoretical Economics,* 152 (1996): 197–215; Kristen Kreiner and Majken Schultz, "Informal Collaboration in R&D: The Formation of Networks across Organizations," *Organization Science,* 14 (1993): 189–209.

[33] To some degree, such fields resemble "social worlds." See Anselm Strauss, "A Social World Perspective," *Studies in Symbolic Interaction,* 1(1978): 119–128.

and propagate knowledge. In such conditions, practices are fairly similar and consequently the barriers *between* different groups are relatively low.[34] In such knowledge ecologies, knowledge that is sticky within organizations can become remarkably fluid outside of them, causing great difficulties for the intellectual-property side of knowledge management. The challenge of plugging these leaks is significant. But cutting off the outflow can also cut off the inflow of knowledge. Living in a knowledge ecology is a reciprocal process, with organizations feeding into each other.

TOWARDS AN ARCHITECTURE FOR ORGANIZATIONAL KNOWLEDGE

The way ecologies spread knowledge helps point to some of the ways that organizations can help to propagate knowledge internally and develop an enabling architecture for organizational knowledge. Social strategies for promoting the spread of knowledge between communities can be described in terms of "translation," "brokering," and "boundary objects"—terms developed by the sociologists Susan Leigh Star and James Griesemer.[35]

Translators

Organizational translators are individuals who can frame the interests of one community in terms of another community's perspective. The role of translator can be quite complex and the translator must be sufficiently knowledgeable about the work of both communities to be able to translate. The powerful position of translator requires trust, since translation is rarely entirely innocent (translators may favor the interests of one group over another deliberately or inadvertently). Yet, participants must be able to rely on translators to carry negotiations in both directions, making them mutually intelligible to the communities involved. The difficulty of doing this makes translators extremely valuable and extremely difficult to find. External mediators and consultants are often called in to provide such translation.

Knowledge Brokers

The role of in-firm brokers, in contrast to that of translators, involves participation rather than mediation. They are a feature of overlapping communities, whereas translators work among mutually exclusive ones. In an analysis of the

---

[34] See John Seely Brown and Paul Duguid, "The Knowledge Continuum," in preparation.
[35] Susan Leigh Star and James R. Griesemer, "Institutional Ecology, 'Translations' and Boundary Objects: Amateurs and Professionals in Berkeley's Museum of Vertebrate Zoology, 1907–39," *Social Studies of Science,* 19 (1989): 387–420.

diffusion of knowledge across networks, sociologist Mark Granovetter noted that overlaps are hard to develop in communities with very strong internal ties. These tend to preclude external links. Thus Granovetter argued for the "strength of weak ties," suggesting that it was often people loosely linked to several communities who facilitated the flow of knowledge among them.[36]

As almost all communities within an organization overlap, those who participate in the practices of several communities may in theory broker knowledge between them. Trust is less of a tendentious issue than with translation. Brokers who truly participate in both worlds, unlike translators, are subject to the consequences of messages they carry, whatever the direction.

Boundary Objects

Boundary objects are another way to forge coordinating links among communities, bringing them, intentionally or unintentionally, into negotiation. Boundary objects are objects of interest to each community involved but viewed or used differently by each of them. These can be physical objects, technologies, or techniques shared by the communities. Through them, a community can come to understand what is common and what is distinct about another community, its practices, and its world view. Boundary objects not only help to clarify the attitudes of other communities, they can also make a community's own presuppositions apparent to itself, encouraging reflection and "second-loop" learning.[37]

Contracts are a classic example of boundary objects. They develop as different groups converge, through negotiation, on an agreed meaning that has significance for both. Documents more generally play a similar role, and forms and lists that pass between and coordinate different communities make significant boundary objects. Plans and blueprints are another form of boundary object. Architectural plans, for instance, define a common boundary among architects, contractors, engineers, city planners, cost estimators, suppliers and clients. Severally and collectively these groups negotiate their different interests, priorities, and practices around the compelling need to share an interpretation of these important documents.

To help produce intercommunal negotiation, organizations can seed the border between communities with boundary objects. The idea-fomenting metaphors that Nonaka describes draw some of their power by being boundary

---

[36] Mark Granovetter, "The Strength of Weak Ties," *American Journal of Sociology* (1976), pp. 1360–1380; Granovetter's argument presupposes that for knowledge to spread, groups cannot simply be related as isolated individuals connected by market; they (and, indeed, markets) must be embedded in complex social systems. This argument appears more forcefully in his critique of transaction costs cited above.

[37] Chris Argyris and Donald Schön, *Organizational Learning* (Reading, MA: Addison-Wesley, 1978).

objects.[38] They work within groups to spark ideas. Once a group has found one metaphor particularly powerful, that metaphor may also serve to foster understanding between groups.

Business Processes as Boundary Objects: Enabling and Coercive

Business processes can play a similar role. Ideally, processes should allow groups, through negotiation, to align themselves with one another and with the organization as a whole. Business processes can enable productive cross-boundary relations as different groups within an organization negotiate and propagate a shared interpretation. In the right circumstances, the interlocking practices that result from such negotiations should cohere both with one another and with the overall strategy of the company. The processes provide some structure, the negotiations provide room for improvisation and accommodation, and the two together can result in coordinated, loosely coupled, but systemic behavior.[39]

Many business processes, however, attempt not to support negotiation but to pre-empt it, trying to impose compliance and conformity through what Geoffrey Bowker and Susan Leigh Star call "frozen negotiation." Here Paul Adler and Bryan Borys's discussion of "enabling" and "coercive" bureaucracies suggests the importance of enabling and coercive business processes. The first produces fruitful intercommunal relations and, in the best case, widespread strategic alignment; the second is more likely to produce rigid organizations with strong central control but little adaptability.[40]

TECHNOLOGY ISSUES

As noted earlier, the ease or difficulty of moving knowledge is a reflection of its social context. Technologies inevitably have an enormous role to play, but they play it only to the extent that they respond to the social context. The desire

---

[38] Ikujiro Nonaka, "The Knowledge Creating Company," *Harvard Business Review,* 69/6 (November/December 1991): 96–104.

[39] For the notion of "loosely coupled" systems, see Karl E. Weick, "Organizational Culture as a Source of High Reliability," *California Management Review,* 29/12 (Winter 1987): 112–127; J. Douglas Orton and Karl E. Weick, "Loosely Coupled Systems: A Reconceptualization," *Academy of Management Review,* 15/2 (April 1990): 203–223.

[40] Geoffrey Bowker and Susan Leigh Star, "Knowledge and Infrastructure in International Information Management: Problems of Classification and Coding," in Lisa Bud-Frierman, ed., *Information Acumen: The Understanding and Use of Knowledge in Modern Business* (London: Routledge, 1994), pp. 187–213; Paul Adler and Bryan Borys, "Two Types of Bureaucracy: Enabling and Coercive," *Administrative Science Quarterly.* 41 (1996): 61–89.

to disaggregate, disintermediate, and demassify, however, is more likely to produce socially unresponsive behavior.

A good deal of new technology attends primarily to individuals and the explicit information that passes between them. To support the flow of knowledge, within or between communities and organizations, this focus must expand to encompass communities and the full richness of communication. Successful devices such as the telephone and the fax, like the book and newspaper before them, spread rapidly not simply because they carried information to individuals, but because they were easily embedded in communities.

Supporting the Informal

One important issue for technology involves the way the local informality found within communities differs from levels of explicitness and formality often demanded between communities—much as the slang and informal language people use among immediate colleagues differ from the formal language of presentations or contracts. The demands for formality demanded by technologies can disrupt more productive informal relations. For instance, in many situations, asking for explicit permission changes social dynamics quite dramatically—and receiving a direct rejection can change them even further. Consequently, people negotiate many permissions tacitly. A great deal of trust grows up around the ability to work with this sort of implicit negotiation. Direct requests and insistence of rights and duties do not work well.

Technologies thus have to include different degrees of formality and trust.[41] The range will become apparent as different types of "trusted systems" begin to emerge. At one end are systems that more or less eliminate the need for social trust. They simply prevent people from behaving in ways other than those explicitly negotiated ahead of time and constrained by the technology. Everything must be agreed (and paid for, usually) ex ante. For high-security demands, such technologies will be increasingly important. People are glad they can trust bank machines and Internet software servers. But if new technologies ask people to negotiate all their social interrelations like their banking relations, they will leave little room for the informal, the tacit, and the socially embedded—which is where know-how lies and important work gets done.

This choice between formality and informality will have repercussions in the design of complex technologies. But it also has repercussions in the implementation of such things as corporate intranets and mail systems. Increasingly, workplaces seek to control the sorts of interactions and exchanges these are used for. Yet these systems in many ways replace the coffee pot and the water cooler as

---

[41] For an insightful view of the interplay between the formal and the informal in the creation of trust, see Sim B. Sitkin, "On the Positive Effect of Legalization on Trust," *Research on Negotiation in Organizations* (1995), pp. 185–217.

the site of informal but highly important knowledge diffusion. Limiting their informality is likely to limit their importance.

Reach and Reciprocity

As continual chatter about the global information network reminds us, information technology has extensive reach. Markets supported by this technological reach spread further and further daily. However, it is a mistake to conclude that knowledge networks, which require a social context, will spread in the same fashion. Technology to support the spread of new knowledge needs to be able to deal not with the *reach* involved in delivery so much as with the *reciprocity* inherent in shared practice. The ability to support complex, multi-directional, implicit negotiation will become increasingly important.

The Internet provides an interesting example of the way people retrofit information technology to enhance its social capacities. It was designed primarily so that computers could exchange electronic information and computer users could exchange files. Early in its development, though, some insightful programmers at Bolt Beranek and Newman piggy-backed e-mail on the protocol for transferring files. This highly social medium superimposed on the fetch-and-deliver infrastructure planted the seed that would transform this scientific network into the social network that has flourished so dramatically in the last few years. E-mail still accounts for the bulk of Internet traffic. Similarly, the World Wide Web has been the most recent and dramatic example that further accelerated the social use of the technology. Its designer, Tim Berners-Lee, a programmer at the CERN laboratories in Switzerland, saw that the Internet was much more interesting if used not simply for exchanging information between individuals, but to support "collaborators . . . in a common project." That social imperative, quite as much as the technology, has driven the Web's extraordinary evolution.[42]

Interactivity, Participation, Learning

One of the Net's greatest assets is that it is interactive and thus has the potential reciprocity to foster knowledge and learning. On campuses, conventional classes now regularly increase not so much reach as reciprocity by using Web pages and listserves (communal mailing lists) to do this. Similarly, well-designed corporate intranets, which supplement more conventional communication, do the same. In particular, these help present and circulate boundary

---

[42] Tim Berners Lee, "The World Wide Web: Past. Present, and Future," [available online]: http://www.w3.org/People/Berners-Lee/1996/ppf.html

objects. New forms of multicasting, such as the "M-Bone" or Multi-Cast Backbone, offer yet denser prospects for such interaction.[43]

When simply combined with reach, interactivity is often merely burdensome. To cultivate true reciprocity (rather than babble), people often find it necessary to introduce limits on the reach. Listserves now increasingly restrict participation, Web sites demand passwords, and intranets erect firewalls. Imposing limits, however, can prove disadvantageous.

Reciprocity is a feature of what Jean Lave and Etienne Wenger (who developed the notion of "communities of practice") refer to as "legitimate peripheral participation."[44] People learn by taking up a position on the periphery of skilled practice and being allowed (hence the importance of legitimacy) to move slowly from the periphery into the community and the practice involved. New communications technologies provide intriguing forms of peripherality. They allow newcomers to "lurk" on the side of interactions in which they are not taking part and of communities of which they are not members. Students, for example, lurk on the sides of exchanges among graduate students and faculty. Novices oversee the Net traffic among experts. Lave and Wenger also showed, however, how vibrant training programs die once newcomers are cut off from such experienced practice. Closing lists to lurkers can have the same results. Consequently, the negotiation of access, of reach, and of reciprocity in such circumstances needs to remain a complex socio-technological challenge and not simply a technological one.

The rewards of reciprocity are high. Technologies that can recognize and to some extent parse how relations *within* communities (where reciprocity is inevitable) differ from those *between* communities (where reciprocity must be cultivated) may actually help to extend reach between communities without disrupting reciprocity within. Understand the challenges of the *between* relation should be ·a significant issue for new design—of both technologies and organizations.

Technology that supports not merely the diffusion of know-what, but the development of know-how and that allows for knowledge to be shared rather than marketed. Curiously, this highlights a pervasive trajectory in the development of communications software, where explicit design strategies for exchanging information are repeatedly subverted by users who press for a social network.

CONCLUSION: DIALECTICAL THINKING

The propagandists of cyberspace have a tendency to speak in terms of discontinuity. The new, they always insist, will simply sweep away the old, so they

[43] See John Seely Brown and Paul Duguid, "The University in the Digital Age," *Change*, 28 (1996): 10–15; John Seely Brown and Paul Duguid, "The Social Life of Documents," *Release 1.0* (October 1995), pp. 1–12.

[44] Lave and Wenger, op. cit.

confidently predict that hypertext will replace the book. (Here they might do well to pay attention to *The New York Times's* confident prediction in the 1930s that the typewriter would replace the pencil. The pencil seems to have won that particular struggle.) Or, as in the issue at stake here, the prediction is that communications technology will sweep away the firm.

Undoubtedly, the present technological revolution will sweep many familiar aspects of life away. Nonetheless, sometimes it is useful to think in terms of "both/and" rather than simply "either/or." This seems particularly true when considering the effect of heterogeneous categories on one another, such as the effects of technologies on institutions,

Instead of thinking of individuals vs. institutions, or markets vs. firms, or start-ups vs. large corporations, it may be more instructive to think of how the two are interlaced. From this perspective, it does not seem as though disintermediation, demassification, and disaggregation are the only watchwords of the future. Community practice, organization, network, and above all organizational knowledge and distributed know-how are equally important.

PART IV

Knowledge, Groupware and the Internet

Chapter 11

The Role of Tacit Knowledge in Group Innovation[1]

Dorothy Leonard and Sylvia Sensiper[*]

Innovation, the source of sustained advantage for most companies, depends upon the individual and collective expertise of employees. Some of this expertise is captured and codified in software, hardware, and processes. Yet tacit knowledge also underlies many competitive capabilities—a fact driven home to some companies in the wake of aggressive downsizing, when undervalued knowledge walked out the door.

The marvelous capacity of the human mind to make sense of a lifetime's collection of experience and to connect patterns from the past to the present and future is, by its very nature, hard to capture. However, it is essential to the innovation process. The management of tacit knowledge is relatively unexplored—particularly when compared to the work on explicit knowledge. Moreover, while individual creativity is important, exciting, and even crucial to business, the creativity of groups is equally important. The creation of today's complex systems of products and services requires the merging of knowledge from diverse national, disciplinary, and personal skill-based perspectives. Innovation—whether it be revealed in new products and services, new processes, or new organizational forms—is rarely an individual undertaking. Creative cooperation is critical.

WHAT IS TACIT KNOWLEDGE?

In the business context, we define knowledge as *information that is relevant, actionable, and based at least partially on experience.* Knowledge is a subset of information; it is subjective; it is linked to meaningful behavior; and it has

[1] Copyright © 1998, by The Regents of the University of California. Reprinted from the *California Management Review*, Vol. 40, No. 3. By permission of The Regents.
[*] We wish to thank Walter Swap, Barbara Feinberg, and three anonymous reviewers for their helpful comments and the Harvard Business School Division of Research for supporting this work.

tacit elements born of experience. Business theorists have, for the sake of convenience, contrasted tacit knowledge with explicit knowledge as if they were distinct categories. J.C. Spender defines tacit knowledge as "not yet explicated."[2] Ikujiro Nonaka and Hirotaka Takeuchi use this distinction to explain how an interaction between the two categories forms a knowledge spiral: explicit knowledge is shared through a combination process and becomes tacit through internalization; tacit knowledge is shared through a socialization process and becomes explicit through externalization.

In this article, we build on Michael Polanyi's original, messier assumption: that all knowledge has tacit dimensions.[3] Knowledge exists on a spectrum. At one extreme it is almost completely tacit, that is, semiconscious and unconscious knowledge held in peoples' heads and bodies. At the other end of the spectrum, knowledge is almost completely explicit, or codified, structured, and accessible to people other than the individuals originating it. Most knowledge, of course, exists in between the extremes. Explicit elements are objective, rational, and created in the "then and there" while the tacit elements are subjective, experiential, and created in the "here and now."[4]

Although Spender notes that "tacit does not mean knowledge that *cannot* be codified,"[5] some dimensions of knowledge are unlikely *ever* to be wholly explicated, whether embedded in cognition or in physical abilities. Semiconscious or unconscious tacit knowledge produces insight, intuition, and decisions based on "gut feel." For example, the coordination and motor skills to run a large crane are largely tacit, as are the negotiation skills required in a corporate meeting or the artistic vision embodied in the design of a new computer program interface. The common element in such knowing is the *inability* of the knower to totally articulate all that he or she knows. Tacit knowing that is embodied in physical skills resides in the body's muscles, nerves, and reflexes and is learned through practice, i.e., through trial and error. Tacit knowing embodied in cognitive skills is likewise learned through experience and resides in the unconscious or semiconscious. While Polanyi addressed tacit knowledge at an individual level, others have suggested it exists in group settings. In fact, Richard Nelson and Sidney Winter suggest that organizations maintain their structure and coherency through tacit knowledge embedded in "organizational routines" that no single person understands completely.[6]

---

[2] J. C. Spender, "Competitive Advantage from Tacit Knowledge? Unpacking the Concept and its Strategic Implications," in Bertrand Mosingeon and Amy Edmondson, eds., *Organizational Learning and Competitive Advantage* (London: Sage Publications 1996), pp. 56–73, 58.
[3] Michael Polanyi, *The Tacit Dimension* (New York, NY: Doubleday, 1966), p. 4.
[4] Ikujiro Nonaka and Hirotaka Takeuchi, *The Knowledge Creating Company* (New York, NY: Oxford University Press, 1995), p. 61.
[5] Spender, op. cit., p. 58.
[6] Richard R. Nelson and Sidney G. Winter, *An Evolutionary Theory of Economic Change* (Cambridge and London: The BelKnap Press of Harvard University Press, 1982).

Much knowledge remains tacit for various reasons. Perhaps its explication would not be beneficial. Unless an incentive is created, there is little reason for an individual or group possessing tacit knowledge that provides an important competitive advantage to explicate "away" that advantage. More commonly, however, people are unaware of the tacit dimensions of their knowledge, or are unable to articulate them. Spender notes various types of "automatic knowledge," such as skilled use of tools (e.g., a computer keyboard) or instinctive reactions (e.g., catching a falling object) or "action slips," as when one starts out to drive on an errand and ends up at the office instead.[7] In all these cases, the physical and mental reflexes operate without conscious direction (or without what Polanyi termed "focal" awareness.)

Moreover, as psychological research has demonstrated, the acquisition of knowledge can occur through non-conscious processes, through "implicit learning."[8] That is, we can acquire knowledge and an understanding of how to navigate our environment "independently of conscious attempts to do so."[9] One intriguing implication is that not only can we "know more than we can tell,"[10] but we often know more than we realize. Furthermore, our efforts to rationalize and explain non-conscious behavior may be futile, if not counterproductive. "Knowledge acquired from implicit learning procedures is knowledge that, in some raw fashion, is always ahead of the capability of its possessor to explicate it."[11] Researchers stimulating implicit learning found, in fact, that forcing individuals to describe what they thought they understood about implicitly learned processes often resulted in poorer performance than if the individuals were allowed to utilize their tacit knowledge without explicit explanation.[12]

Studies on creativity, intuition, and non-analytical behavior suggest three ways that tacit knowledge potentially is exercised in the service of innovation. We speculate that they represent a hierarchy of increasingly radical departures from the obvious and the expected, and therefore are of increasing value to innovative efforts.

---

[7] Spender, op. cit.

[8] Arthur. S. Reber, "Implicit Learning and Tacit Knowledge," *Journal of Experimental Psychology,* 118(1989): 219–235.

[9] Reber, op. cit., p. 219.

[10] Polanyi, op. cit., p. 4.

[11] Reber, op. cit., p. 229.

[12] Much depends, apparently, upon whether the underlying structure is in fact readily accessible, as participants in the experiments deduced incorrect rules from their implicitly learned skills. "Looking for rules will not work if you cannot find them," Reber notes. Furthermore, explicit instructions apparently aid learning only insofar as they match the person's idiosyncratic implicit learning structure. Reber, op. cit., p. 223.

Problem Solving

The most common application of tacit knowledge is to problem solving. Herbert Simon has argued that the reason experts on a given subject can solve a problem more readily than novices is that the experts have in mind a pattern born of experience, which they can overlay on a particular problem and use to quickly detect a solution. "The expert recognizes not only the situation in which he finds himself, but also what action might be appropriate for dealing with it."[13] Others writing on the topic note that "intuition may be most usefully viewed as a form of unconscious pattern-matching cognition."[14] "Only those matches that meet certain criteria enter consciousness."[15,16]

Problem Finding

A second application of tacit knowledge is to the framing of problems. Some authors distinguish between problem *finding* and problem *solving;* linking the latter to "a relatively clearly formulated problem" within an accepted paradigm and the former, which "confronts the person with a general sense of intellectual or existential unease" about the way the problem is being

---

[13] Simon, op. cit., p. 106. Interestingly, when Simon first proposed this concept of expertise, he used as an example the ability of a chess professional to determine a good move after only a few seconds of deliberation because the grandmaster's memory holds innumerable patterns of chess plays and the inherent dangers and benefits associated with the various configurations. The recent match between Gary Kasparov and an IBM computer demonstrated that when all relevant patterns can be codified, a computer can sort even more efficiently than the human brain. For certain kinds of bounded problems, with known rules, explicit knowledge may be more important than implicit.

[14] Allan D. Rosenblatt and James T. Thickstun, "Intuition and Consciousness," *Psychoanalytic Quarterly,* 63 (1994): 696–714.

[15] Rosenblatt and Thickstun, op. cit., p. 705.

[16] Researchers have also found that people organize information into groups of relatedness, called "chunks," in order to retain the information in short-term memory. Chunks themselves are "familiar patterns" that come to be understood through experience as a unit, and as learning continues become increasingly larger and more interrelated. When new stimuli is related to this stored information and recognition of a pattern occurs, ideas and actions appropriate to the situation are elicited from memory. Simon, op. cit. A related theory suggests that cognitive elements in working memory, long-term memory, and short-term memory are represented as nodes in a network. As a person gains more knowledge in an area and begins to make connections between abstract principles and actual events, links between nodes are created and strengthened. Expert's networks may be more efficient as a result of increased speed through network links. See Debra C. Hampton, "Expertise: The True Essence of Nursing Art," *Advances in Nursing Science,* 17/1 (September 1994): 15–24.

considered,[17] to more radical innovation. Creative problem framing allows the rejection of the "obvious" or usual answer to a problem in favor of asking a wholly different question. "Intuitive discovery is often not simply an answer to the specific problem but is an insight into the real nature of the dilemma."[18] Consultants are familiar with the situation in which a client identifies a problem and sets out specifications for its solution, whereas the real value for the client may lie in reformulating the problem. Of course, the more that the consultant's unease with the current formulation derives from his or her semiconscious or unconscious knowledge, the more difficult it is to express and rationalize.

Prediction and Anticipation

Finally, the deep study of phenomena seems to provide an understanding, only partially conscious, of how something *works,* allowing an individual to anticipate and predict occurrences that are then subsequently explored very consciously. Histories of important scientific discoveries suggest that this kind of anticipation and reliance on inexplicable mental processes can be very important in invention. In stories about prominent scientists, there are frequent references to the "hunches" that occur to the prepared mind, sometimes in dreams, as in the case of Watson and Crick's formulation of the double helix. Authors writing about the stages of creative thought often refer to the preparation and incubation that precede flashes of insight. "Darwin prepared himself for his insights into evolution through a childhood interest in collecting insects, the reading of geology, and the painstaking observations he made during the voyage of the *Beagle*."[19]

Similarly, literature on nursing is full of references to the importance of listening to intuition and hunches in caring for patients. For example, the medical team at Methodist Hospital in Indianapolis was able to revive a three-year old boy in respiratory distress because his nurse listened to her "insistent inner voice" and checked on the patient—despite the fact that "logically" nothing should be wrong.[20]

---

[17] Mihaly Czikszentmihalyi and Keith Sawyer, "Creative Insight: The Social Dimension of a Solitary Moment," in Robert J. Sternberg and Janet E. Davidson, eds., *The Nature of Insight* (Cambridge, MA: The MIT Press, 1995), p. 340. They also link problem solving to short time-frames and problem-finding to long time-frames in terms of the gestation period of the thinker. [p. 337] This linkage may be true for scientific discoveries, but there is no evidence that particular types of tacit knowledge utilization are always tied to particular time frames.

[18] Debbie A. Shirley and Janice Langan-Fox, "Intuition: A Review of the Literature" *Psychological Reports*, 79 (1996): 563–584, 568.

[19] Csikszentmihalyi and Sawyer, op. cit., pp. 339–340.

[20] Lynn Rew, "Nursing Intuition: Too Powerful and Too Valuable to Ignore," *Nursing* (July 1987), pp. 43–45.

As these examples suggest, much of the research on tacit knowledge focuses on the individual—perhaps because most investigators are psychologists, for whom the single mind is of primary interest, or perhaps because writers can always probe their own experience for data. For similar reasons, the literature on creativity likewise highlights individual expressions of innovativeness. However, as previously noted, innovation in business is usually a group process. Therefore, we need to examine more closely both tacit knowing and creativity as they are expressed by members of groups—singly and collectively.

CREATIVITY AND SOCIAL INTERACTION

Creative ideas do not arise spontaneously from the air but are born out of conscious, semiconscious, and unconscious mental sorting, grouping, matching, and melding. Moreover, interpersonal interactions at the conscious level stimulate and enhance these activities; interplay among individuals appears essential to the innovation process. In some businesses—notably advertising, games, and entertainment—"the creatives" or "the talent" are separated from the rest of the corporation because it is assumed that creativity and innovation bloom in isolation. However, even in businesses where "creatives" have held elite positions for years, some managers are beginning to question why *all* employees cannot contribute to innovation. One manager in a toy manufacturing company complained that in a recent meeting with 20 people, "nineteen thought they didn't need to be creative."

Studies of people selected because of individually demonstrated creativity refer consistently to their interactions with others as an essential element in their process. One study elicited comments such as: "I develop a lot of my ideas in dialogue,"[21] or "it's only by interacting with other people in the building that you get anything interesting done; it's essentially a communal enterprise."[22] The authors of this particular study conclude that "even in the most solitary, private moment-the moment of insight itself—many creative individuals are aware of the deeply social nature of their creative process."[23]

This social interaction is especially critical for teams of individuals responsible for delivering new products, services, and organizational processes. Before turning to a discussion of how tacit knowledge is utilized by such groups, we present a brief description of the innovation process.

---

[21] Csikszentmihalyi and Sawyer, op.cit., p. 342.
[22] Csikszentmihalyi and Sawyer, op.cit., p. 347.
[23] Csikszentmihalyi and Sawyer, op.cit., p. 349.

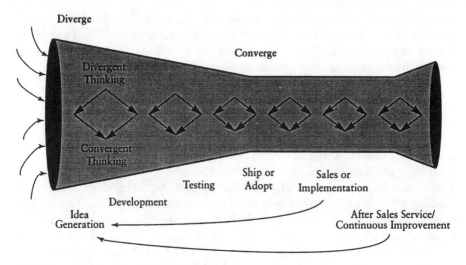

FIGURE 11.1 The Innovation Funnel*: Incremental Cycles

* Based partially on "The Developmental Funnel" in Wheelwright and Clark, *Revolutioning Product Development*, 1992.

THE NATURE OF INNOVATION

The process of innovation is a rhythm of search and selection, exploration and synthesis, cycles of divergent thinking followed by convergence. At the highest level of abstraction, innovation is often presented as linear: idea generation is followed by development, then by adoption or testing, and finally by implementation or after-sales service. However, within this overall pattern, the stages of idea generation through implementation recur at a smaller scale at each step (see Figure 11.1). The innovation pattern thus occurs as fractals, with small decision cycles embedded in large but very similarly structured ones, and with individual choices made within the confines of a hierarchy of prior, larger scope individual or group choices.[24]

The process by which a group or individual first creates options and then chooses one on which to focus efforts occurs during the testing and implementation stages as well as during idea generation and development. Thus creative group activity is not confined to the initial stages of the overall innovative effort but in fact is essential to such downstream activities as launching a new product, implementing a new compensation system in an organization, or improving after-sales service to customers. At any point in an innovation process, then,

[24] See Kim Clark, "The Intcraction of Design Hierarchies and Market Concepts in Technological Evolution," *Research Policy, 14/ 5* (1985): 235–251; Dorothy Leonard-Barton, "Implementation as Mutual Adaptation of Technology and Organization," *Research Policy, 17/ 5* (1988).

managers need to manage both the expansion of thought that gives rise to potentially creative alternatives and the homing in on a viable option. Tacit knowledge has an important role in both stimulating the "requisite variety" of ideas and then in the convergence that permits focus on actionable next steps.[25]

Divergence

One definition of creative synthesis (which underlies the development of many new products, services, or ways of organizing) is the "interlocking of two previously unrelated skills, or matrices of thought."[26] However, research suggests that deep skill takes at least a decade to develop.[27] Therefore, while a particularly talented or ambitious individual may develop deep skills in two or more arenas, most of us will build a single bank of expertise in our lifetimes. This expertise accrues as we experience education, work, and life in general.[28]

In working groups, individuals from different backgrounds (cultures, organizational experience, disciplinary training, preferred cognitive styles) draw upon their pools of tacit, as well as explicit knowledge, to contribute. In fact, it is the tacit dimensions of their knowledge bases that make such individuals especially valuable contributors to group projects; perspectives based on such knowledge cannot be obtained any other way except through interaction. Inaccessible from written documents or explicit expositions, tacit knowledge is protected from competitors unless key individuals leave or are hired away. Moreover, even individuals' explicit statements or suggestions carry with them the weight of unspoken knowledge—mental models, life examples, perhaps physical skills, even unrecognized patterns of experience which people draw upon to increase the wealth of possible solutions to a problem. This experience, stored as tacit knowledge, often reaches consciousness in the form of insights, intuitions, and flashes of inspiration.

When a group of diverse individuals addresses a common challenge, each skilled person frames both the problem and its solution by applying mental schemata and patterns he or she understands best. The result is a cacophony of perspectives. In a well-managed development process, these varying perspectives foster *creative abrasion,* intellectual conflict between diverse viewpoints producing energy that is channeled into new ideas and products.[29]

---

[25] See Donald Campbell, "Blind Variation and Selective Retention in Creative Thought as in Other Knowledge Processes," *Psychological Review,* 67 (1960): 380–400.

[26] Arthur Koestler, *The Act of Creation* (New York, NY: Dell Press, 1964), p. 121.

[27] Herbert Simon, *The Sciences of the Artificial* (Cambridge, MA: MIT Press, 1981), p. 106.

[28] Csikszentmihalyi and Sawyer, op. cit., p. 342.

[29] The term "creative abrasion" was coined by Gerald Hirshberg, President of Nissan Design International. See Dorothy Leonard-Barton, *Wellsprings of Knowledge* (Boston, MA: Harvard Business School Press, 1995), p. 63.

The creation of such intellectual ferment is important to innovation for *a* number of reasons. First, the more options offered (up to a point, of course), the more likely that a frame-breaking perspective will be available for selection. A certain "requisite variety" is desirable for innovation.[30] Moreover, experimental research has demonstrated that a minority opinion offered during group decision making stimulates more innovative solutions to problems—even if the ultimate selection was not one specifically proposed from a minority viewpoint.[31] Apparently, just hearing a very different perspective challenges the mindset of those in the majority sufficiently that they will search beyond what initially appears to be an obvious solution. This may be one reason that *intellectually* heterogeneous groups are more innovative than homogeneous ones.[32] As a recent review of different types of group diversity concludes, "the diversity of information [that] functionally dissimilar individuals bring to the group improves performance in terms of creativity."[33] If all individuals in the group approach a task with highly overlapping experiential backgrounds, they may be subject to "groupthink," i.e., a comfortable common viewpoint leading to closed-mindedness and pressures

[30] Nonaka and Takeuchi, op. cit.

[31] Charlan Jeanne Nemeth, "Managing Innovation: When Less Is More," *California Management Review,* 40/1 (Fall 1997): 59–74; Charlan Jeanne Nemeth and Joel Wachtler, "Creative Problem Solving as a Result of Majority vs. Minority Influence" *European Journal of Social Psychology.* 13 (1983): 45–55; Robin Martin, "Minority Influence and Argument Generation," *British Journal of Social Psychology,* 35(1996): 91–103.

[32] In a review of literature about diversity, Susan E. Jackson, Karen E. May, and Kristina Whitney report that "there is clear support for a relationship between diversity and creativity." See Susan E. Jackson, Karen E. May, and Kristina Whitney "Understanding the Dynamics of Diversity in Decision-Making Teams," in Susan E. Jackson et al., eds., *Diversity in the Workplace: Human Resources Initiatives* (New York, NY: Guilford Press, 1992), p. 230.

[33] Katherine Y. Williams and Charles A. O'Reilly III, "Demography and Diversity in Organizations: A Review of 40 Years of Research," *Research in Organizational Behavior,* Vol. 20 (1998, forthcoming). The authors note that the same cannot necessarily be said of the implementation phase of the innovation process. This review also points out that while "functional diversity has positive effects on group performance," other forms of diversity have been found to have negative effects. Information and decision theories maintain that increased diversity more likely has a positive effect on innovations, complex problems, or product designs, (which are the domains about which we are most concerned here), but social categorization and similarity/attraction theories suggest that diversity is more problematic and can have a negative effect on group process and performance. Much depends, then, not only on the task being addressed but on exactly what kind of diversity is being researched, and through what theoretical lens the material is viewed. Clearly, some kinds of diversity can lead to disharmony. As we suggest in this article, the conflict that arises from intellectual disagreement has to be managed carefully, lest it spill over into personal anger.

towards uniformity.[34] Their tacit as well as their explicit knowledge is similar enough that they neither produce a wide variety of options nor expend much effort on searching.

A popular technique for capitalizing on the respective insights and intuitions of a group of individuals is to conduct a brainstorming session.[35] At IDEO, an international product development firm, brainstorming sessions occur at crucial stages in the product development process and have been shown to lead to important consequences for the organization as a whole.

An IDEO "brainstorm" gathers together a set of staff with diverse skills—human factors, mechanical engineering, and industrial design—to generate product design ideas, often in tandem with the client. The meeting is run by a facilitator and is always held face-to-face. The "rules" are well-known to IDEO designers but are posted visibly: defer judgment; build on the ideas of others; one conversation at a time; stay focused on the topic; and encourage wild ideas. All concepts and ideas elicited during a brainstorming session are recorded on a white board. The principal way that participants share their tacit knowledge is through sketching designs or through visual analogies. For example, an idea for an appliance hinge might be derived from the way in which a boat rudder is maneuvered. Because the IDEO employees share a deep understanding of process, they are generally comfortable both with the highly divergent thinking encouraged in the brainstorming itself and with the vagueness of the initial sketches and analogies as modes of communication. IDEO managers find that their clients tend to underestimate the power of brainstorming—that is, until they have experienced it. Then they are likely to walk away impressed with the profusion of ideas presented.

---

[34] Irving L. Janis, *Groupthink* (Boston, MA: Houghton Mifflin, 1972, 1982). Janis suggests various ways of avoiding groupthink, including assigning someone the role of devil's advocate and inviting into policy discussions outside experts or colleagues not normally included, who would be encouraged to challenge the views of core members.

[35] This technique has been much denigrated after laboratory research revealed that "nominal groups" of individuals attacking a problem produced more, and better, ideas. However, such research relied upon highly artificial problems (e.g., what could you do with a second thumb on your hand?) and enlisted individuals who had no prior knowledge of each other. The group dynamics obviously differ in real world circumstances in which participants know each other well (and therefore do not spend time and energy on self presentation), the problem is actual and urgent, and, most important, their background expertise is relevant and probably essential. In short, in the real world, tacit knowledge is critical to brainstorming and we believe that laboratory research underestimates the power of the technique. See Robert I. Sutton and Andrew Hargadon, "Brainstorming Groups in Context: Effectiveness in a Product Design Firm," *Administrative Science Quarterly*, 41/4 (December 1996): 685–718. Sutton and Hargadon report six important consequences for design firm IDEO as a result of this practice: supporting the organizational memory of design solution; providing skills variety for designers; supporting an attitude of wisdom; creating a status auction; impressing clients; and providing income for the firm.

We may have no choice about managing divergent viewpoints in the creation of today's complex systems of products and services. In a 1992 study of three product lines (cellular phones, optical fiber systems, and refrigerators), Ove Granstrand and others found that the number of technologies and disciplinary bases required to produce these products increased between each successive product generation. For example, the first generation of cellular phones in the early 1980s, required only electrical engineering skills. By the mid-1990s, the third generation of these phones called for a knowledge of physics as well as electrical, mechanical, and computer engineering.[36]

As if the proliferation in requirements for different types of expertise were not sufficient, the design of global products today *also* demands a sensitivity to diverse norms and attitudes. Innovation knows no national bounds. When San Diego, California-based Nissan Design International designers were wrestling with the configuration of the Infiniti J-30, they discovered that their Japanese colleagues were far more sensitive to the front-end or "face" of the car than they, although translating the Japanese tacit knowledge about consumer preferences into information explicit enough for communication (mostly through sketches) took some time and a lot of effort. At last the California-based designers came to understand that the proposed design of a slightly down-turned grill and narrow headlights gave the car's persona a sour appearance to the Japanese designers, reducing its appeal. Very slight adjustments—almost indiscernible to the American designers—raised the design to "a higher level of cultural intelligence," noted NDI President Gerald Hirshberg.[37]

Perspectives at a *group* level can also be brought into juxtaposition so as to increase divergent thinking. John Seely Brown and Paul Duguid point out that when large organizations are conceived as "a collective of communities" with each community having a particular culture and viewpoint, "separate community perspectives can be amplified by interchanges . . . Out of this friction of competing ideas can come the sort of improvisational sparks necessary for igniting organizational innovation."[38]

Whether we seek to increase the divergence of perspectives as a deliberate strategy for innovation or have the diversity thrust upon us as a necessity, we need to manage that rich profusion.[39] Much of the richness derives from the tacit dimensions of the knowledge possessed by individuals in the group. Although

[36] Ove Granstrand, Erik Bohlin, Christer Oskarsson, and Niklas Sjoberg, "External Technology Acquisition in Large Multi-Technology Companies," *R&D Management*, 22/2 (1992): 111–233.

[37] Interview, December 10, 1993.

[38] John Seely Brown and Paul Duguid, "Organizational Learning and Communities-of-Practice: Toward a Unified View of Working, Learning, and Innovation," *Organization Science*, 2/1(1991): 40–57.

[39] See Dorothy Leonard and Susaan Straus, "Putting Your Company's Whole Brain to Work," *Harvard Business Review*, Vol. 75/4 (July/August 1997): 110–121.

diverse explicit knowledge is challenging to harness and direct towards a common goal, it is easier to generate, analyze, and share than is tacit knowledge.

Convergence

At every stage, innovation requires solution, convergence upon acceptable action—and again, tacit knowledge plays an important role. The *process* of innovation has a tremendous effect on the integrity and the system integration of any resultant product or service.[40] In turn, the aggregate knowledge of project members involved in the innovation process has to be coordinated and focused. The degree to which knowledge needs to be actually shared depends upon the nature of the innovation task and how much interdependency exists among subgroups or individuals. Again confining the discussion here to managing the tacit dimensions of knowledge, we suggest that three different types of tacit knowledge need to be managed: *overlapping specific, collective,* and *guiding*. These three form a rough hierarchy from low to high in terms of abstraction.

Overlapping Specific Knowledge

Groups or subgroups of individuals involved in an innovation project may build up shared *specific* knowledge at the interfaces between them—as, for example, of client preferences and attitudes or of particular steps in a production process. This knowledge is overlapping in that only part of each individual's tacit knowledge about the undertaking is shared—that which is essential to the completion of their interdependent tasks. The mechanisms for creating the tacit dimensions of such collective knowledge include shared experiences and apprenticeships.

Observational visits—to customers, to customers' customers, or to potential users of the general class of a given service or product produced by an organizational stimulate innovative ideas.[41] Such "empathic design" expeditions are essentially anthropological in nature. A multifunctional team of individuals who carry with them an acute understanding of their organization's capabilities are directly exposed to the world of potential users and observe how those users

---

[40] Product integrity refers to an internal dimension—namely, the product's structure and function—and an external dimension—the product's performance and the expectation of customers. The process of development affects both dimensions. For a discussion of how the innovation process affects outcome, see Kim Clark and Takahiro Fujimoto, "The Power of Product Integrity," *Harvard Business Review,* 68/6 (November/December 1990): 107–118. See also Marco Iansiti, *Technology Integration* (Boston, MA: Harvard Business School Press, 1998).

[41] See Dorothy Leonard and Jeffrey Rayport, "Sparking Innovation through Empathic Design," *Harvard Business Review,* 75/6 (November/December 1997): 102–113. The topic is also discussed in Chapter Seven of Dorothy Leonard-Barton, *Wellsprings of Knowledge* (Boston, MA: Harvard Business School Press, 1995 and 1998).

interact with their environment. This observation identifies needs about which the users may be unaware and/or are unlikely to articulate. Although the empathic design team members return from the field with very different perceptions (and that, in fact, is the value of sending diverse observers), their observations overlap to create some common—to some degree tacit—understanding of the environment for which they are designing. Individuals from teams that have conducted such anthropological expeditions can explicate some of their observations about the work or home life of those observed, but clearly more knowledge is shared than can be expressed. So, for instance, members' comments about "the pace of work" or the "sporadic communication" are laden with tacit understanding. Such phrases call up specific mental images of routines around the office, household, or factory that are inaccessible to someone who has not shared visits to those same sites.

Apprenticeships are a time-honored way of building shared specific tacit knowledge. Although today most production processes are moved as rapidly as possible from art towards science, even in quite sophisticated processes, some art often remains.[42] A decade ago, a study of the transmission of hybridoma technology revealed that "the *unsaid* is indeed a part of conscious scientific practice."[43] The researchers found that the production of monoclonal antibodies was an artisanal technique. Manuals purporting to instruct in the methodology explicitly recognized the need for apprenticeship:

> The newcomer to hybridization is well advised to learn the technique in a laboratory which is already practicing fusion . . . newcomers to the technique are relatively unsuccessful initially and obtain many hybrids after some practice, although an experienced observer cannot see any difference between the technique used on the first day and in subsequent, successful experiments. The best approach is therefore to learn from an experienced laboratory and practice until hybrids are obtained.[44]

Researchers engaged in the production of the hybridomas talked about getting "a feeling for just what the cells are doing, and how healthy they are by looking at them" and reported gaining that understanding by association with

---

[42] Moreover, even in high-volume, highly automated processes, workers' tacit knowledge about the way that particular equipment works and their ability to problem solve is critical to continuous improvement. See Gil Preuss and Dorothy Leonard-Barton, "Chaparral Steel: Rapid Product and Process Development," *Harvard Business School Case 9-692-018.*

[43] Alberto Cambrosio and Peter Keating, "Going Monoclonal: Art, Science and Magic in the Day-to-Day Use of Hybridoma Technology," *Social Problems,* 35/3 (June 1988): 244–260.

[44] H. Zola and D. Brocks, "Techniques for the Production and Characterization of Monoclonal Hybridoma Antibodies," in John G.R. Hurrell, ed., *Monoclonal Hybridoma Antibodies: Techniques and Applications* (Boca Raton, FL: CRC Press) quoted in Cambrosio and Keating, op. cit., p. 248.

experienced individuals. "The professor says: these are healthy, those are not. You learn by association, without knowing what you are looking at."[45] In such an apprenticeship, much explicit knowledge is conveyed from expert to novice, but tacit knowledge grows through shared observation and from mimicking behavior, even without knowing why.

The newer such technologies are to the world, the more important apprentices are to the innovation process. The faster the innovation cycle, the less likely that knowledge will be captured explicitly. The director of an advanced development group commented that his researchers were likely to be "stuck for life" with a technology they created because the knowledge base moves so fast it is never totally captured in any explicit form. Once responsible for a given technology, the researchers remain the key repository for not only the original concepts, but for undocumented refinements of the technology made by downstream recipients. Of course, observers may aver that all aspects of the technology *should* be captured explicitly, but as the pace of innovation accelerates, such capture is increasingly difficult. Not only has knowledge not progressed to the point of easy codification (i.e., the process is still an art), but tacit knowledge that is a prerequisite to exploiting the technology can constitute a competitive advantage.

Collective: System Knowledge

Collective tacit knowledge is developed communally, over time, in interactions among individuals in the group. It exists more or less complete in the head of each group member who has been completely socialized into the group. One form of collective tacit knowledge encompasses the entire production system, allowing individuals to contribute to innovation without explicit communication because they understand at a systemic level how all the individual operations in an organization fit together. The more that tacit knowledge about operations is diffused and shared, the harder is imitation. This is why companies such as Chaparral Steel or Oticon invite competitors to visit and observe, convinced that no one could imitate their success from absorbing explicit knowledge.[46] Even if some individuals leave the organization, a shared "net of expectations" created through organizational routines and accepted standards remains.[47] Moreover, these expectations are conveyed through artifacts as well as through behavior. Thus, for instance, in any design shop, one sees models and prototypes embodying tacit knowledge about successful and unsuccessful attempts at innovation.

"Taken-for-granted" collective tacit knowledge often appears in the form of unconscious norms; individuals draw on it unawares. Members of a

[45] Cambrosio and Keating, op. cit., p. 249.
[46] See Preuss and Leonard-Barton, op. cit.; John J. Kao, "Oticon (A)," Harvard Business School Case 9-395-144.
[47] See Scott D.N. Cook and Dvora Yanow's account of three flute workshops in "Culture and Organizational Learning," *Journal of Management Inquiry,* 2/4 (1993): 373–390.

"community of practice" develop implicit ways of working and learning together.[48] Researchers at the Institute for Research on Learning noted in one study *a* particular norm of behavior that aided informal communication: they called it "storking," the practice of sticking one's head up over the office cubicle to query someone in a nearby cubicle.[49] Adding a few inches to the cubicles could have provided more privacy—but would have interfered with the behavioral norms of the group. While such "communities" often go unnoticed, much work depends on their informal, shared use of "non-canonical" practices,[50] that is, norms of behavior and activities that are unacknowledged by the larger organization. According to John Challenger (executive vice president of Challenger, Gray & Christmas, a Chicago-based consultancy) this kind of collective tacit knowledge is essential to how people communicate and, by extension, how they innovate. He claims that down-sizing presents a particular risk for "company Alzheimer's." A firm's success depends not only on the skills and knowledge at any given point in time, but on "memories," the intangibles of collective business experience, triumphs and failures, culture and vision.[51]

Perhaps the purest form of collective tacit knowledge is that possessed by a team or group whose process *is* the product.[52] Their individual knowledge bases are complementary but have to be shared and merged for innovation to occur. An orchestra or a sports team that plays so far beyond the ordinary that their performance constitutes an act of innovation, harnesses their individual tacit knowledge to serve a shared mental model of perfection.[53] Such groups of people (including business teams) feel bonds of shared accomplishment that are

---

[48] For an explanation of "community of practice," see Jean Lave and Etienne Wenger, *Situated Learning: Legitimate Peripheral Participation* (New York, NY: Cambridge University Press, 1991). For an application of the idea to organizations and businesses, see John Seeley Brown, "Changing the Game of Corporate Research: Learning to Thrive in the Fog of Reality," Raghu Garud, Praveen Rattan Nayyar, and Zur Baruch Sapira, eds., *Technological Innovations: Oversights and Foresights* (Cambridge, UK: Cambridge University Press, 1997), pp. 95–110; John S. Brown and E. S. Gray, "The People Are the Company," *Fast Company*, (premiere issue), pp. 78–82; Etienne Wenger, "Communities of Practice: Where Learning Happens," *Benchmark* (Fall 1991), pp. 82–84.

[49] Helga Wild, Liby Bishop, and Cheryl Lynn Sullivan, "Building Environments for Learning and Innovation," *Institute for Research on Learning Report to the Hewlett-Packard IRL Project*, Menlo Park, CA (August 1996).

[50] Brown and Duguid, op. cit.

[51] See "Fire and Forget?" *The Economist*, U.S. Edition, April 20, 1996, p. 51. Similarly, Freda Line, the membership manger of Britain's Employers Forum on Age (EFA), points out that many down-sizing companies have had to hire back as consultants those employees who have taken early retirement. It is not so much the skills and experience that are needed, but many of those people "understood the crucial development history of their businesses—a vital part of corporate memory." See Tim Dawson, "Firms See Downside of Down-Sizing," *The London Times*, June 1, 1997.

[52] See Mihaly Csikszentmihalyi, *Flow* (New York, NY: Harper & Row, 1990).

[53] Csikszentmihalyi, op. cit.

inexpressible except in exultation and excitement in the mutual achievement. Together they have created something that no one of them (or even the group of them, absent this collective tacit knowledge) could have—but that is nevertheless dependent upon their individual contributions.

Guiding Tacit Knowledge

The more innovative the new product, process, service, or organizational form, the less likely that the objectives have been spelled out in detailed specifications, simply because it is more difficult to anticipate all needs and possible interactions in a radically new product or process. Individuals creating and implementing an innovation need to exercise judgment and make dozens of decisions. In their own initiative about how to reach the agreed-upon objectives. Lacking guidance, individuals may rely on their own ideas about the new product or process when making a particular decision, and their efforts may go in many disparate directions. The group must be guided by an understanding of purpose that extends beyond explicitly stated goals.[54] Such a vision or product concept keeps the school of fish swimming in the same direction, as it were.

Although such guiding visions must of course be explicit, they are often highly metaphorical or presented at a high level of abstraction, so that much of their significance is tacitly understood. Ford Motor Company used the phrase "contemporary luxury" to rally their hundreds of diversely skilled development troupes around a central concept for the 1988 design of the Lincoln Continental. The word "contemporary" helped to distinguish their design from the boxy, large images associated with past conceptions of luxury cars.[55] Nonaka and Takeuchi recount how Honda project team leader Hiroo Watanabe coined the phrase "Automobile Evolution" to inspire his designers, and the team continued the metaphorical conceptualization with the product concept "Tall Boy." The process resulted in the revolutionary Honda City, a car that was both "tall" in height and "short" in length.[56]

A guiding concept need not be expressed in words to be powerful in aligning individuals during innovation. A group symbol or logo often carries significance far beyond the visible. Moreover, creative research on "totemics" has revealed the power of aesthetics to tap into collective tacit knowledge. Angela Dumas uses "visual, object-based metaphors" to help new product developers converge on a general image for a line of products. The team members find common aesthetic and functional attributes—a similar "feel"—in an otherwise

---

[54] See discussion of guiding visions in H. Kent Bowen, Kim B. Clark, Charles A. Holloway, and Steven C. Wheelwright, "Development Projects: The Engine of Renewal," *Harvard Business Review*, 72/5 (September/October, 1994): 110–120.

[55] H. Kent Bowen, Kim B. Clark, Charles A. Holloway, and Steven C. Wheelwright, *The Perpetual Enterprise Machine* (New York, NY: Oxford University Press, 1994), p. 74.

[56] Nonaka and Takeuchi, op. cit., pp. 12–16.

disparate group of objects, e.g., paintings, furniture, wine glasses. The resulting "totem" helps coordinate design decisions.[57]

BARRIERS TO GENERATING AND SHARING TACIT KNOWLEDGE

Were the process of eliciting and managing the flow of the tacit dimensions of knowledge easy, innovation would still not occur effortlessly—but it would be much less of a challenge. Multiple barriers exist both to the stimulation of divergent thinking and then to the coalescence of that thinking around a common aim.

Obviously, if individuals who possess tacit knowledge important to the innovation are either actively discouraged from participating or censor themselves, none of the benefits suggested above can be realized. Individuals rewarded for hoarding their tacit knowledge will do so. In organizations where expertise is highly regarded, but mentoring and assisting others is not, rational people may be unlikely to surrender the power they gain from being an important knowledge source—especially since sharing tacit knowledge requires time devoted to personal contact.

Inequality in status among participants is also a strong inhibitor to sharing, especially when exacerbated by different frameworks for assessing information. Nurses often hesitate to suggest patient treatments to physicians, not only because the doctors have higher status, but because the nurses base their diagnoses on different knowledge bases. Dr. Richard Bohmer has speculated that nurses' ability to assess a patient is based on observation over time, i.e., longitudinal data gathered from standing by a patient's bedside. In contrast, a physician makes a judgment based on cross-sectional data, such as blood tests, ultrasound results, and x-rays.[58] Thus, the nurses' intuition about a situation draws on very different tacit knowledge, and they have neither the laboratory data to back up hunches nor the status to insist on the validity of their perspective.

Distance (both physical separation and time) renders sharing the tacit dimensions of knowledge difficult. Although technology may offer a partial solution, much knowledge is generated and transferred through body language, physical demonstrations of skill, or two- and three-dimensional prototypes that can be interactively shaped by a group of people. Howard Gardner has suggested a number of "intelligences," beyond the usual ones tested, that are more difficult to express over distances: spatial, kinesthetic, and interpersonal.[59] Furthermore, although research is scanty on the topic, a certain level of personal intimacy may

[57] Angela Dumas, "Building Totems: Metaphor-Making in Product Development," *Design Management Journal*, 5/1 (Winter 1994): 70–82.

[58] Personal communication, December 1997.

[59] Howard Gardner, *Frames of Mind: The Theory of Multiple Intelligences* (New York, NY: Harper Collins, 1993).

be necessary to establish comfortable communication of tacit knowledge. Internet-based friendships suggest that intimacy does not depend wholly on physical co-location, but it remains to be seen whether such friendships are based enough in reality to mimic the mutual understanding born of face-to-face encounters.

All of these barriers operate against the generation and sharing of the explicit as well as the tacit dimensions of knowledge. Some barriers, however, specifically inhibit the growth and transfer of tacit dimensions. First, working groups often exhibit a strong preference for a particular type of communication—most often (at least in most business situations) communication that is logical, rational, and based on "hard" data. As numerous studies of thinking styles have shown, individuals have strong thinking style preferences—for particular types of information—"hard-wired" into their brains and reinforced over years of practices and self-selection into certain careers.[60] Even if an individual could make some of the tacit dimensions of his or her knowledge explicit in the form of a physical demonstration or a drawing, such information would rarely be given a hearing because such evidence is not regarded in most business settings as relevant or useful unless backed up with analysis. Imagine how difficult it is in the ordinary product development meeting to introduce relatively inarticulate preferences that are based on largely tacit knowledge. As Microsoft's Tom Corddry noted about the design of new multimedia products, computer programmers never offer a suggestion about a product feature without telling you the rationale. In contrast, a visually talented artist may offer several drawn options for a screen design, "tell you which one they like—and stop!"[61] Artists find it extremely difficult to explain just why a particular pattern, rhythm, or color is preferable in a product design. In many companies, only the top managers dare express a preference without data to back it up. The point is not that such unarticulated preferences, opinions, and tastes are always correct, rather that the more diverse a collection of viewpoints shared, the more likely that the eventual solution will challenge the status quo.

Individuals possessing deep knowledge may also fear trying to express the inexpressible and failing. "No one," they may reason, "can appreciate the experience I bring to this problem; therefore, I will appear foolish and this is too high a price to pay." Operators in factories and plants sometimes hesitate to explain their apparently uncanny ability to foretell when a piece of equipment is about to fail. A lime kiln operator once interrupted an interview to hurry off, exclaiming simply "something is wrong; she [the kiln] doesn't sound right." Later pressed to explain, he could not—or would not—explicate further what sound he heard the revolving kiln make that caused him to hasten to make adjustments. "It's nothing scientific," he said somewhat defensively. "Nothing an engineer would believe. I just know."[62]

[60] Leonard and Straus, op. cit.
[61] Interview, February 28, 1994.
[62] Interview, November 1984.

Yet another barrier of special importance to managing tacit knowledge is the uneasiness of the group members that their colleagues will draw upon life experiences to express emotional rather than intellectual disagreement. For abrasion to be creative, it must be impersonal. After a review of relevant research, Lisa Hope Pelled suggests that group diversity based upon highly visible differences (gender, race, age) leads to more emotion-based disagreements, while more subtle forms of diversity (educational background, personality) are more likely to lead to intellectual disagreements.[63] This model suggests that the more that diversity in tacit knowledge is sought from individuals selected because of readily observable differences, the more difficult it becomes to ensure that the tacit knowledge is heard, is valued, and is targeted towards the innovation.

MANAGERIAL IMPLICATIONS

The value of tacit knowledge to the firm has been demonstrated.[64] Although it is much easier to stimulate, combine, and communicate the explicit dimensions of knowledge than the tacit, there are numerous situations in which tacit knowledge cannot or will not be wholly converted into explicit. Managing tacit knowledge is thus a significant challenge in the business world—and it requires more than mere awareness of the barriers.

The above descriptions of tacit knowledge in divergent and convergent processes suggest some mechanisms by which such knowledge is created and tapped. Brainstorming aids in divergent thinking if participants are encouraged to make suggestions on the basis of intuition and insight—as well as analysis—and to convey their suggestions through drawings and analogies. However, much divergent thinking occurs naturally, just because individuals approach a task from such different experience bases. The more radical the desired departure from status quo, the more fruitful it is to solicit discussion by individuals from varied intellectual perspectives. Managers thus can calibrate the level of divergent thinking that they encourage by varying the number and disparity of tacit knowledge

---

[63] Lisa Hope Pelled, "Demographic Diversity, Conflict, and Work Group Outcomes: An Intervening Process Theory," *Organization Science*, 7/6 (1996): 615–631. Pelled lumps creative idea generation, decision making, and problem solving together in her definitions of cognitive tasks and considers group tenure, organizational tenure, education, and functional background to be job-related diversity. "The more job-related a particular type of diversity is, the stronger its relationship with substantive conflict will be. . . . The more visible a particular type of diversity is, the stronger its relationship with affective [i.e., emotional] conflict will be." [p. 3] The literature reviewed by Williams and O' Reilly [op. cit.] seems to concur. The claim that diversity is beneficial for groups is based on variation in individual attributes such as personality, ability, and functional background.

[64] Especially Nonaka and Takeuchi, op. cit.; Leonard-Barton (1995), op. cit.

bases brought to bear on the task. However, they must manage the ensuing tendency towards chaos and keep the abrasion creative by depersonalizing conflict.[65]

Managers can also use tacit knowledge to aid convergent thinking, by creating guiding visions and concepts for groups involved in innovation. Collective tacit knowledge is created through shared experiences such as trips to customer sites and deliberate apprenticeships. Some degree of natural convergence occurs in so-called "communities of practice," in which unconscious work norms guide much of the interactions among members. Managers interrupt these tacit work practices at their peril, and savvy managers may make good use of them in the service of innovation.

Many of the barriers to the sharing of tacit knowledge are the same ones that inhibit innovation in general: hierarchies that implicitly assume wisdom accrues to those with the most impressive organizational titles; such strong preferences for analysis over intuition that no one dares offer an idea without "hard facts" to back it up; and penalties for failure that discourage experimentation. Managers thus can encourage the full exploitation of tacit knowledge by paying attention to the environment they are creating, by encouraging respect for different thinking styles, by understanding the distinction between intelligent failures and stupid mistakes, and by allowing their employees to "fail forward" where appropriate.

Not all tacit knowing is valuable or even accurate. Although we may not be able to judge the knowledge itself, we can certainly see the *results* of the knowledge (just as in astronomy we deduce the presence of a black hole or even a distant planet by its effects on other bodies.) The effect of tacit knowledge embodied in physical skills is especially visible. In any operation, different individuals using the exact same machinery may produce very different output, just as skiers or tennis players vary in performance using the same equipment. New operators in a factory are often assigned to watch particularly skilled workers so as to absorb tacit knowledge. More cognitively based skills can also be modeled. At American Management Systems, junior consultants in the Organizational Development and Change Management practice work alongside and are coached by "shadow consultants," more experienced senior consultants with years of experience. As one junior consultant said, "the hardest thing about organizational development is that people have to have their own experiences to really understand it. They have to begin to embody the processes."[66]

Cognitive skills are also open to assessment, as individuals and teams are judged by their "track record" of performance. Organizations hire individuals and groups not for their explicitly expressed knowledge alone, but for their anticipated overall impact on the performance of the organization. Such people

---

[65] For suggested ways of producing "light instead of heat" in very disparate groups, see Leonard and Straus, op. cit.

[66] Dorothy Leonard and Sylvia Sensiper, "American Management Systems: The Knowledge Centers," Harvard Business School Case N9-697-068.

often have a reputation for being "good managers" or "creative artists," much of which derives from the tacit dimensions of their knowledge.

Managers may also implicitly judge the value of tacit knowing by assessing individuals' abilities to *communicate* some of the tacit dimensions to their knowledge—through prototyping, drawing, demonstrating, expressing ideas through metaphors and analogies, or mentoring in general. At a California company producing video games, the manager in charge of product development values individuals he calls "Gepettos" (named after Pinocchio's famous puppeteer "father") because of their ability to develop other talent and to instill some of their own tacit knowledge in new employees through informal apprenticeships. Managers who wish to encourage this kind of diffusion of tacit knowledge set up systems that encourage, enable, and reward the disseminators.

Tacit knowledge, like all knowledge, can become outdated. By the time the obsolescence is obvious and proven, the organization will be in trouble. Therefore, one reason that managers import diverse perspectives is to serve as a check on the application of tacit knowledge to current innovation. The more rapidly moving the knowledge base involved, the more critical it is to bring people in from outside the group—either as new hires or as visitors.

CONCLUSION

Tacit knowledge is a tremendous resource for all activities—especially for innovation. The tacit dimensions of *individual* knowledge are not publicly available except as embodied in people to be hired, and the tacit dimensions of *collective* knowledge are woven into the very fabric of an organization and are not easily imitated. Therefore, tacit knowledge is a source of competitive advantage. The creativity necessary for innovation derives not only from obvious and visible expertise, but from invisible reservoirs of experience.

Our understanding of tacit knowledge and its relevance to innovation is nascent. This article presents the barest outlines of a path towards that understanding but may serve to instigate more discussion. Clearly, many different fields of inquiry are relevant, including ones as diverse as design, cognitive psychology, group dynamics, and information technology. In order to understand the potential and complexity of collective tacit knowledge, we shall need to practice what we study—interacting through metaphor as well as analysis and through mutual apprenticeship as well as structured intellectual exchanges. We shall have to confront in the field of business the delicate, imposing task known best to poets and artists—expressing enough of the inexpressible that the communication effort becomes invaluable.

Chapter 12
Knowledge Management and Collaboration Technologies[1]

INTRODUCTION

The concept of organizational knowledge as a valuable strategic asset has been popularized recently by economists, management theorists, consultants, and executives. The enterprise which leverages its intellectual resources can focus that power on critical challenges, fostering innovation and potentially altering its competitive landscape. Leading firms therefore are finding that, to remain competitive, they must efficiently and effectively create, capture, locate, and share their organization's knowledge and expertise, and have the ability to bring that knowledge to bear on problems and opportunities. We refer to the development and leveraging of organizational knowledge to increase a firm's value as *knowledge management*.

While the business case for knowledge management is becoming widely accepted, few organizations today are fully capable of developing and leveraging critical organizational knowledge to improve their performance. Many organizations are so complex that their knowledge has become fragmented, difficult to locate and share, and therefore redundant, inconsistent, or not used at all. In today's environment of rapid change and technological discontinuity, knowledge and expertise which can be shared is rapidly made obsolete.

The management of organizational knowledge is fundamental to effective performance, and collaboration technologies can play a central role. In particular, our research is directed at learning how these technologies can support and improve knowledge management in three areas:

- Distributed learning
- Communities of practice
- Enterprise knowledge management

While conceptually related, each of these themes presents a unique perspective on the creation, acquisition, management, and application of organizational knowledge using collaboration technologies.

- *Distributed Learning* employs collaboration technologies to deliver training and education to geographically dispersed individuals and groups. Specific subject

---

[1] Reprinted by permission of Lotus Institute.

303

knowledge can be made accessible and formally presented and transferred in a highly efficient and convenient manner, enabling people to integrate training and education with their day-to-day work responsibilities.
- *Communities of practice* comprise people who engage in similar work practices. While these people may work either as teams or within different organizational units, they have a common need to capture, share, and leverage their collective knowledge related to that practice.
- *Enterprise knowledge management* refers to the need for an entire organization to share and leverage knowledge among and across different knowledge communities and organizational units.

WHAT IS KNOWLEDGE?

It is fashionable to distinguish between data, information, and knowledge. Data typically represent symbols or facts out of context, and thus not directly nor immediately meaningful. Data placed within some interpretive context acquire meaning and value as information. Knowledge is the meaningfully structured accumulation of information.

Knowledge may be categorized as *explicit* or *tacit*.[2] Explicit knowledge can be formally articulated or encoded. Therefore, it can be more easily transferred or shared, but is abstract and removed from direct experience. Textbooks and software code are examples of explicit knowledge. Tacit knowledge is developed from direct experience and action and is often referred to as knowledge-in-practice. It is highly pragmatic and situation-specific. Tacit knowledge is subconsciously understood and applied, difficult to articulate, and usually shared through highly interactive conversation, story-telling, and shared experience.

Nonaka[3] proposed that while knowledge must be internalized and made tacit to be truly understood and applied to practice, it is best exchanged, distributed, or combined among communities of practice by being made explicit. Once

---

[2] The tacit-explicit knowledge continuum has also been more precisely modeled as a set of knowledge levels or stages. For example, Hubert and Stuart Dreyfus ("From Socrates to Expert Systems," *Technology in Society*, Vol. 6, 1984, p. 217) define 5 levels of knowledge (novice, advanced beginner, competence, proficiency, and expertise) which differ by the extent to which action goals, plans, and rules are context-specific and consciously formulated.

Roger Bohn ("Measuring and Managing Technological Knowledge," *Sloan Management Review*, Vol. 36, No. 1, Fall, 1994, p. 61) has defined eight stages based on the extent to which cause, effect, and control feedback for some process may be articulated and measured. James Quinn ("Managing Professional Intellect: Making the Most of the Best," *Harvard Business Review*, Vol. 74, No. 2, March, 1996, p. 71) differs between knowledge about, knowledge how, and knowledge why, with knowledge of why something occurs being the deepest and most contextual.

[3] Nonaka, Ikujiro and Hirotaka Takeuchi, *The Knowledge-Creating Company: How Japanese Companies Create the Dynamics of Innoration*, Oxford University Press, New York, 1995.

shared, explicit knowledge can be internalized and made tacit again by reapplying it to practice. This constant cycle of tacit creation leading to explicit combination and exchange enlarges the total knowledge base of the organization.

Converting explicit knowledge into tacit tends to occur naturally as a by-product of action. However, making tacit knowledge sufficiently explicit to be recorded, documented, and efficiently shared and reapplied, especially outside the originating community, is perhaps the greatest and least understood knowledge management challenge.

THE ROLE OF COLLABORATION TECHNOLOGIES

The creation, sharing, and combining of knowledge within and among different knowledge communities, therefore, requires the coordinated management and exchange of tacit and explicit knowledge. Zack[4] found that sharing tacit, contextual knowledge requires using highly expressive and interactive communication modes such as face-to-face conversation, storytelling, and shared experiences. However, when communicators already share an interpretive context, less interactivity and richness is required. Communication in those situations is more focused on explicit, factual knowledge conveyed via leaner and less interactive communication modes such as electronic mail, computer conferences, and shared electronic repositories of explicit knowledge.

Effectively applying collaboration technologies for knowledge management requires fitting the richness and interactivity of the communication mode to the degree of shared contextual knowledge. At one extreme, the dissemination of explicit, factual knowledge within a community having a high degree of shared contextual knowledge can be accomplished through access to a central electronic repository. However, when interpretive context is moderately shared, or the knowledge exchanged is less explicit, or the community is loosely affiliated, then more interactive modes such as electronic mail or discussion databases are appropriate. When context is not well-shared and knowledge is primarily tacit, communication is best accomplished using the richest and most interactive modes such as video conferencing or face-to-face conversation. Collaboration technologies may also be useful to help structure or coordinate interaction to maximize learning and sharing among a community, by automating particular communication techniques or rituals.

Therefore, in cases where knowledge can be explicitly encoded and recorded, or where interactive context is well-shared, collaboration technologies can play a central role in its acquisition, combination, interpretation, and dissemination. Where knowledge is primarily tacit, these technologies support the personal interaction required for its sharing, creation, and explication.

---

[4] Zack, Michael H., "Interactivity and Communication Mode Choice in Ongoing Management Groups," *Information Systems Research*, Vol. 4. No. 3, 1993, pp. 207–239.

CATEGORIES OF KNOWLEDGE MANAGEMENT APPLICATIONS

From our research, we have defined two categories of knowledge processing applications for collaboration technologies: *distributive* and *collaborative* (Figure 12.1). *Distributive* applications maintain a repository of explicitly encoded knowledge created and managed for subsequent distribution to knowledge consumers within or outside the organization. These applications exhibit a sequential flow of information into and out of a central repository, structured to provide flexible access and views of the knowledge. Their primary focus tends to be on the repository and the explicit knowledge it contains, rather than on the contributors, the users, or the tacit knowledge they may hold.

Collaborative applications are focused primarily on supporting interaction among people holding tacit knowledge. This may be a simple directory of individuals within or associated with a community of knowledge. It may also take the more interactive form of a knowledge brokerage—an electronic conference or discussion space where people may either search for knowledge by posing questions (e.g., "Does anyone know. . .") or advertise their expertise. The most interactive form supports direct communication through discussion databases, computer conferences, and real-time collaboration technologies. These applications directly support interaction and collaboration within and among knowledge-based teams, enabling "teams of teams" to form across knowledge communities.

In contrast to distributive applications, the repository associated with collaborative applications is a by-product of the interaction, rather than the primary focus of the application. This repository of messages is dynamic and its content emergent. The ability to capture and structure emergent communication within a repository provides a more valuable, enduring, and leverageable knowledge by-product than the personal notes or memories of a traditional conversation or meeting.

Collaboration technologies, therefore, can support a well-structured repository of explicit knowledge while enabling the management of tacit knowledge.

Knowledge Management Applications

Distributive

Collaborative

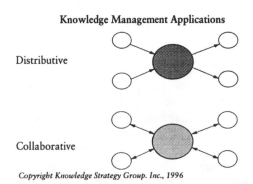

Copyright Knowledge Strategy Group. Inc., 1996

FIGURE 12.1 Knowledge Management Applications

The *knowledge repository* represents a valuable means to manage the explication, sharing, combination, application, and renewal of organizational knowledge.

THE ARCHITECTURE OF KNOWLEDGE MANAGEMENT APPLICATIONS

Knowledge comprises two components: knowledge *structure* and information *content*. Structure represents a framework used to arrange information to make it meaningful, while content represents the information itself. Knowledge structures therefore provide the context for making sense of information.

A knowledge repository also can be defined by its structure and content. The structure reflects the way in which each "knowledge unit" is classified and indexed for retrieval or association with other units of knowledge. The repository structure is defined by the format of the knowledge unit, the indexing scheme, and the inter-unit links. The actual knowledge units represent the content of the repository

We use an information architecture or "pipeline" framework[5] (Figure 12.2) to describe how a repository of explicit knowledge can be effectively created and

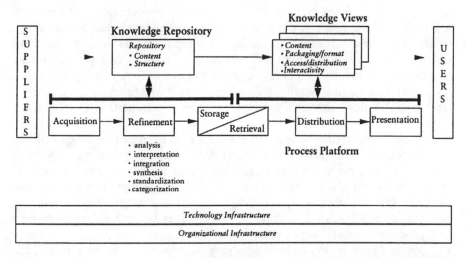

adapted from Meyer and Zack, 1995

FIGURE 12.2 The Architecture of Knowledge Repositories

[5] Zack, Michael. H., "An Information Infrastructure Model for Systems Planning," *Journal of Systems Management*, Vol. 43, No. 8, August, 1992, p. 16; Meyer, Marc H. and Michael H. Zack, "The Design and Development of Information Products," *Sloan Management Review*, Vol. 37, No. 3, Spring. 1996, pp. 43–59.

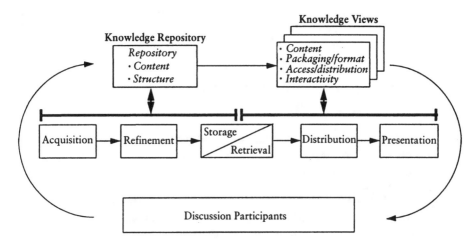

FIGURE 12.3 The Architecture of Interactive Knowledge Repositories

managed. Information and knowledge can be acquired from many different internal and external sources. That knowledge then is subjected to value-adding processes such as labeling, indexing, sorting, abstracting, standardization, integration, re-categorization, as well as the process of making the knowledge explicit. The knowledge is stored in an integrated repository. It may be accessed in a variety of ways and its content combined, restructured, and presented in a variety of new contexts depending on how that repository has been designed and the mechanisms for distributing and presenting its content. In highly interactive exchanges, the users and suppliers comprise the same group of people, continually responding to and building on each individual's addition to the discussion database. The flow continually loops back from presentation to acquisition (Figure 12.3).

A well-structured repository allows for a high degree of viewing flexibility. If the repository is conceived as a knowledge "platform," then many different knowledge views may be derived based on the particular content, format, and medium by which it is presented to the user.[6] A knowledge platform may also consist of several different repositories, each with a structure appropriate to a particular type of knowledge. These repositories may be logically linked to form a composite or "virtual" repository.

Various information technologies may be applied along the pipeline, but they should support the seamless movement of information and knowledge into and out of the repository. For quantitative data, the repository resembles a data warehouse which may be fed by various production systems and tapped by information reporting, mining, and analysis software programs. For richer forms of data, the process can be supported by collaboration technologies which provide

[6] Meyer and Zack, ibid.

appropriate mechanisms for capturing text, sound, graphics, and video; categorizing and indexing that information to provide the appropriate context and structure within the repository, and providing customizable views of the knowledge in the repository. As the knowledge becomes less precise, the use of structured discussion databases and multi-media presentation formats becomes the appropriate means for collecting and exchanging narrated experience.

Collaboration technologies such as Lotus Notes® offer a natural environment within which to build a repository for rich, explicit knowledge. Input is captured by forms for assigning various labels, categories, and indices to each unit of knowledge. Document databases offer flexibility as to both content and structure. Content may range in richness and include video, sound, graphics, rich text, numerical analysis, or raw data. The structure is flexible enough to create "knowledge units," indexed and linked using categories that reflect the structure of the contextual knowledge and the content of factual knowledge of the organization, displayed as flexible subsets via customizable views.

Collaboration technologies, employed in this manner, can be used to develop knowledge maps which identify key sources of expertise, or databases with pointers to important content. The technology can support the creation of shared memory and interpretive context essential to effective communication.

CASE STUDIES

We have used this framework to design and study knowledge sharing applications that support teamwork, enterprise-wide knowledge navigation, distributed learning, and electronic publishing. In all of these cases the technology has been extremely useful in managing organizational knowledge. Three representative cases are described below.

Distributed Learning

As part of a study to identify appropriate learning models for use with collaboration technologies, the Lotus Institute developed a distributed learning program for a major public accounting firm. The program provided education and training on advanced accounting services to new hires. The students were located in different offices around the world, and most had never met in person. The course objectives were to present key accounting concepts, to provide guidance for marketing the service, and to coach students on how to integrate subject-matter experts into an engagement.

The course was conducted using a combination of traditional study/response as well as electronic group interaction and team projects. The course lasted six weeks, and all students followed the same structured course syllabus and work schedule.

The material was delivered through the *Lotus Learning Network*, a Notes-based application comprising several cross-linked repositories: a course syllabus, a student profile database, a library of readings, a subject matter (lesson) database, and a discussion database. All repositories except for the discussion database represented distributive applications whereby the content was developed primarily for efficient and convenient delivery to the students. The discussion database added an interactive dimension by enabling the students to discuss the content of those repositories as well as initiating discussion around lessons, group projects, or other topics of interest.

The pilot project successfully demonstrated the value of the technology for distributed learning. Training was clearly more convenient and less costly than traditional co-located classes. However, delivering training to students also responsible for performing their normal work responsibilities often created priority conflicts. This suggested that course material should be more closely integrated with the real-world engagements to which the students are assigned.

Future studies will examine issues such as the effects of self-pacing *vs.* instructor-defined schedules, the role of the instructor/facilitator, groups having social relationships among the students *vs.* those without, highly-structured *vs.* less-structured course content, and identifing learning situations for which the reflective interaction provided by collaboration technologies is most appropriate.

Communities of Practice

The Lotus Institute helped to develop a Notes-based application to document and share a wide range of practice-based knowledge among the members of a major consulting firm. The objective was to equip the field consultants with all the knowledge they would need to successfully perform an engagement. The approach was to develop "knowledge packs" for each line of business, which included a portfolio of pertinent information such as marketing presentations, sample proposals, subject knowledge, industry information, prior engagements, market research reports, and client history. This information, previously held in three-ring binders, now was brought into a common repository together with knowledge packs for two dozen other lines of business.

The project posed several challenges. One was to create a common navigation tool with cataloging, indexing, and mapping capability across the various knowledge repositories to make the repository content more easily accessible. A second was to make the database design scalable so that it could be extended throughout the consulting practice and then to the tax and audit practice areas. An additional challenge was to rationalize the increasingly complex classification of the knowledge being stored. A final challenge was to define the appropriate roles and responsibilities for managing the repository.

The project, which is still underway, has provided a proof-of-concept for creating an in-depth electronic knowledge repository which is portable, easily accessible, and quickly updated, and which provides a common location for the intellectual capital of the firm.

Enterprise Knowledge Management

The Lotus Institute is working with another professional services firm attempting to build an enterprise-wide knowledge management capability. They are concerned with issues similar to the previous two cases but at a greater level of complexity related to scaling up to the enterprise level. For example, they are trying to identify the best approaches to building large-scale knowledge repositories that extend across multiple and heterogeneous repository technologies such as Lotus Notes, relational databases, object-oriented databases, and legacy applications. They are likewise concerned with the best practices for capturing, retrieving, and indexing content, and for building knowledge taxonomies that extend across communities of practice. In their preliminary planning, they are trying to determine what application template conventions, dictionary elements, object structures, and interfaces are required for knowledge categorization and navigation.

OUR FINDINGS

From these and other studies, we have identified several overarching issues which must be addressed in order to maximize the quality of the design and implementation of these knowledge management applications.

Application Complexity

The first issue which must be addressed is to identify the level of complexity of the application. The greater the complexity, the more effort, time, and resources will be required to understand the knowledge processing requirements and to develop and implement the application.

Knowledge management applications form a continuum from low to high interaction complexity. Teamwork is the most interactive and complex application context, because team activities span the entire tacit/explicit knowledge processing cycle. The teams we have worked with have had an opportunity to establish a well-defined social community and shared context to support the use of the technology, and this has played a key role in the success of the application.

Electronic publishing, in contrast, is perhaps the most straightforward. It represents the one-way distribution of explicit knowledge, for example a human resources policy manual, which it is assumed will be applied in practice. The user community may be loosely affiliated, related only by their need for access to the same knowledge repository, but not necessarily supported by a social community. Moderate interaction may occur between user and publisher to clarify the application of particular knowledge as needed.

Distributed learning and enterprise-wide knowledge navigation, while reflecting different knowledge management issues, similarly represent a middle case: moderately interactive cycles of locating or distributing explicitly encoded knowledge, together with electronic discussion to discuss and interpret its content. The distributed learning and enterprise-wide knowledge communities we have worked with vary in the strength of their social affiliation and shared context, although at the very least all belong to the same company and functional area within those companies.

Repository Design

A critical issue influencing success across all of our experiences is the ability of the organization to define a repository structure that reflects the structure of contextual knowledge tacitly held by the organization. In most organizations, those structures are neither well-defined nor widely shared, and resolving this issue is essential for implementing technologies that explicitly encode organizational knowledge.

A related issue is that complex knowledge management problems may require support through multiple repositories. These repositories may differ based on the degree of interactivity required, the volatility of the content, the degree of familiarity of the knowledge domain, or the basic structure of the knowledge itself.

Knowledge Accessibility

We have also discovered that even where knowledge repositories exist, they often are not well identified or easily accessed. Navigation capabilities must be created to access knowledge repositories throughout an enterprise. These repositories should be linked at the knowledge-unit level to promote rapid access and support ad hoc navigation.

New Organizational Roles

Organizations must create new organizational roles to support the knowledge pipeline process. Traditional organizational roles typically do not address either knowledge management or the cross-functional, cross-organizational process by which it is created, shared, and applied. These new roles have few existing models to imitate, and they create a significant power shift regarding the control of knowledge assets. This combination of role ambiguity and power uncertainty can spell disaster if change is not managed appropriately. If done well, however, the results can be extremely positive.

Our framework suggests new roles within the organization, regardless of the application. The organization must create a role which entails overall responsibility for the knowledge management architecture, infrastructure, and process. Each stage of the process represents additional knowledge management roles which must be explicitly addressed.

Acquisition for distributive applications requires knowledge finders and collectors. Capturing verbal knowledge held as stories will require transcribers. Documenting observed experiences may require organizational "reporters". Interactive applications require recruiters and facilitators to encourage and manage participation.

Distributive refinement roles include analysts, abstractors, classifiers, editors, and integrators. In interactive applications, the structuring and indexing of the communication is often performed by the communicators themselves, using guidelines built into the application, supported by a conference moderator. Assuring the quality of the knowledge being acquired requires quality assurance personnel and reputation brokers.

The distributive repository must be managed by a knowledge librarian or "curator," while the interactive repository is usually managed by a moderator or facilitator. Others must take responsibility for access, distribution, and presentation. Each role requires unique skills and expertise.

Appropriate Organizational Climate and Context

Beyond creating specific knowledge management roles, organizations must create a social climate and work context which supports and encourages knowledge creation and sharing.[7] Leading-edge firms maintain a *culture* which promotes knowledge creation by encouraging information sharing, openness and trust, cooperation and collaboration, continual search for knowledge and truth, risk taking, experimentation, and a respect for others' knowledge and expertise. These firms exhibit *norms* that encourage organization members to search for or develop new ideas, share ideas, and accept others' ideas. They maintain *rewards* and *incentives* for information sharing and learning. They also exhibit a *social climate* which fosters a spirit of camaraderie, and *mechanisms* which encourage the formation of diverse and organizationally distributed communities of interaction, within which individuals can commit to collaboration and knowledge sharing.

Organizations which effectively manage knowledge employ or develop *people* who have the appropriate level and diversity of knowledge, skills, and experience regarding interaction and human relations, as well as the task, and a commitment to learning. These organizations design *tasks* to be engaging, to

---

[7] Zack, Michael H. and James L. McKenney, "Social Context and Interaction in Ongoing Computer-supported Management Groups," *Organization Science*, Vol. 6., No. 4, July-August, 1995, pp. 394–422.

provide sufficient variety to enable learning opportunities, and to offer sufficient discretion and autonomy to enable experimentation and opportunities for learning.

Effective Knowledge Management Processes

Organizations which manage knowledge effectively exhibit four process characteristics. These organizations:

1. apply maximum effort and commitment to creating, sharing, and applying their knowledge;
2. apply an appropriate level and mix of skill, knowledge, and expertise to problems and opportunities;
3. employ an organizational and technical knowledge processing strategy appropriate to the situation;
4. engage in effective communication as evidenced by the reliable, accurate, timely, and meaningful exchange of information and knowledge.

Organizations can reorient or enhance their knowledge management processes by two types of intervention: technical or social. With a technical intervention, the organization focuses on building an *information infrastructure* to improve its ability to identify, store, manage, distribute, and communicate information and knowledge. A social intervention attempts to improve its *social infrastructure* to produce greater creativity, collaboration, trust, and ability to change, enabling more effective communication and sharing of tacit knowledge.

CONCLUSION

Creating competitive advantage today requires developing and leveraging organizational knowledge. Leading-edge firms consider their knowledge to be a strategic asset, and actively and explicitly manage it as such. These firms have cataloged their knowledge by creating so-called knowledge maps, which represent the location, content, and value of the firm's knowledge whether stored in physical or electronic media, embedded in technologies or information systems, or held within the minds of employees. They also have developed standards for measuring and evaluating the quality and value of their knowledge; for representing, encoding, and storing that knowledge; and for indexing and labeling knowledge for effective access. They have created social climates that encourage knowledge sharing. Finally, they have provided the appropriate technical infrastructure.

Effective knowledge management also demands effective communication. Collaboration technologies can play a central role in this process by facilitating the sharing, documentation and dissemination of organizational knowledge. Leading-edge firms are using collaboration technology explicitly to create, store, share, and apply their organizational knowledge to increase business value.

ABOUT THE AUTHORS

Michael H. Zack is a Research Fellow of the Lotus Institute, a partner in Knowledge Strategy Group (Cambridge, MA), and the Joseph G. Reisman Research Professor at Northeastern University College of Business Administration. His research and consulting focuses on the use of information technology to improve the creation and flow of information and knowledge within and among teams, organizations, and industries. He received his Master's degree from Northwestern University (Kellogg) Graduate School of Management and his Doctorate degree from the Harvard Business School.

Michael Serino is a Research Fellow of the Lotus Institute and a partner in Knowledge Strategy Group (Cambridge, MA). His research and consulting focuses on the use of information technology to support organizational transformation and knowledge management. He received his Master's degree from Harvard University and his Bachelor's degree from Hamilton College.

Chapter 13

Creating Knowledge through Collaboration[1]

Andrew C. Inkpen[*]

Increasingly, the creation of new organizational knowledge is becoming a managerial priority. New knowledge provides the basis for organizational renewal and sustainable competitive advantage.[2] A failure to create knowledge and manage it as a critical organizational asset may account for the declining performance of many well-established firms. However, our understanding of the organizational processes surrounding knowledge creation and management is rather limited. By examining knowledge creation through alliance strategies, this article provides insights into how firms manage knowledge. Understanding the process by which new knowledge is created poses a fundamental challenge to the development of a learning organization.[3]

In the past five years, the number of domestic and international alliances has grown by more than 25 percent annually.[4] Peter Drucker has suggested that the greatest change in the way business is being conducted is in the accelerating growth of relationships based not on ownership but on partnership.[5] Many firms have now realized that self-sufficiency is becoming increasingly difficult in a business environment that demands strategic focus, flexibility, and innovation. Alliances provide firms with a unique opportunity to leverage their strengths with

[1] Copyright © 1996, by The Regents of the University of California. Reprinted from the *California Management Review*. Vol. 39, No. 1. By permission of The Regents.
[*] Support from the Carnegie Bosch Institute for Applied Studies in International Management is gratefully acknowledged.
[2] J. B. Quinn, *The Intelligent Enterprise* (New York, NY: Free Press, 1992).
[3] The notion of the learning organization is explored in detail in P. M. Senge, *The Fifth Discipline: The Art and Practice of the Learning Organization* (New York, NY: Doubleday, 1990); P. M. Senge, C. Roberts, R. Ross, B. J. Smith, and A. Kleiner, *The Fifth Discipline Fieldbook: Strategies and Tools for Building a Learning Organization* (New York, NY: Currency/Doubleday, 1994).
[4] J. Bleeke and D. Ernst, "Is Your Strategic Alliance Really a Sale?" *Harvard Business Review*, 73 (January/February 1995): 97–105.
[5] P. R. Drucker, "The Network Society." *Wall Street Journal*, March 29, 1995, p. 12.

the help of partners. In essence, alliances provide firms with "a window on their partners' broad capabilities."[6] Through this window, alliances create the potential for firms to acquire knowledge associated with partner skills and capabilities. This knowledge can then be incorporated into the firm's systems and structures. Without an alliance, access to the partner's skills would probably be restricted, limiting opportunities for learning.

Many firms enter into alliances with specific learning objectives.[7] Although learning through alliances can and does occur successfully, it is a difficult, frustrating, and often misunderstood process. The primary obstacle to success is a failure to execute the specific organizational processes necessary to access, assimilate, and disseminate alliance knowledge. Successful firms exploit learning opportunities by acquiring knowledge through "grafting," a process of internalizing knowledge not previously available within the organization.[8]

When firms internalize alliance knowledge, new knowledge is created. For example, Sony Corp. has recently formed various alliances with computer and telecommunications firms in an effort to forge new technology linkages for its consumer electronics products.[9] These alliances provide Sony with access to a wealth of new knowledge, such as how to manage product development cycles in the computer industry (which are much faster than in consumer electronics). The challenge for Sony and other firms involved in such alliances is to incorporate disparate pieces of individual knowledge into a wider organizational knowledge base.

Organizational learning is a systems-level concept that can become useful only when its component parts are thoroughly understood and brought down to an operational level. Unless individual knowledge is shared throughout the organization, the knowledge will have a limited impact on organizational

[6] G. Hamel, Y. Doz, and C. K. Prahalad, "Collaborate With Your Competitors—and Win," *Harvard Business Review,* 67 (January/February 1989): 133–139.

[7] There is a growing body of research dealing with learning and alliances. See J. Badaracco, *The Knowledge Link: Competitive Advantage Through Strategic Alliances* (Boston, MA: Harvard Business School Press, 1991); G. Hamel, "Competition for Competence and Inter-Partner Learning Within International Strategic Alliances," *Strategic Management Journal.* 12 (1991): 83–104; B. Kogut, "Joint Ventures: Theoretical and Empirical Perspectives," *Strategic Management Journal,* 9 (1988): 319–322; N. S. Levinson and M. Asahi, "Cross-national Alliances and Interorganizational Learning," *Organizational Dynamics,* 24 (Autumn 1965): 50–63.

[8] Huber has explored the various ways by which organizations are exposed to new knowledge: congenital learning experiential learning, vicarious learning, searching, and grafting. Of specific interest in this study is grafting knowledge from outside the organization's boundaries; for example, through mergers, acquisitions, and JVs. See G. P. Huber, "Organizational Learning: The Contributing Processes and a Review of the Literatures," *Organization Science,* 2 (February 1991): 88–117.

[9] D. P. Hamilton, "Sony Expands in Computer-Linked Gear: Effort Requires Shift in Go-It-Alone Tradition," *Wall Street Journal,* April 14, 1995, p. A8.

effectiveness.[10] Thus, organizational knowledge creation represents a process whereby the knowledge held by individuals is amplified and internalized as part of an organization's knowledge base.[11]

Radical changes are occurring in the competitive environment. Some of the forces that firms must deal with are deregulation, technological discontinuities, the emergence of trading blocks, and global competition. To deal effectively with these forces, firms must refocus their resources and in many cases, radically change how they do business. To create effective strategic change, managers must generate new knowledge. For example, the telecommunications industry was for many years a cozy, protected market dominated by AT&T. The breakup of AT&T into the Regional Bell Operating Companies (RBOCs) was designed in part to stimulate new services and competition. However, a decade after deregulation, the RBOCs find themselves under a fierce assault from a host of unlikely competitors: energy companies, railroads, cable TV firms, and small start-up firms that are all poised to offer phone services. For the RBOCs to survive, they must create and harness new technological and marketing knowledge for products and services that did not exist a few years ago. In many instances, this involves the formation of strategic alliances to gain access to the skills of other firms.

THE RESEARCH STUDY

This research study examined two main questions: Do alliance parents recognize and seek to exploit alliance learning opportunities? and What organizational conditions facilitate effective or ineffective learning? The sample of alliance organizations for the research consisted of 40 American-Japanese joint ventures (JVs) located in North America and involved interviews with their managers. All of the JVs were suppliers to the automotive industry and, with two exceptions, all were startup or greenfield organizations. In terms of ownership, 17 ventures were 50–50, in 15 ventures the Japanese partners had majority equity, and in eight ventures the American partners had majority equity.

The automotive industry at the supplier level provided an interesting context for a study of learning and knowledge creation. Ongoing structural changes

---

[10] D. H. Kim, "The Link Between Individual and Organizational Learning," *Sloan Management Review*, 35 (Fall 1993): 37–50.

[11] I. Nonaka has written extensively in the area of knowledge creation. See I. Nonaka, "A Dynamic Theory of Organizational Knowledge," *Organization Science*, 5 (February 1994): 14–37; I. Nonaka, "The Knowledge Creating Company," *Harvard Business Review* 69 (November/December 1991): 96–104. Nonaka and Takeuchi have argued that one of the limitations of organizational learning theory is its failure to develop the concept of knowledge creation. See I. Nonaka and H. Takeuchi, *The Knowledge Creating Company: How Japanese Companies Create the Dynamics of Innovation* (New York, NY: Oxford University Press, 1995).

in the industry have contributed to what could be referred to as a learning imperative for North American automotive suppliers. With domestic automakers under pressure from transplant Japanese firms, North American suppliers have found their traditional customers increasingly more demanding in terms of cost and quality. This situation, coupled with increasing foreign investment, has created increasingly difficult competitive conditions for automotive suppliers. As a result, this industry was fertile ground for a study of knowledge creation. Many of the American partner firms in the study, struggling to compete in an industry in transition, saw their JVs as a point of leverage for the development of new skills and capabilities.

Five cases from the initial study were selected for further study. Several criteria were used to select the cases. Of particular interest was the alliance learning potential created by the JVs and the motivation of the American parents to exploit the potential. Differences in JV performance, partner history, and the source of JV management were other criteria used in the selection of cases. Overall, the issues faced by the managers associated with these Jys were representative of alliance issues in general.

EXPLOITING COLLABORATIVE KNOWLEDGE

There are four critical knowledge management processes used by firms to access and transform knowledge from an alliance context to a partner context: technology sharing; JV-parent interactions; personnel movement; and linkages between parent and alliance strategies. These processes create connections for individual managers through which they can communicate their alliance experiences to others and form the foundation for the integration of knowledge into the parent's collective knowledge base. As individuals interact through the various connections, the interactions become larger in scale and faster in speed as more and more actors in the organization become involved. This process has been described as a "spiral" of organizational knowledge creation.[12] In the spiral, knowledge starts at the individual level, moves up to the group level, and then to the firm level. As the knowledge spirals upward in the organization, it may be enriched and extended as individuals interact with each other and with their organizations.

Although the knowledge management processes are not complex or difficult to understand, the lack of complexity should not be associated with a lack of effectiveness. The creation of organizational knowledge requires the sharing and dissemination of individual experiences. Each process provides an avenue for JV parent managers to gain exposure to knowledge and ideas outside their traditional organizational boundaries. The processes deal with both operational and strategic knowledge and taken together, provide a comprehensive view as to how

---

[12] Nonaka, op. cit., 1994.

TABLE 13.1 Knowledge Management Processes and Types of Knowledge

Knowledge Management Processes	*Types of Knowledge*	*Examples of Knowledge Potentially Useful to American JV Parents*
Technology Sharing	Explicit	• quality control process • product designs • scheduling systems
JV-Parent Interactions	Explicit Tacit	• specific human resource practices • expectations of Japanese customers
Personnel Movement	Tacit	• continuous improvement objectives • commitment to customer satisfaction
Linkages Between Parent and Alliance Strategies	Explicit Tacit	• market intelligence • visions for the future • partner's keiretsu relationships

alliance knowledge can cross organizational boundaries and become the basis for knowledge creation in parent firms.

Tacit and Explicit Knowledge

Organizational knowledge creation involves a continuous interplay between tacit and explicit knowledge.[13] Tacit knowledge is hard to formalize, making it difficult to communicate or share with others. Tacit knowledge involves intangible factors embedded in personal beliefs, experiences, and values. Explicit knowledge is systematic and easily communicated in the form of hard data or codified procedures. Often there will be a strong tacit dimension associated with how to use and implement explicit knowledge.

Table 13.1 shows the four knowledge management processes and the primary types of knowledge associated with each process. The table also provides examples to help clarify the tacit and explicit dimensions. Two of the knowledge management processes, JV-parent interactions and linkages between parent and alliance strategies, create the potential for both explicit and tacit knowledge to be created. Technology sharing provides access primarily to explicit knowledge. Personnel movement, while it could be associated with explicit knowledge, will be most effective as a means of gaining access to tacit knowledge.

Technology Sharing

In the cases studied, parent firms had put into place various mechanisms to gain access to JV manufacturing process and product technology. The most

---

[13] Nonaka and Takeuchi, op. cit., 1995.

common approach was also the most straightforward—meetings between JV and parent managers. In one case, monthly meetings were held, with the location alternating between the JV and one of the American parent plants. In attendance at the meetings were plant managers, heads of quality control, R&D managers, the VP manufacturing at the American parent head office, and several senior JV managers. In addition, quarterly R&D meetings were held involving the JV and American parent. The manufacturing vice president of one of the American parent's said that "while he hated to admit it, the quality of the JV product was superior to that in the parent." As a result, he initiated a program with his plant managers about the need to improve quality and customer service.

Access to partner technology skills also occurred through direct linkages between Japanese and American partners. In two cases, there were regular visits by American parent personnel to Japanese parent facilities. Consistent with the argument that Western firms find it difficult to undertake activities not fitting prevailing notions of what the company is about,[14] an American parent president expressed frustration at the lack of tangible output from these visits.

> Our engineers go to Japan and come back with some good ideas but nothing ever happens. They [the American engineers] are too protective of their technology and way of doing things. It drives me crazy when I visit a Japanese partner plant. They are doing the same things we are with one-third the employees. I tell our people here but they can't do it.

Despite this frustration, the president recognized the value of the Japanese technology and decided to initiate some changes within the parent operation. To capitalize on the Japanese partner's fabrication knowledge and ability to operate with fewer equipment operators, the American president invited several Japanese engineers to the United States to train parent engineers. The Japanese engineers brought very detailed equipment designs that would allow the American firm to replicate their manufacturing process. When no visible progress was made on designing new equipment, the American president decided to contract the design and manufacturing of the equipment to the Japanese partner. An American engineer would be sent to Japan to learn about the equipment so it could be installed in the United States.

In another case, the partners signed a very broad global technology agreement. Both partners agreed to be completely open in sharing both product and manufacturing technology For example, the JV had developed a specific process technology that was considered proprietary (so proprietary, in fact, that a section of the manufacturing line could be closed off behind dark curtains if necessary).

---

[14] G. Hedlund and I. Nonaka, "Models of Knowledge Management in the West and Japan," in P. Lorange, B. Chakravarthy, J. Roos, and A. Van de Ven, eds., *Implementing Strategic Processes: Change, Learning, and Cooperation* (Oxford: Basil Blackwell, 1993), pp. 117–144.

The American parent was actively studying the process to incorporate in its own plants. With this technology-sharing agreement, there were explicit terms on licensing and royalties only for product technology. For manufacturing technology, such as the proprietary process above, there were no established financial terms. The American parent may ask to borrow a Japanese partner engineer for a few weeks. When this had happened in the past, there was never any financial considerations involved because, according to a manager, "it all comes out in the wash." The American partner recognized the need for reciprocal commitment and tried to make the technology sharing a two-way relationship, as a parent manager explained:

> When we give something to the Japanese partner, they will return it tenfold. If we are not coming up with anything, they will not give us anything in return.

Not all the American parents were interested in access to Japanese partner technology. In one case, a Japanese partner offered to share its manufacturing technology with its American partner. The Japanese partner had developed some proprietary process technology and was willing to share it at no cost. The technology was used in the JV and was very visible to American partner managers. The offer was communicated in a written memo from a JV manager to the American partner president. The American firm never followed up on the offer. Why was the offer refused? One JV manager's opinion was that "the people from the American parent do not want to learn because they see the JV as an upstart."

JV-Parent Interactions

The JV-parent relationship plays a key role in knowledge management. In addition to the technology-sharing initiatives discussed above, other JV-parent interactions can create the social context necessary to bring JV knowledge into a wider arena. JV-parent interactions can provide the basis for what have been referred to as "communities of practice."[15] A community of practice is a group of individuals that is not necessarily recognizable within strict organizational boundaries. The members share community knowledge and may be willing to challenge the organization's conventional wisdom. Communities emerge not when the members absorb abstract knowledge, but when the members become "insiders" and acquire the particular community's subjective viewpoint and learn to speak its language. In this study, the insiders were the American managers who recognized the strategic benefits of collaboration and who were prepared to accept the JV as a legitimate basis for fostering learning. As an example, a manager in one case explained, "over time the JV has become grudgingly accepted as

[15] J. S. Brown and P. Duguid, "Organizational Learning and Communities of Practice: Towards a Unified View of Working, Learning, and Organization," *Organization Science*, 2 (February 1991): 40–57.

more people have been exposed to the JV. Now, there is high regard for what is going on." In this case, the elements of a community emerged when a cross-section of parent and JV managers recognized that the Japanese partner was not a threat but a valuable partner.

Visits and tours of JV facilities were an effective means for parent managers to learn about their JVs. JV managers were generally convinced that differences embodied in the JV were visible and parent managers would appreciate the differences if they spent more time in the JV. However, visits were not always utilized effectively, as a JV manager explained:

> Plant managers have been invited and some have visited. However, the American parent organization is so lean that these people have little time to invest in learning. . . . A group of 1st line supervisors spent two weeks in the JV. They spent time learning about the JV systems and took videos and notes back to the parent. They went back to the parent plants and nothing happened. . . . The Japanese partner, on the other hand, sends many people to the JV with a learning objective. They are not afraid to ask questions and spend a lot of time in the JV doing that. There are always Japanese people visiting, both from Japanese parent divisions and from Japanese parent world headquarters. It is not always clear what they are here for. Sometimes they just observe, other times they ask a lot of questions.

An effective utilization of a JV visit occurred when the American parent sent several managers to visit the JV to study the JV's human resource management systems. In contrast to most of the American parent plants, the JV was a non-union operation with a hybrid mix of Japanese and American human resource practices. The American parent was establishing a new non-union operation and decided to use the JV as a model. With the JV managers support, the visiting managers spent several days studying the JV and then incorporated much of their knowledge in the new non-union plant.

Customer-supplier relationships between the JV and the American parent also created a basis for extensive JV-parent interaction. In one case, the American parent substantially increased its quality because of pressure from the JV customer, which in turn was under pressure from its Japanese transplant supplier. Until the JV was formed, the American parent had not had any extensive interactions with Japanese customers. In supplying the JV, and indirectly becoming a transplant supplier, the American parent was forced to evaluate some its manufacturing operations.

The customer-supplier interchanges were not always amicable. In one case, the JV acted as both supplier and customer for the American parent. Neither relationship was considered satisfactory although it was a rich source of knowledge for the American parent. As a customer, the JV had so many quality problems with the American parent's products that most of the business was shifted to an outside firm. As a supplier, there were also problems. In one instance, the parent asked the JV to carry out a special order because they were behind in their deliveries. The JV refused the business because of concerns about the product quality. The reaction from the American parent was "those [JV] people are too inflexible and going too far with the quality issue."

Personnel Movement

The rotation of personnel between the alliance and the parent can be a very effective means of "mobilizing" personal knowledge. Rotation helps members of an organization understand the business from a multiplicity of perspectives, which in turn makes knowledge more fluid and easier to put into practice.[16] In this study, the rotation of interest was a two way movement of personnel between the JV and parent. If there is only one-way movement, such as from the parent to the JV this was not considered rotation.

Interestingly, none of the cases studied had an explicit process of rotation between the JV and the parent. However, in four cases, there was an informal system of personnel movement between the organizations. For example, an American parent promoted a JV manager to a staff training position at parent HQ. Several engineers also were promoted. In four cases, senior managers were transferred to the JV when the JV was formed. The careers of these managers were considered closely linked to the American parent and not just the JV. In one JV, the Chief Operating Officer of the JV came from the American parent to act as mentor for the younger JV management. This manager will eventually return to the American parent. In another JV two plant managers spent time in the JV and then returned to plant management positions in American parent plants. The chairman of the American parent in this case told one of the managers that he wanted him back in the American parent to "do some of the things he has learned here [in the JV]."

The attitude of the Japanese parent sometimes constrained rotation. In one case, the Japanese parent preferred that JV personnel not move to the American parent. The Japanese parent saw the JV as distinct and separate from the American parent. Despite this concern, the American parent has moved personnel from the JV to the parent. In another case, personnel were willing to move from the parent to the JV but less willing to return to the American parent. This prompted the American parent to ask its JV not to "poach" any more personnel from the parent.

Linkages Between Parent and Alliance Strategies

The degree to which the parent and alliance strategies are linked plays an important role in the management of alliance knowledge. A JV perceived as peripheral to the parent organization's strategy will likely yield few opportunities for the transfer of alliance knowledge to the parent. A JV viewed as important

[16] Nonaka, op. cit., 1994.

may receive more attention from the parent organization, leading to substantial parent-JV interaction and a greater commitment of resources to the management of the collaboration. To maximize exposure to partner knowledge, alliance partners must go beyond the narrow confines of the JV agreement. In two cases, the JV functioned like a related division of the American parent, with the parent focused on managing the partner relationship, not just the JV itself. According to the president of one of the American parents:

> The JV is treated exactly the same as our other divisions. The JV participates in all our meetings and all of the JV's salaried employees have the same benefits as their counterparts at other divisions. This makes it easier to move people back and forth between the JV and parent.

In this case, the relationship between the partners was getting much stronger. The JV started off strictly as a transplant supplier and relatively independent of its American parent, relying extensively on the Japanese partner for product technology and marketing support. Over the years, the JV became less independent as ties between the two partners increased. Plans were underway to jointly explore several new international options. Both parents realized that pooling their knowledge made sense given the ongoing consolidation in the global automotive industry.

Another case illustrates a deepening of the ties between the JV and American parent. When the JV was formed it was initially presented as a Japanese company to the transplant customers. The JV evolved into a much less "Japanese" firm and through its American parent's contact, had developed a substantial amount of business with domestic customers. The objective, remarked a JV manager, was for both the JV and the parents to benefit.

Through strategic linkages between the JV and the parent, the partners can gain important insights into each other's businesses. For example, an American parent won a contract to supply a part but was unable to meet the target cost. The parent decided to use its JV to produce the parts because of the JV's superior process technology. This type of linkage indicates that the American parent has internalized the differences between the parent and JV. It also opens the door for more knowledge sharing and cooperation in the future.

With these strategic linkages, there is an assumption that the linkages are consistent with the strategic goals of the parents and JVs. If a JV is in a business unrelated to that of the parent, linkages may not be possible and alliance knowledge may have limited value to the parent. In all the cases examined for this study, the JVs were in a similar business and the opportunities for synergy were substantial. Nevertheless, I would classify only two of the JVs as highly integrated with their American parents.

FACILITATING FACTORS

Why do some firms actively seek to leverage alliance knowledge while others make only a minimal effort? Why are some firms more effective at leveraging alliance knowledge? There are six factors that facilitate effective knowledge management: flexible learning objectives; leadership commitment; a climate of trust; a tolerance for redundancy; creative chaos; and an absence of performance myopia.

Flexible Learning Objectives

The collaborative objectives of the JV partners are a key element in alliance knowledge creation. However, it is not enough to enter a JV with a learning objective. Initial learning objectives may have little impact on the effectiveness of knowledge creation efforts. This is not to suggest that learning objectives are unimportant. If learning objectives are associated with the formation of a JV, a parent firm may enter more actively into the search for knowledge. However, if the initial learning objective is not correctly focused and management is unwilling or unable to adjust the objective, knowledge management efforts may be ineffective. For example, in one case the American partner had a very explicit technology learning objective. However, this firm's knowledge management efforts were weak and inconsistent because the firm did not have a clear understanding of its partner's skills. While the partner was highly skilled in specific manufacturing technology areas, its success was also the result of skills in other areas such as customer management and scheduling. The American partner was unwilling to adjust its original, narrow technology learning objective. Rather than reorienting the learning objective, parent management saw the differences between the parent and the JV as irreconcilable. According to the president of the American partner, "the JV is in a different business than us. They do not have traditional customer relationships."

In another JV the situation was almost the reverse. The American parent was interested in forming a JV primarily to gain access to the Japanese transplant market. When negotiations to form the JV were started, American parent management made it clear that they were only willing to be involved if they managed the JV. According to the JV president, "we have a quality reputation which we should be able to carry over to the JV." But, after working together for several years, American parent management realized that alliance knowledge could be important to their firm and greater effort was made to gain access to the JV operations and JV partner knowledge. The American parent formed its JV with a weak learning objective that grew stronger with exposure to the JV partner.

In several cases, the American firm did not have an initial learning objective until skill discrepancies became obvious and unavoidable. For example, an American firm that had prided itself on its high quality product status found its quality lacking once it formed its JV:

Initially, we thought there was nothing to learn from our partner. We thought we were better than anybody. When we first went to Japan we thought our partners wanted a JV so they could learn from us. We were shocked at what we saw on that first visit. We were amazed that they were even close to us, let alone much better. We realized that our production capabilities were nothing [compared with the Japanese firm]. We realized that we were not world class. Our partner was doing many things that we couldn't do.

As a starting point, a firm must have a learning objective. However, if the initial learning objective is based on an incorrect and inflexible assessment of partner competencies, learning and knowledge creation efforts may be ineffective. Ideally, as a firm builds a relationship with its partner, the learning objective will become more focused and ambiguity about the partner will disappear.

Leadership Commitment

Top management's role in managing knowledge should be one of architect and catalyst.[17] While multiple advocates are important,[18] there must be at least one strong champion of knowledge creation in a leadership position. The leader's role is especially important in initiating linkages between parent and alliance strategies. In one JV, the primary impetus for this close relationship came from the president of the American parent. The president had a longstanding personal relationship with the chairman of the Japanese partner. The president was committed to building the JV relationship and leveraging the JV experience to strengthen the American parent business. Through the president's efforts, both explicit knowledge management efforts designed to transfer specific technologies were initiated as well as more exploratory exchanges of personnel and ideas.

Another example illustrates what happens when leadership commitment weakens. The CEO of the American parent joined the parent shortly after the JV was formed. In the JV's initial years, there was a moderate amount of ideas shared between the two firms, primarily because the JV was formed as an offshoot of a licensing agreement between the Japanese and American partners. After joining the American parent, the CEO found a deteriorating relationship between the JV and the American parent. To improve communication, regular "differences meetings" between the two sides were set up. For example, one issue discussed was the American parent's role in performing some intermediate manufacturing for the JV. JV management accused the American parent of poor quality and high prices. After a few meetings, the CEO stopped attending and no more meetings were held. From the JV president's perspective, the American parent was aware that there were technology differences between the two firms.

[17] G. Hedlund, "A Model of Knowledge Management and the N-form Corporation," *Strategic Management Journal,* 15 (Special Issue 1994): 73–90.

[18] E. C. Nevis, A. DiBella, and J. M. Gould, "Understanding Organizations as Learning Systems," *Sloan Management Review,* 23 (Winter 1995): 73–85.

When the American parent people come to the plant they can see the differences but they tend to rationalize them: you have new machines, you have only one customer, etc. The real problem is that their management does not have to deal with the same customer demands as us.

A lack of top management commitment was also seen in another case, as indicated by a comment from a JV manager.

The top American partner people come in once or twice a year. They are impressed with the venture and will go back to headquarters and tell their managers: go do this Japanese stuff. The problem is they do not back it up with support. For example, the first plant manager was transferred to Europe and told to 'do the Japanese stuff.' He put together a proposal that would cost $200,000. The plan died at that point.

Climate of Trust

A climate of trust between both the JV partners and between the JV and parent organizations is critical to the free exchange of information. Trust between the partners appeared to be both a function of top management involvement in the relationship and a history of cooperation prior to the formation of the JV. In one case, a JV manager suggested that the high trust relationship between the "patriarchs" in each partner was critical to the partner relationship. In another case, in response to a question as to the single most important factor in ensuring an enduring partner relationship, the American parent president indicated that a long history of cooperation was essential. This supports other research findings that a history of ties between alliance partners generates trust.[19] If there is no such history between partners, initial trust may become precarious.

Mutual trust was also important between the JV and the parent as a basis for sharing and cooperating. JV managers indicated that the JVs were viewed by parent middle managers with distrust. In three of the cases, the JV-parent relationship had evolved into a high trust relationship. In one of the other cases, there was a high level of distrust about the nature of the relationship and the motives of the two organizations, as illustrated by the following JV manager statement:

The American parent typically screws up and asks the JV to smooth things over. They [the American parent] cannot meet a commitment. We have helped them lots of times, what have they done for us?

---

[19] R. Gulati, "Does Familiarity Breed Trust? The Implications of Repeated Ties for Contractual Choice in Alliances, *Academy of Management Journal,* 38 (February 1995): 85–112.

Tolerance for Redundancy

Redundancy means the conscious overlapping of company information, activities, and management responsibilities.[20] Redundancy encourages frequent dialogue and, as Peter Senge argues, dialogue is a key element of collective learning.[21] In a dialogue, complex issues are explored with the objective of collectively achieving common meaning. Dialogue involves conversations and connections between people at different organization levels. Inevitably, as issues are debated and assumptions questioned, dialogue will lead to some redundancy in information. Without a tolerance for redundancy, sharing of ideas and effective dialogue will be difficult.

The knowledge management processes discussed earlier involved elements of redundancy. Much of the discussion revolved around concepts such as sharing, interaction, and integration, all of which imply the transfer of knowledge between individuals. Managerial tolerance for redundancy was not consistent across the cases. In one case, the regular attendance of JV managers at meetings involving parent division managers could have been seen as redundant given that the JV was initially formed with a narrow mandate to supply one transplant firm. However, the attendance continued and, eventually, the mandate of the JV widened to the extent that the JV became an integral division within the organization.

In another example, the American parent president realized that the parent had to make a large commitment in managerial time when the JV was formed if the JV was going to be successful and if the parent was going to directly benefit from its JV involvement. While this commitment was initially costly, the result was a JV closely integrated with the parent's strategy and a clear overlapping of roles.

In a case of low tolerance for redundancy, the JV general manager actively promoted the JV as a training ground for parent managers. With the exception of a few instances, the parent was unwilling to incur the minimal expense of sending key parent managers to the JV on a regular basis to experience the JV firsthand. This type of action could have been seen as wasteful and not directly associated with successful JV management. However, allowing individuals to enter each others' areas of operation promotes the sharing and articulating of individual knowledge, which can lead to problem generation and knowledge creation.[22] In this study, the Japanese parents frequently took the opportunity to send Japan-based managers to visit the JV, probably because of a greater tolerance for redundancy and because in Japanese firms life-long learning is an explicit element in the career path of Japanese managers.

---

[20] Nonaka, op. cit., 1994.
[21] Senge, op. cit., 1990.
[22] I. Nonaka, "Redundant, Overlapping Organizations: A Japanese Approach to Managing the Innovation Process," *California Management Review,* 32/3 (Spring 1990): 27–38.

Creative Chaos

Chaos is created naturally when an organization faces a crisis, such as a rapid decline in performance.[23] Chaos can also occur when differences or discrepancies disrupt normal routines. Chaos increases tension within the organization and focuses attention on forming and solving new problems. The job of managers in the knowledge creating company is to orient the chaos toward knowledge creation by providing managers with a conceptual framework that can be used to interpret experience.[24]

Most of the JVs between Japanese and American firms in the automobile supply industry were formed in the late 1980s. For many suppliers, this was a time of chaos. With the domestic automakers under pressure from Japanese firms, many suppliers found their traditional customer base shrinking. In one case, the problems in the auto industry strengthened the JV-parent relationship, as a JV manager explained in 1991:

> With the downturn in the auto industry, the JV is now starting to beat the other parent plants. They are losing money and the JV is clearly superior in terms of quality and efficiency. The American parent can no longer ignore the differences between the JV and the American partner plants.

However, in several of the other cases, there was a great deal of suspicion at the middle management level about why the JVs were formed, as the following quote from a JV manager suggests:

> There are still people with the attitude 'these guys from Japan are not going to show me how to run a JIT plant.' It is still hard for Americans to admit that there may be something worth learning from Japanese firms.

The impact of crisis-induced chaos on knowledge creation is difficult to assess. A crisis associated with serious financial problems may not lead to managerial reflection.[25] However, if chaos is invoked or manipulated *creatively* by top management, it can be a powerful motivator. For example, one JV participated in corporate level meetings with other parent divisions. By showing superior quality indicators to parent plant managers, the JV manager was able to send a very powerful signal. In fact, by treating the JV as a related division and encouraging interaction, managers were in a much better position to challenge what is taken for granted. In contrast, the situation at another company involved conflict over

---

[23] Nonaka, op. cit., 1994.

[24] Nonaka, op. cit., 1991.

[25] On this point I disagree with Nonaka. Based on his observations of Japanese firms, Nonaka suggested that crisis-induced chaos can stimulate knowledge creation. My observations involving financial crisis suggest that crisis shifts down knowledge creation efforts. The explanation may lie in differences between Japanese and Western firm approaches to knowledge creation.

the role of the JV as a parent supplier and customer. While this provided an excellent opportunity to leverage the resultant chaos, parent management chose to use the experience as an excuse for lessening interaction between the parent and JV.

Performance Myopia

Managers seeking to create knowledge must cope with confusing experiences.[26] One such "experience" for JV parents was the assessment of JV performance. Several managers in the American parent companies pointed to the poor financial performance of the JVs as evidence that learning was not occurring, or could not occur. More generally, a myopic preoccupation with short-term issues was a common characteristic of the American partners. Although it is too simplistic to describe Japanese management as long-term oriented and American management as short-term oriented, the Japanese partner firms in this study appeared to focus on customer satisfaction and product quality rather than on profit-based performance. Consistent with other studies,[27] the Japanese firms seemed less constrained by issues of share price and by impatient boards of directors than their American counterparts. While North Americans focused on the bottom line, the Japanese focused on improving productivity, quality, and delivery.

When a firm is heavily focused on financial performance issues, learning will often be a secondary and less tangible concern. In the poorly performing JVs, American managers found it difficult conceive that learning could be occurring in the face of poor performance. A JV manager described a situation involving performance and learning:

> The American parent's emphasis on the profitability of the JV clouded their judgment. They just could not see past the startup period. The losses distorted the attitudes of the American parent. Learning was never allowed to surface. Their attitude became, they [the Japanese partner] don't know anything so how can we learn from these people?

In the face of poor JV performance, there will be a reluctance to commit to or even try out proposals generated at the JV level. More importantly, when either learning or performance are less than satisfactory, there are implications for the assessment of the other objective. Poor performance can lead to myopia, which then acts as a barrier to knowledge creation, unexploited learning opportunities can lead to perceptions of unsatisfactory JV performance.

---

[26] D. Levinthal and J. G. March, "The Myopia of Learning," *Strategic Management Journal*, 14 (Winter 1993): 95–112.

[27] For example, see J. C. Abbeglen and G. Stalk, *Kaisha: The Japanese Corporation* (New York, NY: Basic Books, 1995).

IMPLICATIONS

Successful organizations must be able to create, gather, and cross-fertilize knowledge across individuals and operating units. One potential avenue for creating knowledge is collaboration. Properly managed, alliances can be very powerful vehicles for the creation of new organizational knowledge.

Effective Knowledge Creation

Effective knowledge creation through alliances depends on two main elements. First, there are the organizational processes that firms can use to access and transform knowledge from an alliance context to a parent firm context. While these knowledge management processes are not complex, there was substantial variance in the extent to which firms in this study were actively seeking to exploit the knowledge potential of their JVs. Some parent managers were unable or unwilling to appreciate both the simplicity and the potential of these processes. Simple actions, such as visiting a JV and interacting with JV personnel, can be strong stimulants for learning. Despite the high cost of visits, the Japanese partner firms in this study were much more willing to send visitors to their JVs than were the American partners.[28]

The second element necessary for knowledge creation is an organizational climate that facilitates the effective implementation and utilization of the knowledge management processes (this incorporates the facilitating factors discussed above.).

While a balance between the knowledge management processes and the facilitating factors is necessary there is also the question as to which management processes are most important. Does a firm need to be good at all the processes to create knowledge or will an "unbalanced" approach to knowledge management work? The answer depends on the type of knowledge sought and the strategic value attached to JV knowledge. A firm seeking access to manufacturing process technology may use a very different approach than the firm interested specifically in product market positioning knowledge. The firm with a learning objective that covers a broad spectrum of knowledge will probably employ a broad knowledge creation strategy. No two firms will attach the same value to JV knowledge and, therefore, each firm will have to tailor its knowledge management strategy to its own objectives. Similarly, it is unlikely that all of the facilitating factors will be present in equal strength in any firm. The challenge is to develop an organizational climate that fosters knowledge creation and is consistent with collaborative objectives.

---

[28] One interpretation of the Japanese partners' willingness to send visitors to the JVs is that the visits provided an opportunity to learn about the American marketplace and business environment. Obviously, the American firms had little to learn in this area.

The Cost of Knowledge Creation

An issue that cannot be ignored is the cost of knowledge creation. The four knowledge management processes used by firms to access and transform alliance knowledge involve costs for the knowledge creating firm. Therefore, a decision to initiate knowledge creation efforts must be balanced with the cost of doing so. For example, visits and tours of JV facilities were identified as a simple and effective means for parent managers to interact with JV managers. While visits and tours can be effective, their cost cannot be dismissed. Given the uncertainty associated with any knowledge creation effort, it is not surprising that parent managers in this study raised questions about the value of visiting the JV plants.

Nevertheless, Japanese firms appear to be more willing to make the investment in knowledge creation than American firms and also are willing to accept incremental developments of knowledge.[29] As a result, Japanese firms may be in a better position to assess the cost-benefit tradeoff of knowledge creation processes. In contrast, American firms tend to seek knowledge in large discrete steps and there is often a reluctance to experiment and deviate from prevailing notions of what the company is about. Consistent with this perspective, a manager in this study suggested that Americans tend to look for "home runs" before new knowledge is considered worthwhile. The problem is that since potential projects are frequently evaluated against an ideal situation, many organizations fail to undertake any knowledge creation projects. This home run mentality, coupled with the failure to recognize the value of incremental learning, provides additional insights into why parent learning was low even when the potential for learning was high. Much of what could be learned from the JVs in this study was of an incremental nature and closely linked to the Japanese partner's business philosophy.

A further issue associated with alliance knowledge is that partner firms may have to take steps to protect their core technologies. To protect themselves from the learning objectives of their partners, firms may have to be cautious in transferring their technologies to alliances. Firms can also institute measures to limit the transparency or openness of their skills to their partners. These measures include the establishment of gatekeeping roles, limiting the number of partner personnel involved in active alliance management, and controlling key operational tasks in the alliance.[30]

A difficult question for any firm instituting knowledge creation structures and processes is: At what point has an optimal level of learning been reached? In other words, when does the cost of creating new knowledge exceed its benefit? Because knowledge creation and its benefits may be separated in time, or the benefits may be masked by intervening forces, assessing the true cost of knowledge creation efforts will never be easy. However, ignoring the cost entirely may

---

[29] Hedlund and Nonaka, op. cit., 1993.
[30] Hamel, op. cit., 1991.

lead to inefficient knowledge creation. Assuming the cost is prohibitive may mean no new knowledge is created.

CONCLUSION

Knowledge creation is a dynamic process involving interactions at various organizational levels and it encompasses a community of individuals that enlarge, amplify, and disseminate their knowledge. It can be haphazard and idiosyncratic and should be viewed as a continuous process, rather than one with identifiable input-output phases. It may occur unintentionally and it may occur even if success cannot be assessed in terms of objective outcomes. Given its haphazard and idiosyncratic nature, firms may view resources committed to knowledge creation as extravagant and wasteful. The view here is that the ability to create knowledge and move it from one part of the organization to another is the basis for competitive advantage. While not all knowledge creation efforts will be successful, some will yield surprisingly important results. Also, not all knowledge creation efforts will have immediate performance payoffs. However, over the long term, successful knowledge creation should strengthen and reinforce a firm's competitive strategy.

Index

Butterworth-Heinemann Business Books . . .
for Transforming Business

*5th Generation Management: Co-creating Through Virtual
Enterprising, Dynamic Teaming, and Knowledge
Networking, Revised Edition,*
      Charles M. Savage, 0-7506-9701-6

*After Atlantis: Working, Managing, and Leading in
      Turbulent Times,*
      Ned Hamson, 0-7506-9884-5

*The Alchemy of Fear: How to Break the Corporate Trance
      and Create Your Company's Successful Future,*
      Kay Gilley, 0-7506-9909-4

*Beyond Business as Usual: Practical Lessons in Accessing
      New Dimensions,*
      Michael W. Munn, 0-7506-9926-4

*Beyond Strategic Vision: Effective Corporate Action with
      Hoshin Planning,*
      Michael Cowley and Ellen Domb, 0-7506-9843-8

Beyond Time Management: Business with Purpose,
      Robert A. Wright, 0-7506-9799-7

*The Breakdown of Hierarchy: Communicating in the
      Evolving Workplace,*
      Eugene Marlow and Patricia O'Connor Wilson,
      0-7056-9746-6

Intuitive Imagery: A Resource at Work,
John B. Pehrson and Susan E. Mehrtens, 0-7506-9805-5

The Knowledge Evolution: Expanding Organizational Intelligence,
Verna Allee, 0-7506-9842-X

Leadership in a Challenging World: A Sacred Journey,
Barbara Shipka, 0-7506-9750-4

Leading Consciously: A Pilgrimage Toward Self Mastery,
Debashis Chatterjee, 0-7506-9864-0

Leading from the Heart: Choosing Courage over Fear in the Workplace,
Kay Gilley, 0-7506-9835-7

Learning to Read the Signs: Reclaiming Pragmatism in Business,
F. Byron Nahser, 0-7506-9901-9

Leveraging People and Profit: The Hard Work of Soft Management,
Bernard A. Nagle and Perry Pascarella, 0-7506-9961-2

Marketing Plans That Work: Targeting Growth and Profitability,
Malcolm H.B. McDonald and Warren J. Keegan, 0-7506-9828-4

A Place to Shine: Emerging from the Shadows at Work,
    Daniel S. Hanson, 0-7506-9738-5

Power Partnering: A Strategy for Business Excellence in the 21st Century,
    Sean Gadman, 0-7506-9809-8

Putting Emotional Intelligence to Work: Successful Leadership is More Than IQ,
    David Ryback, 0-7506-9956-6

Resources for the Knowledge-Based Economy Series

> *The Knowledge Economy,*
>   Dale Neef, 0-7506-9936-1
>
> *Knowledge Management and Organizational Design,*
>   Paul S. Myers, 0-7506-9749-0
>
> *Knowledge Management Tools,*
>   Rudy L. Ruggles, III, 0-7506-9849-7
>
> *Knowledge in Organizations,*
>   Laurence Prusak, 0-7506-9718-0
>
> *The Strategic Management of Intellectual Capital,*
>   David A. Klein, 0-7506-9850-0

The Rhythm of Business: The Key to Building and Running Successful Companies,
    Jeffrey C. Shuman, 0-7506-9991-4

Setting the PACE® in Product Development: A Guide to Product And Cycle-time Excellence,
    Michael E. McGrath, 0-7506-9789-X